FOOTPRINTS

FOOTPRINTS

David Foot's lifetime of writing

Stephen Chalke

Foreword by Scyld Berry
Preface by Mark Foot

CHARLCOMBE BOOKS
in association with
FAIRFIELD BOOKS

Charlcombe Books
125 Garnet Street, Bristol BS3 3JH
tel: 01174 523760

Fairfield Books
Bedser Stand, Kia Oval, London SE11 5SS

Text © David Foot and Stephen Chalke
Photographs © as listed on page 8

First published 2023

ISBN: 978 1 7399293 4 3

Printed and bound in Great Britain by
CPI Antony Rowe, Bumpers Way, Chippenham SN14 6LH

Contents

	Foreword by Scyld Berry	9
	Preface by Mark Foot	10
1	Introduction	12
2	First Steps into Writing	20
3	Diary of a Young Journalist	40
4	The Never Forgotten Afternoon	54
5	Country Reporter	64
6	National Service	78
7	Bristol Evening World	88
8	Drama Critic	108
9	Peter O'Toole	126
10	Going Freelance	136
11	Local History	158
12	Back to the Theatre	168
13	Outsiders	180
14	The World of Books	192
15	Harold Gimblett	202
16	Allsorts in a Busy Working Life	214
17	Cricket Reporter	228
18	Great Innings	244
19	Football	256
20	Boxing and Other Sports	270
21	Cricket History	284
22	Intimate Portraits	308
23	Siegfried Sassoon	328
24	Battling On	340
25	Obituaries	356
26	Last Footsteps	370
	Index	380

BOOKS BY DAVID FOOT

Books written as David Foot
Famous Bristolians (1979)
From Grace to Botham – Profiles of 100 West Country Cricketers (1980)
Harold Gimblett – Tormented Genius of Cricket (1982)
Cricket's Unholy Trinity (1985)
Sunshine, Sixes and Cider – A History of Somerset Cricket (1986)
Viv Richards (1987, *a book for younger readers*)
Hungry Fighters of the West (1988)
Country Reporter (1990)
40 Years On – The Story of the Lord's Taverners (1990)
Somerset Cricket – A Post-War Who's Who (1993, *with Ivan Ponting*)
Beyond Bat and Ball – Eleven Intimate Portraits (1993)
Wally Hammond – The Reasons Why (1996)
Fragments of Idolatry – from 'Crusoe' to Kid Berg (2001)
Sixty Summers – Somerset Cricket since the War (2006, *with Ivan Ponting*)
Footsteps from East Coker (2010)

Books written as a ghost
Ladies' Mile, *Victoria Hughes* (1977)
Gardening My Way, *John Abrams* (1978)
Viv Richards, *Viv Richards* (1979)
Zed, *Zaheer Abbas* (1983)
Skateaway, *Robin Cousins* (1984)
Learn Cricket with Viv Richards, *Viv Richards* (1985)
Shep, *David Shepherd* (2001)

Books containing chapters by David Foot
Facets of Crime (1975)
Murder in the Westcountry (1975)
Strange Dorset Stories (1981)
Strange Somerset Stories (1984)
Westcountry Mysteries (1985)
Wiltshire Mysteries (1989)

David Foot ghosted memoirs by Leslie Gardiner and his son John (privately published) and George Dowty (unpublished) and wrote several booklets. He also wrote much of the text of 'Rough and Smooth – Cider's Story' by Mark Foot.

For advice about the availability of these titles,
please ring **01174 523760** or email: **stephen.chalke@hotmail.co.uk**

About this book

David's output was extraordinary. Inevitably, among his writing, there is a sizeable chunk of workaday journalism that does not warrant reproduction, but there is so much on so many subjects that has stood the test of time. In compiling this book, I have been spoilt for choice.

My selection has been guided by three factors: the quality of the writing, the need to capture the full range of his work and a desire to show the story of his life as a writer: from adolescent ambition through journalistic apprenticeship to full maturity.

I have divided the book into chapters. Initially these are chronological; later, as David's writing career develops, the demand of chronology becomes secondary to the thematic categories. This allows the book to be read in one of two ways: either from first to last, as the story of a writer's life, or dipped into, according to one's special interests.

Each chapter begins with an introduction by me, usually incorporating short extracts from David's work. This is then followed by pages in which his writing is left to speak for itself. Some of the selected pieces are complete; others are extracts from longer works. As David knew only too well from his own journalism, such decisions can sometimes be influenced by the demands of page layout.

There has been an especial joy in unearthing some of David's private writings and also in retrieving his finest work for newspapers and magazines. He wrote a number of outstanding books, from which I have drawn extracts, but these books are already in print so I have not let them become the dominant element of the mix here.

In transposing his newspaper articles into this book, I have made some small tweaks: correcting misprints, reducing the number of paragraph breaks, occasionally standardising points of style. At all times I have stayed true to the spirit of the original writing.

David wrote two particularly fine books of what he called 'intimate portraits', essays of some five or six thousand words, mostly on sportsmen. To demonstrate his special touch in this form, I have reproduced in full one of these, the longest entry in this book, on Siegfried Sassoon. If I could keep only one piece of David's writing, I think it would be this. His compassionate humanity, his worldly wisdom, his sense of time and place and his felicitous way with words shine in every sentence.

Stephen Chalke
Bristol, 2023

Acknowledgements

First and foremost I am grateful to Mark Foot for encouraging me to write this book, then undertaking the demanding task of sorting through his father's work. This categorising of the great heap of newspaper and magazine articles into themed boxes made my task so much easier. I am also most grateful to him for writing the preface. Quite simply, the book would not have happened without his unwavering enthusiasm.

Scyld Berry, a great friend of David, has been a champion of the book from the outset and has played a vital role in encouraging its completion. I am most appreciative of this support and of his pitch-perfect foreword. When I thanked him for it, he replied simply: "I owe it to the old boy!"

I am also most grateful to all those who have read the book, or sections of it, ahead of publication and have offered much helpful feedback as well as corrections to my sometimes careless typing: Stephen Brenkley, Susanna Kendall, Stephen Lamb, Nigel Llewellyn, Douglas Miller, Ivan Ponting, Linda Saunders, David Smith, Richard Whitehead and, above all, David Woodhouse who, in the midst of a busy life, read the book three times. If any errors still lurk in the text, please do not blame them – or David Foot. They are my responsibility.

Many of the photographs come from David's own collection. In addition I would like to thank the following for permission to use copyright images:

    Graham Morris for the picture of David Green on page 228;
    Getty Images for the picture of the Yeovil crowd on page 54;
    University of Bristol/ArenaPAL for the pictures of Peter O'Toole on page 126 and the bottom picture of 'The Room' on page 108;
    Performing Arts Images/ArenaPAL for the top picture of 'The Room' on page 108;
    The Longfellow-Stanshall family estate for the picture of 'Stinkfoot' on page 168;
    SWNS (Sportspix) for the picture on the front cover.

Finally I would like to thank Matt Thacker and the team at Fairfield Books for co-publishing the book with me. Matt took on Fairfield Books when I retired from full-time publishing, and I am delighted with the way he is carrying forward the flame. Their current list of titles can be found at:

    www.thenightwatchman.net

Foreword
by Scyld Berry

"Good morning, David."

Slight pause.

"You don't sound quite your sunniest this morning." Spoken very gently.

How does he know, on the basis of three words, that I dropped two catches yesterday and didn't take a wicket?

David Foot, I believe, was the dearest and most decent of men because he was so sentient. The only child of a rural family, born and growing up between the World Wars, without earphones on and screens to stare at, he was fully alert to his surroundings, and human beings, and also trees. "I love trees," he used to say, "and words."

Has anyone gone on to write so many published words as that East Coker lad? Maybe one or two. But I would guess that nobody has written so many published words of such quality. There was never an ungainly sentence, such was his "feel", let alone a bad or waffly paragraph. In his prime, which lasted at least 50 years, he would compose up to 5,000 words a day if he was writing a book, like his biography of Harold Gimblett, which opened the public's eyes to the stresses of professional cricket.

This book would be in addition to a weekly column on local life, which he would type in the morning then post, before attending a cricket or football match, perhaps for more than one newspaper, then off to the theatre for a review for the *Guardian*. If anyone has written more published words per day then it cannot have been on such an enormous variety of subjects, as you will see in this book: every facet of life from boxers and the homeless to Peter O'Toole and, lest you think he could not address the heavyweight world of politics, Harold Macmillan before he became Prime Minister.

How do you do it, David?

Being also the most self-effacing of men, his face would crease into smiles and he would say: "I'm just an old fraud." The furthest I pushed him was when he replied that, having typed a paragraph, he would read it through, make any corrections, and that was it. Some eye, some ear, some sentience.

Little of human life escaped his eye until the end came. "I love words," he would continue to say, "but I can't remember them any more." Thanks to David's family, and Stephen Chalke, the finest of them are here enshrined.

Preface
by Mark Foot

It was extraordinary that Dad, from his background, became a writer. Due to the Depression he was a single child, whose family for hundreds of years had worked on the land as agricultural labourers, woodmen and gamekeepers. No one before him had been educated beyond the age of twelve.

I was four years old when the *Bristol Evening World* closed, and Dad took the decision to go freelance. Life was difficult, with two young children to support, but he was fortunate to have a resourceful and capable wife. Two lodgers were taken in, and Mum found market research work that could be fitted around the family and Dad's erratic hours. He was afraid to turn anything down in case it wasn't offered again.

Journalism was very different then. There was competition to get local stories out; newspapers were printed on site, with sellers on the streets. Shorthand and typewriters were used, and finding a phone when away from home was often an issue. Research was difficult, leading to hours in libraries. As a freelance he had to think up ideas, research, place and write them to earn enough for us to survive. At one time he was using a dozen or so aliases. One edition of the magazine *Gloucestershire Life* carried four features by him, all under different names.

I can't recall ever being remotely aware of the pressures they must have felt. My younger sister Julia and I had a wonderful childhood with our loving, fun parents. Dad would work every day and several nights a week, but we would see him when he was working at home and often we would go in the car to interviews. On Sunday we would have a roast dinner or go for a walk.

The escape was camping and, later, caravan holidays to the continent. These were magical times. Luckily we still have the family ciné films. When the camera was turned on him, Dad would often do a funny trip that still amuses us. How he never fell over is a mystery to us all!

His grandfather had wanted him to be a car mechanic, but that would not have been a good fit. We had a succession of cars that used to break down. Andy Wilson, the former Gloucestershire cricketer, offered us his reliable Rover, but Dad rejected it; he said it was far too grand for him.

When time allowed he entertained us with magic tricks and playing the piano, favouring improvised jazz, often based on hymns from his days in the church choir. He carried on the family tradition for gardening. At meal times Mum would proudly announce, "These are from Dad's garden."

Dad had time for everyone. He would pick up hitch-hikers, sometimes letting them camp in the garden. Once, when he drove a camper to Temple Meads train station, he was surprised to be asked a favour: "Could I have your socks?" Dad, naturally, took them off and gave them to him.

Saturday, when he reported on football, was the only day he was properly paid. To improve the family finances he would cover as many papers as possible, several for the away team. For years I went with him, to phone through copy as he wrote and dictated other copy as well as reporting for *Radio Bristol*. It was amazing how quickly he could write.

Dad would bring colleagues back from cricket and football, and Mum would make sure they were fed and watered. The house always had visitors from all sorts of backgrounds. I remember with embarrassment how, when Vivian Richards came to the house, Dad proudly told him of my latest batting score! He left the two of us in the front room, the shy Viv and the starstruck me; for ten minutes we just looked at each other and smiled.

Regrets, I suspect, were few. He never got to write his anti-war play or to walk with the family the length of the old Somerset & Dorset railway line. Possibly he regretted that his book *Country Reporter* did not become a TV series – and that he was not present when Somerset won their first silverware, the Gillette Cup, on my wedding day. Nevertheless, he hid a radio under the top table and got an article or two out of the day!

He didn't have a big ego; he got life in proportion. He was curious with good instincts, doing his own thing, totally trusted, caring and kind. He kept in touch with people, writing letters to villagers, school teachers, as well as sacked football managers and others, when he felt they could do with a warm word or two. He appreciated kindness and was very moved when colleagues from all around the country turned up at his surprise 80th birthday party.

Mum needs a very special mention as without her love, flexibility and support, he couldn't have crammed in as much as he did.

After getting over the shock of this book he would be thrilled that Scyld Berry has written the preface and Stephen Chalke has taken on the writing, editing and publishing, a near impossible task that very few, if anyone else, could have done so brilliantly. I can hear Dad say as he always said when seeing a complimentary piece: "They are my mates, they are just being kind."

You can read the book and make your own judgements about Dad's writing. We, his family and friends, remember him above all as someone you wanted to be with, whatever your background or age. He was a good listener, a good talker, empathetic – a kind soul with a fantastic sense of humour. He had that twinkle, and so much more.

1
Introduction

The idea of this book, in the beginning, was a simple one – to collect some of the best of David Foot's work in a single volume, with the emphasis on his cricket writing. It was his loyal and admiring readers in the world of cricket who would, I figured, want to read such a book.

I suggested the idea while David's son Mark, Scyld Berry (the *Daily Telegraph* cricket correspondent) and I were in the front room of David's old house in Westbury-on-Trym, Bristol. David had died the previous year, and now Anne, his wife of 65 years, had gone, too. Our immediate task that morning, a somewhat melancholic one, was to work out how best to find homes for David's extensive collection of cricket books.

The three of us had come together several years earlier, persuading David to write a memoir of his life. He was eighty years old, the creeping onset of dementia was draining away his confidence, and he protested repeatedly that he could not do it. But we kept at him, chivying him in our distinctive ways, and the result was the beautifully written *Footsteps From East Coker*, a volume which I am immensely proud to have published. What better than to follow this by gathering up some of his writing in a celebration of his life's work?

Mark undertook to sort out all of David's papers. I had sometimes accompanied David into the loft study where he worked, seeing for myself the piles of books, files, tapes and other clutter that made it hard to move around the room. So I was expecting plenty from Mark, to supplement my intended trawl through the published books and the various newspaper archives.

Mark patiently and lovingly set to work, separating the various elements of his father's writings into large storage boxes that he transferred to his house in Nailsea. He invited me to inspect them, and I was immediately overwhelmed: in part with astonished joy at the scale of it all, in part with nervous trepidation. What on earth had I let myself in for?

Not only had David cut out and kept a vast proportion of the newspaper and magazine articles he wrote, sticking the cricket reports and theatre reviews into scrapbooks, but he had also retained a mass of private, unpublished writing: his school exercise books, the diaries he kept during his teenage years, his observations on National Service life and some poignant reflections on his late-life dementia. And they were not casually scribbled diaries and observations; they were carefully crafted pieces, written as if to be read one day.

The first box I explored, reflecting a passion of my own, contained David's writing on the theatre. For six years, from 1956 to 1962, he was the drama critic of the *Bristol Evening World*, then from 1969 to 1992 he reviewed regional productions for the *Guardian*. The years at the *Evening World* were pivotal ones for the theatre in England, and the quality of David's grasp of what was going on – both the new writing and the dying days of music hall – struck me at once as outstanding. He befriended the young Peter O'Toole, he had for his deputy a none-too-serious Tom Stoppard, and he penned the first-ever review of the first production of a play by Harold Pinter. I knew at that moment that this book had to encompass much more than cricket.

The second box I tackled contained David's early writing. Here were the diaries, some short stories and his 'Billet Notes' from National Service. These were his formative years, not recalled in old age as he had done so evocatively in *Footsteps from East Coker* but vibrantly alive with the aching uncertainties of adolescence, captured in the still-developing prose style of his youth.

David, revisiting these diaries late in life, wrote in the front of one of them how embarrassed he was by what he had written: the immaturity of his idealism about journalism, the prejudices of his provincial adolescence, the self-importance. Yes, to a 21st century reader, there are one or two passages that jar, and his earnest declarations of socialist faith are naïvely expressed, but – as he acknowledged repeatedly – he had not yet encountered much of the world. In all other respects I was deeply moved by the quality of the diaries. Here was someone, coming from a humble background, who was determined to make it as a journalist, using his private writing to develop the skills he required: observing the world around him with a sharp eye, recording it all with a proper formality and constantly analysing himself in the quest to make a success of his career.

Not only was this book to cover a wider range of topics than cricket, I now realised that it would also be the story of David's lifetime of writing: from the little top-floor bedroom in East Coker where he wrote his diary at night through journalistic apprenticeship and years of freelance insecurity, forward to the establishment of his unique, much-loved style and a national reputation. With the world of journalism undergoing radical change during his career, the book would also reflect something of the social history of print journalism in the last seventy-five years.

There were six more boxes, all full to the brim: cricket, football, local history, research notes for his books, unpublished and privately published works, letters of commission and rejection – and a whole box of short stories, plays, comedy sketches and television documentary scripts from the years when, after the sudden closure of the *Evening World*, he was setting out to make a living as a freelance writer.

I immersed myself in it all, not only relishing the best of David's prose but gaining constant insights into his life as a journalist and writer. He was a good friend, I knew in some detail the outline of his life story, and I had read all his books. Yet I was being taken by these boxes into a more intimate relationship. The whole experience has been both fascinating and exciting.

*

David George Foot was born in East Coker, a South Somerset village, on 24 April 1929. From the local school he passed the entrance test to attend the grammar school in Yeovil where he stayed till the summer of 1946, leaving to take up a five-year apprenticeship at the Yeovil-based offices of the *Western Gazette*. On completion of the five years he was called up for his two years of National Service in the RAF.

The *Gazette* was a staid publication, set in its ways, and in the spring of 1955, 18 months after his return from National Service, David on a whim hitch-hiked to Bristol, turning up at the *Evening World* offices to ask if he could report on cricket for them. There was no vacancy but, as he was leaving, he was called back and offered a position as a news reporter. So he settled in Bristol, later in the year marrying Anne Stacey, a farmer's daughter from the hamlet of Littleton, close to Compton Dundon.

The *Evening World* was in a circulation battle with the *Evening Post*, and for seven years David threw himself into the excitement of it all – the multiple editions each day and the rush to meet deadlines. He was not only a news reporter but soon enough the drama critic and, in time, the assistant sports editor, covering Bristol City's football matches and the cricket of Gloucestershire and Somerset.

On a Saturday afternoon in January 1962, while David was reporting Bristol City's match at Halifax, the *World* closed with immediate effect. David opted – at the age of 32, married with two young children – to see if he could earn a living as a freelance writer. At first he took whatever work he could get, even reviewing local pop concerts for *Melody Maker*. As his verdict on a performance by The Who at the Yeovil Liberal Club makes clear, he was not always a natural fit for the role.

The going was hard for a few years, during which he put in long hours, often on projects that came to nothing, but gradually he built a reputation and a contacts book and was able to focus on the work he most enjoyed, particularly sport, theatre and local history. He also developed the skill of ghost-writing, producing books for a wide range of characters: from the great West Indian cricketer Viv Richards to a retired lavatory attendant, Victoria Hughes, whose tales of the nocturnal life around the ladies' toilet on the Bristol Downs captured a revealing and previously unrecorded aspect of the city's history. These glimpses of life beneath the respectable surface always fascinated David, and he contributed several chapters to local books on historic crimes.

So often at the heart of David's work was his ability to engage people from all walks of life in conversation. A letter from the writer Jilly Cooper, after David interviewed her on local television, put it perfectly: 'It was a lovely interview, you are so easy to talk to and, watching it back on the machine, I was horrified to see how much you made me talk.'

Cricket was the number-one passion of David's life. In his early diaries his ambition, stated clearly, was to become a cricket writer. He played in his school eleven, then for East Coker and the *Western Gazette*, and during his freelance years he ran an occasional Sunday side called The Bristol Badgers, made up of various cricketers, footballers, actors and journalists.

His breakthrough as an author came when the former Somerset batsman Harold Gimblett, one of David's first heroes, asked David to ghost-write his autobiography. David suggested that Gimblett start by talking into a tape recorder – but, before they got down to the writing, Gimblett committed suicide. Some months later David was presented with the tapes. Gimblett had suffered from nervous problems during his career, and the tapes took David into the darkest corners of a sportsman's mental life. With great sensitivity, never flinching from the truth, he crafted *Harold Gimblett – Tormented Genius of Cricket*, a book that, at a time when the mental health of sportsmen was rarely discussed, was ground-breaking.

Among the many tributes to the book was one from Alan Gibson, a fellow West Country writer. While saying it was 'one of the best cricket books I have read for a long time', he went on to accuse David of a reluctance to work seriously at his writing, suggesting that he would be happy 'knocking off copy' for the *East Coker Mercury & Advertiser*. I republished this review in a collection of Gibson's writing, and I now regret that decision – not just because it upset David but because, having worked through these storage boxes, I think it is untrue. Yes, David was a fast writer, he let the words flow out of him, that was the way he wrote, but that did not make him a lazy writer. Yes, to earn a living, he often had to complete jobs quickly, to knock off copy as Gibson put it, but he worked long, long hours throughout his career. When the writing mattered, he cared greatly about it. So much in the boxes tells me that.

After *Harold Gimblett* there followed several further cricket books, notably two volumes of what David called 'intimate portraits': *Beyond Bat and Ball* and *Fragments of Idolatry*. Each contained a set of essays on sports people, mostly cricketers, with the focus of the writing not on their achievements, certainly not on their statistics, but on the inner men, many of them troubled characters. Among them was Siegfried Sassoon, whose complex personality David approached through the cricket the poet played for his local village side.

David returned to the scenes of his *Western Gazette* apprenticeship in a lightly fictionalised memoir, *Country Reporter*, that was published in 1990. A joy to read, it captured a lost world of rural journalism with a gentle, observant humour. The BBC planned to create a series from it, in much the same genre as 'All Creatures Great and Small'. Scripts were commissioned, David received a considerable advance for a paperback edition of the book, but a round of spending cuts, forced by the ill-fated launch of an unsuccessful soap opera, led to its abandonment.

By the 1990s David's working life increasingly focused on cricket – his books and his reports of county matches for the *Guardian* – though he continued to cover football in winter and to write regular columns for the sports pages of the *Western Daily Press*. He remained in Bristol from 1955 till his death in 2021, with his work retaining a strong West Country feel. If in his youth he dreamed of being a star reporter on Fleet Street, he had no such hankering in later life. He had a melancholic streak, but he was proud of his roots and he drew strength from the closeness of his family.

By the turn of the century, entering his seventies, he was conscious that his memory was going. He would tell how he would go into the kitchen and be blank about what he had come for. Outwardly he maintained that it amused him, but it is clear from his private writings that, when despatched to cover cricket and football, he was terrified that he would not be able to produce his copy with the required speed and accuracy. He took a pride in his work, and even little slips sent him spiralling into despair. Yet, as his editors kept insisting, his work was superb.

In a *Radio Bristol* interview, to promote *Country Reporter*, he looked back at his younger self. "It may be a weakness," he said of his desire to be a journalist, "but I was genuinely, incorrigibly romantic. I wasn't very versatile. I still can't mend a fuse, I can't put up a bookshelf. I'm hopeless. My wife has to do all that around the house. The only tools I could really feel at home with were the typewriter and the dictionary. I loved words. I still love words. And I'm happiest of all when I'm bashing out words on a typewriter, surrounded by my family preferably."

That love of words shines through everything he wrote. And it explains the sadness we all felt when, in his final years, he used to say, "The only thing I was ever any good with was words, and now I can't find them."

In 2010 he signed off from his last regular journalism, his column in the *Western Daily Press*. Later that year *Footsteps from East Coker* was published. After that, he penned an occasional obituary till his memory loss proved too great. He died on 25 May 2021, at the age of 92.

*

I first encountered him in the mid-1990s when, in a mid-life change of direction, I left employment in adult education to become a writer of cricket books. In that formative period, when a new world was opening up for me, I read *Beyond Bat and Ball*, and I was mesmerised by it. I had never before read a book that brought cricketers to life in this way. The prose was beautiful, there was such a vivid sense of time and place, and at the heart of each portrait was a man with something of a paradox or mystery at his core. Alongside the standard cricket books of that period it shone out like a beacon.

I finished up publishing my first book myself. It left me having to learn many new processes, not just layout and printing but how to sell a cricket book. I rang David for advice. Other writers as busy as David would have found me a pest, perhaps David did, but patiently he offered me valuable tips. His instinct with everybody was to be kind and helpful, making him the most popular of writers on the cricket circuit.

Three years later, having had several dealings with him by then, I was promoting my third book during the Cheltenham Cricket Festival. I asked him if he was working on a book himself, and he said yes, a sequel to *Beyond Bat and Ball*. I enquired whether he had a publisher, he said not yet, and without a thought I offered to do it.

So it was that I became the publisher of his last books. He was the easiest author to work with, providing immaculate copy at all times. We only argued once – over the royalty I proposed to pay him.

"No, no, no," he protested. "You can't pay me that much … No, you certainly won't. I won't accept it." Happily I got my way in the end.

David was the most sweet-tempered of men, never one to want a fuss. It is a silly memory, but I recall an occasion when we were having a pub lunch. His salad had a dressing that he started spitting out, complaining that it was like grit. He called over the barman and queried what it was.

The man replied, then asked him if he liked it. "Yes, very nice, thank you," he said politely before continuing to spit it out. It was so David.

Yet, ironically, his writing had none of that quality. He was prepared to venture into dark places and tell the truth. With another writer it could have been salacious, exploitative, but with David, beneath the surface of his sentences, there was always such a rich vein of human compassion. He was never seduced by the trappings of wealth and power; he came from the soil of a rural working-class and he never betrayed the values of his honest upbringing.

Journalism was David's chosen profession, and he was quietly proud of that. I had come to writing from a different background, and I harboured reservations about the cut-throat world of newspaper reporters. "I don't think you're an admirer of journalists, are you?" David would sometimes suggest to me, and I could never quite deny it. Yet, reading through his body of work in preparing this book, I would answer him differently now. Good journalism – telling fascinating stories vividly and accurately in well-crafted English without exploiting or sensationalising people's lives – is a gift and it enriches us. David did all of that superbly, and he had every reason to be proud of his calling.

So would David have approved of this book? It is a question I have asked myself repeatedly as I have reverently typed out his prose. If he were alive, a strong part of him would have been embarrassed by it. He would have felt that far too much fuss was being made of his humble efforts. But there was another side of him, kept largely hidden, that treasured the compliments, the glowing reviews, the awards. They reassured the 'inner' village boy, who remained forever a little uncertain of himself.

Would he have wanted his diaries and private writings to appear in print? That is a harder question. The first thing to observe is that, instead of penning a note saying how embarrassed he was by some of what he wrote, he could have thrown the diaries away, and he never did. Secondly, and most importantly, I think he would have done the same as me if he had been in my shoes. He would have wanted to reach as close as possible to the heart of his subject. And he would have done so, as I hope I have, with affection.

David was a truth-teller, and I have tried to follow his example. I have revealed his times of struggle and his setbacks – even his failures – as a writer. For me, they only reinforce my admiration for the values that steadfastly underpinned his life: the hard work, the respect for his calling, the loyalty, humanity and compassion.

2
First Steps into Writing

Luck At Last - *'My first literary effort (age 10)'*

15-year-old David sketches and profiles the 1944 Somerset Amateurs

David was an only child, born into a rural world that was still feudal in many respects. His father was an estate worker; his mother had been a parlour maid. Their little cottage, clad in Virginia creeper, was without electricity and running water and had a two-seater lavatory at the top of the garden. Yet, as David was to reflect in his late-life memoir *Footsteps from East Coker*, they did not complain about their lot.

> None of the cottage dwellers seemed to. Perhaps it never entered their heads, back in the thirties, that they might ever aspire to better days, better furniture, better suits of clothes. They were resigned to the restrictions of the way they lived; they seldom pondered improved escape routes and more money, however marginal, from the squire's steward on a Friday night.

The Foots did not talk much at the meal table – 'The lack of conversation in village homes, especially then, was commonplace' – so, as an only child, David listened to and watched the world beyond his family home.

> I used to lie in my small bedroom and wonder about my future. Verandah Cottage, a listed building and centuries old, had been my rock. As for my educational reflections, I was convinced that the village pub just across the road, had – especially in the earlier years – been my most effective academy of learning. I used to lean out from the front bedroom window and, at closing time, would crane to catch the words of intimacy being exchanged, the hushed invites, the fumbled guilty kisses, the cruder fragments of carnal intent. This was where I learned so much about life, its transgressions and bodily excitement. I was an avid listener and learner.

This late-night fascination seems to have provided the inspiration for a short story written when he was still at the village's elementary school. Called 'Luck at Last', only one page of it survives – written with childish care in red ink, with David's adult hand adding in a paragraph break: 'My first literary effort (age 10)'

The story starts at closing time in a public house, going on to describe the central character Sid Fry as he makes his way home:

> Somehow Sid stumbled to his lodgings, looking like nothing on earth. His hair was streaming down over his eyes, his face was the resting place of many large ugly bruises – the results of colliding with the wall – and his clothes were torn. (He was bad tempered, and had tried to start several foolish fights.)

Picked in an emergency for a local football team, Fry's lack of fitness – 'caused by so many cigarettes' – makes him a wretched failure. Then he sees an advertisement from another club for a goalkeeper and takes to practising with a group of boys and a goal marked on a wall. Here the fragment ends. Almost certainly the young author was planning a triumph for his Sid.

David begins *Footsteps from East Coker* by describing this first story, mentioning the red ink. He says he wrote it at the age of eight and sent it to *Strand*, the literary magazine that first published Conan Doyle's Sherlock Holmes stories. It came back, rejected, within days.

It is a charming tale of his childish naïvety but, as with so many of our memories of childhood, while it retains an emotional veracity the details do not tally with the surviving evidence.

David says the story he sent to *Strand* was not 'Luck at Last' but 'a superficial psychological tale about a geeky young man called Clarence'. All his life David preserved these early stories, along with his school reports and many of his exercise books, including neatly drawn maps of the Far East and carefully explained chemistry experiments. From these it is clear that 'Clarence and the Carnations' was a much later story. More adolescent in theme and style, it was written in blue ink in a well-developed hand. It is in a brown envelope on which the adult David has written:

> Early effort – the dreadful CLARENCE. Sent, when still at school, to STRAND mag of all things. Back came cruel, brief reply from Editor. 'Don't waste our time or your stamps.'

'Clarence and the Carnations' tells the tale of Clarence Appleyard, a young office worker who is ungainly in appearance and awkwardly self-conscious in manner. Yearning to be successful with women, he goes to bed one night and drifts into a blissful dream in which all his tormentors are kind to him. He finds himself sitting on a wedding throne, being presented by a beautiful bridesmaid with 'a charming bouquet of rare, multi-coloured carnations'. He places one in his button-hole, waking to find himself alone in bed in his pyjamas. In his despair he decides not to get up and go to work.

> When an anxious landlady later knocked and peeped in at the door, she made the astonishing remark that she could smell faintly but unmistakably some sweet-scented flowers like, perhaps, carnations. Clarence started. Something made him look down at his pyjamas. Sticking from the top pocket was a beautiful carnation.

David may have chuckled in later life at his naïvety in sending off such a story to *Strand*, but with admirable tenacity he continued to send his writing to magazines and newspapers. Even at this early age he was determined to be a writer, and he was not going to give up in the face of repeated rejection.

His education went well. From the village school he won a scholarship, complete with book and bicycle allowances, to Yeovil Grammar School. His termly reports suggest a hard-working pupil, usually near the top of his class, particularly in English.

In January 1944, at the age of 14, he began to keep a diary. Initially it was just a few words each day, but he kept it going without lapse for five years, with each diary growing in size till in 1948 he bought a large hardback book and wrote seven or eight hundred words a week.

A typical entry at the start of his first diary is:

> Didn't get on too well at cross-country – Boys' Club.

But by June his diary-writing has developed. The handwriting has shrunk, and the words are filling all the space available each day, with David not only recording the titbits of his own life but reporting on momentous international events:

> Thomas in awful temper in gym. Invasion going well in spite of heavy losses. Wiped Germans out of all hiding places. Beat Boys' Brigade by about 20 runs. I made 5* and 16, 6 wickets, 2 catches.

Also surviving from that year are David's meticulous pre-season pen portraits, complete with a drawing, of the members of a local cricket team, the Somerset Amateurs.

> Gumage: Owing to his war-time duties, he is restricted in his matches but he makes up for it when playing on account of his opening partnerships with Sawtill and his fine short-leg fielding. Height only 5 ft 4 ins.

David played for two years in the school cricket eleven. In his last year, when he stayed into the sixth form to improve the grades of his matriculation, he helped to produce the school magazine, penning reports on the year's lectures and on the staging of a mock sitting of parliament. Then, as the year drew to a close, he obtained an apprenticeship at the *Western Gazette* in Yeovil.

The headmaster during his final two years was a still young Denys Thompson, a pioneering English teacher who had been a Cambridge associate of FR Leavis, the great champion of English studies as a civilising force in society. David was not taught English by Thompson, but it was to his study that he went when he sought permission to leave school two days before the official last day on Thursday 1 August 1946. It was a scene described in *Country Reporter*, David's largely autobiographical account of the young Matthew Fouracre's five-year apprenticeship on a local paper.

> 'I wondered, sir, if I might leave a couple of days early – Tuesday instead of Thursday. There is probably nothing much for me to do here. And ... I'd ... like to –"
>
> "See the Indians at Taunton?"
>
> Till then, I had never thought him in any sense a cricketing man. He had these thick, book-wormy glasses, a pallid, lugubrious face verging on the cod-like features of a younger and rather taller Leslie Henson, and he appeared to glide round, ever tugging at his gown, in vague introspection. He was gentle and remote: and we never saw him on match days.
>
> 'Let me see, Fouracre, you've been in the 1st XI this season, haven't you?'
>
> 'And last, sir.'
>
> 'Have you made many runs?'
>
> 'I got 16 against Dorchester when we were up against it, sir.'
>
> 'Was that your top score?' he asked in a tone which I felt was unreasonably dismissive.
>
> 'Well, no, sir. I also got 16 when we played Huish's on the county ground at Taunton. Mr Sparks gave me run-out and afterwards told me he'd made a mistake.'
>
> The headmaster clearly disapproved of superficial conversation. 'Did you stay on for a whole year in the sixth form just to play cricket?' I fancy that he was close to adding that, considering my token batsmanship, I'd have been advised to leave a year earlier. He had the good grace to remain silent.
>
> 'No, sir. I needed another credit for matriculation. So I took my English again.' I knew immediately it was the wrong thing to say.
>
> 'Do I assume that English is not one of your better subjects?'
>
> 'It's my best, sir,' I blurted out. 'But I took so long on my essay last year that I never got round to the grammar.'

Given permission to leave, David recorded the trip to the cricket in his little pocket diary:

> Went to Taunton to see the Indians play – enjoyed every minute.
> Indians all out 64. We replied 250 odd for 5 (Gimblett 103).

At some point afterwards he wrote a fuller account, 'A Day with the Indians', on two lined sheets of paper. It was his first report of a day's cricket.

Within a fortnight of this, David was reporting for work at the *Western Gazette*, beginning a five-year apprenticeship at the bottom of the journalistic profession. A staid eight-page broadsheet, with a front page made up of small advertisements, the newspaper came out every Friday.

His week as a copy-boy consisted of such mundane tasks as running up and downstairs delivering messages, collecting galley proofs and going out to buy packets of cigarettes for the sub-editors. His pocket diary for 1946 allowed room for only brief impressions of his first week's work:

> MON 12 AUG: Started at Gazette at 7.30. Arose early this morning – will it continue? Everything was strange but I'm settling down. What swanks the sub-editors are – Lanham uses words he can't pronounce, Elliott hangs his coat on a 'hanger'.
>
> TUES 13 AUG: Getting into the swing of things – keeping my eyes open – and my ears (surprising what one picks up in the Sub-Editors Room!) I have taken fancy to Mr Pike, although I'm not sure his job; he's a sleepy-eyed but sympathetic person.
>
> WED 14 AUG: Have to arise at 5 tomorrow. Well, I must try anyway. Freddie Mills knocked out the Swede Nilsson in the first round.
>
> THUR 15 AUG: Country startled by squatters, people without homes of their own, grabbing forbidden disused Army huts – started in Yeovil now. Lines were busy in office. Busy time today, 6.30 am – 5.50 pm.
>
> FRI 16 AUG: Wages, after deductions, £1 – 2 – 4. *(£60 in today's money – about £3,000 a year.)* Not too good but I'm very lucky to have got a job in the circumstances, even if it's plenty of drudgery to start with. They are much too Conservative in politics at the Gazette for my liking.

Soon he was given Saturday work, reporting on Yeovil's rugby matches. This gave him the chance to increase his earnings by sending copy to other publications:

> SAT 19 OCT: I had my hands full – covering the Yeovil v Bridgwater rugger match for Football Express, Echo, Evening Post and subsidiaries, Sunday Despatch and Express, Taunton Weekly and of course Western Gazette. My biggest to date – kept busy till 7.30 pm.

Relying on a bicycle had its downsides, but he was not complaining:

> MON 2 DEC: Never known such weather. I have now got wet through every day for three weeks.
>
> WED 4 DEC: I am realising now that I love my job – wouldn't change it for anything. Sending through football and rugby copy on Saturdays is my greatest thrill.
>
> SAT 7 DEC: Got wet through again reporting but it was worth it.
>
> END OF DECEMBER: <u>My Personalities of the Year</u>: Politics & Diplomacy: E. Bevin, who – although he left school at 12 – has shown himself to be perhaps our greatest Foreign Minister. Sport: Sydney Wooderson for his brilliant run in Oslo, and Bruce Woodcock – should soon be world champion. <u>Myself</u>: I have left school but as yet do not regret it. Love my job though dumped with all the 'spade work'.

David's pocket diary for 1947 was slightly larger. As his work grew more demanding, he gave up writing each day, sometimes filling three days with a single entry. The topics included his thoughts on religion and the monarchy, his struggles as chairman of East Coker's boys' club, his embarrassment when two of his friends are caught stealing his father's pears, and his observations on the staff at the *Western Gazette*. Always it was an opportunity to write, and he did so with formality and discipline.

Eager to extend his vocabulary beyond that of his home life and the village boys' club, he resolved to write down and learn the definitions of three new words every day, in a notebook that also survives:

> ABJURE – renounce or retract
> ACERBITY – vitriolic speech
> ACME – culminating point of achievement

He was playing adult cricket now, not only for East Coker but also for the *Western Gazette*. He was a middle-order batsman, but on a never-to-be-forgotten afternoon in June he was given a rare chance to bowl his off-breaks and took seven wickets. In the following weeks more wickets followed:

> My amazing success with the ball continues. In the last 3 matches I have taken 14 wickets at a cost of 47 runs. I have now taken 30 wickets for the season.

There were runs, too. Given the rough pitches on which they played, an innings in double figures was a source of pride:

> I got 14 against the Yeovil Post Office on Monday. I was most satisfied as the bowling was good. I got a chance, for the first time this season, of executing a few cover drives.

As well as reporting on rugby matches, he was responsible for writing up stories from East Coker and the nearby villages. None carried a by-line, it would be a while before the name of David Foot would appear against anything he wrote, but as an ambitious 17-year-old he enjoyed his first experiences of sitting in meetings with reporter's notebook in hand.

He was still sending his short stories for publication. One, written somewhat in the style of MR James, was a macabre story, with a twist in the tail, set at night-time around a village church. Once more he tried the *Strand* magazine. With the new sophistication of his working life, he included in his typed copy some of the shorthand abbreviations he had learnt: t for the, ws for was, bn for been, durg for during. It was clear from his diary that he had high hopes for it:

> I sent them what I thought was one of my better efforts in short-story writing: 'The tower and the tombstone'. With that brilliant title and some subtle wording in the covering letter, about having left school but a short time, I thought I stood a slight chance of getting the story accepted. How wrong I was!

Back came another impersonal rejection letter, though this one had a handwritten note at the bottom: 'We've had this sort of short-hand spelling and do not want it again.' In his diary David dwelt long on his reaction: first mirth, then semi-anger, finally pride in being 'one of the few' to draw a personal reply from the 'celebrated editor'.

Eventually, after more rejections, the story saw its way into print in a Saturday edition of the *Bristol Evening World* in October 1949, at least two years after it was written. His reward was a cheque for 30 shillings and the joy of seeing his name in bold in the middle of the page – though not his real name. The *Western Gazette* did not allow that. It was 'The Tower and the Tombstone' by David Coker.

A DAY WITH THE INDIANS

August 1946

We were breaking up for the summer vacation on the Thursday; I was breaking up for the last time. On the Wednesday, the Indian tourists were due to play Somerset at Taunton. I made up my mind that I would see that match, to see the celebrated Indians and, of course, my Somerset heroes.

The train puffed out of Hendford Halt at 10.02, and I found myself jammed between two powerful masculine forms, in the corridor. The train was packed but, for once, I did not give a second thought to my discomfort, the fact that I had paid 5/7 for a sardinish position in an intolerably stuffy train or to the merits of the G.W.R. in general. I was excited like an infant waking up on Christmas morning. I knew wonderful thrills were in store for me – thrills that only this grand old summer game can produce. The train puffed on.

I didn't see the hedgerows and fields, villages and stations that we passed. I saw Frank Lee's familiar stance at the wicket, I saw the coloured Indians darting about the field, I saw the numbers rattle up on the varnished scoreboard. And I trembled with excitement. My fellow sardines must have felt it.

At long last the train drew in at Taunton. I am quite sure that I was the first person out of the corridor and onto the platform. How I did it I'm not at all sure. I am, however, dimly conscious of sticking my elbows in one man's eye, of tripping over two suitcases and of nearly knocking a baby out of her mother's arms. Manners were a thing of the past.

Half-running – perhaps more than half – half-walking I reached the ground. Oh good Lord! a queue. But I was in luck. A children's queue 'à la droite' (there, who said French was never useful) was moving rapidly. After a bit of quick thinking I pulled out, from my pocket, an extremely crumpled and faded Yeovil School cap. I joined, a little self-consciously I admit, the children and in less than no time found myself in the County Ground. I had reached almost fever point by this time.

Already the ground was packed but I found a spot where, with my legs tucked up under me, I could sit on the ground. Physical discomfort meant nothing as then. Unconsciously, I glanced at the clock above the scoreboard. Oh dear! I still had 20 minutes to wait. I waited but how I do not know. Programme racketeers and a heated argument on 'Blasphemy' behind me, after someone had shouted "For Christ's sake, get out of the way", intrigued me at different times.

At 11.30 sharp the Somerset side took the field and I clapped until my hands were sore. Yes, there went the Indian batsmen, slick, carrying themselves excellently. There was the tall, swarthy Mushtaq Ali and the short, dapper Merchant, a millionaire. From that point until the luncheon interval my aching eyes were trained both on the 13 men and also on the 22 yards of wicket. Each man who went onto the field underwent a thorough scrutiny from me – thanks to the field-glasses.

I went to Taunton hoping for thrills and I truly got my fair share. Merchant, the most consistent and stylish of the Indian batsmen, was out to the third ball of the match, snapped up behind the stumps by Luckes off a fastish one from Andrews. The crowd went wild. I couldn't believe my eyes. For once, I did not mind missing the artistry of India's greatest batsman.

Shocks and thrills galore were to follow. Mushtaq Ali, becoming a little too aggressive, was bowled by an Andrews 'special', Amarnath was caught in the slips by Lawrence off a Buse spinner, Hafeez the youthful handsome student was bowled almost first ball by Andrews, Hazare was taken in the slips off Buse, Mankad – opening batsman in the first Test – was bowled by a Buse 'beauty', and Sohoni was well caught by Longrigg off Andrews. All this, which looks incredible on paper, happened in less than an hour.

The Nawab of Pataudi, the elegant captain who had gone in No. 3, gallantly tried to hold the side together but, becoming bored with his role, he was unfortunate to raise one. The last two stayed for a time until the last ball before lunch when Hindlekar was brilliantly caught on the square-leg boundary when powerfully hooking Andrews. The Indians were all out for 64. My cucumber sandwiches went down well.

At 2.30, the Tourists took the field alongside the Somerset idol, broad-shouldered Harold Gimblett and the almost comical, pathetic-looking, defensive Frank Lee. The crowd was in for a treat. For three hours the two batted soundly giving not a chance until Lee was run out quite unnecessarily. After him came my own favourite, tall R.J.O. Meyer – delightfully aggressive as usual, gripping the long-handle from the start. He was out as one might expect – on the boundary. Castle who followed him was out to a good one from Sarwate. Lawrence, the humorous diminutive Yorkshireman qualified for us, paid for his undue enthusiasm (incidentally, unable to get a house, he sleeps with his wife in a caravan). Gimblett, moved by Lee's dismissal, coolly passed 100 and then gave an easy chance to extra cover. The day finished on a little more sober note; Skipper Longrigg survived, however, an appeal for a behind-the-wicket catch in the last over.

I left the ground happy, with violent cramp ... but contented and thrilled with the Cider County.

MAN WITH THE IMPERIAL BEARD

written in 1947, this is the first hand-written entry in 'Every-Day Cameos', a collection in a hardback notebook of some early, unpublished pieces

I was making one of my frequent visits to the Town Reading Room on a bright summer's morning when I first saw him.

The door had opened and a dainty but purposeful little step had hastened by me. I instinctively turned, and immediately I saw the man his character interested me. He was positively brimming over with personality. One didn't have to contact him to acquire that knowledge.

Intentively, almost impatiently, he turned the sober pages of *The Times*. He found what he was seeking and peered earnestly forward.

By this time I was deeply interested ... I sized the man up. He wore a white drill suit and panama hat and unique, gold pince-nez with a black cord. But I have left his most striking possession to last – a fine, ginger imperial beard. He was a dapper, little fellow of 5 ft 6 inches or thereabouts. There was something, it seemed, fascinatingly distinguished about him.

I hazarded a guess at his profession. Novelist of foreign origin or overseas newspaper correspondent, I thought at first. Yet there was the touch of the artist or the musician about him.

With his unchanging look of apathy, he coughed politely, closed *The Times* and moved over to a seat. Momentarily, I got the impression of a cold, callous, unscrupulous businessman. It passed. The man opened a portfolio and took out some papers. After a few moments' intense concentration, he began writing. There was now, very faintly, the look of a man clinching a lucrative deal.

He ceased writing, re-read with supreme care and pocketed his pen. The papers were slipped back into his portfolio and he rose. Still with that intent, almost distant, look he walked briskly out. I was really intrigued. I sincerely hoped that I would see the man again. I did – several times.

Two or three more times I saw him in the Reading Room; each time there was the same procedure. The last occasion, however, curiosity got the better of me. I 'got to work' on the *Manchester Guardian* – next to *The Times*. My enterprise was not in vain. The scrutinised one – the novelist, author, musician, artist, sculptor, stock-broker – was studying ... the racing form.

Of course! He was a gambler – the retired, debonair continental sort. I admired the man even more. I have always had a secret respect and admiration for the cool, uncompromising, ruthless better.

I spotted him once coming out of a hotel, once at a bookstall. Every time, although unconscious of the fact, he got an interested audience – not only from me.

Regretfully I completely forgot my eccentric 'friend' until a column story appeared in the *Daily Express* on 11th September 1947. That must have been six months since I saw him last,

The story told how a William Henry Coulson had sent a telegram in Italian to his separated wife. The unsigned telegram said: 'Domani sera moriro'. His wife, with a very superficial knowledge of Italian, believed it to mean 'Tomorrow evening I shall arrive'.

She communicated with her solicitor and, upon his advice, sent a reply to her husband, saying that she did not wish to see him; that divorce proceedings were already instituted.

Conscience smote her. She studied her husband's telegram again and, with the help of an Italian dictionary, re-read the three words. The correct translation she discovered was: 'Tomorrow evening I shall die.'

And in his 17th century house, Virginia Cottage at Bradford Abbas, the husband was found dead beside a jar of cyanide.

Police found every room piled high with sporting journals and litters of betting slips. Everywhere there were wine and whisky bottles; the garage was stacked with empty beer crates. He had three photos of his wife on his dressing-table.

The villagers were questioned. Not one had entered Virginia Cottage, ever. Tradesmen were met at the door and invariably offered a glass of wine.

Villagers knew well, though, the sight of the short, stocky man in a white, spotless drill suit and panama hat which he always wore – regardless of the weather. They knew him as the man with the fine imperial beard and the gold pince-nez which dangled from his neck on a black cord. He was never seen inside the local tavern but was often carrying a barrel of wine under each arm.

At the Inquest, his wife Sylvia Constance Coulson stated that they were married in 1932 when her husband was a clerk in the London branch of the National Bank of India ... retired a year later, seven addresses in five years ... came to live in Bradford Abbas in 1937 ... married life not happy ... he was sometimes amiable, sometimes quarrelsome ... wife left him for last time in June.

He died in solitude, unhappy and penniless. But if it is any consolation to him now, let me tell him that for me, at least, he brought colour and personality into a drab community.

I MEET A SADISTIC KILLER

The second entry in 'Every-Day Cameos', this is David's write-up of an encounter, probably in 1945, with the infamous Neville Heath, a conman who was hanged the following year for the brutal murders of two young women. Police later confirmed to David that Heath had been in Yeovil at the time.

I am very sorry that I have left this story so long before recording it. This is, I am sure, my most sensational. It's a pity I'm a little vague at times.

I must have had a year still to go at school. I was about sixteen. It was a coldish late afternoon – Autumn, I think – and I was enjoying an ice-cream at Hannam's, West Coker Road. I'll cut out the frills and tell the story simply.

He came over towards me from the other side. I hadn't noticed him approach. Some of his conversation is still pretty lucid. First of all, he asked me about the times of the buses. Then a few general remarks.

I was taking him in fairly thoroughly. He was fairly tall, handsome – in fact, very good-looking in a kind of way – and had fair, wavy hair. His tight lips struck me. He asked me about my school and asked where it was. He said he would probably be calling to see the Head about a collection for some charity. This seemed very strange and stuck in my memory. He asked me my age and said I looked younger.

The man's obvious keenness for conversation began to slightly embarrass me. He asked me where I lived. I told him in the country and he wondered how far away. He thought it must be very dull there. Surprisingly, he confided in me that he was craving for excitement and asked in some kind of way where he could get it. Then he said something about I wouldn't understand. I began to think him rather abnormal. I swear that I am telling truth and not letting the pen run away with me.

I suggested, very naïvely I realise now, that he might want night-clubs. He shuffled at me. Then he half made a suggestion to me, as far as I can remember, and decided "You would be too scared." I didn't know a lot about life then – it's very vague.

I cannot remember what followed but he seemed to get, quite suddenly, impatient and stalked off. The man's face held in my memory – till this day.

Some time after, I opened my daily paper. A large head and shoulders took up most of the front page. At once, before I looked at any wording, I recognised – without doubt – the man as the same one as I had seen outside Hannam's. Good God! I read the story. 'NEVILLE HEATH WANTED FOR MURDERS'.

Nothing will ever shake my belief that I met Neville Heath.

THE TOWER AND THE TOMBSTONE

Bristol Evening World, 1 October 1949

I'm not easily frightened, but as I write these lines my whole body trembles and the nib of my pen, controlled by an unsteady grip and somewhat incoherent mind, scratches almost drunkenly about the paper.

Twilight was fast descending into complete darkness as I ascended the short hill which led up to the ancient village church. I was a comparative 'foreigner' to the district and it was my first visit to this fine building.

Admittedly, it was a late hour to go sight-seeing, but I desired to say I had entered the church's porch before leaving that part of the country on the morrow.

The night was very still and, on one side of me, the sombre row of almshouses looked especially forbidding. Alas! I was young and curious – even fearless I thought then.

So I moved forward into the winding church path. A thick yew hedge on my left and bushy shrubs on my right almost obscured whatever light was left in the sky. And though I was out of doors the atmosphere was strangely hollow; my normally light-footed steps seemed surprisingly resonant on the path.

*

I heaved open a creaking iron gate and found myself in the churchyard, filled with tombstones of all shapes and sizes. Some, beaten back by the ageless wind, lay almost horizontal. Others leaned at various degrees towards the ground.

Those stones appeared to me like sinister figures, crouching and waiting. But I chided myself for being fanciful – caught up in the compelling powers of my own imagination.

Then it was that I first heard the sound – a dull, metallic tapping from somewhere above me.

I glanced up into the church tower and in time saw a faint flicker of light from one of the windows.

*

I passed between two or three of the crumbling, ivy-covered tombstones and reached the side door of the church. The tapping was much louder.

Peering in, I could just make out the inner door of the tower, standing half open. Intrigued by the noise above, I began to feel my way up the spiral staircase. It was not pleasant, but I gained some consolation in the knowledge that I was not alone in the tranquil church.

I must have mounted sixty or more steps before I came to the end of my quest – the clock-room.

The dusty interior was partially lit by a solitary candle stump and, as the weak flame flickered, so a thousand little shadows danced about the four walls. The pendulum of the big clock swung to and fro in one corner and the clock's heavy weights, suspended in mid-air, looked grotesque in the half light. All this I saw in a second.

*

Then, as I moved further into the doorway, I saw the figure of a man winding the chimes, his large frame half bent over the handle. His body was facing me but his eyes were staring fixedly at the boards below him.

He immediately struck me as being extraordinary. The candle was in such a position to give a fairly good view of the man and I could see that he wore a heavy, velveteen coat and a filthy pair of tight breeches. His dust-covered boots were little more than half laced and both had splits across the toes.

Obviously he had not heard me approach, for he steadily continued to wind – tap – tap – tap –

But then he stopped to rub his aching back, and pulled himself up straight. His facial features shocked, even horrified me. The man had sharp, deep-set eyes, a large, twisted Roman nose, and thin, treacherous lips. There was a week's beard on his face.

He looked more like a character conjured up by Dickens than a product of the 20th century.

*

Slowly he became conscious of someone in the doorway. He brought those terrifying eyes to bear on me and, simultaneously, took on a bitter scowl.

Like some ludicrous creation of a caricaturist, he glowered at one who dared to cross his threshold. It was an unbearable moment.

I managed to make some effort at a friendly gesture – an unconvincing smile. It was a bombshell. The man evidently interpreted the smile as a form of ridicule. I had ignited every particle of fire and evil within his soul.

His sudden spring to action was as surprising as it was unforgettable and ghastly.

He released his grip on the chimes' handle and made a snarling rush at me. Instinctively, I hurled myself to one side.

Oh God, it was terrible. Unable to check his impetus, he was flung right through the doorway. With a number of piercing, agonising cries, he tumbled out of sight down the steps.

My mind went nearly numb, but I remember that soon the cries turned to muffled groans, then nothing more than the thuds of his body against the stone structure of the stairway.

*

Minutes must have elapsed before I grabbed the candle-stump and raced down the steps after him.

But the unbelievable truth is that there was no-one at the bottom, no sound save that of two owls, hooting somewhere above.

Obeying instinct, I ran back past the tombstone, down the winding path to the almshouses. A benign old man bade me come in and listened to my rather fantastic story. Now and again, he gave a little smile which seemed to reassure me.

When I had finished, he said: "You've got plenty of 'magination and no mistake. The old devil up in the church was 'xactly like old Jake Spragg, sexton here, hundred years ago. Mysterious sort. Must have heard of him, 'cos he be disappeared just like you said.

"Funny, really – a young feller, like you might be, was first to tell of it."

I tried to stammer out that this was no imagination, but he went on: "That young 'un didn't live long to tell the tale, though. Week or so later, he died, queer like. There's his grave-stone up there now, second in from the gate, on the right.

"Well, pleased to have seen you. Always likes to talk about the strange happenings of the old days. What's yer name?"

"Tom Saunders," I told him.

He gave a significant chuckle. "You know, you'll be tellin' me next yer second name is Benjamin."

"It is," I said, surprised.

*

Back on the road I hesitated. I was uneasy. Everything that had happened was bewildering and incomprehensible. Making a brave decision, I retraced my steps up the winding church path and through the creaking iron gate.

Striking a match, I made for the second tombstone on the right. I got down on my knees and peered at the inscription.

It read: 'Here lyeth the body of Thomas Benjamin Saunders, who died in extraordinary circumstances, February 8th, 1859.'

For the second time that night I tore away from the tower and the tombstone.

EXTRACTS FROM 1947 DIARY

January 5 – I've just had the idea of starting a Boys' Club magazine. At the moment I'm fired with enthusiasm. Of course, I would 'appoint' myself editor.

January 16 – A character who has always intrigued me is Mr Hawkins, who has a filthy little newsagent's shop opposite the Gazette. Always sleepy, drowsy. I had never known what to make of him – until today. He's a dipsomaniac. Really drunk. I had to cut the band from the papers for him and count the change. All in the shop were laughing at him. He was sobbing like a child. Bloodshot eyes, dishevelled hair – a Dickens character!!

February 26 – Mr W. Stevens put me on to the fact that Mr James Baker of Naish Road had just completed 75 years service at East Coker factory. He was eating kippers when I arrived. It was the hardest job in the world to take down what he had to say – he wandered off at a tangent so much – but I think I interested Coker readers.

February 28 – I am terribly run down – toothache, pimples, general aches and pains, lack of energy, languid, nausea, neurotic. I must sound terribly morbid but it's the truth. I have read before that adolescent years can be hard. They are!!

March 2 – Oh the satisfaction, the pride, the joy, the enthusiasm. I have quite unexpectedly received a cheque from 'Sporting Record' today for a few short local sports pars I sent them recently – nothing less than £1 – 7 – 6d. I sent the pars in ink, little thinking that they would be used.

March 10 – Walter Hammond, England and Gloster captain, has handed in his official resignation from 1st class cricket. This great player deserved a better 'nunc dimittis' than he got in Australia. Not a classic captain, perhaps; was no good at after-dinner speeches. On the field he had no great imagination. Nevertheless, a great cricketer and one who will go down with 'Cricket's Greatest'.

March 24 – After having been at the Western about 6 months, I have just about summed up the paper and its personalities. The paper is Conservative and unenterprising. Punctuation is bad, sentence construction poor. One thing that has impressed me is the high standard of intelligence of all the journalists I have come into contact with – not just glamourised, flashy gentlemen as the screen and fiction would have us believe.

March 27 – Had my biggest assignment. Covered the A.G.M. of the Yeovil cricket club. Complimented on effort by John Goodchild jnr of all people. Felt quite important with my note-book and pencil at meeting.

April 26 – Played cricket for Gazette v Compton House and made 13. A happy debut. It was a lovely day and I got a real kick out of playing cricket again.

April 30 – All my old cricket enthusiasm has returned. Today driving the ball hard against the wall, I had the misfortune to break a window. Just like old times.

May 1 – Police are tightening up on the vice racket. The great increase in homosexuality is also causing alarm. One of the Sunday papers has printed a letter from a prostitute in defence of her profession. It's logical! I am longing to go to London and see for myself what it is really like down Piccadilly way at night – without, of course, doing anything silly.

May 16 – What a thrill it gives one on a Thursday to watch papers being actually printed ... the large machine gradually gaining speed until one is sure the strain will tear the paper. Our machine prints more than 36,000 per hour.

May 26 – Spent a most enjoyable day at Taunton, watching Somerset-Gloucester match. Impressed by Tremlett. It was boiling hot all day; I came home red as a berry. Facilities at the County Ground are bad – at times our view was completely blocked.

May 28 – Had an interview with J.G. Sanders regarding the parish's forthcoming 650th anniversary. He was in bed with a bad throat. Rather fancied myself sitting on corner of bed with note-book and pencil. Mr Goodchild jnr (chief reporter) has offered me 10 days holiday which I think is quite reasonable.

May 30 – Went to Gymkhana, carnival and sports at North Coker – or rather picked up the results and listened to a foul address by Mr E.H. Northover, propaganda officer of the Conservative Party. Attacked the miners' four hours less a week – I only wish he'd been sent down the mines. He was one of the real old Tories – not a thought of his own, a spluttering, obstinate, pig-headed, old gas-bag! Honestly, I was ashamed to be seen listening to him.

June 8 – Played for Coker 2s v Queen Camel yesterday. We made 111 and they 14. I had good day. Made 9 and bowling took 7-7.

June 26 – Got a very good story in, just in time for publication. A heifer had climbed to the top of 150ft Monument at Curry Rivel. The animal had climbed 179 steps and by the time it had been spotted, it was thoroughly frightened. It was finally assisted on its descent – backwards!

July 4 – Have been notified that I have been granted deferment from military training for a time. I should have liked to get training over. People may think I am trying to avoid service. I'm very conscientious.

July 30 – Played for East against West Coker tonight. Made 7 but bowling to sloggers Lucas and J. Stroud had 19 knocked off me in one over. They took me off! I should think so. I lost the game for them.

August 14 – A great pit disaster has occurred at Whitehaven. Over a hundred men have been killed. It accentuates once again the many great risks taken by miners. Three men came out alive after being entombed for 21 hours, and one actually asked for the latest racing results.

September 16 – I am ravishingly hungry for new knowledge but don't feel able to absorb any. I am also becoming more self-conscious and not so easy a conversationalist as I used to be. One maddening drawback is my inability, at times, to concentrate. I find myself just listening to a jumble of words that mean nothing. A book I'm reading, 'Journalism – A to Z', has renewed all my journalistic keenness. I fear I've slacked a little lately.

September 18 – I am beginning to size up the subs. 'Cherry' Lanham now takes an almost embarrassing paternal interest in me – but I'm sure it's only because I've sold him some cheap eggs. Cleverly I like best of all – the 'furtive' way he asks me to get him cheap 'gaspers' and 'medical remedies' is most amusing.

September 25 – I went up the Court today. One of the cases concerned Denzell Lucas, West Coker, accused of stealing asbestos piping from Liberty Hall. He pleaded not guilty unsuccessfully but was let off with costs. I expect he was mad to see me there – but I had little sympathy. He knocked 19 off my bowling towards the end of the season!

September 29 – I seldom get a free night now. Either I have to cover a meeting in town or attend one of the dratted ones I belong to in the village. The boys' club for instance: this is, I feel, a darned nuisance at times. They are a pretty rough bunch of fellows on the whole and they do get occasionally in an ugly mood. Most of them have reached the age when they take a great pleasure in hearing their own voices. One will start an argument over almost nothing and some of the others think it a 'swell' idea to play the committee up. On the whole, though, I think I've been a quite successful chairman. Some times the psychological stuff works wonders on them – force rarely.

October 27 – Show business is in my veins again. The gang are working on a new show which Donald Murley and myself have written. We have got several provisional engagements. 'Stingy' Murley is certainly a man of ideas and fine imagination. He would make a very good script writer.

November 14 – Went to Street to see Yeovil play. Atrocious game on the whole. What I enjoyed most about the day's outing was a talk I had with McCormack of the 'Post'. He told me, as good as, to get out of the 'W.G.' He said it is living in a world of 500 years ago. Journalism really starts when you are working for a bigger paper, when you meet people. Imagination and knowledge of human nature are more important than shorthand and fact! He said that getting drunk was part of one's education.

November 17 – The story of the week is the Royal Wedding. Despite the courageous but ridiculous efforts of the 'Daily Worker' to denounce the monarchy, there is a festive, austerity-free air about the whole place. The papers are 'splashing' every scrap of wedding news – presents, dresses, who's coming, route of the procession. I am far from a die-hard Royalist, but I must admit that all this popular emotion rather gets into my veins.

November 29 – We went to Ilchester tonight to put on a 2-hour show for the British Legion. The audience was appalling – incredibly dumb. Jokes that we had laughed at for hours at rehearsals didn't force a mutter. Any intelligent joke or hint of sophistication went begging. Visual humour, alone, got appreciated – that only slightly. It was a great disappointment after all our work – some of our material was very clever. We learnt a lot.

December 20 – For some inexplicable reason, I have lately become again very self-conscious. I thought I had got over all that. I must shake off my inferiority complex. I think it often does more harm than good to psycho-analyse oneself.

December 31 – My year at the 'W.G.', while not particularly exciting, has been good ground-work. I've earned just as much money from linage as from my own paper. I've learnt a lot of the tricks of the trade. 'Sporting Record' regularly take my pars of local sport at 5/- each but I have yet to get one of my stories accepted.

3
Diary of a Young Journalist

JULY, 1948 — July 12 to 18

15 THURSDAY — St. Swithin

As the result of an earthquake in Japan last week, several thousands were suddenly, without warning of any shape or form, struck down stone dead. Now this sort of thing must really make all reasonable people wonder. We must be realists. Diabolical though the thought is, I believe that there is some monstrous power that can strike us down at will.

This power (call it Satan if you like) is continually struggling against a weaker power — Goodness.

What can we do in the matter? Very little. It's a terrible thought.

16 FRIDAY

I heard some evangelist talking in the borough the other day. He informed us that the day was near at hand when again the whole world would be destroyed. If that does happen, all I can say is that there could be nothing better.

What is the logic in our existence at the moment. Wars seem bound to go on eternally.

When I was younger, I was very happy, innocent & contented. Why? Because I had never heard of that foul word POLITICS. Now I am beginning to realise that while there is not a common ideology, there will not be common peace and prosperity.

But there will never be a common ideology.

17 SATURDAY

We were not made sheep-like. We think, usually, in the way nature intended us to. And nature did not make us all the same.

Therefore the trouble seems to lie with our creator. Now we are back to the old question of Genesis, Chapter 1. Hang it all, cut this phoney philosophy, Foot. You know the whole thing is miles beyond you!

40

> I commence the New Year fired with journalistic ambition.

So begins the diary that David wrote in 1948. He is eighteen years old, turning nineteen in April, in the second of his five years of apprenticeship at the *Western Gazette*. His writing opportunities at work are limited and mundane, and he turns to this diary to express himself more freely.

He buys a much bigger diary than in previous years, two foolscap pages for each week, and he abandons completely the constraint of writing separate entries for each day. Gone are the trivial details and the brief mentions of his own cricket. Now he uses the diary to write at length on chosen topics, a single subject often extending over the full two pages of the week – perhaps 750 words written in blue ink in a well-formed hand. Every day of every week is filled to the last line. 'I hate to see blank pages,' he admits.

In one instance, when he describes a week's holiday – a day at Taunton watching the Australians, followed by a seven-day trip to London – he runs the account across four and a half weeks of the diary.

> Never have I had a more exciting, adventurous, wholly enjoyable, interesting and educational seven days ... which is a rather verbose way of saying that I have just passed through the best week of my life. At last I've got something to write about.

This London trip is a step into a new world for him, and his account of it brims with excitement from first to last. He is alive to everything he witnesses, his writing flowing with unbridled energy.

> The tenses in this narration are shocking but why worry about trivialities when I am in such a whirl and <u>time</u> means little.

With a relative, with whom he stays in Harrow, he visits the Houses of Parliament, Madame Tussaud's, the zoo, but these are not the sites he most wants to see. He is much more enthralled when he watches speedway among a 90,000-strong crowd at Wembley Stadium, listens to the soapbox speakers at Hyde Park Corner, joins the bustling Sunday throng in the Petticoat Lane market and slips into a risqué revue at the Windmill Theatre, where 'the girls have orders to play to the sweating front rows'. Then on the last day he takes the tube to Stepney Green:

> I fell hopelessly in love with the dirty East End. Bethnal Green, which a policeman described to me as "a stinking market with the scum of the earth on the street corners", is undoubtedly a filthy place. This was the first time I had been in the heart of a slum – it was just as bad as anything I had ever read about.

> Educationally I found this last day's tour of the filth and extensive bomb damage to be of great use. I shall go home to East Coker, a sweet-smelling, open, spacious paradise, a more thoughtful young man.

The year is an eventful one around the world: Mahatma Gandhi assassinated, the state of Israel created amid violence in Palestine, Berlin blockaded by Soviet troops, the launch of the National Health Service, an unsuccessful government attempt to suspend capital punishment. David uses the diary to explore his thinking on all these topics. Politically he leans to the Left, sometimes strongly, but with no great certainty of conviction:

> I'm apt at times to be a little inconsistent in my political credo. But I'm still comparatively young and should still be LEARNING. The time is yet to come when I am mentally equipped enough to form honest opinions.

In sport Don Bradman's Australians go unbeaten all summer, London stages a surprisingly successful Olympic Games and the world of boxing is beset with controversy. David writes at length about all these, twice offering a detailed analysis of the state of the England cricket team.

> Nevertheless, although England are plumbing the depths, they still get affectionate support from millions of their countrymen. Nearly everyone tries to listen to the wireless or enquires every ten minutes "How's the Test going?"

Always David takes the diary seriously. He writes last thing at night, seated on the bed in his little room at the top of Verandah Cottage:

> There's only four square yards of it, but it gives me a feeling of beautiful simplicity, security and peace.
>
> There are the four walls of yellow distemper – bright to the tired eye ... the pretty but cheap, little wash-stand (no bathroom as yet) ... the rather clumsy, oaken chest-of-drawers ... the little, 'primitive' window ... Not a cupboard in the place so I improvise by keeping some of my wardrobe behind a curtain on one of the walls. Then, by the side of my bed, a large pile of my old school books, for ever bringing back grand memories, a batch of sporting and film journals, and let's see ... a book on Socialism, 'The Amazing Theatre' by Jimmy Agate, one of Neville Cardus's cricketing books and my priceless files.

Sometimes he finds the inspiration for a diary entry in episodes from his own life. As chairman of the East Coker Boys' Club, one who prefers the 'whispered word of warning' to 'soap-box shouting', he is plunged into a crisis when a boy fires an air-pistol out of the door and accidentally hits another boy in the head:

> One moment he was laughing, joking and playing table tennis with me; the next, had the pellet found a more porous part, he might have been dead.

Later in the year David is in trouble again. Fed up with his 'rusty, creaking bicycle that seemed to sustain a hundred mishaps a week', he overhears a fourteen-year-old boy called Taylor trying to sell a brand new bicycle to a friend for five pounds. The friend can only manage four so David, 'making a split-second decision', steps in to buy the new bike for five pounds and sell his old one to the friend for four. 'A neat deal'.

'Now come the repercussions,' he writes. The mother of the boy who has bought his old bike storms into the *Gazette* office, saying that her son was 'under strict orders never to have a bicycle' and, furthermore, the four pounds was stolen from her. David ends up that evening in their house, 'a condemned cottage', arguing with the grandfather, 'a fat old Cockney with chronic asthma'. He takes pity on them, returns the four pounds and leaves the house with his old bike. The 'neat deal', of which he was so proud, unravels further when Mr Taylor, the father of the other boy, complains that his son has been taken advantage of by David, selling the new bike for much too little.

> So that's as far as the bicycle transaction has gone. I'll have to pay another pound or two to Taylor, and I'm dumped once again with my beastly, old bike.
>
> Let me give you a little philosophical advice, Mr David Foot. You leave business to the businessman. And thank God you're not one. For as soon as you become a trader, and deal in money, you begin to lose your soul, your friends and your own happiness.

Early in the year David writes with appreciation of the *Western Gazette*, calling the provincial paper 'the finest training-ground possible for the aspiring top-notch scribe' and commenting on how much he is learning about all aspects of the newspaper business. Yet it is not many weeks later when he is railing against the dullness of the paper, with its front page filled with advertisements of auctions.

At the start of the year he is often in the office. Then, when he does get out, he is attending funerals, Conservative fetes and the annual meetings of the ladies' skittles league and the beekeepers' association.

This last assignment sees him in hot water when the Secretary of the Association ('a certain Mr Turner, a fiery Scotsman') writes an angry letter to the editor about David's 'totally incorrect' report. Summoned by the chief reporter to answer the charge, David is not helped when he cannot decipher his shorthand notes. So bravely he opts to visit the complainant:

> I was really a bit scared. If I was proved wrong, I would be humiliated and I would be cast as unreliable.
>
> At 7.30 that evening, there was a trepid tap on the door of 35, West Coker Road – the residence of the aforementioned Mr Turner. I sighed momentarily with relief when his wife answered the door. Could I see Mr Turner? The lord of the manor duly made his appearance. "Yes?" "I'm from the Western Gazette –" Splutter, crash, bang. "You are, are you – come in." I breathed something about having a breast-plate. "Who was the reporter in question?" "Me" – spluttering again.
>
> For 45 minutes we talked, in which time he told me that the Association unanimously agreed that the report was rank impudence. But though that grey-haired Scottie argued for minute after minute, the only real thing he put before me as incorrect was the chairman's name – TOULD for Gould.
>
> I was pleased with myself and began to gain confidence. I pointed out that the decision to make any feature of a meeting prominent rested with us (the office) entirely. His main grouse seemed to be the fact that I made quite a lot of the discussion over finances. He also thought some trivialities, that I completely ignored, should have gone in.
>
> Briefly, he had no really concrete argument against the report. It was a victory for me (stop that trumpet-blowing).

David has a burning desire to succeed as a writer. When he goes to the cinema to see a film in which Gregory Peck, as a journalist, pretends to be a Jew in order to understand anti-semitism, he comes home inspired:

> The film greatly renewed my ambition to reach the top of the penning profession. I didn't mean to use 'top'. I've no false illusions of travelling that far. What I meant was – will I ever

become a real, a REAL journalist? Will I have the opportunity of writing 'specials', getting to the heart of human nature?

I think I can say that I've got, generally speaking, a very placid temperament. But there are streaks of real fire, of initiative and determination, within my make-up.

Cricket is unquestionably his first love:

As summer approaches each year, I experience two great longings. One is to get out in the open with leather and willow. The other is to become a cricket writer. I am able to fulfil the first wish; perhaps, one day, my second desire will be answered. I love cricket and despite what our American friends say about a game that is quite beyond their comprehension, I am sure that it stands alone, high on the pinnacle of sporting life.

Those two ambitions, to get to the heart of human nature and to write about cricket, found in time the perfect outlet in his ground-breaking biography of Harold Gimblett – so it is a delightful coincidence that his first article on cricket, albeit without a by-line, should be a brief feature on the Somerset batsman.

Thirty-five years on from this diary, his Gimblett book would receive a glowing review in the *Wisden Almanack* from John Arlott. So there is a further lovely happenstance in David's second published article being the report of a game at which Arlott is providing the crowd with commentary. It gives David the opportunity to introduce himself to the great broadcaster:

In his deep, warm voice, rich in wit and West Country dialect, when he wasn't sleeping, drinking beer or signing autographs, he kept a 2,000 crowd amused. I got his autograph, telling him that, with a little forging, I might at least get a few articles accepted.

He appreciated that.

Seventy-five years on, the autograph survives among David's papers, recording a special moment when the eager youngster from East Coker touched fleetingly a master of his craft.

For all his ambition and his lectures to himself to work hard and learn as much as he can, David's diary is never many pages away from a fresh expression of his self-doubt:

Will I ever make a journalist? I'm quite unable to form an opinion. Sometimes, after receiving perhaps an occasional word of praise, I feel, literally, on top of the world. I can write ... I've a natural flair for news ... I could show some of my colleagues a thing or two ... I would make a first-class sports scribe.

> Then I sober myself. Maybe I am stumped for a lead ... there's a fearful inaccuracy ... I may realise just how atrocious my shorthand is. Anything of these incidents will sober me.
>
> Will I ever be a success at my profession? Can I write, after all? I don't get such a lot of practice, and somehow I don't think I'm as fluent as I used to be. How do I compare with the rest of the Editorial Office? Most of them have vastly better shorthand, and some of the copy they churn out is better than I could ever compose.

Then, maintaining the conceit that this diary was addressed to the world:

> All this must make terribly dull reading.

Fifty-two years later, in March 2000, David got out the diary and was appalled as he read through it. In the front of it he wrote:

> I'm so ashamed at some of my personal observations of those immature days. Some dreadful, smug, self-righteous, patronising comments – and all that ghastly romantic nonsense about journalism.

He returned in 2003, adding a second shudder of horror:

> I am thoroughly ashamed of some of my observations in this, one of my very few diaries. Was I so parochial, so naïve and, worst of all, so bigoted? There are anti-semitic sentiments, and even a hint or two of appalling teenage snobbery. A few of my more subjective thoughts seem, at this distance, painfully self-conscious.

Yes, it is 'painfully self-conscious' in places, with all the earnestness of late adolescence. Despite that, the entries demonstrate how alive he was to the world around him and how much thought he was giving to his writing. Words were important to him; he was never going to be content with becoming a jobbing hack.

The diary ends with a reflection on his year-long endeavour:

> I have filled another diary and enjoyed it. It is full of the laughter and tears of one's average day-to-day life. I never intended to make this a literary masterpiece – one that I could look back on with pride. I merely wanted it to serve as a fairly thorough record of my life.

EXTRACTS FROM 1948 DIARY

Graham Heathcote

The same age as David but living away from home, Heathcote reports on Yeovil sport for the Bristol Evening World. His dramatic departure in May opens the door for David to take on his work as a side-earner.

January – I find Graham ('Flash') Heathcote, young 'Evening World' Yeovil staff reporter, an interesting study. His good points: (1) a fine writing style, (2) the imagination and general knowledge of an older man, (3) a 'classic' example of the 'sensationalist'. His bad points: (1) inaccurate, (2) unco-operative, say fellow reporters; (3) unscrupulous, which, of course, does not pay when one is a district reporter, when your critics are on your door-step and when you may need the help of some-one whose assistance you may have abused in the past.

'Flash' walks at an incredible pace with head down, complete with broad-brimmed brown trilby, bent low on chest. I like him for his moments of confidence, when he shows he's 'human' and not the 'artificial' pseudo-Yankee he likes to think he is. (He reads masses of American magazines and I think that he's becoming, journalistically, a little too American.)

In these moments of confidence, he strikes me as if he's a very lonely, young man, yearning for home life (he hates 'digs').

June – It's not often the reporter himself finds the headlines. This is exactly what has happened this week. It was, I suppose, inevitable. Graham Heathcote was an unusual type, to say the least. Without boasting, I believe I can honestly say that I was the only reporter who could get on with him. He had a great many faults but, because I thought I understood him, I found he confided more in me than in anyone else.

As a young man, he appeared to be rather unco-operative, inclined to be indiscreet and, at times, morose. I put him down as neurotic. He was extremely fascinated by tough American films and American literature. His adoration for the Yankee way of life was, I fear, his undoing. Leaving a note, saying "I'm through – Heathcote" for his editor, he packed his bag and disappeared.

He has now been picked up by a police 999 car in Oxford Street at 2 a.m. I think he was obstreperous and when searched – for loitering suspiciously – was found to have a loaded revolver with quite a lot of live ammunition.

Well, Graham got a £10 fine and lost his job as well. He has probably ruined his career. And, while quite a few seem to be gloating over this 'interesting affair', I think his case really pathetic.

Graham, at Yeovil, was a very lonely person and I think he yearned for happy family life. Despite the 'little dream-land of America', I found he had a very human side at times. "I've bought some coffee today to send home to my mother" ... "I used to like nothing better than to field at cover-point" ... "All the Yeovil press are against me, but I know I can beat them all." The latter was a mixture of persecution mania and sheer conceit.

I wonder if I shall see him again. I hope so.

> *They do meet – at the National Union of Journalists conference in Bridlington in 1951. Graham Heathcote, working for the Daily Mirror, is 'a lot more mature,' David writes. 'He is now a member of the PARTY – a devout worshipper of the Kremlin's way of life.'*

Life and Death

The first of his two weeks of annual holiday takes David to Southbourne, near Bournemouth, with his mother. When he witnesses an attempt to resuscitate a drowned man, he uses it as an opportunity to develop the observational skills necessary to be a reporter.

July – I had a very worthwhile experience on the beach. I saw a young man very nearly die. Going out for a swim one afternoon, I saw several looking out about 25 yards where two or three on a raft were beckoning to the shore. I didn't take much notice but when the raft came in, I saw that there was a man stretched out full-length on it. He had fallen off a raft, couldn't swim and had, I gathered, been in the water for a minute or so before being grabbed.

I had a grand-stand view. I watched for an hour or so while beach attendants rendered, till they sweated, artificial respiration. The tension was terrific. A couple of hundred had gathered in a large circle, some of them stripped to the waist. They spoke in whispers. No-one who watched the sweating attendants, fighting to save the life of one of their cousins, looked anything but white and grim. There was the dramatic moment when the mother and father came on the scene and hysterically had to be led away. Previously, I had asked one of the first young men on the scene about the casualty and he said it was his brother. Another brother was praying. I am not merely being dramatic and letting my imagination run away with me. I watched the scene as a reporter. I observantly noted every emotion of the onlookers.

The strain was terrible. Then the young fellow – his body black and blue by the vigorous massage – began to struggle. We knew he would live, and we sighed. Gradually he began to moan. Before he really came round, they bundled him into an ambulance and took him to hospital.

While that gathering watched the fight for human life in silence, little children nearby, in complete contrast, laughed and shouted and made sandcastles. <u>They</u> were very much alive.

Harold Gimblett

*He is not given a by-line, but a century by Harold Gimblett
gives David his first chance to submit an article on cricket.*

July – Harold Gimblett scored his 28th hundred for the County today and has now beaten the record of Lionel Palairet of scoring most centuries for Somerset. I've written a stick-and-a-half pen-picture of Gimblett for the 'WG' and I'm rather proud of it. The style's reminiscent of Neville Cardus at his best ... it's a good job no-one else ever reads this diary!

Wally Elliott (bless his heart), although he may not be a brilliant sub, has good qualities. He was not too ruthless. One of my sentences about 'Palairet being the West Country doyen of the game' and another talking about 'Gimblett and his glorious cow-shots in the early days' came out, however.

How I long to become a cricket scribe. I may be far from talented, but I have the assets of knowing the game pretty thoroughly both as a player and critic, increasing my knowledge of the past men's great deeds and genuinely loving everything connected with this great game.

Road Accident

*Although David reports this second hand, he relishes the
telling of the tale, seeing quickly its potential as a news story.*

November – I believe the following story is authentic. I doubt if we shall ever know for certain, though.

Travelling in his little car somewhere near Crewkerne a week ago, Gordon Hosie (Adv Dept) went to pull round to one side and a huge streamlined job gliding along behind hit its little brother a resounding slap. Gordon and his little car rocketed across the road and he was very lucky to get out unhurt. Indignantly, he went across to meet the chauffeur, equally red-faced. The latter told Gordon that he was in the wrong, that he did not show his indicator.

Gordon grabbed a bystander who confirmed that the chauffeur's comment was untrue. Thereupon, the driver of the big car said that everything would be paid for and put right. There was no need to make any fuss. Gordon was not having that, however. He insisted upon ringing the Police. The chauffeur certainly did not receive that with enthusiasm but, after he had realised that money alone was not enough to turn Gordon, he relented. He did, without success, stress that his male passenger was in a great hurry.

The Police arrived and, after Gordon's particulars had been taken, he went on his way. Next morning, the Police rang him to check two or three points. They now understood, they said, why the chauffeur was keen to move on as quickly as possible. The car was not properly insured, the driving licence was at fault and the tank had red petrol in it.

But did Mr Hosie know who the distinguished gentleman in the big car was, asked the Police. No? Why, Lord Beaverbrook.

The Beaver has, of course, got a farm fairly near here. There is every reason to believe Hosie's tale. What a story! John Fenner and myself thought about flogging it to the 'Daily Worker'.

Home Life

Life in the Foot household moves forward in 1948, with David's father starting his own gardening business. Yet the adolescent David, alive to a wider world, is often frustrated by his parents.

May – I went to see Bill Smith, parish councillor and Labour man, to check on something I was putting in the paper. Now Bill and myself have more than a few common beliefs – however much I may not agree with some of his attitudes – and it was not particularly unnatural when I brought home a couple of books to read. One was Strachey's 'Why you should be a Socialist'. I did not necessarily agree with the views of the writer but brought it home as part of my education.

Jokingly I showed it to my father. He was silent for a time, then became serious and got in an ugly mood. Made such comments as "You'd do best to keep away from Smith – he won't do you any good nor his party" ... "He'll get you the sack in the Western Gazette."

July – I suppose this is a big day in the history of our family. We have a Ford 10, bought from Mr Dodge at a fairly reasonable price, and we are now tolerating the bitter glares of the envious neighbours. I have not ridden in the car yet. Father has been very fortunate in getting a licence right away and not having to carry an 'L'. I'm not sure if this is for the best, though. He likes to give the impression that he is a fully-fledged driver when, in fact, he is very uncertain.

We have known very hard times when every penny counted. It seems a little ironic, however, that whereas we now have a car to call our own, we still have to go 100 yards to fetch our water and bathe in a cold, hard enamel tub – if we are lucky.

December – Christmas is essentially a time for joyous family life but if ever there is a time in the year when there is friction in the Foot household, it is on December 25th. The trouble is that it is all really so very childish.

Morning usually goes comparatively smoothly. Mother gets in a bit of a flap over the preparations for the big dinner and, to crown it, Father often stays in the Helyar Arms and is late for the feast.

After this, tension gradually mounts. Father goes to sleep in the front room and Mother wakes him up. He lights his cigar and Mother cannot bear (or so she says) the smell. So she goes out in the cold kitchen to sulk for an hour or so. Hardly a pleasant word comes after that.

Yes, I know the routine off by heart. Without a word of a lie, I daresay we are one of the most miserable families in East Coker on Christmas Day.

A By-Line At Last

*David spends the year longing for his first by-line.
But when it comes, he is not thrilled.*

November – For the very first time in my short journalistic innings, I am getting a by-line – and I'm as a child who is getting a tricycle for Christmas. Yeovil FC supporters are producing a brochure for a jubilee occasion. Local sporting journalists are contributing and quite by accident I was asked whether I could hastily bash out anything about the club's 'guests' – those soldiers, stationed at Houndstone, who helped Yeovil out.

December – Yeovil Town's Silver Jubilee programmes are now on sale – complete with articles by Kemble, Voyzey, Sibley and what I have now decided is a poor one from me.

This is not a question of mock modesty. I just do not think my article on 'Soldiers in Green' is good enough. It's a lazy piece of writing. For the first time I have my by-line to the effort and, boasting apart, I do not think the writing is worthy of me (it's as bad as that!).

In humble defence I gave the article no thought and wrote it in well less than an hour. Wasn't quite sure what was wanted so I wrote in a 'don't-carish' frame of mind. There was not half enough concentration.

I was told to write it snappily and bring in some humour. I feel I made the fatal mistake of being inclined to force the latter. One of my similes, in which I introduce gorgonzola cheese (heaven knows why in a soccer article), I am quite ashamed of.

GIMBLETT MAKES CRICKET HISTORY

David's first published article on cricket (without a by-line)
Western Gazette, July 1948

As Harold Gimblett raised his bat, after scoring his 28th hundred at Frome this week, to acknowledge the cheers of the crowd, he knew that, if figures are anything to go by, he is the greatest batsman Somerset has ever introduced to the cricketing fraternity. He had broken the record of Lionel C.H. Palairet, that West Country player who used to thrill crowds by his prodigious strokes all over the field half-a-century ago.

Gimblett's comparatively brief but colourful County cricketing career began in the same town – Frome – on May 18th, 1935. To say this debut was sensational is an under-statement. Brought into the Somerset team at the last minute as a replacement, at No. 8, this unheralded rosy-cheeked, broad-shouldered farmer proceeded straightway to make the cricket purists shudder, but the majority of the 'rustic' element at Frome that day to cheer themselves hoarse.

Treating Test bowler Nichols and the rest of the Essex attack with utter contempt, Gimblett wielded a bat as nature and village-cricket enthusiasts intended him to. He had three figures to his name in 63 minutes and the 'Lawrence' trophy was his. Many think it a pity that his play was 'developed' – from the unorthodox to something more orthodox, elegant and safer.

Whether Harold Gimblett should be an opening bat will long be a matter for speculation. But the fact remains, his name will go down among the great batsmen, 'one with a touch of genius' in the opinion of R.C. Robertson-Glasgow; he will for many summers remain the idol of West Country crowds and many glorious runs will flow from his bat before he oils it for the last time.

COUNTY TEAM BEAT YEOVIL

David's first report on a cricket match (again without a by-line)
Western Gazette, August 1948

In the opinion of John Arlott, well-known cricket commentator, Yeovil's new sports ground at Brimsmore has great possibilities. Watching the Bill Andrews testimonial game on Sunday, he told a representative of this paper that, although not ready at the moment, the ground would certainly in the near future be worthy of county cricket. He did think, however, that the great size of the field was apt to be a disadvantage.

Most of the keen, appreciative crowd of 2,000 stayed until the last ball was bowled. In fact, the closing overs were the most exciting of the game. Batting painfully slowly, at times, against the wily slows of Wellard and West Indies' player Cameron, Yeovil scrambled together 117 for nine wickets in nearly three hours batting before declaring. A more disastrous start could not have been made, Tetlow and Seward being back in the pavilion with not a run being scored. E.J. Freeman, White and Commander Hodges pulled the side together, however, and Ward made a breezy contribution towards the close.

Scoring often at two runs a minute, Bill Andrews' team really set about Yeovil's attack. Hill and Stephenson showed us some aggressive stroke play, and they were ably assisted by Pothecary, Wellard and Vickery. It was only appropriate that Arthur Wellard should smite the first six on this ground. Fielders were lost over the brow of the hill as they hunted for the ball.

Scores: Yeovil, 117 for 9, dec. (Freeman 29, Ward 28 n.o., White 19, Commander Hodges 17, Wellard 3-32, Cameron 3-25); Bill Andrews' XI, 119 for 10 (game was 12-a-side!) (Stephenson 29, Pothecary 22, Hill 19, Wellard 19, Vickery 11, Scriven 4-20, White 2-15).

Somerset played county cricket on the ground, known as Johnson Park, between 1951 and 1970. It was here in 1969, in the first year of the Sunday League, that off-spinner Brian Langford bowled his allotment of eight overs without conceding a run.

4

The Never Forgotten Afternoon

(above) The Yeovil crowd cheering their team's fairy-tale triumph
(right) Player/manager Alec Stock

For David the foggy afternoon in January 1949 was 'the nonpareil of my sporting life'. On the famously sloping Huish Park pitch his beloved Yeovil Town, of the Southern League, beat the mighty Sunderland in the fourth round of the FA Cup.

David was 19 years old, working as a copy-boy on the *Western Gazette*, too junior to be entrusted with the reporting of the game. Nevertheless he played a bizarre and never-to-be-forgotten role in transmitting regular updates to the outside world. He told the story in later life in features for the *Guardian* and, lightly fictionalised, in a chapter of *Country Reporter*.

Somerset has never been noted for its soccer. At the time Yeovil Town were a mid-table club in the Southern League, playing against such sides as Hastings United and Merthyr Tydfil. They were mostly local men, part-time footballers who worked during the week. Sunderland, by contrast, were a permanent presence in the all-powerful First Division, with six league titles to their name. Their post-war activity in the transfer market, signing Ivor Broadis and Len Shackleton for what were then eye-watering sums, led to their being nicknamed 'the Bank of England club'.

In the first two rounds of the Cup Yeovil had beaten fellow non-leaguers, Romford and Weymouth. They were the only remaining non-league side in the third round, and they triumphed 3-1 over Bury of the Second Division. Their reward was a home tie against the mighty Sunderland; it was the greatest sporting event in the Somerset town's history.

The regular reporter for the *Western Gazette* was in great demand from numerous publications, looking to make a tidy sum from the afternoon. However, he had a problem. An army of rival reporters were due to descend on the ground and there was only one telephone. Cunningly he and David drew on their local knowledge to devise a plan. The reporter, high up at the back of the stand, would lower sheets of paper through a small hole for David, stationed below in the gents urinals, to reach up and receive. From there David would run to the local butcher's shop where he would phone out each breathless update. Working to an agreed schedule, the procedure was carried out more than a dozen times during the afternoon.

It was a story that was perfect for David's delightful imagination and, with the extra freedom of fiction in *Country Reporter*, he was able to embellish the tale with some humorous, if not always wholesome, details.

Yeovil won 2-1 after extra time, with goals from player/manager Alec Stock and Eric Bryant. Their reward was to be drawn away to Manchester United who, in front of more than 81,000 spectators at Manchester City's Maine Road ground, ended the fairy tale by winning 8-0.

David's first opportunity to tell the story of the triumph came in 1973 when he persuaded the *Bristol Evening Post* to let him write a series, 'The Great Games', about memorable matches played by local teams. Yeovil's giant-killing was a tale made for the stirring hyperbole of a local newspaper.

> There has never been a more romantic story in the history of West Country soccer. Glovers and aircraft workers from Yeovil, farmers from Pendomer and Hardington Mandeville still relive every minute of it ... the day Colonel Joe Prior's much-vaunted Sunderland came to Somerset and saw their FA Cup aspirations frenetically brushed aside by a team of upstart Saturday afternoon footballers.
>
> It was a fantastic game – in a fantastic setting. A town with a population of less than 25,000. And here were 15,000 of them crammed around this intimate, gently sloping pitch. Many of them sat on beer crates, encroaching almost onto the playing area.

For the next 54 years, till 2003, Yeovil remained in the ranks of non-league football, sometimes winning the Southern League, other times sinking into the tier below that. The Cup threw up further moments of giant-killing glory, though none against a top-division club. Home ties against Arsenal, Norwich and Queens Park Rangers were all lost 3-0.

Alec Stock went on to have an illustrious career in football management, taking in spells at Arsenal and AS Roma and famously leading QPR, then in the Third Division, to a fairy-tale triumph in the 1967 League Cup Final. By the time of the West London club's visit to Huish Park in January 1988, Stock had retired from management and was on the board at QPR, an added piquancy to the fixture that did not escape David.

By this time David was an established *Guardian* sports writer so he had no difficulty persuading the sports editor to visit his 'land of memories' with a feature on the 1949 game. Further features followed when Yeovil moved to a new ground in 1990, on the 50th anniversary of the Sunderland match in 1999 and when the club were promoted to the Football League in 2003.

Inevitably there was repetition from feature to feature, but always David injected fresh touches. One time he recalled a Christmas scene from the 1930s, with 'the bizarre background of carol singing from the adjacent Victorian school competing with the throaty agricultural cheers', another time there was a flashback to the old ground where 'Tesco's tills now ring on almost the spot where Alec Stock scored his only goal of that season.'

David was especially fond of Stock, writing a beautifully crafted portrait of him in *Fragments of Idolatry*:

> I continue to see him in my mind's eye dapper in appearance, solemn of face, never lacking an old-world courtesy when a stranger with a market-day accent wishes him good-morning, walking briskly down to the bank in Yeovil's pale winter sun; or maybe knocking on the solicitor's door, just over the cobbles from the parish church, to tell the gawky Dickie Dyke, the office boy, that he'd be needed to play against Sunderland but it wouldn't affect his bible-class attendance the following day. Alec was a man for all seasons and occasions.

That foggy afternoon in 1949 was a perfect medium for David, half a century on, to express his lingering melancholy about the passing of the less 'sophisticated' rural world in which he had grown up:

> Those were the days when the Somerset market town rattled to the sound of Aplin & Barrett's milk churns and there was more commotion from cussing drovers and herded shorthorns than from the antiquated traffic. Middle Street had not yet succumbed to pedestrianisation and the half-timbered George Inn continued to protrude quaintly onto the pavement. On the outskirts was Westlands, where the Lysander and the Whirlwind were made and where, once a year, Somerset came to play cricket alongside the hangars.
>
> The football club was called Yeovil and Petters United before 1945 and dubbed 'The Glovers' because the town was once home to more than 30 glove factories. On bleak winter Saturday afternoons the country folk tumbled out of the bus near The Three Choughs, crossed the road and bustled up Tabernacle Lane to the Huish ground, just round the corner from Nick Collins's cider pub.

During their 16-year stay in the league Yeovil Town rose briefly and valiantly to the second tier. Now, at the close of the 2022/23 season, they have been relegated from the fifth to the sixth tier of the pyramid, the National League South, to play against such sides as Bath and Eastbourne. I suspect that in his heart David felt that was pretty much where they belonged. Despite the rare days of glory, rural Somerset folk are not given to delusions of grandeur.

THE LAND OF MEMORIES

Previewing Yeovil v Queens Park Rangers in the FA Cup Third Round
(Two years earlier Michael Heseltine had resigned as Minister of Defence
in a dispute over the Yeovil-based helicopter manufacturers Westland)
The Guardian, 9 January 1988

Long before Yeovil built helicopters, when young, resourceful, golden-haired Mick Heseltine would only have reaped a passing mention in the local public prints as the possessor of a good left foot, the south Somerset market town made a living from gloves, cheese and, intermittently, from presumptuous winter deeds on a coarse strip of grassland, mythically described as resembling the hazardous foothills of the Mendips.

Most of the glove factories have now gone and the dairy products have found another home. But there is still the football club, playing these days in the Vauxhall-Opel competition, lower than the GM Conference, a temporary station it accepts with a slightly embarrassed, or maybe disdainful, shrug.

QPR will be wise to ignore the down-grading of a team which has already knocked 13 League clubs out of the FA Cup, most famously Sunderland and most recently Cambridge in the last round.

From that solicitous Saturday in 1938, when I stood on a beer-crate next to the corner flag to lend boy-soprano ecstasy to the triumph of Yeovil and Petters over Brighton and Hove, I have missed few of Huish's stirring cup battles.

Romance clouds and distorts the memory: all the ties were for me an amalgam of valour and stunning skills, manifested by a bunch of broad-vowelled glove-cutters, storekeepers and farmers' sons.

By the time of Sunderland's visit, in January 1949 for the fifth round, I had progressed from beer-crate to the aromatic allure of gents' lavatories. The transition reflected acquired professional status. I was by now a newspaper copy-boy, hands poised – doubtless in suspicious circumstances – above the urinals to snatch the latest batch of purple prose, lowered by string from the lofty, miniscule, ill-equipped press box, down the back of the crudely creosoted old stand.

This was journalism, the Street of Adventure: and Alec Stock, too. My brief was to sprint out of the ground to Mr Rowsell's butcher's shop, where I had hired a phone for half a crown. And, between the pork chops and with hands hygienically far removed from the food, I breathlessly dictated to the nation my sports editor's account of an historical match.

Somehow, with both journalistic and sentimental instinct, I also contrived to see both Yeovil goals and to be back in lavatorial position for the successive despatches of footballing literature – impertinently embellished by me in partisan joy. As young, weekly newspaper reporters, we knew all the players. We accepted that most of them would soon be chasing off afterwards to skipper Nick Collins's pub 200 yards away in Wellington Street – and we would be there, too, as we fancied his daughter; that beanpole centre-half, Les Blizzard, would want only to celebrate with a double helping of Beswick's fish and chips; that abstemious Dickie Dyke, the last-minute choice as goalkeeper who ran a bible class on Sundays, might make an exception and treat himself to just a half.

That smart Mr Stock was an especial favourite. He walked with a limp and I was never quite sure how good a player he was. He didn't score many goals – but I, and most of the wonderfully delirious 17,000 spectators heaved at that ball at the same time as he did for Yeovil's first goal. It was a mighty, multi-assisted, maybe supernatural effort and not even a keeper as agile as Johnny Mapson was going to stop it.

Afterwards we crowded into the steamy dressing room where weary, naked men re-enacted Eric Bryant's winning goal and told him he should stop lumping sacks of corn for a living. Big, bald Stan Abbott, the timeless trainer, pushed the big, chipped enamel teapot towards me. "Here, give the lads a drink." It was my proudest duty.

Stock was 27 then, still looking like an army captain. We'd watched him over the weeks, helping to cut the grass and mark the pitch, counting the takings – before his own bath – and paying the players. There wasn't too much to pay, of course: the week's wages came to £65.

Now he comes back today, with the QPR party, his tortured allegiance masked behind that embracing miner's-son smile of his. Those of us who traded jokes with him nearly 40 years ago and were invited home for a supper of tomato sandwiches think we know where his heart will be this afternoon.

Jack Gregory, actually a former captain of QPR, was Yeovil's first professional manager in 1922. George Patterson, the Scottish international who used to read Burns to the local reporters over morning coffee, was the most civilised; Ron Saunders and the present manager, Brian Hall, are the most single-mindedly dedicated and taciturn. The managerial spectrum has been as wide at times and as engagingly bizarre as the playing staff.

There is a green-and-white fanaticism and warm-hearted loyalty at Huish, unique among non-League clubs. Palace, Bury, Gillingham, Sunderland, Southend, Bournemouth, Exeter, Brentford and Cambridge know all about it.

ON DUTY IN THE URINALS

Country Reporter (1990)

My afternoon's work got harder, less romantic. Ron had been optimistic with his typed timetable of calls. It took longer than either of us had imagined to phone over the acceptable soccer clichés of the day. By half past three we were running late – and I was out of breath.

Often on my return to the ground, the lavatory was full and I had to take my turn before getting into position for the 'drop'. Several times, the copy was already dangling on the string two feet below the hole. I'd let out my self-conscious shout 'I'm waiting, Ron' and down would come the next batch. The stench of urine, influenced by the strong content of Bruttons, intensified. It was joyful relief to run close to the dressing rooms on my way back to Mr Rousell's. The aroma of liniment brought sweetness to the acrid recesses of my nostrils.

*

Just once, when back in the lavatory, I had to lurch over the shoulders of a burly farmer with apparent prostate trouble. I snatched at and spilled my slip catch. It was calamitous. I gingerly extricated the soaked paper from the improvised trough, read what I could of the contents and memorised it. The facts, as relayed on Mr Rousell's phone, were suspect but the narrative fizzed with interest. Alec Stock was the scorer – and the shopful of housewives cheered. I said he hit it with his right foot and got it wrong. I took a chance and said the pass came from Ray Wright (all the passes seemed to come from him) and got it right. The main thing was that I named the scorer correctly. I just didn't get names wrong.

There were two more scorers. But my lavatorial catching never wavered again and Ron's feverishly scrawled longhand was retained intact. Sunderland equalised and then Eric Bryant, who I used to see humping sacks of corn during my weekly village calls at Martock for the *Gazette*, won the tie to make history for a non-league club, in extra-time.

*

My mother was unmoved by the drama and frivolities of the day. 'It's egg-in-nest, you'll like that,' she said. It was the high-tea meal, left over from the war years.

She knew I was due to phone someone else's reports from the family butcher's. But as she carefully eased the egg into its nest, she considered for the first time the size of the football crowd and the complications of the phoning operation. With perfunctory brevity I told her of an afternoon spent for the most part in the men's toilets at Huish.

Her reaction was immediate. She pushed the plate away from me as I was about to take my first mouthful.

'Before you do anything else, take some hot water from the kettle on the fire and thoroughly wash your hands.'

The tone of her postscript was even more reproachful. 'I just don't know what Mr Rousell thought of you.' For my part, I trusted that he never knew.

ALEC STOCK

Fragments of Idolatry (2001)

Peasedown St John is a long way from Loftus Road, Highbury and Roma, three of his ports of professional call. The village is functional, its cottages and little terrace houses daubed by the greyness that symbolises the community's past deprivations. When he motors home, with the wreaths and the memories of youth, he pulls in the car and gazes across the vast, haughty undulations of the Mendips. This is where he comes to reminisce: about those little, isolated homesteads and the families who once lived there, below in the valleys. "Look, down there, see that house, that's where …" He points out, with an almost unspoken eloquence, the sites, now verdant, of the numerous pits that used to scar this sublime landscape. He reminds you it's birdnesting time and those were the lanes where once he went in search of eggs. He shows you the three woods where he played, the direction of the best chestnut trees; the knowledge of natural history he acquired in the exciting process of self-discovery is apparent in a sustained enthusiasm for the countryside.

His mother had eight brothers and three sisters. All the brothers were miners; virtually every man in the parish was. They would come up on the early cage on a Saturday morning. The flush of expectancy was defiantly visible through the caked grime on their faces. The brothers lived more or less next door to each other. Their shift finished, they would tear off their blackened clothes in the backyards. Then, as part of an uplifting ritual, they'd move into the kitchen. The water was warm, waiting for them in the tin bath in front of the roaring fire. Around the fire was positioned the polished brass guard and on it were the football shirts, red and yellow, aired and ironed. The brothers would pull on their shirts, already in spirit out on the field, their increasing animation offsetting aching limbs from their subterranean labours. Kitted out and clean, they'd sit down to dinner. "A proper knife and fork job," as Alec recalls.

Peasedown Miners played in the Western League. They were big and strong: and notorious. It was said oppositions needed to be equally fearless to play against them. The Miners were rejuvenated by the soap suds and a good meal; they were now ready to do battle. It was for most of them the highlight of their week. Saturday's fixture was the way to spit the coal dust out of their lungs – and make their aggressive statement in the pure air, after being cramped and cowed in the belly of the scarred Mendip hills. In Stock's words: "They were like birds set free." In one of the local pubs hangs a photograph of a victorious Peasedown team. The caption graphically tells us that every player came from within a mile of the nearest local pit.

This was Stock's first club, certainly in affection. His father was on the committee. He himself marked the pitch on Saturday mornings. The family involvement was extended to his mother who made two big enamel cans of coffee for the teams at half-time. Alec would run home to collect them; his father would hand one to the visitors and Alec, with his little strides and a sheepish grin that reflected importance and pride, would take the other can to the home side. His reward was a generous measure of coffee, poured into the lid for him by the goalkeeper. The pattern didn't change. In those more basic days, the players never left the field at the interval. There was precious little shelter for them if it was raining, and it was too far to troop back to the pub which served as their changing-room.

He was devoted to his parents who made willing sacrifices for him. Their abiding resolve was that he should never go down the pits. He won his scholarship at the village school and wondered what his future might be. Children left their fathers to worry about the ominous political implications of the times. His father was 'dead Labour'; they all were. Peasedown had an insular communal warmth, a defiant independence of spirit, and he liked that.

GOODBYE TO THE GREAT LEVELLER

The Guardian, 5 May 1990

So it's farewell to the climbing boots, the pitons and the skis, which mythmakers would have us believe are stored with the corner flags. Tears will cascade down Somerset's beloved mountainside. After today's match against Telford at Huish the slope is being dug up.

Alec Stock and many of his legendary side that beat Sunderland in 1949 will be there to see the last kick and eavesdrop on the last engaging exaggeration, in West Country burr, about non-League soccer's most famous field, where the incline, wing to wing, is said to be anything from three to 15 feet. Six is a fair compromise.

Here Yeovil and Petters played, and then Yeovil Town. Here the glamorous footballers such as Len Shackleton stumbled, and familiar cigarette-card faces turned ashen white as they stepped out of the team's coach for their first sight.

*

Now the ground is being sold. Yeovil are moving out to a £3.2 million site where once the troops were stationed at Houndstowne camp. It is six times as large, complete with executive boxes, a gymnasium, administration block and sports shop. There will be seating for half the 9,000 capacity.

Forty-one years ago I stood, a junior reporter, with Stock in his poky office, where he paid the players, helped the bald trainer Stan Abott make the tea in a large brown enamel pot, and wondered whether he would ever have enough time left over to play on the Saturday. Now we were looking at the ground again, up the hill, swapping small-town gossip.

"Nick Collins, who kept the pub down the road, was the best we had. He's sadly very ill now – I visit him when I can … Arthur Hickman, our big full-back … ah, yes, his wife was Huish's most vociferous fan. After one game she told me she'd had a wonderful time. Someone in front of her had been shouting at Her Arthur and so she had her own back, burning holes in his overcoat with her cigarette end."

Stock is as companionable as ever. He has a story for every club he managed, every player he signed. "I liked Roma, you know, because they had the same colours as my home village, Peasedown … Rodney Marsh? No real trouble – you simply had to get inside his skin … Stan Bowles? The only problem was his gambling, for heaven's sake." And then inevitably back to intimate Yeovil, where Alec and his teacher wife grew begonias, and Dickie Dyke, the boy from the bible class, took it so matter-of-fact when asked to play in the next round against Manchester United.

I walked from top to bottom of Huish only the other day, stopping to pick the dandelions and blow the seeds away, just as I had in the Thirties. Some of the advertisements were also the same as when I stood to watch Dave Halliday and Tommy Lynch.

My daughter has bought me a chunk of Huish turf for a birthday present. Alec approves – especially if, in my own back garden, I get the angle right.

5
Country Reporter

For the young David, with dreams of becoming a top-name Fleet Street reporter, his years on the *Western Gazette* provided him with a training in the essentials of journalism that he never regretted. Yet, as he later reflected, his time there 'went on too long'.

It was the most staid of weekly newspapers, with little opportunity for an ambitious writer to develop any kind of individual style. Three of the ten pages were filled with small advertisements, and much of the rest was taken up with standard features: round-ups from around the villages, weddings and funerals, reports of rotary clubs, scout groups, young farmers' dances. There were court cases, mostly petty offences – 'Took Dead Man's Ladder', 'Motor-Cyclist Struck Cow' – written up soberly. It was in the main a gentle, rural world. A report, written by David, of a woman trapping her finger in a sash window and phoning the emergency services ran to 350 words.

There was no emphasis on the identity of the writers. David's articles, cut out and preserved, are sometimes credited – 'by D.F.' or 'by D.G.F.' – but are often without by-line at all. Far more alluring for the ambitious young writer was the *Bristol Evening World* which, in May 1949, printed David's 650-word piece on the start of his village's cricket season. Even then, contracted to the *Western Gazette*, he had to assume the nom-de-plume of 'David Coker', as he did when the *World* printed his short story, 'The Tower and the Tombstone', later in the year.

In August 1951, at the age of 22, he completed his apprenticeship, which led immediately to the activation of his delayed National Service. His last contribution to the *Gazette* was a lengthy and surprisingly colourful piece marking the 300th anniversary of the birth of the naval explorer William Dampier of East Coker.

Returning in September 1953, more aware of the wider world, David was ever on the lookout for stories that gave him the opportunity to write with more flair. 'Ghosts of a Clock Room' was his offering on his first week back – more than 500 words describing a visit to East Coker Church's tower where he counted all the names that people down the ages had scratched on the walls. One assumes the ghost story mentioned was his own, 'The Tower and the Tombstone':

> It was evening when the last few names were counted. Having been forewarned that a macabre ghost story was once published about that very room, the reporter gazed about him. The eight bell-ropes, which hung down into the belfry below, were being fanned by a slight breeze coming in from a broken window-pane

and setting a hundred shadows dancing on the walls of the dimly-lit room. On one side the big clock pendulum swung to and fro, sounding like relentless footsteps that never got any further away.

Amid his reports of tropical fish-keeping and an 85-year-old gardener, he wrote about an ancient murder in a smugglers' cave and a mysteriously silent manor house. And he stretched a story of a squirrel chased up a telegraph pole by a cat to 350 words.

I was captivated by the human warmth and aged aura but was ready to move on. At the *Gazette*, amid its many accepted virtues, no editorial was too boring, no word too long, no front page of advertisement any different visually from the previous year (or generation, we sometimes thought). "Don't try any of that silly, fancy writing, David, and you can be here for life." In fact, the next week I was gone.

I was due a Friday off and took the bus to Bristol before impulsively stepping into the lift for the editorial department of the *Evening World*, part of the Northcliffe chain of brash provincials and despised, I have no doubt, by the varied editors and executives of my weekly.

Thirty-five years later David returned to these *Western Gazette* years in *Country Reporter*, his semi-fictionalised account of his apprenticeship: the bicycle, the funerals, the early girl friends, the afternoon in Yeovil Football Club's urinals. It was beautifully evocative of time and place, and the BBC saw the potential to create a long-running drama series out of it, as they had done so successfully with the Yorkshire vet James Herriot's 'All Creatures Great and Small'.

They commissioned six scripts from Keith Waterhouse, who served an apprenticeship on the *Yorkshire Evening Post* at the same time as David's apprenticeship at the *Gazette*. A paperback edition of the book was published, with David for once in his life being paid a sizeable advance, enough to afford the building of an extension to his house.

Then the BBC hit a funding crisis, triggered by the money they had spent on an ill-fated soap 'Eldorado', and the project was cancelled. All that remains are two pilot scripts. Set in Yorkshire, with many of David's best stories reworked, they retain little of the flavour of the original. They disappointed David, though he was too polite to say so.

Country Reporter is the most delightful of books. Sensitively adapted for television, it could have been a great success.

WESTERN GAZETTE

Footsteps from East Coker (2010)

At the *Gazette*, newspaper tuition was really minimal. It was assumed that no-one would ever want to leave the paper. Those in authority were kindly and benevolent, while intolerant of any glimmer of literary enterprise. Every news story was a parody of the last one – in style and phraseology. Any tentative flight of imagination was instantly condemned and spiked. "Now let's see, that was a nice write-up of yours on the county court case, young David. Took no liberties with the evidence. Your shorthand must be coming along. We must give you a few more courts to cover. The trouble is we have to be so careful. No-one ever sues the *Western Gazette* for an inaccuracy, you know."

"I'm sure that is so, Mr Lanham." By this time I had gained enough self-confidence, still not too much, to slip in a gentle slither of sarcasm. Mr Lanham, in his blue suit and with his demeanour of non-conformist, non-contentious goodness, saw my throwaway as nothing but confirmation of the paper's worthiness.

Above all, we were taught the virtue of accuracy. Length was discussed in 'sticks', not columns. If we were reporting the local Tory's speech at the Party's summer fayre, we were asked for six sticks of copy, and that was what was delivered. At a funeral service – and I attended so many of them that I tended to dream of coffins rather than goalposts – it was not enough to get the Brigadier's surname and rank right; it was obligatory for me to check and re-check the ex-military man's three initials, in the right order. Far too often, I stood in church porches, the rain pouring off the brim of my brown trilby, as I was patronised by a dignitary who thought I should know his name without having to ask for it. Was he, in his view, more important than the deceased?

My seven years at the *Gazette* taught me so much about human nature. It ensured that I would remain in life an unshakable egalitarian. It also demonstrated the weakness of a paper or one of its reporters being too deferential. That has nothing at all to do with bad manners or misplaced aggression. It is a measure of self-esteem and human dignity.

I had no regrets about working at this newspaper. It just went on too long and there was no encouragement if a reporter occasionally stretched himself with a decent image and dared to tiptoe beyond the accepted literary parameters.

SOME BRIEF 'STICKS'

Extracts from articles written for the paper between 1949 and 1955

Dour struggle at Yeovil

As I came away from the Recreation Ground on Saturday, after seeing Wellington beat Yeovil by the odd try, an old stager, one who had experienced the thrill of Twickenham on more than one occasion, came across and said of the match: "That was Rugger in all its glory." It was a very apt summary. Few of the spectators could have but admired the spirit with which those thirty mud-plastered 'demons' slid for the ball. It was, in my opinion, the toughest game this season. The two uncompromising and robust packs gave the crowd plenty of excitement, and though stoppages were frequent, when the players either had mud rubbed from their eyes or had their cuts and bruises attended to, play was quite fair.

Eleven brothers

Central figure in the England-West Indies 'lively wicket' controversy, Old Trafford groundsman Harry Williams, one of the most experienced in the game, is the brother of Yeovil's groundsman, Gerald Williams. Although opinions may differ about the Manchester wicket, vaguely described as 'sporting', it is a fact that instructions were given to the groundsman that the pitch was not to be watered during the week preceding a match, and that use of the heavy roller was forbidden.

From a chat with Gerald Williams this week, it was very obvious that he was far from a novice. One of eleven brothers, all at one time engaged in preparing cricket wickets, he has been 'in the game' all his life. "I was even working on a ground before I went to school," he told me.

Tropical fish-keeping

"Come in and see my Hyphessobrycon Innesi," said Yeovil tobacconist, Mr N. Stainer. With this linguistic accomplishment a representative of this newspaper was introduced to the fascinating subject of tropical fish-keeping – a hobby fast gaining support in the district.

Mr Stainer's text-book precision and profound interest in his subject was typical of every keeper of tropical and coldwater fish interviewed this week. "It's a serious business which gets right into your blood," one said. For some months a small band of enthusiastic fish-keepers have been toying with the idea of starting a Yeovil and District Aquarist Society to promote and stimulate interest in what one wife ruefully described as "an obsessing pastime".

Funeral of a Gipsy Queen

After the service in the cemetery chapel the long line of mourners moved to the graveside. Although it was pouring with rain, many stood with bared heads. As the coffin was lowered a profusion of sprays was dropped upon it. Intimate members of the family muttered their own prayers and vows. Then, after the new 'queen' and others had left, half-a-dozen men stood in a circle around the graveside. They produced a bottle of beer and solemnly passed it from man to man, each taking a short drink.

Cobbler for 70 years

While the rest of the world rumbles by outside, there is a link with a more peaceful age in the cellar of 61, South-steet, Yeovil, where Mr H.B. Dicks carries on the cobbling business he started fifty years ago. But it is a link that will soon be severed for at 82 Mr Dicks thinks it is time to retire.

Sat in his little Dickensian cellar, surrounded by his tools, boots and shoes to be repaired and boots and shoes to be collected, Mr Dicks reflected about his life when a representative of this newspaper called to see him. All the time he was hand-sewing leather to the soles of a pair of shoes with the dexterity of a man who has loved and practised his craft for a lifetime.

A visit to East Coker Church tower

Almost 4,000 people since the late 19th century have climbed the age-worn, spiral stone steps of the East Coker Church tower to the quaint little clock-room and written their names on the four walls there.

To be precise, the clock-room has 3,617 signatures. And, on a matter of statistics, it took a reporter two hours four-and-a-half minutes of patient checking to arrive at that figure. The names are written in chalk, crayon, pencil and even, in one case, ball-pen. Some, scratched on the wall with stubs of pencil, are hardly decipherable; others, mostly among the earliest 'entries', are the work of copper-plate specialists.

The Messiah

Whether or not it is possible for a school choir of 30 voices to give an effective performance of 'The Messiah' is a matter of opinion, but it was done with some success at Yeovil School on Monday. The singing of the boy choristers, trained by Mr Harold Sinclair, the school music master, showed an understanding of the spirit underlying the great Handelian choruses and there was one outstanding virtue in their singing – every word could be heard clearly.

East Coker honour William Dampier

Next month the villagers of East Coker, Yeovil, celebrate the 300th anniversary of one of their most famous ancestors. Here, in 1651, amid the fragrant lilacs and wisteria of this delightful parish, was born William Dampier, one destined to take his place among the greatest English explorers and navigators.

Dampier knew both fame and infamy. It might be said that at one time he reached the zenith of his calling. He was regarded as one of the most brilliant navigators of all time. Were there not occasions when his name was on the lips of everyone who really counted in this country? Was he not the guest of a Queen, thrilling Her Majesty with tales of the hazardous ocean? Like many great men, Dampier made big impressions and big mistakes! The lamentable truth is that he experienced the extreme humiliation of a court-martial. He lived to see himself despised by his crew. During his life at sea he was often dogged by ill-fortune; fate was rarely kind to him. Although he knew the glamour and glory of being recognised as a leading authority on sea matters he died in debt ... and in an unknown grave.

The tale of the murdered woodman

Go to Pendomer, the tranquil, detached hamlet not far from Hardington and you can be sure that before long one of its inhabitants will be telling you the tale of 'the murdered woodman'.

You cannot easily associate Pendomer with murder. With its mellowing church, dating back to 1440, its little thatched cottages and the warm friendship of the people who live in them, this little village has an air of serenity. But it is hard to deny the macabre pages of its history; hard to deny that a man who laughed and drank with the people of Pendomer was shot dead one moonless winter's night.

Of course, it's some years back – back in fact in the reign of George III. There was then a good deal of disquiet in England. Smuggling was proving a lucrative activity for some virile young men with a lust for adventure. There were three such men in the East Coker area. They spent much of their time in an artificial cavern, hidden by the undergrowth of Penn Wood.

But a vigilant young woodman is said to have stumbled on the secret. When none of the lawless occupants were about he entered the cave and discovered many kegs of spirits! The woodman could not miss such an opportunity. He supped freely and fell to the ground in a drunken stupor. But back, alas! came one of the smugglers. He found the woodman and shot him on the spot.

A RIDE WITH THE DEAD

The young reporter is sent to cover a funeral – 'an important story for the Gazette'.

Country Reporter (1990)

'Tomorrow there is a big funeral at Charlton Mackrell at 2.30. Miss Emily Pomeroy ... P for Peter ... O ... M for Mother ... EROY. Have you got that? Good. A pillar of the church and local community' (it was as if Mr Chapman was already dictating my report for me). 'There will be a lot of mourners. You will need to be at the church forty-five minutes at least before the service starts. Don't miss anyone. Every name, every initial.' He suddenly looked at the yellow tie I was wearing. 'And maybe a more sober colour would be appropriate tomorrow, don't you think?'

I checked the direction next day and cycled off towards Ilchester. That was only about halfway and I realised with some concern that the church was farther away than I had imagined. The wind was against me and there was a drizzle blowing into my face. My trilby wouldn't stay on; after retrieving it from a puddle, I determined never to wear it again, at least not until I got to Fleet Street.

At last I came to a sign post, marked 'Charlton Mackrell', pointing ominously up a narrow country road. By now I was thoroughly wet and uncomfortable. I feared that the pages of my notebook were sodden. And then my misery was compounded when my cycle began to bump and lurch on the unkempt road. It very soon dawned on me that I had a fast puncture in my front tyre.

I wasn't at all sure how near I was to the church but I sensed that my chance of making contact with any mourners on the exterior side of the porch was decreasing by the minute. I threw my faithful but wounded racer against an elm trunk. It was a time for drastic decision – though I couldn't quite think what. I started to run.

Almost at once I heard the sound of some kind of traffic behind me. This had to be my opening lesson in journalistic resourcefulness. I stood in the middle of the narrow road and thumbed down the driver.

The rain dripping down from my tangled hair partly obscured my vision. But it didn't take me long to realise the enormity of my blunder. For I had stopped the hearse. I was vaguely aware of another car with a few occupants behind.

The driver of the hearse poked his head out of the window, tilting back his battered, almost comic, peaked cap as he did so. 'What's the trouble, lad? We've a burial to catch. And we've got the body inside.'

An undertaker's assistant with a sense of humour offered a glimmer of hope. What alternative was there, in any case? 'Dreadful thing's happened. Just had a puncture – and I've got to get to the church in time. I'm from the *Gazette*.'

'Climb in. Here, Bill, move over. The lad's got to get to the church on time.' He hummed the appropriate sentimental song as I squeezed in alongside them. 'That makes the four of us. A nice number. Us three – and the body. The other bearers will be waiting for us at the farm. We drop 'em off afterwards to do the milking. They keep their dark suits in the cow shed.'

The hearse chugged along the rough country road at a respectful pace. I had started to dry myself with my big white pocket handkerchief. There was time for some panicky contemplation. If I didn't get to the church before the coffin, what chance did I have of taking all those names? The driver interrupted my troubled train of thought.

'Surprised the *Gazette* is bothering with thissin.'

He shouldn't have been, I felt. 'Oh, I understand this is a really big funeral. A lot of people coming.'

'I don't think so, lad. Just two or three of the family. And they're in the Austin 7 behind. Poor old Herbie Masters has been past it for years. Nobody remembers him no more. Tha's what's sad about old age.'

'Herbie ...?'

'That's it, lad. Herbert Ambrose Masters, aged ninety-one. Funeral Charlton Adam Church, 2.15pm, Tuesday.'

My heart was pounding. Was there really a Charlton Adam, as well?

'Oh dear, sorry. Can I get out? Where's Charlton Mackrell, please? That's where I should be.'

The driver retained his jocular manner. 'So many Charltons, inn't there? Could have been worse for you, though. Could have been bloody Charlton Athletic!' He was now irritating me, but he continued. 'Look out across that hedgerow, by this gate. There 'tis. Next village. But 'fraid I can't take you all the way. Old Herbie were an Adam man.' Another little chuckle.

I stammered my thanks and left the other three occupants, including the lamented and long-forgotten Mr Masters. I ran back to the five-bar gate and looked across in the direction of Charlton Mackrell Church. It didn't seem quite so far that way. I climbed over the gate and headed across the middle of a field. Not quite as the crow flies – more like the way an anxious, soaked cub reporter stumbles.

DIANA AND A FUTURE PM

The young reporter invites Diana, a waitress at the Cadena restaurant with 'lovely reptilian hips' and 'a complicated life', to join him when he is sent to report a Conservative Party fete where Harold Macmillan is the guest speaker.

Country Reporter (1990)

As we neared the well-heeled Ham-stone village, she turned to me. 'I won't let you down.' I felt I should have been saying it to her.

We had no difficulty finding the big field where the autumn fayre was taking place. A woman with the face of an ageing point-to-pointer was on the gate taking the shilling admissions. 'From the *Gazette*,' I said grandly and she waved us through. Diana was impressed, I could see. We had got there with time to spare. So we had a go on the treasure-hunt and I skittled for a pig. I knocked down seven pins. The farmer, who had taken my sixpence, said: 'Bad luck, son. Only just missed the landlord.' The sticker-up in his shirtsleeves, rolled back the skittles. 'I'll get back to do the milkin' now, boss. See you later on.' Sticking-up was an occasional therapy he enjoyed. It was usually worth five bob at the end of the night.

They found a lad to take over and I paid sixpence for Diana. She put two skittles off the improvised alley and scattered a little group of idle observers. 'Got to do a bit better than that, miss.' Everyone laughed. Something told me my dream-tart hadn't been so happy for a long time.

At four o'clock I went in search of the Tory officials. I found them with their big blue rosettes and their solid tweeds. 'Has Mr Macmillan arrived yet? I'm from the *Gazette*. We've been invited to report the speech.'

The hard-eyed secretary was peering suspiciously at my companion. It wasn't the most hospitable of scrutinies. Diana had presence but perhaps not class. In the intuitive ways of a middle-class woman, the secretary could also see Diana as too much of a distraction among the sherry glasses which I could just spy laid out for committee and VIPs on a trestle table inside the marquee. 'This ... is my friend. She's very keen to hear Mr Macmillan.'

'Oh dear, now that's a pity. We have just the one place for the press in the front row. Maybe your – er – friend wouldn't mind standing at the back.'

As a boy not long out of school, nurtured in rural ways, I was hardly well versed in social etiquette. But I felt that a slight was being perpetrated. I became consumed with a hitherto unknown sense of gallantry. 'Well – em – no, I don't think that would be quite right. We'd like to be together.

I'll stand at the back as well.' This produced an awkward silence and I produced a daring card. 'I'll do my best to hear. But you will have to forgive me if I don't get it all quite right.'

The secretary left us abruptly. She flounced back towards the marquee entrance and was soon in tetchy, intense conversation with a male member of the committee. He looked in our direction. He lingered over Diana. Their eyes met; he nodded in an almost guilty fashion and they exchanged smiles. The conversation with the secretary went on. Then she returned.

'We have had a word about it. And we think we can perhaps squeeze in one more place in the middle of the front row. It isn't going to be easy.' She didn't need to add that; it was implicit in her frigid voice.

Everyone, or at least everyone with a big blue rosette, started moving into the marquee. The enthusiasm was even more muted. 'You had better come in with the rest of us. We are going to have a glass of sherry with our special guest before he delivers his speech.'

Diana darted a look at me. She took my hand and squeezed it. She looked quite strikingly flash, she looked adorable and, for one fleeting moment, she looked very vulnerable. If I had possessed more confidence myself, I'd have hugged her and led her forward with an assertive step. She recovered and assumed once more that untutored, rather brash poise.

We walked into the big tent together and joined a long line for the introductions. The sherry was offered us off a silver salver. It was sweet, good quality. Diana drank it with eager gulps, fast as I emptied a Cadena coffee cup on one of the mornings I was on stolen time. She ran her tongue along her lips to savour the final taste. I wanted to see her do it again.

There were so many snatches of sycophantic small-talk that it took a long time for us to reach the head of the queue. A constituency official, briefed by the displeased secretary, said to Mr Macmillan: 'This is a young fellow from ... the local weekly newspaper. A very good paper, too, sir. He is keen to report your speech. Will that be in order?'

I wanted to say: 'Hang on, you pompous so-and-so. You invited us here and your association is after the publicity. I could have been watching Stocky leading out Yeovil Town.'

The Member for Bromley put out his hand. There was a caricaturist's droop to the moustache but he was still a formidable and handsome figure. He really was an amalgam of Eton, Balliol, the Guards and the Athenaeum. He seemed to be enjoying the adulation of the party workers, dispensing the pleasantries in a languidly attractive voice. He was wearing an impeccable Savile Row suit, a blue handkerchief protruding from the breast pocket. There were more women than men pressing forward to meet him.

'And this must be your – your young lady. Charming gel. Yes, charming.'

Diana possessed an innate eloquence without needing to speak. She compressed a whole evening of innuendoes into an almost coy smile. He was still absorbing himself in this tangible communication of silence as he was being introduced to the next couple.

The speech, when it came, was as thespian as it was political. He measured his pauses, caressed and elongated his carefully fashioned phrases. He turned to every corner of his audience; each party follower felt he was talking specially to them. I had heard Wolfit and Donat on the wireless, and now thought of them both. In that slightly weary country-squire manner, he transfixed his disciples. He wasn't averse to stirring alliteration and a poetic, rehearsed afterthought. Some of his ideas were a good deal more liberal in concept than the regional faithful were used to. But he was an adept performer. He never went too far. There was enough traditional Conservatism to placate the momentarily startled members of his flock. He extolled the way Somerset farmers had kept tilling the land during the war; one could detect the murmurs of approval all around. At the end there was prolonged applause. Mac beamed and gave a theatrical bow. He was much loved.

Diana and I were sitting between the divisional chairman and a person I assumed was Mac's agent. I took down my shorthand notes with professional aplomb. Diana watched me with increasing admiration; once or twice she jerked my arm playfully. For most of the time she watched the speaker.

On the bus, going back to Yeovil, she said to me: 'Didn't he talk well. I think I could vote Conservative, you know. A snooty lot, though. Did you see that committee chap in the blue suit? Made a pass at me. Silly little twat!' Mock scorn one moment, a little slip in dignity the next.

I didn't like to hear about that smarmy little official in the blue suit. I suppose I was jealous, something I had never experienced before. It wasn't what you expected at a Tory rally, among the tweeds and the polished voices.

JOY AGAIN ON THE VILLAGE GREEN

by 'David Coker' (David Foot's first newspaper article with a by-line)
Bristol Evening World, 9 May 1949

Our village took up the willow again on Saturday. Once more, there was the excitement and air of expectancy as we prepared the pitch, the thrill as a lofty six sailed into the Mill Pond, the cheers of encouragement from the villagers seated beneath the sturdy sycamore, a cricketer's agony of mind as he beheld his wickets shattered behind him.

This traditionally English game is part of our village's way of life – we couldn't exist without it. To us, cricket in the big town or city, with the perfectly mowed outfield and chemically-treated wicket, its painted stands and members' enclosures, is completely foreign to the true spirit of this great game.

When we think of cricket, we see the typically rural spectacle in the field at the back of the hostelry, on a sunny Sunday afternoon. We see the crudely-prepared wicket, with its two or three unavoidably bad patches, and around it the fresh, green grass, of undulating meadow land spotted with buttercups and dandelions.

To us cricket-lovers, the winter months are cold, cheerless and void, only temporarily warmed by pleasant memories of how our forefathers wielded the bat in days gone by. Surely there can be no subject but cricket that brings such a flow of reminiscences, encourages such an inexhaustible collection of anecdotes, such contentment of mind and escape from our colourless daily lives.

Now summer is almost here again. For some weeks we have been pushing the mower, pulling the roller, oiling the bats, whiting the pads, repairing the benches, and even improving the pavilion's sanitary system.

It is cricket time, and it has not taken us many hours to recapture the youthful enthusiasm and vitality of a bunch of schoolboys.

What is it that makes this game – equally enjoyed by the Lord of the Manor and the hardy man of the fields – so great, so distinct? The principal reason, I believe, is that cricket more than any other game brings out character.

Perhaps we will watch the ruddy-faced farmer setting about the attack from the first ball he receives, as if to indicate that he wishes to hurry off and milk the cows as soon as he is out.

Maybe, there will be an inoffensive-looking little clerk, eternally frustrated in the home by a buxom wife, who will momentarily express his latent adventurous spirit by dancing down the wicket to clout a fast bowler.

Just as likely, we will see the village blacksmith, with massive shoulders and bulging muscles, ignoring the impatient advice of youngsters on the boundary, and continuing to put a copy-book straight bat to every ball, fast or slow.

Perchance the landlord will send down his faster one with all the accuracy of the good skittler that he is, or the vicar will gain the especial respect of his parishioners by holding a 'red-hot' drive at silly mid-off.

There is a lot in the game on the village green that is missed at Lord's or Kennington Oval ... the fever-pitch excitement as the secretary posts the team on the notice board ... the subsequent comments, words of praise and otherwise ... the unpretentious but romantic old pavilion, with numberless tales of crushing defeats and one-run victories ... the player at square leg in corduroy trousers.

We had it all on Saturday. The sun shone bright and clear and the ground looked a picture. To both sides of us, a row of beeches and sycamores introduced peace and security to the scene. Close by the pavilion, two poplars swayed gently to and fro in the slight breeze. A narrow, winding stream rippled playfully on its way past the far boundary, on down to the picturesque village mill that could just be seen raising its head above the brow of a hill.

And as Tennyson said the brook goes on for ever, so we pray will countrymen continue to gather on a Saturday to bat and bowl. It means a good deal to us.

6

National Service

R.A.F. FORM 1394.
(Revised December, 1951.)
(For issue only to National Service Airmen and Airwomen not on regular engagements).

ROYAL AIR FORCE
BRIEF STATEMENT OF SERVICE AND CERTIFICATE ON DISCHARGE

1. Surname ...... FOOT ...... Official No. 2528404
   Christian Names ...... David George ...... Rank on Discharge ...... LAC
2. Period of whole-time service. From 27.8.1951 To 20.9.53
3. Trade in civil life ...... JOURNALIST ...... 4. R.A.F. trade on entry ...... U/T RAD TELST
5. Details of any R.A.F. trade training ...... Operations Clerk
6. R.A.F. trade on discharge and brief description of duties. (vide A.M. Pamphlet 51.)
   Assist in the air traffic control of aircraft, and the provision to aircraft of flight information and airness service. Plots aircraft movements, transmits and receives R/T messages connected with aerodrome control.

7. Assessments of Conduct, Proficiency and Personal Qualities during service:—

	Exemplary	Very Good	Good	Fairly Good	Poor
(a) Conduct	EXEMPLARY				
	Exceptional	Very Good	Good	Fairly Good	Poor
(b) Ability as tradesman/aircrew*		VERY GOOD			
(c) Ability as supervisor in his trade					
(d) Personal Qualities:—					
(i) Leadership				FAIRLY GD	
(ii) Co-operation			GOOD		
(iii) Bearing (to be assessed "Very Smart," "Smart," or "Untidy")				a UNTIDY	

8. Medals, Clasps, Decorations, Mentions in Despatches, etc. ...... NIL
9. Reason for Discharge ...... Termination of National Service
10. REMARKS. (This section to be used only to amplify Assessments, trade qualifications, etc., where necessary.)

11. DESCRIPTION ON DISCHARGE
    Height ...... 5 ft. 9 ins. ...... Colour of Hair ...... D. BROWN
    Complexion ...... RUDDY ...... Marks or Scars ...... VAC. L. ARM
    Colour of Eyes ...... BLUE

12. National Service airmen are liable to undergo part-time service—See notice overleaf.

UNIT DATE STAMP
2 5 AUG 1953
R.A.F. STATION THORNEY ISLAND

Signed ...... Rank ...... F/Lt
Commanding 2 A.N.S. THORNEY ISLAND

Signature of Airman/Airwoman ......

(*4742—1203) Wt. 34406—BJ 923 3,600 Pads 12/52 T.S. 839

For David, with his journalistic ambitions and pacifist leanings, National Service was a frustrating waste of two years. Having completed his five-year apprenticeship before being called up, he was already 22, older than most of his fellow conscripts and often older than the power-drunk drill instructors. This did not always make life easy for him.

He reported first to RAF Padgate in Lancashire to be fitted out, then was sent to Hereford for initial training, a gruelling ordeal full of mindless discipline and parade-ground square-bashing. From there he was despatched to Hendon in north-west London, awaiting placement. With a credit in French in his School Certificate, he applied to and was accepted by a newly created Joint Services School for Linguists, being sent to Coulsdon in Surrey to learn Russian.

> We weren't told much in advance. But the general belief, accepted in naïve wonderment, was that we would be treated during the course in effect as civilians. We would miss all the nauseating excesses of 'bull' and would benefit from the relative comfort of 'undergraduate' tuition.
>
> "We're on a great skive," one newly found mate assured me in intimate tones, "and we'll be officers in everything but name. No drill parades, no prats with two stripes belting out the orders. Plenty of weekend passes. And at the end a cushy time when we'll be pretending to be interpreters or monitoring signals from ships in the North Sea."

It did not turn out that way. Run by the army, there was still plenty of monotonous drill, and the Russian, often taught by hard-to-understand East Europeans, proved tougher to master than his school French. After four months David asked to be taken off the course, spending the rest of his service time at Thorney Island, near Portsmouth, where his official duties were to 'assist in the air traffic control of aircraft and the provision to aircraft of flight information and distress service' – or, as he put it in *Footsteps from East Coker*, 'plotting navigation hazards and distributing pre-flight chocolate to trainee aircrew'.

Throughout the two years, deprived of outlets for his writing, David recorded his experiences – first on sheets of paper, then in a large exercise book which he labelled 'Billet Thoughts', with the sub-title 'A Mixture of the Objective and Subjective'.

There are early expressions of homesickness, accounts of trips into the West End of London, reflections on the death of two airmen in a crash, tales of hitch-hiking and late-night train journeys that go wrong. He has his wallet with precious photographs stolen, he takes a trip home to marvel at the newly installed indoor toilet, and he accompanies a fellow conscript, a single-minded Methodist, to a Remembrance Day service at Westminster Central Hall. There are also fifteen pages entitled 'With Me They Served', lengthy and penetrative descriptions of nine of his fellow conscripts – or, as he puts it, 'interesting studies in human nature'.

Late in his time at Thorney Island the base starts a magazine, and David volunteers an article about Phyllis Dixey, who had been the 'Queen of Striptease' at Soho's Whitehall Theatre during the war. Now in early middle age, her popularity in decline, she was appearing in her 'Peek-a-Boo' show in Portsmouth. With a reporter's initiative, he manages to arrange an interview, arriving backstage 'expectant, excited, a little bit scared'. Unfortunately Dixey's husband/manager, an older man, controls the occasion, limiting the star to a few bland remarks, but at least the evening revives David's journalistic spirit. His nine-page account ends with him on an overnight train home to Yeovil:

> Flushed with the hot injection of whisky, I spent much of the uncomfortable journey musing over the night's events. I remember one partly inebriated soldier who was boasting about his amorous adventures of that same night. He turned to me and asked: "Did you have a woman tonight?" As casually as possible, I said: "Yes, I've been with Phyllis Dixey." Of course he didn't believe me.

So ends the last entry in 'Billet Thoughts'. It is followed by a postscript, written in a much older hand:

> Reading these jottings in 2012 (60 years later) I'm quite embarrassed – at my unformed judgements and level of naïvety. At times I write like a wide-eyed child, appallingly conventional. But that is understandable for an East Coker graduate! I was really a good deal more radical than that. And I was emotionally maturing.
>
> On occasions the flashes of writing are a modest revelation. I even like some of the insights. All the stories are authentic and they made an impression on me. Memories trickled back. I saw forgotten faces again. It pleases me that I sat down all those years ago and recorded my gentle adventures. My enthusiasm for observation suggests I might turn into a decent reporter.

BILLET THOUGHTS

Extracts from writing during National Service

First impressions

Twelve dejected souls are slumped across their ill-made beds. They are my new brothers – my companions in depression. Together we arrived at Padgate for the RAF's dastardly initiating ceremony. I've now been in for just over 24 hours. And I'm thinking of one subject – DESERTION!

Even as I write these incoherent sentences, I well realise that the difficulties of doing those things I planned – reading and writing – are great.

Five yards from my bed, a loud-mouthed young man is singing an obscene song at the top of his voice. Another is showing off his knowledge of profane limericks. The room is full of futile chatter and typical lewdness. This is Service Life, with its colour, its humanity, its immorality, its companionship.

Drill instructors

I never used to think of myself as vindictive in nature; now, I have my doubts. I know what it feels like to be blinded by resentment for the first time in my life.

My first billet corporal was a Scot called Tait. He was about 22, with what must have been the loudest voice on the Station. He pronounced Foot to rhyme with boot and every word was spoken slowly, sharply, deliberately. For almost the whole time, he was a picture of austerity, unsmiling and severe.

This hard-bitten facade struck me quickly as a pose; I believed he was actually a lonely fellow. As the miserable days went by, so the cold exterior began to melt. Towards the end, he would even sit on our beds and listen to our idle chatter. He had a twin brother, also a drill instructor, but apart from that very few friends, it seemed. He didn't smoke or drink and frowned on bad language. There was the Presbyterian touch about him.

Just when you felt you were gaining his confidence and were beginning to like him, he would become conscious of the lessening friction between us. This, he appeared to argue with himself, was bad for discipline. He would immediately 'freeze' and become detached and unsympathetic again.

My trouble really started when I moved to 'D' Flight. This time my billet corporal was Roberts. His name was the most feared among all the recruits on the Station. Roberts was a Welshman but there was no great trace of it in his voice. He was well-built and had done some boxing in the Services. He was previously in the Merchant Navy. In civilian clothes he looked quite good-looking but there was a bestial hardness about the eyes.

I was fortunate only to experience his rule for a couple of weeks. Those poor fellows who had known him longer were completely cowed. There was a strained stiffness about the billet. All the character and individuality were destroyed. He swore continually; he bullied and cajoled. And when I, a newcomer, joined his billet, he literally rubbed his hands and 'set into me'. The fact that I refused to shake in my shoes or put on a penitent expression riled him. He used every known word of profanity, he picked every possible fault he could with one's work.

He was passionately hated and I am certain many of the recruits would have celebrated his sudden death. I did not think any one man could have such wickedness in his heart. It makes one lose faith in humanity.

There were other DIs. Just a few of them treated you as humans. But almost without exception they were bumptious fools, naïvely abusing their suddenly acquired power. Most of them would have been helpless in a normal civilian job. They had few interests outside the 'square'.

A late-night coffee stall in Soho

If stranded in the West End late at night I used to make for this stall, run by a fat, blowsy, Italian-looking woman and her daughter. The drink and food had no special virtue. A cup of tea, from a chipped and lipstick-stained cup, sufficed. The enjoyment of the visit sprang from the varied splice of humanity gathered before the liquid-stained counter.

The gamblers came across from the smoky, tense atmosphere of a Dean Street basement. They were morose and laconic. They rarely joined in the general jollity. Instead, they nervously sipped their hot tea. Their minds were on the trick they had just lost or the inexpert throw of the dice.

Then there were the 'criminals' – some in garish attire, others obviously in a much less fortunate 'social' position. Generally they were the less imaginative, rough-tongued variety – the cat burglars and less-skilled car thieves. Their uneasy, shifting eyes told the full story of the hazardous life they led. The callous words of cynicism they uttered showed that they expected little.

The prostitutes 'talked shop' openly, brazenly, shamelessly. They joked of their patrons' whims, of the 40 shilling fines at Marlborough-street, or the latest nail-fight between two of their less neighbourly sisters. Their faces and bodies had lost the attraction that had once assisted them. But they took their degenerating downhill slide philosophically.

During my months in London I have reaped much benefit from the text book of life. But nowhere have I found a more informative chapter than at the Dean Street coffee stall.

Character study – number 4

Harold was a sturdy countryman. He had a big red face and healthy complexion. He walked with the carefree gait of a farmer's son. When he shook hands, his big, strong fist radiated friendliness. Harold was a Cornishman. When I first met him at Hendon, where he worked as a batman-waiter, he offered me a Cornish pasty. After that, he simply HAD to be a friend of mine.

Time and again I find myself admiring the general good nature of West Countrymen in the services. They seem to move in an atmosphere of conviviality. But maybe I'm taking this local pride a stage too far!

During my stay at Hendon I took the opportunity to study Harold quite closely. He had so many qualities to admire; he was frank, open and sincere. As he spoke he breathed the pure, unspoiled air of the country. He was completely unaffected by the slick, artificial sophistication of the town. I envied him his winsome manner and simple charm. I could never see the uniform he was wearing; rather could I see a colourful rustic garb slung loosely over his broad shoulders.

But, alas, these words of eulogy have a bitter twist. Before I left Hendon, Harold gradually unfolded the inner side of his life.

Because of unrelenting friction at home, normal relations with his parents were a thing of the past. In fact, he stayed with the foster parents of his girl, a young lady, which – judging by the tone of her letters which Harold insisted on quoting – was a far from suitable match. Yet, Harold could see virtue where there was none – or little.

Worse still, he was a juvenile delinquent and, I believe, a Borstal boy. Obviously, he was reticent in such matters. I think none the less of him now that I know his wayward record but, all the same, never have I received such a surprise in my favourite occupation of character summing-up.

Talking in his sleep

from a Bristol Evening Post article, August 1986

I did my National Service with a young man called Hughes. He came from direct ecclesiastical background and was due to go Keble College, Oxford himself, as soon as he'd done with the RAF, as the first steps towards ordination. For much of our time together his behaviour was impeccable. He read the Good Book at night as he sat on his billet bed. He confided his hopes to become a missionary. Never have I seen so much genuine goodness in one person. There was a touching gentility that he extended to everyone, even insensitive drill instructors.

One evening he began talking in his sleep. He woke the whole billet – 22 of us. He went into a monologue that lasted ten minutes. It amounted to a tirade against evil-doers in the world. That was fine. But he couched his indictment in the most appalling language any of us had ever heard. We just let him go on, mesmerised by the ferocity of his attack. Then he dropped back into a deep sleep. The next morning none of us had the courage to tell him.

But at times I wonder whether he ever made bishop.

A plane goes down

After the customary time-check, the young navigator-trainees finished drawing their equipment from me. The pilots came over, also, for their flying rations of chocolates and sweets. One of the Wellingtons, I could see from the board, was being taken up just for testing by Fl Lt Marshall. I had come into contact with him once or twice. A big, well-built man who hailed from Canada, he was friendly in his quiet way.

Sometimes I used to wonder whether the pilots had any misgivings about their job. Compared with the jet-controlled death-traps, Wellingtons could not be described as unsafe. And yet everyone knew that the plane had long since had its day. Frequently it was giving some sort of trouble.

*

As I handed out the sweets and chocolates to the pilots, I used to think of them, without being unduly sentimental, as brave men. They were also very human. Few of them conformed to the popular caricature of the typical flying man – wild, carefree, indifferent to the manifold dangers of the air. They were always concerned – without being worried – about the planes they were flying.

They looked on being airborne rather as a duty than a pleasure. They were anxious to get back as punctually as possible. Most of them were married with families and, as they took their rations, I would hear them talking with pride of the minor domestic things which help to make up a happy married life.

Like every other night, they finally left and the briefing-room was still. I could just hear the monotonous click of the teleprinter, sending and bringing in its signals, from along the corridor.

The Duty Flight Commander was Fl Lt Moyle, a tall, blond, strikingly handsome officer, who spoke little but was always a model of politeness and treated everyone whether they were Air Marshal or AC2 as a gentleman. Rumour had it that he was a devout Salvationist.

The pilots had been gone about an hour when the buzz on the Duty Flight Commander's desk sounded. In his typically unruffled way, Fl Lt Moyle listened in. I sensed a slight change of tone in his voice – one of concern. I heard him mention the plane 'Black Dog' and the fact that the pilot was Fl Lt Marshall.

By this time, through the sliding door which divided my office from his, I was watching him intently. I realised that something had gone wrong.

He told the Air Traffic Control that he would contact the police and get a message flashed across the camp, requesting the Rescue Crew to report immediately. Efficiently, dispassionately he went about the urgent business.

At one point, he turned to me and said: "I'm afraid Black Dog is down in the deeps." Then to himself: "I wonder whatever went wrong." But apart from that one expression of concern, he betrayed no emotion. Once or twice, however, I saw him looking ahead into space, lost in profound thought. Was that the Salvationist in him, offering up a silent prayer for the safety of a brother-officer?

*

Slowly snatches of news reached us. There had been a leading aircraftsman up in the plane with Fl Lt Marshall. He only had a fortnight to go before demob. Then the first black news. The LAC had been killed and Marshall was in a very bad way. The unpleasant, sickening drama was gripping me like a vice. My mind was obsessed by the tragedy.

*

I came off duty about midnight and went across to the cookhouse for a bite to eat. Some of the Crash Crew were also there – wet, sand-stained, smeared with oil. They looked a dejected crowd. Judging from the clothes some of them were wearing, they were in the process of going to bed when they were suddenly beckoned to the crash.

Reports, during the next day or so, were few and far between about Marshall. It appeared that both his legs were in plaster and that he had other injuries. But there was a very good chance of recovery. As so often happens in the case of shock, his slightly improved condition was short-lived. He became the second fatal victim of the crash.

And so, once again the frightening uncertainty of life was brought vividly home to me. One moment I had seen Fl Lt Marshall; the next he was dying.

In some ways it does us all good to feel the proximity of death. It helps to eliminate some of our less prepossessing qualities. It helps us to re-adjust things into their true perspective.

Lena Horne

From the first moment when I saw the café-au-lait figure of Lena Horne and listened to her enchanting singing of blues, I fell in love with her. I remember her doing but one three-minute number in a star-studded American musical. For me, she made the picture.

And then Lena came to England for a short season. She topped the bill at the Palladium. Needless to say, I went to see her, even if I only paid five shillings to stand.

She was last to appear on the programme. After a brief announcement she made a sober entry from the wings and broke into her first song, an unusual one with a strange tempo and an equally strange presentation by her.

I could not take my eyes off her. My previous contact with her – on the films and radio – really gave no indication of her personality. There can never have been another singer like her.

The emotional impact of her singing is overpowering. She lives every song she sings. One moment she is screwing her face into unbelievable agony, the next she is radiating a glowing, carefree personality. Now she is a tiger, now an angel.

Audience reaction was interesting. People didn't know whether to laugh or cry. At first her weird facial contortions appeared almost comical. Yet, as she sang on, she began to captivate and, in fact, hypnotise the audience.

She purred at them, snarled at them, whispered soothingly at them, vocally spat at them. As she sang, the girl from a Brooklyn slum forgot the outside world. She was singling out and magnifying every word – making it sound fifty times more powerful.

All the time, her willowy figure was moving gracefully. Although she remained by the microphone, in spirit she was down in the stalls, up in the circle. She was singing to every individual in the audience.

Lena wore a tight, glittering white gown. She never once spoke to the audience during the act. At the end of one of her more emotional numbers she acknowledged the applause by murmuring to herself in the heartbroken mood of the song. She took several encores, each time moving on and off the stage in a distinctive way, half run, half shuffle.

During her songs Miss Horne looked at times strikingly beautiful. Her sensuous body was always moving, maybe with sophisticated poise, maybe to the beat of primitive rhythm.

Five shillings is a lot to spend on a show when one is in the Services. But, without the slightest suggestion of a grudge, I would willingly have given twice that amount. To me, she was very, very cheap at the price.

Going backstage to interview Phyllis Dixey

I was told to enter. I held my breath as I went forward, trying vainly to remember my opening gambit. But I was due for disappointment.

My eyes were not to feast on the famed Phyllis. Instead, I came face to face with a little man (about 5 ft 2 or 3 inches) with big glasses and a cod-like face. He was wearing a faded dress-suit and spoke with what appeared to be an affected American accent. The dressing room itself was not a lot bigger than a lavatory cubicle. It was cluttered with a trombone, a couple of changes of clothing, golf clubs and the usual theatrical paraphernalia. This midget room boasted a big radiator and, not unnaturally, the atmosphere was stifling.

The little man gave me an outstretched hand, fairly casually, half looking at a piece of paper on his dressing table at the same time. He knew all about my visit; after all, I was soon to discover he was Miss Dixey's husband. He told me, with the conceited air of one who knew the way to handle the Press, that he could give me most of what I wanted and, anyway, Phyllis wasn't much good at this sort of thing.

I was inwardly annoyed that I had been palmed off with her publicity manager-husband. But he seemed to like to talk and rattled away. He talked as if he were Miss Dixey's father and not her husband: "Of course, Phyllis is a really nice kid – and clever. Do you know that she arranges all the dances and knows more about the lighting than I ever will? ... She's really an ACTRESS. She's appeared in intellectual plays, you know. But the public want to see her in this kind of stuff." Thinking no doubt of the coffers, he sighed hypocritically.

During our talk – or rather his – Miss Dixey made her bow. She came in, smiled, shook hands and answered one or two questions. She was more or less as I had imagined her. About 45. Well-preserved figure. Smooth skin. Benign eyes. A sensuous suggestion about the mouth. I could imagine that, stripped of her abundant grease-paint and other means of camouflage, she would look middle-aged and rather weary.

Husband Jack Tracy, who apparently revelled in the role of spokesman, was in no hurry for me to leave. He led me down to the wings where the girls were about to go on for the opening tableau.

"We're one happy crowd here. I can tell you that we pay our girls top wages. Like to keep them contented. And they're nice girls too – no messing about. Here come and meet them," he commanded.

With that brief warning, I found myself shaking hands with the six to eight girls who were in the opening number. They were in varying stages of undress. I was surprised to be told that one was only 15 years old.

7

Bristol Evening World

Bristol Evening World
Saturday, February 23, 1957
No. 8506 — Price 2d.
LATE NIGHT

BRISTOL HOUSEWIFE, 54, IS FOUND BATTERED TO DEATH IN BATHROOM

Police: We're Anxious to Contact Husband

By PAT KAVANAGH, BRUCE PERRY and DAVID FOOT

Police throughout Britain are trying to trace a lorry driver whose 54-year-old wife was found battered to death in the bathroom of her home in Bristol today.

The body of Mrs. Ethel Mary Elms, of 5 Allison-avenue, Brislington, was found lying fully clothed on the bathroom floor. She had severe head injuries caused by a number of blows from a heavy weapon.

Chief Det.-Insp. Jesse Pane, called from his bed to take charge of the investigation, went to the house. Later, after a consultation with Mr. F. W. Hicks, Deputy Chief Constable, he issued this statement:

"We are anxious to contact the woman's husband, John William Elms, aged 44, who is missing from his home. A description of Mr. Elms, a lorry driver, has been flashed to Scotland Yard and police forces throughout the country. He is believed to have a relative living in the East End of London. The description reads:—

Height 5ft 8ins.; proportionate build; fresh complexion; brown hair greying at the temples and bald on top; blue eyes; usually wears horn-rimmed spectacles, believed to be wearing a grey chalk-striped suit, fawn mackintosh and brown trilby hat.

Son Found House in Darkness

The discovery of the body of Mrs. Elms, who had lived in the house for about 15 years, came when her 12-year-old son John arrived home shortly before midnight and found the house locked and in darkness.

Knowing that his mother, whom he had not seen since lunchtime, should be in, he went to the police station. Police officers accompanied him home and broke into the house, to find Mrs. Elms lying dead in the bathroom.

There were no signs of a struggle in other parts of the house, and the weapon used in the attack was missing.

"It is obvious that whatever happened occurred only in the bathroom," said Chief Insp. Pane after he had visited the house with Det.-Insp. Reginald Hicks and other detectives.

Immediately dozens of police

CID MEN IN THE CASE
Chief Insp. Pane   Insp. Hicks

"CHIEF DET. INSP. JESSE PANE, deputy head of Bristol's CID. He worked all day yesterday, went home to bed at 11 p.m. last night, was called up to take charge of the investigation soon after midnight in the absence of Chief Det. Supt. Melbourne Phillips, who is on leave.

DET. INSP. REGINALD HICKS, in charge of CID for the Bedminster Division—Brislington is in his area. Bristol's last murder—that of a girl in an air raid shelter about five years ago —also took place in the Bedminster Division.

officers were concentrated in the vicinity of the terraced crescent. They began to search the area, yard by yard for any trace of the weapon of Mrs. Elms' assailant.

They combed the gardens of the neighbouring houses, and chicken-runs and hen-coops in a wooded dell stretching for a quarter-mile behind Allison-ave.

Chief-Insp. Pane took a statement from John and interviewed residents of Allison-ave. Later he went to the City Mortuary to watch a post-mortem examination. Wood-he-headed returned to headquarters and Brislewell he immediately went into conference with the Assistant Chief Constable.

His statement giving news of the search for Mrs. Elms' husband followed.

Neighbours told the police today they heard no screams or disturbance from the small terraced house where Mrs. Elms has lived with her husband and 12-year-old son John for about 15 years.

Mrs. Elms was a quiet woman of medium height. She had red straight hair and wore heavy glasses. Neighbours described her as "very much an ordinary housewife, keeping mostly to herself."

Devoted to Her Son

She was devoted to her son, said neighbours.

The boy goes to school at Wick-road, Brislington, where he is a good scholar, coming second in his class. He previously went to Broomhill School, Brislington. The husband, Mr. Elms, had

Continued in Back Page (A)

QUEEN MOTHER TO SEE GYPSY LOVE IN WEST STEEPLECHASE

Queen Elizabeth the Queen Mother is visiting the Beaufort Hunt Point-to-Point Steeplechase, at Didmarton, next Saturday, to see her horse Gypsy Love run in the first race.

"She is only coming for the day," said an official at Badminton House today.

She will drive from Windsor to Badminton in the morning and have lunch with the Duke of Beaufort Hunt. Her car will return to Windsor after the races.

It will not be the first time the Queen Mother has seen Gypsy Love run. The eight-year-old horse was the point-to-point steeplechase bought several years ago and March, 1954.

has been in the Duke of Beaufort's stable for some time. Various members of the Duke's household have been hunting on the horse this year.

Lt.-Col. R. S. Baker, secretary of the Beaufort Hunt, said today that Mr. O. Balding, of Weyhill, Andover, had been engaged to ride the horse in the first race at 2 p.m.

The Queen Mother has visited

BRISTOL DOCTORS
March 4 Protest Talks

Bristol doctors are to meet on March 4 to discuss strike action following their pay claim. Bristol doctors have pledged their support to the British Medical Association's threat to resign from the National Health Service. A resolution of support is likely to be sent to the BMA from the Bristol meeting.

Police at the Front

Policeman at the front door of 5 Allison-avenue, Brislington.

...and at the Back

A policeman stands guard in the back garden.

TODAY'S WEATHER

Dull, rain.
Further Outlook: Rain.
High Water at Weston: 1.11 p.m. today; 2.3 a.m. and 2.49 p.m. tomorrow.
Lighting-up time: 6.9 p.m. today to 6.37 a.m.; 6.11 p.m. tomorrow to 6.35 a.m.

Son-in-Law of 'Archers' Actor Found Shot

ANTHONY Brainbridge (29), son-in-law of the late Robert Mawdsley, the original Walter Oxbred of the BBC "The Archers," was found dead with a gunshot wound in Quantley Wood, Daneway, near Stroud, last night.

Mr. Brainbridge, who lived at Melton Mowbray, Leics., was, it is understood, on holiday at Oakridge Lynch, near Stroud. He went out about 10 a.m. yesterday and as he did not return, the police made a search.

In 1956 Mr. Brainbridge joined the staff of Petfoods Ltd., Melton Mowbray. He was married and had a daughter of 11 months.

Henleaze Man Hurt

David Davis, 32, of 192, Lake-road, Henleaze, was taken to Southmead Hospital suffering with head injuries and concussion after falling from his cycle.

FISHPONDS BOY BADLY INJURED

Richard Pinnegar (9), of 18, Snowdon-road, Fishponds, is officially ill in Cossham Hospital after a collision with a car today. His injuries include a severely lacerated forehead.

POSTMAN ATTACKED BY 2 DOGS

FREDERICK Cochran, 63, a postman, of Lisburn-road, Knowle, was found lying injured on a garden path today after two dogs were alleged to have attacked him and thrown him to the ground. City Ambulance rushed him to the BRI with chest injuries, severe shock and abrasions to the hands and legs. He is detained for observation.

At the time of the incident, he was delivering letters in Ruthven-road, Knowle.

Mrs. Grace Davis, of 11, Ruthven-road, said she saw two dogs set upon him. "They rushed at him, but he managed to fight them off. Then they went for him again and he was thrown on the ground, very heavily with his pack around his neck.

"I ran over and managed to get him to my house. Then he collapsed in great pain."

HALF-TIMES

Bristol Rovers NIL, Barnsley NIL
Bury ONE, Notts Forest ONE
Chelsea ONE, Bolton NIL
Hartlepools NIL, Crewe NIL
Arsenal ONE, Everton NIL
Manchester Utd. NIL, Blackpool NIL
Bournemouth NIL, Colchester NIL
Chester ONE, Southport ONE
Ipswich THREE, Newport TWO
Walford TWO, Reading TWO
Wrexham THREE, R.Q'n TWO
Carlisle THREE, Gateshead NIL
Oldham ONE, Hull NIL
Sheff W TWO, Manchester C ONE
West Brom ONE, Luton NIL
Chelmsford TWO, Crystal Palace NIL
Leicester ONE, Port Vale ONE

One Friday in the spring of 1955, frustrated by the limitations of his work at the *Western Gazette*, David hitched his way from East Coker to Bristol. He had submitted reports on Yeovil sport to the *Bristol Evening World*, and he had an idea that the paper might be looking for a new cricket reporter. So what better than to turn up in person and present his credentials?

There was no vacancy for a cricket writer. With his spirit crushed David started to leave the room, only for the news editor to call after him: "Fancy a job on the news side?" Five minutes of formalities later, he was taken on as a reporter.

> Now it was a matter of hitching lifts back to East Coker, warily telling Mum and Dad that I was leaving them shortly, and handing in my notice. The latter wasn't as difficult as I'd expected. Suddenly I was consumed with a feeling of freedom and adventure. In a perverse way I'd enjoyed the weekly's enforced chores and restrictions, even when standing in dozens of church doorways to take mourners' names. But now, as I saw it, I was about to become ... a proper journalist. I was halfway to Fleet Street.

The *World* had begun life in October 1929. It was the second, after the *Newcastle Evening World*, of a string of evening papers set up by Lord Rothermere, owner of the *Daily Mail* and *Daily Mirror*. His aim was to offer an 'up-to-date newspaper' to 'add enormously to the interest and intensity of life throughout the West Country' and 'free readers from the stranglehold of second-rate publications a quarter of a century behind the times'.

They were fighting words, which Rothermere had the funds to back with the building of the art-deco Northcliffe House in the city centre, equipping it with 'the most modern machinery outside London', and providing his new paper with a generous budget for offering attractive gifts to readers. Inevitably the established papers fought back, there was much newspaper politics, and by 1955, when David arrived, the *World* was locked in a circulation battle with the *Bristol Evening Post*, a battle that it was not winning.

On his first morning the news editor sent David to interview a woman in Old Market who was trying to set a new record for non-stop playing of the piano. "Just two or three paragraphs. And one other thing, Mr Foot. You're not working for the *Western Gazette* any longer. Short sentences, don't waste words. You are writing for passengers on the bus."

His first day of reporting did not end, however, after the printing of the last edition. Late that night he was in a café in Park Row when a brawl broke out, involving several prostitutes. The police were called, and David, back in his bedroom, wrote it up for an article that appeared next day.

He was staying in the YMCA, close to the *Evening World* building, and this proximity led in July to his being entrusted with a major story:

> In the middle of one night there was a knock on my door. I hesitated, aware of the prowlers, before opening it. John Bennett, the paper's film critic and assistant editor, was there. He'd just returned from a cinema premiere and was in a state of some anxiety. He blurted out that there had been serious floods in Weymouth overnight, that caravans had been washed away and lives were in danger.
>
> Weymouth was marginally in our circulation area. This was, however, a big story and we needed to be there. John had checked the emergency list of reporters and saw that I lodged nearest to the office and the office car. He said he had arranged with the night-watchman to open up the garage. "You do drive, don't you?" he asked as an after-thought.
>
> I dressed in a frenzy of expectation. So far I had never been entrusted with the office Ford Pop. So I'd be learning – and thinking – on the job. I stuffed a virgin notebook into my pocket and made sure I had enough coppers for the phone calls I knew I would have to make.

At one stage, early next morning, with the deadline approaching and no word from David, it looked like it might be his last big assignment, but he came through with a stirring piece. His reputation was enhanced.

Soon enough, he was being trusted to write not only major news stories but also investigative and opinion pieces on topical issues, such as the influx of West Indian immigrants into the St Paul's area. He also drew material from his personal life, filling two full columns with the story of how, after his wedding in October, Anne and he had been unable to shake off the confetti and hence keep to themselves the fact that they were on honeymoon:

> The harder we tried to retain our secret, the less successful we were. Those little bits of coloured paper haunted us throughout the week. But now, on reflection, I can see that there is something to be said for sharing a honeymoon secret with the world.
>
> For we would not have really missed for the world the sweet, understanding smiles of those charming French chambermaids. Nor the way one head waiter at a Dinard hotel took one look at us as we entered in what we thought was a suitably unromantic manner: *"Bon soir, Monsieur-Madame. May I recommend a wine? A special wine, tres excellent for, em – a honeymoon."* We gave up.

The following year he became the newspaper's drama critic. The year after, he was assigned to Bristol City's football matches, home and away. He also covered cricket. All these roles gave him the opportunity to write at length on subjects he loved and to express opinions.

David's marriage to Anne produced two children, Mark and Julia, and he was happy at home and at work. But it was not to last. The *World* was losing its battle for survival, and it came to an end with edition number 9,993 on Saturday 27 January 1962. That day David travelled on the Bristol City team coach to the Shay Stadium in Halifax. Through the afternoon he phoned regular updates back to the paper: City one up after three minutes, Halifax leading 3-2 at half-time, an equaliser in the 69th minute. Then:

> Nine minutes from time TAIT scored a brilliant individual goal. It was the kind he has scored twice before this season. He gained possession 40 yards from goal near the touchline and then moved diagonally towards the goal. He successfully held off a challenge and finally shot past the advancing Knowles into the net.

It was a thrilling victory, taking City close to the two promotion places in Division Three. The headline on the front page read: TAIT'S LATE WINNER FOR CITY IN A 'THRILLER'.

At much the same time, back in Bristol, the *Evening World* staff were summoned to the canteen, where a statement was read, informing them that the paper was closing. The *Football Final* of the *Pink 'Un* was its very final edition. David's description of City's winning goal might well have been the last words ever written for the paper.

The team coach stopped for a bite to eat at a hotel in Buxton.

> Fred Ford, the City manager, the warmest-hearted of old-style football bosses, suddenly got up as we all finished our apple tart. "Right, then. Quiet for a moment. Now some of you may have heard that the *Evening World* has closed. So no more David Foot with his fair reports, kidding us he's seen the same game as us. But we'll miss him. Now I want you buggers to get on your feet and drink a toast to him and his paper."
>
> The players were all standing, offering their obligatory digs and personal jokes which they liked to trade. Pro footballers could be exuberant in insult but the reporters liked to think it was offered in affection. After that we had a brief spontaneous song or two, with Alex Tait, schoolteacher-turned-centre forward, and myself taking it in turn in discordant jollity at the hotel's off-key piano.

EARLY WEEKS AT THE EVENING WORLD

Marathon Pianist

First article, Evening World, April 1955

Marathon pianist 'Musical Marie' Ashton's limp fingers fell away from the keyboard just after 11 o'clock on Saturday night. She had done it – completed 132 hours of non-stop piano playing and set up a new world record. But what a struggle it had been! She had started off well enough last Monday morning. Yet, by Saturday, she looked a pathetic sight. Her eyes were black with fatigue; her hands were bandaged; her reluctant fingers moved by instinct.

Maria, portly mother of two, attracted a crowd of 20,000 during the week. Towards the end they saw her retinue fighting to keep her awake. She had to be vigorously massaged. Then, after she had played the National Anthem and collapsed over the piano at Shepherd's Hall, Old Market, Bristol, she was driven away in an ambulance. For Maria, it was sleep – the first for nearly a week.

First Night as a Reporter

Footsteps from East Coker (2010)

I had not yet found any accommodation so had booked myself into the YMCA, just round the corner from my office, for a few nights. They directed me to the overflow annexe, which happened to be an erstwhile women's reformatory. It was constructed like one. The aura of authority still persisted; so did the smell of cheap disinfectant.

I went searching for a nearby café late that night and found one still serving modest, greasy suppers. It was populated by half a dozen women with pale, unhealthy complexions and language guaranteed to extend my vocabulary of enforced expletives. I soon realised it was where the prostitutes came when their back-seat-in-the-car work was done.

That night they were in an ugly mood. Their voices were raised and some of them began to fight. A glass door was smashed and before long half a dozen police officers arrived. I remained mesmerised. This was Bristol at its most seedy, and I was determined not to move. Several of the women, their thick lips smeared with the remnants of crudely applied lipstick, appeared to be into their sixties. They continued to hire out their arid bodies because it was the only trade they knew. The arguing continued, and some of the offenders were unceremoniously carted off to the station.

I went back to my cramped bed and wrote it up. Not too long ... short sentences ... just right to read on the bus on the way into work. I would never have dared to turn it into a news story for the *Gazette*. But I was given a frisson of pride to discover that the *World* had used it on page three with a two-column intro GIRLS EJECTED AFTER CITY CAFÉ INCIDENT. All my own work. I was in business.

First By-Line

In a private piece, written at the time, David reflects on the first time an article appeared in a newspaper under the name 'David Foot' (June 1955)

I must thank June Sampson for my first by-line. It was because she asked me to take a job off her that I found myself interviewing Vic Oliver. I saw him in his dressing-room for about ten minutes. As he was in a Folies Bergère show, I wrote a piece about the difficulty of a male getting back-stage. It took me about half an hour to turn in six folios. Then I went off for a hot-dog before bed.

I thought possibly I might warrant a by-line but I wasn't very confident. In my unforgivable conceit, I was longing for one. Remember I had never had a proper one in my life. An odd essay or short story, for which the evening papers had grudgingly given me a pittance, had gained me 'David Coker'. A few pieces I wrote for the East Coker parish magazine had presented me with one or two 'DGF's. Even the Western Gazette had been good enough to bolster my ego with those three magic intitials from time to time. But 'David Foot' ... never.

Next morning I was thinking of Vic Oliver again. By this time, that elusive by-line was looming up quite big. I had not written my story in the first-person but I felt it was rather a personal story – and the *World* likes that kind of thing. Then I thought, however, of several pieces I had written in the last few days – and for which I got nothing.

I had felt certain that my name would have appeared at least once during the West of England tennis championships which I had covered throughout the week. I remembered the way I had anxiously bought a *Pink-Un* on the evening of the finals ... and my naïve disappointment at finding nothing signed.

The first edition comes out at about 11 o'clock. All morning, the suspense had been mounting. I'm sure my re-writes suffered. When the chance came, I hurried out of the office and wandered along Colston Avenue. It was a long wait.

Then the sellers came out of the *World*, shouting their wares. This was when I had to be cool, calm, blasé. I ambled across the road and handed two pennies to the vendor. In exchange, he gave me a crisp, neatly-folded paper.

With great self-control, I opened it. Immediately, my eye rested on the by-line. Yes, it was there ... page 3. Nearly a column story. I sensed that I was flushing with pride. I stood there on the corner of Colston Avenue and read it from top to bottom. It was my work and there was my name to prove it.

I didn't decide rightaway that I was the *World*'s star writer. But I did start thinking about sending the article home as soon as possible to show Anne and my parents. I hadn't stopped to ponder on whether I had any cause to be jubilant. I didn't propose to be analytical.

The trouble with a signed story is that there is no escape. Your reputation can soar on the strength of it – and it can take a nasty tumble. There was no chance to wriggle clear under the cloak of anonymity.

I read my first by-lined story rather furtively. The last thing I wanted to happen was for anyone I knew to come round the corner and catch me wallowing in my superficial glory. I can remember how funny and unfamiliar the by-line looked.

There was still the real test to come. How would my colleagues react? I folded the paper as small as I could and tucked it completely out of sight in one of my pockets. I couldn't let anyone think I had rushed out to buy the morning rag. But I feel that my initial excitement would have been considerably blunted if I had not bought the paper off the street, if it had just been mundanely handed to me inside the office.

For what reasons I know not, but it needed a big effort from me to enter the office. I suppose I was now self-conscious and a trifle dubious of the reception I would get. I had already discovered that there is a good deal of friendly banter about the respective abilities of the various reporters.

My return to the office was via the back-door. I lingered in the lavatories before finally rushing into the reporters' room and sitting down, red-faced and guilty. I waited for someone to say something. No-one did. Then it dawned on me: the papers had not reached the reporters yet. All my harrassed confusion and diffidence for nothing.

Then the papers came. Heads were buried in the pages. I picked up one and gazed nonchalantly at one of the sports pages. I glanced from colleague to colleague. Several of them were on page 3. The agony passed. Later, my dear patronising Miss Sampson said: "Didn't you know you'd get a by-line? Oh yes. Of course, I get so many of them (authentic quote). I'm glad I didn't go. It was really a story for a man."

One thing worried me about it. The subs had changed my 'a reporter' to ME and I. It made me look a bit cocky, going out of my way to hog a by-line. But I suppose, truly, I had tried desperately hard for that first one.

Girls Make Vic So Hard To See

First article to carry the by-line 'By David Foot', Evening World, June 1955

It's the hardest job in the world to see Vic Oliver back-stage at the Hippodrome this week. The trouble is that he's appearing in the Folies Bergère revue, 'Pardon My French'. Also in that rather saucy, very arty affair are a lot of curvaceous young ladies.

Doormen at theatres have an intuitive sense. They have a number of strict orders to carry out. One of the cardinal rules is "Keep an eye on loitering stage-door Johnnies." The extreme gallantry of those young gentlemen, who once made sweeping bows and lavished flowers and presents upon comely Gaiety Girls, is, alas, a thing of the past, it appears.

So it was that my humble request to see Mr Oliver became at first a demoralising experience. There were polite coughs, discerning looks.

After explanations, however, all was well. The helpful personal manager of Vic Oliver ushered me up the stairs. This time, the quizzical glances came from scantily-dressed young ladies, who spied a stranger in the house.

I blew my nose, fidgeted with my wrist watch and tried, reluctantly, to look the other way.

Composure was restored in Mr Oliver's dressing-room. He was courteous, friendly. He pulled up a chair and, impromptu, started talking of his first love – music. His youthful ambition was to become an accomplished musician. He has achieved it – but passport to fame has been the gag-book rather than the baton.

What made him switch to comedy? He drew deeply on his cigarette and there was a momentary look of sadness. Then he reminisced: "I was a musician until I was 36. But then there was an enormous slump in good music ... Well, I had to eat and I had a family to support."

He came to England in 1936. He got his first broadcasts, and people liked this new comedian with the foreign accent and a fiddle which he seldom gave himself the chance to play. Now he has more than 1,100 broadcasts to his credit.

Of his act at the Hippodrome he said: "You have to adapt yourself to your audience. With this kind of show you have to be a little risqué."

Of his dual talents: "Audiences are funny. Some would never listen to me play or conduct. Others would never listen to me tell jokes. Always try to give the public what they want."

Of his beautiful 'feed', Vanda Vale: "You'd never believe how she got into the act. I advertised for someone who would walk across the stage for a gag during my piano playing. Vanda, who is only 17, applied and got the job. She had just left the Royal Academy of Dramatic Art and wanted to be a serious actress. I tried her with a bit of cross-talk, and her spontaneous wit was so good I had to keep her in the act."

I also discovered that Miss Vale is a vicar's daughter and is to open a bazaar at Frome at the weekend. It seems that she is another to make a profitable switch – from the legitimate stage to the halls and a load of promised contracts.

Being sent to Weymouth

Footsteps from East Coker (2010)

The floods were as bad as John Bennett had warned. My basic newspaper training came to my aid, and I stopped at Weymouth's police station for the duty sergeant and his augmented staff to tell me what exactly was happening. Frank, an experienced reporter from the *Daily Express*, was already there. He sensed I was a young lad not too sure how to tackle my assignment. "Leave your car here and come along with me," he said. That kind of generous spirit was something I recurrently met and valued. I'm not at all sure that it still exists in the reportage world of laptops and impersonal facades of token communication out on the stories as eager agency journalists need ruthlessly to compete with a declining number of staff men.

As usual there were conflicting reports of the flood damage. But by 7.30 a.m. I had enough for my first piece. It ran to more than fifteen hundred words. There was no time for any fancy descriptive phrases, although alliterative images like 'raging rivers' slipped in. I wrote of ruined holidays and chalets floating past like so much matchwood. I quoted the Chief Constable and members of the council and some of the victims I had already seen in the pre-dawn confusion.

Back in the *World* office, my lengthy first-edition copy was running late with no more than a hurried transfer-charge call and message from me that it would soon be on the way. Reg, the news editor, was apoplectic as he swore to no-one in particular: "Where the bloody hell is his copy? Does he even know our edition times? Why did we get him out of bed? He's probably never covered a big story before. When it comes, we'll probably have to rewrite the whole lot. Christ, what a disaster!"

Even as he blasphemed, I was on the phone dictating, partly from my notes, partly off the cuff. It was the first really big story with which I'd ever been entrusted. And it was OK. Even from the pavements of Weymouth, running with floodwater as they still were, I imagined I could hear Reg and the room full of subs sighing in unison with relief. My report was spread over the front page and two pages inside. I wrote of the rescue work that had already begun and of holiday plans in ruins. I wrote of 600 homeless people. (It was a justifiably hazardous statistic I had heard mentioned. There was no chance yet to verify it.) It helped that by accident I also found a family from Bristol, bedraggled and miserable. The human interest, lifeblood of popular journalism, wasn't ignored.

The *World* seemed pleased apparently with the mature way I handled the floods. I visited the holiday caravan sites and the river banks that had burst. I latched on, privately triumphant, to every distressed family with an address in or near to Bristol. I motored to Bowleaze and Lulworth Coves.

"You gave us a scare but it all worked out well. Think we'll leave you down there for a day or two. Let's see, don't you come from near Weymouth?"

"Well, 25 miles away at least. But happy to stay with the story, Mr Eason."

The *World*, desperate of necessity to look after their pennies, suggested I should stay with my parents. I was proud of my proper newspaperman's status and willingly agreed. Some of the fellow reporters were altogether more pointed. "That's the one trouble with our paper – it's run by mean sods. You should have been put up in a Dorset hotel." I was in no mood to complain. The scope of the story meant more to me than where I was going to sleep.

Weymouth Flood

from report, Evening World, July 1955

Weymouth, which yesterday was a seaside report full of gay holidaymakers, is today a town of misery, with 600 people homeless, after hours of fierce thunderstorms and cloudbursts. Little more than 15 miles west, flood waters burst the banks of the rivers Brit and Asker, bringing disaster to the little holiday town of Bridport (population 5,509).

Weymouth holidaymakers had their holiday plans shattered in a few minutes. Caravans collapsed like matchwood. Solid stone walls were sent crashing across roads. Streams turned overnight into raging rivers, ploughing their way through back gardens, caravan sites, side streets, leaving a trail of wretchedness and destruction.

At one caravan site at Eden Garden Orchard, near Upwey, 17 caravans were tossed over on their sides by the rushing water. One was sent hurtling downstream for 100 yards.

Talking Point

June 1956

Mr Ted Leather MP gets up and says: "Racial prejudice could wreck the British Commonwealth. I defy you to find one country in the world that can afford it less than this one." Those are courageous and sincere words. And they follow those of Father Huddleston, who has had English consciences nagging ever since he returned from South Africa.

We like to think of ourselves as good democrats. Ask anyone in Bristol what he thinks of the colour bar and he affects horror and bristles with indignation. Yet it does exist in this country – and in the city of Bristol.

I have seen it myself. Not blatantly. But it is there just the same. On a double-decker bus, there was an empty seat next to a Jamaican worker. Into the bus stepped a girl. She looked at the empty seat, turned her head.

*

The know-alls and reactionaries will shout: "You're steering on dangerous ground. We don't like the look of the political aspect." Yet it's not a question of politics but of world citizenship. Or living together.

If we all try to exercise a little more understanding and tolerance, we shall be heading the right way. And the brave words of Father Huddleston will not have been wasted.

Tommy Steele

June 1957

The Hippodrome has never known anything like this before. An audience, with a surprising number of schoolchildren, yelled and clapped to the powerhouse beat which stridently dominated this show. And they licked the feet of the boy they came to see.

Tommy Steele's singing might be gibberish for all you know. But if you can't hear a word, you can applaud him for his technique, remarkable as it is. He grips his guitar like a sten gun. He shakes his blond, unruly hair as though he is subject to periodic convulsions. He does ungainly dance steps. He has no finesse. And yet he is a great success. With his Steelmen – excellent musicians in their vigorous way – he has the most antagonistic liking him by the end of his incredible act. That means he is a STAR – and that is why so many people in show business are jealous of him.

Here is another point. Despite the flailing of arms and legs, he is essentially modest and unaffected. That reaches the audience.

Tom Graveney

from a report of Gloucestershire v Yorkshire, Bristol, May 1958

Tom Graveney has played many fine innings for his county and country. But seldom has he shown his stature more than against Yorkshire at Bristol yesterday, when for two hours and 20 minutes he shielded the other Glo'shire batsmen and assembled 65 runs at the same time. It carried his county to a great three-wicket win.

The atmosphere was tense. But the crowd's good-nature did not desert them. They whooped as Trueman flashed a bumper near Meyer's head; they ironically clapped as Close dropped the ball several times as he moved up to bowl.

... Wardle and Illingworth were now on top. And so much depended on Graveney. He was nearly bowled before he had scored; he might have been caught by Trueman perhaps. But, despite his task, he seldom lived dangerously. With true Yorkshire fervour, lbw appeals sounded out loud and frequent in the decisive overs of the late afternoon. The umpires were not to be swayed, however. In assessing this Glo'shire win, the innings of Graveney will live in the memory.

Peter Wight

Opening of a 'sporting profile' of Somerset's Guyanese cricketer, August 1958

Ruddy-faced farmers with the froth of Somerset ale still on their lips were gazing through the tavern window of the County Ground, Taunton. Their minds should have been on haymaking and the approaching harvest; one or two had stolen time, with scant regard for agricultural economy, from the local market. But there was a look of contentment on their faces. They liked what they were seeing.

And the object of their interest was a slight figure, whose natural grace of movement at the wicket and innate grasp of stroke-play forced one rural observer to remark with a deeply ruminative air: "So he be Peter Wight. He looks a good 'un. Can't he just use the willow."

Yes, it was the elegant West Indian in one of his early matches at Taunton. Since then, many other Somerset folk have stopped – and held up their prosaic work – to applaud him. He is not a dynamic opener in the Gimblett or Barnett groove; he is not a swashbuckling wielder of the blade in the Wellard tradition. But he can still, by the crispness and style of his stroke-play, fire the imagination of a crowd.

ADVICE TO THOSE ABOUT TO GET MARRIED

Evening World, August 1956

Would anyone like to see my scars? I have five of them and they are my proudest possession. The unimaginative might be content to call them blisters. I prefer to inflate my chest and think of them as the grim legacy of a day in the fields. My haymaking wounds.

They have been with me now for over five weeks. But, latterly, my morning inspection has confirmed a morale-weakening fear. The scars are disappearing. And I feel like the jaded, complexion-conscious belle who sadly realises in October that the becoming sun tan is going out of her life for another year.

My nap-hand of scars have, you see, served me handsomely. They won me sympathy and admiration. I got blissfully blasé over remarks like: "Poor devil, they must hurt like mad!" or "Just shows you don't fight shy of a hard day's work."

Sometimes I would fish for compliments. With an ostentatious gesture, I would make sure that my maimed hands were seen. An occasional dramatic wince as I gripped a pan or a cup of canteen tea worked wonders.

And now this invaluable, ego-boosting evidence of manly toil will soon be lost. I shall be left only with my memories – plus an unshakable resolution that I shall never become a farmer. You don't get three-week blisters from tapping a typewriter.

Of course, I began my haymaking – part of my holiday – with so much enthusiasm. It was a novelty, an invigorating experience in the open air. Couldn't I remember those gay, enticing posters of the war days, which had land girls vying with Hollywood starlets in the glamour stakes? If these girls could do it, so could I.

I prided myself on my ability to do a man's-size job. So with preconceived ideas of how I would take things in my stride, I presented myself to the farmer. To get the authentic touch, I had gone without my shave that morning. And I wore my oldest trousers.

The haymaking corps, with an earnestness that staggered me, climbed aboard the tractors. One of the young members gave me a queer look, one rather of disapproval, and laconically said: "You need a shave." Just the beginning of a day's disillusionment.

Those tractors throttled into life – and jerked forward. I gripped the back of the seat for grim death. The others lit cigarettes. I find it hard to remember in detail what happened for the remainder of the day. Things were not too bad at first. But in the sweaty, itchy, back-breaking period that followed I worked by instinct. Will-power and pride carried me through.

We were loading bales of hay onto the wagons for most of the time. That wasn't so bad when the wagon was nearly empty and the body was still fresh. But those bales began to weigh eight or nine hundredweights each, I decided. And as the load towered over the wagon so the effort had to be super-human to get the bale up.

I urged and heaved, puffed and cursed. The sweat ran into my eyes and my tongue felt like sandpaper. Once, rather like the dying man having his last kick, I pugnaciously stuck the pick into the bale and went to toss it up.

But it didn't go. I went instead ... onto my knees.

More hardy members of the corps roared at my Chaplinesque antics. They made funny remarks which I found singularly unfunny. And the annoying thing was they were not collapsing on their knees. They were lasting the course.

The farmer, a kindly man, asked me if I was enjoying myself. I lied with a conspicuous lack of conviction and looked with pained horror at the bevy of blisters which were already making their mark. But nobody seemed to notice. Nobody had time to notice.

I have always been the farmer's protagonist whenever a belligerent town-dweller has argued, ignorantly, about rural economics. Now my support for the agriculturist has risen threefold.

He must be the most rugged, the most dedicated, the most tireless worker in the world. And the toughest master of the novice. You join the corps and you're one of the team. There's no half-time, no tea break and no stop for a chat. If you want to talk you do it as you work. Myself? I didn't feel like talking.

It was 10 p.m. when the last wagon rattled through the farmyard towards the Dutch barn. Dusk was very beautiful to me. My work was over and I'd passed the test. Perhaps it was the steak I had eaten the previous day; my stamina had seen me through.

Back at the farm the beer tasted good. The bath felt good. So did I when the farmer's son, John, gave me a pat on the back. In his good-natured way he had always been the sternest critic of the would-be agriculturalist. He hadn't thought I was 'cut out' for it.

But it's a hard life ... So you want some advice, son, about getting married? Listen! Think first of the father-in-law. If he's a civil servant, a bank clerk or an insurance agent you are on a good thing.

But me? I married a farmer's daughter.

BRISTOL CITY FOOTBALL CLUB'S NEW REPORTER

Footsteps from East Coker (2010)

The City man had gone from the *World* and there was a vacancy for me. What appealed, after the years of objective reporting, was the opportunity to be able to express an opinion in print. I didn't have simply to regurgitate the platitudes of the local Member of Parliament as he lectured blandly to the transfixed faithful. I could actually say if the centre forward had a stinker.

My first game at Ashton Gate was against Liverpool, then in the Second Division. I hadn't met any of the Bristol players and the only Liverpool one I would have recognised was the wonderful Billy Liddell whose picture I had previously cut out and put in my scrapbook. In addition I knew from my cigarette cards that the visitors played in red shirts – although I had forgotten that, because of a clash of colours, they'd have to change their strips for this visit to the West Country

It was the days of the *Pink 'Un* and the *Green 'Un*. I was confronted, on my debut, with 2,000 words of crisp commentary dictated straight into my phone. Nothing except perhaps the goal-scorers was written down. It struck me as a challenging exercise and I was up for it. That was until 20 minutes into the game when I recognised Billy Liddell – in a white shirt. And wasn't that tall, strong player at the other end of the field John Atyeo? In red?

In panic I realised I had been describing all the wrong players – and wrong teams – for 20 minutes. I sank deep into my hard Ashton Gate seat and evaluated my options. Dare I tell George Baker, my affable sports editor, what calamitous, inaccurate commentary I had offered our readers, and would I be now worth keeping on the staff? Or should I just pretend that everything was fine, hoping that no-one would notice? Perspiring freely, I opted for bluff. My duplicitous decision succeeded, and there wasn't a single complaint. What conclusion do we draw about readers' powers of concentration?

The *Pink 'Un* was on the street less than half an hour after the final whistle. I marvelled many times over the proficiency of the system, inevitable literals excused. In those early exchanges with Liverpool, no-one had scored. So who was going to berate me for that burst of emergency fiction? No-one, blissfully, had even noticed.

MAGIC BILLY LIDDELL TOUCH BEAT THE CITY

Bristol City 1 Liverpool 2

from Monday's post-match report, Evening World, August 1957

Hush, you City fans, hush! Temper those harsh words which you began to utter rashly as soon as the final whistle sounded – and you knew that Bristol City had suffered a home defeat in the first game of the season.

It very nearly wasn't a defeat at all. If Liverpool hadn't such a skilled soccer craftsman as Billy Liddell, who could wander out disconcertingly to the empty wing and then land a centre on a threepenny piece, the City would have shared the points.

There were only six minutes left when Liddell, with a speed which made a mock of his age, doubled back to pick up a loose ball on the left. He steadied himself, measured his pass and sent the ball plumb onto the eager head of Tony Rowley.

And for the second time in what was, basically, a fairly even game, Rowley found the net. Each time the man behind the pass was former Scottish international Liddell, the idol of Anfield, the Peter Pan of the North West.

In the centre he found Jackie White marking him tightly, so he resorted to the game he likes best, the style of play which takes him out to the wings to pick up those stray balls which look like going into touch.

The City failed to learn the lesson that Liddell, that crafty veteran, pointed out on his previous visits to Bristol. You can't afford to give him an inch. Play Liddell out of the game and the Liverpool forward line, which he supervises so effectively, can become a negative force.

*

Bristol City did not play badly. Nor, to be fair, did they play particularly well on the whole. But the missing cohesion is not unusual in the first match of the season.

And remember this. Liverpool are a really good side. They will win a lot of points before next Spring. It will not surprise me if they return to the First Division.

Yet this was no easy game for them. Taking the match right through they only just had the edge on the City. I was quite resigned to a draw as the closing minutes went by and thought it would not be unreasonable.

But Liddell had other ideas.

FOOTBALL REPORTS

The opening sentences of eight football reports, Evening World

Bristol City 3 Bristol Rovers 2 – *October 1957*

Derby Day came to Ashton Gate on Saturday and with it a glow returned to the faces of the recently solemn home supporters. For, like last season, the League table was no guide. Bristol City came out of this rugged, high-speed, wholehearted display by all 22 players victorious by the odd goal in five. No, it wasn't a game brimming with text-book delicacies and precision moves. It was, instead, full of cut-and-thrust, red-blooded tackling and pulse-racing attacking play.

Bristol City 3 Bristol Rovers 4 – *February 1958*

Once again the southern banks of the Avon are stilled. The Battle of Bristol has been fought – and won. Ashton Gate is deserted as the Wembley-inspired glitter sweeps northwards across a hoarse, cup-happy city. I don't ever want to see a more exciting, throbbing, dynamic tussle between two Bristol clubs. For my money it was a game and a half. It was a tingling, tantalising 90 minutes. There were 22 stars – if, by stars, one means players who gave absolutely everything.

Bristol City 1 Sheffield United 4 – *March 1958*

I didn't know so many people eat oranges at football matches. There seemed to be an interminable supply of missiles directed on the bravest man at Ashton Gate on Saturday – Bob Mann, of Worcester, who left the field in the middle of 13 burly police officers. Mr Mann continued to smile at times as the scorn of nearly 20,000 rabid City supporters was loudly expressed.

Bristol City 4 Swansea Town 0 – *October 1958*

Mrs Wally Hinshelwood proudly led her young son, Paul, down from the grandstand after the game. It was the first time he had seen his father play. "He'll be a family mascot from now on," said mother. For the little winger silenced every one of his hardened critics with a second half exhibition of football artistry as devastating as any he has ever turned in. By the end of the game Swansea's left back, Lawson, was giddy from his vain effort to counter the speed and bewildering footwork of Hinshelwood.

Bristol City 2 Sheffield United 2 – *February 1960*

One looked almost in vain for something resembling an oasis in the barren, often cheerless desert of Ashton Gate on Saturday. But the grimly tempo-slowing tons of sand had the final word – they ruined this game as a spectacle and broke the spirit of the more constructive football long before the end. We had the rather farcical situation of a Sheffield United forward advancing in full cry on the City goal, then stumbling pathetically as his ankles sank in the sand.

Middlesbrough 6 Bristol City 3 – *February 1960*

I experienced an apparent mirage, no doubt brought on for a change by the intense cold of the North East, for the first 20 minutes of the second half. It showed Bristol City as a side immeasurably better than the opposition. During this period of near-gold football, the City dazzled in their approach work. They found each other with unerring precision; they nonplussed one of the best defences in the division. It was all very bewildering. Through the filmy haze of the mirage one could hear the Middlesbrough supporters chastising their team for losing its grip on the game. There was even an element of panic in the raucous accent nearby which shrieked: "We're going to throw away both points." Alas, it didn't last.

Bristol City 3 Port Vale 4 – *October 1960*

Those who attach importance to omens possibly saw some significance in the incident half an hour before the game when a sheet of asbestos roofing crashed onto the terracing in front of the press box in the main stand. Bristol City's luck was out, and after Casey's injury 15 minutes from the end the home team lost the lead and then the game. Reporters had a difficult time and it is hard to decide which demanded the greater concentration – shielding their notebooks from the driving rain or keeping count of the goals which arrived with indecent haste in the second half.

Bristol City 2 Queen's Park Rangers 0 – *November 1961*

Alec Stock, a mixture of urbanity and country good health as becomes a well-publicised football manager nurtured in the West Country, came 'home' on Saturday – not to talk about the exhilarating air of his beloved Somerset but of anaemia. And the anaemia he spoke of belonged to his forward-line. He knew they were never in the game at Ashton Gate.

PINK 'UNS AND GREEN 'UNS

The Guardian, June 2009

The trouble about writing for newspapers, a craft that has brought me a modest and often stimulating living, is that it has now lost its inherent sense of excitement. These days we see reporters sitting bleary-eyed and po-faced, hunched in awkward posture over their laptops, a piece of temperamental equipment that I have so far done my best to resist. Technology is inexorably taking over, with journalists having increasingly to work for the internet as well as the printed page. As someone who still remains at times cussedly loyal to an old manual typewriter, I recoil from such modern and impersonal traits.

My happiest days were in the 1940s and 50s when the pink 'uns and green 'uns continued to circulate around the country, providing a cherished Saturday tea-time ritual, this symbol of post-war's insatiable hunger for sporting news. The evening paper I worked for miraculously got its bundles of pink 'uns into the vans or on to the streets within 20 minutes of the final whistle. It was an extraordinary achievement and, in the days when I was still a schoolboy buying a copy in such eager expectation, I even imagined the papers were hot to the touch. The print used to come off on my fingers, a badge of fulfilment.

Later it was my turn to come up with the words, too. Nothing was more journalistically pulsating – more dramatic in its way than the murder trials and the police chases that had once filled our notebooks. But this was different; it actually recorded in graphic detail the build-up to the winning goal at Ashton Gate. The football public, many of whom had already watched the match – beer now on their breaths, boyish thrills in their veins – were back again, in the pavement queue, ready to live the 90 minutes all over again. Remember those were days before television's sprawling interest and radio's blanket coverage.

Fanatical fans jammed the newsagents, loose change jangling in back pockets. They exchanged their trite opinions with their mates as they waited: the missed chances, the penalty save, the blind referee. Nowadays, you can hear it all, shallow, repetitive, biased, on the radio phone-ins. But surely it was much more fun when the supporters had to make do with just those austerely enunciated BBC results and then the sporting prints hot off the presses.

Up in the frequently minuscule press boxes, whether in my case at Eastville or Halifax's Shay, where once I saw pram wheels protruding through the concrete of the terracing, I regularly gabbled away as I dictated in strict chronological order nearly 2,000 words of endeavour from 22 players of markedly varying talent. The writer's job was always to give the game rather more gloss than it deserved. There was no time to write so we merely talked into the phone. Back in our offices, a skilled copytaker typed our words for the compositor. It was frantic stuff. Literals got into our reports because there was no time to correct them. Nor was there time for long words or pretentious prose. The discipline served us well.

Sports editors would look for the fastest typist they could find. At times those duties in our office were entrusted to a fiery, likeable, talented Scottish reporter called Charlie, even if he resented being pulled away from his favoured Saturday afternoon residency at the Artichoke pub. It should be added that he liked a drink and was on this occasion more garrulous than usual with his waspish verbal running commentary. Towards the end of the report of my finest purple prose, it was the custom to offer a few paragraphs of judgement on the game. It carried the sub-heading 'David Foot comments'. Charlie suddenly saw scope for a literary liberty and typed 'David Foot belly-aches'. The saucy observation wasn't spotted and got into the paper.

I mention it only because the improvising copytaker was Charles Wilson, later to become editor of *The Times*. Maybe on reflection he had some sympathy for me. In any case, he once offered me a job in Fleet Street. I stayed contentedly to churn out my affectionate clichés on Shadow Williams and Jantzen Derrick instead.

The pink 'uns and green 'uns gradually receded and most of them disappeared for good. They became an uneconomic commercial indulgence while the street-corner vendors, with their distinctively throaty entreaties, saw no future in competing with the garages and supermarkets. And what was the point, anyway, in producing a newspaper whose contents had already been superseded by the radio reports and interviews?

Some of us much regret their passing. Apart from the sheer throbbing professional enthusiasm and the aim to get the sports papers on the street when some of the players were still pulling off their mud-caked boots, there was a sweaty romance that will never be recaptured in the computer age. My old pink 'un, cluttered as it was with typographical lapses, was not fashioned for literary awards. But it was fun – and it was exciting. And where else would I have got the editor of *The Times* to work for me?

8
Drama Critic

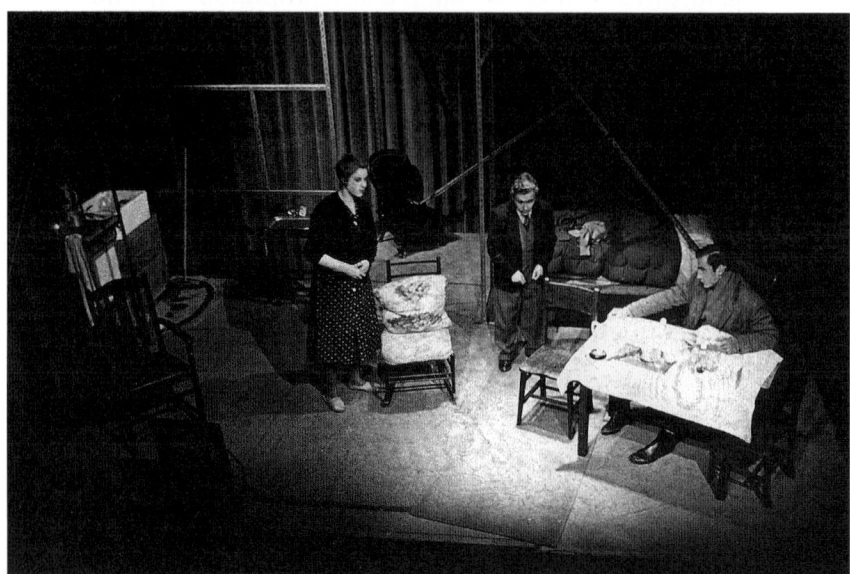

'The Room' by Harold Pinter, Bristol University Drama Department, May 1957

During the first year of David's time as a general reporter on the *Bristol Evening World* he was occasionally asked to file theatre reviews. They were mostly those that Dennis Bushell, the drama critic, could not fit into his diary, productions by such ensembles as the Bristol Cathedral School Drama Group or the Bristol Commercial Travellers' Dramatic Society, requiring pieces of just 200 or 250 words.

If Bushell was on holiday, David stood in for him at major performances. One, for which he was given 600 words, was a visiting production of *Macbeth* starring Paul Rogers, a respected Shakespearean actor who had spent crucial years in Bristol. David had not studied at university, he had little experience of such reviewing, yet he rose with panache to the challenge.

So it was no surprise that, when Bushell departed the *Bristol Evening World* in October 1956, 'leaving journalism for industry', David was promoted to the role of drama critic. He was responsible for reviewing all the city's productions, professional and amateur, and writing related feature articles. Tom Stoppard, eight years his junior, joined the *World* two years later and served as David's deputy. According to David, the *World*'s news editor Reg Eason had 'filched' Stoppard from the rival *Post* by taking him to lunch and offering him the role of motoring correspondent: 'Tom couldn't drive a car, but he took the job.'

Bristol in the 1950s was a major hub of regional theatre. The Bristol Old Vic Company, established after the war at the Theatre Royal, was highly regarded, launching the careers of many actors. The university had established the first drama department in the country, and there was an influential theatre school. The Hippodrome staged everything from Shakespeare to variety shows, while the city boasted a plethora of amateur and student groups for David to visit.

Newly wed and living in a one-bedroom flat not far from Horfield Prison, David was fascinated by the thriving world of amateur theatre, as he recalled in *Footsteps from East Coker*:

> I used to produce a weekly column for the amateur stage. Harassed producers would confide in me. There seemed to be a surfeit of flirting within the company and marriages, affected in some cases by the pseudo-romantic dialogue and sexy nuances on stage, collapsed permanently.
>
> Anne and I attended church halls in most of Bristol's suburban outposts. We travelled on the bus. In the middle of winter we were sometimes so cold that we deliberately rode an extra stop or two on the way home. It wasn't an aspect of journalism much to

my liking. But I tried to review the plays with a measure of kindly encouragement. I'd knock out my half a dozen paragraphs in front of the one-bar electric fire as my young wife poached an egg for us.

Yet what a time it was to become a drama critic! The theatre was on the cusp of a revolution, the conservative world of drawing-room dramas being subverted both by 'angry young men', writing plays of gritty social realism, and by experimental writers who challenged reality with forays into the absurd. Some mainstream critics denounced this new writing, yet David came with no such 'stuffy preconceptions' and saw straightaway its importance.

He was not always convinced by the more unconventional offerings from the continent. He thought Eugène Ionesco's *Rhinoceros*, in which all the inhabitants of a French town gradually turn into horned beasts, was 'a disquieting and hilarious experience' that 'partially misses as a piece of theatre'. But he warmed to Samuel Beckett's *Waiting for Godot*, and he loved Bertolt Brecht's *Mother Courage*, calling it 'a staggering masterpiece'.

He was excited by the 'real human beings' in John Osborne's *Look Back in Anger*, by the 'uninhibited garrulity' of Brendan Behan's *The Hostage* and by the authenticity of the rural working-class characters in Arnold Wesker's *Roots*. In reviewing these works, he had the advantage of knowing that at least some national critics had already seen worth in them. He had no such background when he went to the University Drama Department's production of a play by a first-time writer, a one-time schoolmate of postgraduate student Henry Woolf.

Woolf had been for supper at David's house, extolling the pioneering work of the department. He urged David to come and review the forthcoming production of his friend's play, which he was staging in the small theatre that the department improvised in an upstairs room in the Wills Building. He explained how his friend, an actor in repertory in Bournemouth, had written the play, *The Room*, in just two days.

'A hit,' David declared it in an enthusiastic 240-word review – 'I'm so glad I didn't miss this production' – adding that Woolf's friend 'should go on writing.' Little can David have imagined that many years later he would be telling with amusement how, in his first months as a young drama critic on the *Bristol Evening World*, he had penned the first review ever to be published of a work by Harold Pinter.

How well his judgements have stood the test of time. When reviewing Shelagh Delaney's *A Taste of Honey*, he praised the play's vitality and compassion but also noted its imperfections:

> Miss Delaney, a worldly 19-year-old, writing her first play, made her heroine pregnant by a coloured sailor, etched the mother as a gin-inclined tart, added a drunken layabout and a homosexual student ... Yet the play does not erupt into another display of adolescent invective in the interests of realism. With its undeniable poetic quality, its concern with real people, its Salford vowels, cruelness and belly-laughs, it gives the Old Vic a vital start to the season ... Miss Delaney is a probationary dramatist; this is perhaps on occasions an untidy and immature play. But it has originality and tremendous theatrical impact. This is working-class drama at its best.

Later the same year David was at the Hippodrome to review Delaney's second play, *The Lion in Love*, which was on a short provincial tour before heading for London, and he was less forgiving of its imperfections:

> Miss Delaney, who tasted success with honey, has not noticeably progressed. Her second play is again North Country and working class. It contains some humour and some warmth; the writing is generally fluent; and the play again breathes life. But its sum total is not impressive. Breakfast-table banter and belly-aching and a pervading aura of marital misery are in danger of making this piece little more than an elongated music-hall joke.

Always a gentle soul, hating to give offence, David will not have enjoyed writing this, especially as three days later he was reporting the early closure of the play's run, the cast's hopes of West End glory dashed.

> Indifferent public response and lukewarm press criticisms have doubtless influenced the premature burial of 'The Lion in Love', a story of marital misery ... "If only we'd gone to London I think we should have clicked," said Somerset-born actress Sheila Allen.

Two months later, with a largely changed cast and some rewritten dialogue, the play opened at the Royal Court Theatre, but the London critics shared David's doubts and it closed after only three weeks. It would be twenty years before Delaney would write for the theatre again.

David was always uncomfortable with controversy. He was in the thick of it when he penned a highly critical review of the world premiere of a farce *Meet Mr Tombs*, which had been written, directed and acted in by Richard Lawrence Griffith. Under the headline 'The Author Needs to Get Busy Again on this Farce', David called it 'a bitty, often unfunny, cliché-ridden piece ... a rather uninspiring story ... all a bit embarrassing – only the French can do this sort of farce and make it amusing.'

David's review was mild compared with the one in the rival *Evening Post*, which called it 'one of the biggest flops in recent experience', adding that the show 'debased the coinage' of theatre. The script was 'witless, artless, vulgar and depressing, completely devoid of invention or imagination'.

Within hours of David's review appearing, the *Evening World* received a vitriolic letter from Griffith – 'a highly excitable Welshman,' according to David. 'The general opinion in this city,' it began, 'is that your theatre critics are a lot of silly, stupid, petty frustrated writers.' After several more paragraphs of invective, it ended: 'To me, they're a lot of cowards who hide behind their ridiculous pens.' What ensued was recalled by David in *Footsteps from East Coker*:

> My news editor pondered the author's letter: "This is one for Mr Stoppard. I think we'll let him loose on this Mr Griffith fellow. There's mileage in the brimstone."

Stoppard began his lengthy response by saying he could 'see the author's point of view'. He then let the Welshman loose with an even longer rant about his critics before subtly skewering him with the word 'humble':

> Griffith said: "I am a humble boy from Wales, with very humble beginnings, very humble. I have made a fortune in my 17 years in show business. I have a Jaguar, a mansion in Swiss Cottage, a hotel at Holborn and three girls at private school."
>
> Humbly, he went on: "I did not do all that by being a — fool. I wrote it because I thought it was a good play, and I directed it because I have engaged directors in the past who have made an ugly mess of things."

Tom Stoppard soon moved on from the *Evening World* – though not according to Katherine Kelly, a professor at a university in Texas. In her 1991 work 'Tom Stoppard and the Craft of Comedy', she asserted that the author had continued to submit reviews to the paper under the pseudonym 'David Foot':

> It suggests that Stoppard had begun playfully to fictionalize himself in a way that becomes a writer of fiction rather than a reporter of facts. The name 'David Foot' may have been Stoppard's parody of 'William Boot', the bumbling reporter in Evelyn Waugh's novel about journalism, 'Scoop'.

When David told the story in *Footsteps from East Coker*, he prefaced it with 'a slightly shamefaced confession':

> My overall regard for academia has never been as high as it should be. It comes, I suppose, from my own deficient depths of proper scholarship and a loitering feeling of inferiority, often there though seldom bothering me.

It is hard to look at the arc of David's writing and think his work would have developed better if he had been to university. These were golden years for local journalism. Not only was the *Bristol Evening World* one of two evening papers that appeared every weekday in the city but it could afford to employ a drama critic who not only reviewed all the productions but was given licence to write widely on theatre. For David this even involved occasional trips to Stratford-upon-Avon, where in April 1959 he reported on the first night of a new *Othello*, produced by Tony Richardson and starring the great American singer Paul Robeson, now in his sixties.

David was responsible for a weekly column, 'Through The Stage Door', in which he was given free rein to express opinions, interview actors and explore themes. In April 1957, with television sets now in more than half of British homes and with every week bringing news of the closure of another theatre, he asked 'Is Variety Dead?' and 'Is Panto Losing Its Hold?'

He was a great admirer of Max Miller, the 'Cheeky Chappie' whose mix of sentimentality and earthy humour was loved by working-class audiences. Twice he reviewed his concerts, one time interviewing the ageing entertainer in his backstage dressing room.

More poignantly David reviewed the Hippodrome's pantomime for Christmas 1960, *Aladdin* with music by Cole Porter. It was not, in David's opinion, the best of shows. The music, though 'agreeable', was 'not memorable', and the comedy was 'banal'. The day was saved for him by the star of the show, George Formby, in the role of Mr Wu.

Shortly before the Christmas Eve première, the ukelele-playing Lancastrian comic was told his wife was in a coma, close to death, but he went on stage regardless. Then, after her cremation in Blackpool, he drove through the night in time for the next day's matinée. The strain took its toll of Formby's fading health, and in mid-January he was too ill to continue, returning to Lancashire where he had a heart attack and died. Just as David had written the first review of a Harold Pinter play so, in all probability, he had penned the last review of a performance by George Formby.

The following winter, when the Hippodrome's pantomime was *Robinson Crusoe*, David was altogether more enthusiastic, celebrating without inhibition another of the comic stars of the age.

> This is the best pantomime Bristol has seen for years. And it belongs to Norman Wisdom. His clowning is a consummate art. The style verges on Chaplin and some of the other great comics. For sheer personality and mime he has no equal on the English stage. His comedy comes from within. It has heart – and warmth. There is no barrier at the edge of the footlights. Contact with the audience is made immediately.
>
> We have seen some of his 'business' before; we hope we shall go on seeing it for ever. I double up at his torture drum-set. I convulse at his deceptively simple but brilliant piece when he becomes fascinated with his own voice over the microphone. In short, I think Wisdom's the tops.

David was privileged to be paid to watch a generation of performers who would soon pass from the stage – Max Miller, Gracie Fields, George Formby – yet he also witnessed stars of the future, none greater than Peter O'Toole whose two formative years at the Bristol Old Vic coincided with David's first years as the *Evening World*'s drama critic.

Many future stars passed through Bristol in those years. Harry H Corbett's Macbeth at the Theatre Royal ('There have perhaps been more flamboyant and physically dynamic Macbeths but from the moment he starts recoiling from Banquo's ghost his tormented soul is often brilliantly conveyed') was his last role before appearing in a one-off sitcom for the BBC's *Comedy Playhouse* in the role of Harold Steptoe. Leonard Rossiter's 'lodging-house caretaker' in *The Hostage*, long before his appearance as the lecherous landlord Mr Rigsby in *Rising Damp*, was prophetically described by David as a 'made-to-measure part'.

Rossiter, while appearing in *Richard II*, was the subject of a 'Through the Stage Door' column in which David revealed him to be, like Peter O'Toole and Tom Stoppard, a kindred spirit in his love of cricket:

> Rackhay is the name they give the narrow alley-way which leads up to the stage door of Bristol's Theatre Royal. It is also, if you ignore the undulating cobbles, vaguely in proportion with a cricket strip. And there, during a break in rehearsals this week, I found character actor Leonard Rossiter doing his stuff with left-arm medium-paced deliveries aimed venomously at two vegetable crates, one balancing indecorously above the other.
>
> Mr Rossiter's enthusiasm for cricket is not hard to trace. As a schoolboy he went near to gaining a county trial for Lancashire. Now his desultory appearances are limited to captaincy of the

Old Vic XI, a side which varies considerably in talent according to the cricketing merits of the 'floating' members of the Company.

He tossed the ball to a fellow bowler and returned, slightly out of breath, to the 'pavilion'. In the dressing-room he retrieved a half-smoked cigarette from his pocket, combed his Bolingbroke-styled hair and pondered on his working career, both as an insurance inspector ("Claims department – far more interesting") and an actor.

These columns gave David the opportunity to explore beyond the front-of-stage stars. In one piece, combining work with a family trip to the seaside, he reported on the 'bitter disappointment' of a Punch and Judy show. In another he shone a spotlight on Daisy Gomez, the one-time dancer who made her living as a theatrical landlady on Park Street. Here was David in his element, and the editor gave him almost a whole page to tell the tale.

> I had heard so many depressing tales of dreary theatrical digs, where lonely, hungry, sad-eyed theatrical girls ravenously bolt their beans on toast, that Daisy's rooms came as something of a surprise. The rooms were neatly decorated ("all my own work") and furnished. It could so easily have been your own home. And it's the homely atmosphere that she has gone out of her way to cultivate. For show business is full of loneliness and melancholy – beyond the sequins and tinsel.
>
> Daisy is, in fact, loved by everyone who stays there. They like to share their problems with her. Share her washing up and ironing, too. There's something so refreshingly homely where you might expect everything to be artificial. Can you imagine Moira Shearer washing her hair in the kitchen sink here? Well, she did. And that immediately makes her doubly human and lovable.
>
> Daisy has got sincerity, too. When, several years ago, an all-negro cast came to Bristol with 'Anna Lucasta', there was some difficulty in accommodating everyone because of the colour bar.
>
> That made Daisy bristle with indignation. She proceeded to put up as many as she possibly could – even though they were sleeping on the kitchen table and on the floor. But at least they had a room for the night.

The *Evening World* closed in January 1962, during the run of Norman Wisdom's *Robinson Crusoe*. David would not return to regular theatre work till 1969 when the *Guardian* took him on to review West Country productions.

Paul Rogers as Macbeth
Theatre Royal – Evening World, April 1956

This was a performance when superlatives would not be abused. Despite the utter, unrelenting morbidity of the theme, one was held spellbound. It struck terror into the auditorium; the stage became a pool of blood … and yet. Oh! what a morbid fascination we all had.

It has been said that Shakespeare wrote this play for two characters alone, that he merely sketched the others. Yet how adroitly is it written. The speed is unslackening. One can find not a single situation, hardly a movement, which might be called superfluous. Although there is so much outward violence in this bloodbath of a play, it is really the inner conflicts between the worse and the better natures of Macbeth and his Lady that make the story.

Paul Rogers's Macbeth is a magnificent study of an ambitious, storming, tormented man. He can be diabolical in the plotting, yet troubled and sickened when thoughts of virtue nag him. Rogers is superb in the Banquo ghost scene, when the full horror of the situation grips him.

Coral Browne spits out her words and must be quite one of the most petrifyingly-pagan Lady Macbeths Bristol has seen. There she is at her husband's side, goading him with that ruthless, frenzied resourcefulness of hers. Her first entrance down the dimly-lit steps impresses and she continues to eject venom until Shakespeare fades her out in a cloud of remorse.

Look Back in Anger by John Osborne
Theatre Royal – Evening World, April 1957

Phew! At times this play is as brutal and savage as a jagged piece of glass being scraped across one's bare heart. It's squalid as a sewer-alley. It's salacious as the most lurid page of a Sunday newspaper. But it's real – excitingly real. Those in it are real human beings. Sordid tenement rooms like this do exist. The bitter mixed-up kid complex of Jimmy Porter is a malady of this age. And it does us no credit to pull our hats down over our eyes and pretend we can't see what's going on around us.

Producer John Moody, who has a great regard for this play, has probably done nothing better since coming to Bristol. He knew there could be no compromise with such a subject. He has pulled out all the dramatic stops – and this angry piece of theatre is a triumph.

I know Peter O'Toole will forgive me if I say that he has something of Porter about him. Not the bitterness, the warped outlook, the striving for expression. But the rasping, colourful turn of phrase, the contempt for convention, the outspoken streak. This is far and away his toughest role. He started with a suggestion of the self-conscious last night but played some of those punchy scenes with brilliance.

Wendy Williams, agonisingly uncertain of which way she should turn, gives one so much of the pathos of Alison. This is just one more star performance from this so-promising young actress. Phyllida Law is best when she sheds her sophistication for the garb of a mistress – and then she's terribly good. Barry Wilsher, too, shows how good he can be with a fine study of the Welsh lodger. And Joseph O'Connor is once again seen in the kindly part he plays so well.

Just now and then John Osborne betrays an immaturity in his writing. But thank heaven for a realistic play which allows us to forget the cosy warmth of the drawing-room.

The Room by Harold Pinter

Bristol University Drama Department – Evening World, May 1957

One can never be sure about these private University productions – quality varies so much. Last night the climb up Park Street was rewarded. I'm so glad I didn't miss this production.

Henry Woolf, whose quiet work as a character actor has caught our eye before, here introduces himself as an intelligent and sensitive producer. He introduces, too, an old school friend of his, Harold Pinter, who as a writer should go on writing. 'The Room' was completed in two days by this 26-year-old Bournemouth repertory actor. In those two days he gave his play a strange macabre atmosphere, a commendable quality of natural dialogue and a dramatically powerful climax which stabs at the conscience.

The audience, who could so easily have ruined the evening, behaved admirably. They warmed to the early unconscious humour, yet went deathly still as the play became more and more taut.

Acting was admirable. Susan Engel, an Old Vic Theatre School student, excelled as the dowdy wife, and in their various ways Henry Woolf (mysterious landlord), David Davies and Auriol Smith (loquacious young couple), George Odlum (blind negro) and Claude Jenkins (silent, morose husband) all made their contribution.

One feels the spiritual significance of the end without being completely happy about the way it is expressed. The writer should have left slightly less to the imagination.

The producer appeared disappointed that the set could not be improved. He need have had no such disappointment; it was adequate.

Waiting for Godot by Samuel Beckett
Theatre Royal – Evening World, December 1957

One might be smart and say that Godot kept everyone waiting just a little too long. The two tramps' utter futility and indecision as they fidget beneath the symbolic tree is, in the second act – so very similar to the first – in danger of inducing the audience to fidget as well. For threequarters of this remarkable play I was convinced it was an intellectual leg-pull. And yet, as I left the theatre, I realised my hasty conclusion amounted to a criminal injustice.

'Waiting for Godot' entertains in spite of itself. Go to treat it as just a joke – and you will have plenty to laugh about. Go to be stimulated and you will probably find it a carping commentary on modern society. Guest producer, Denis Carey, puts it succinctly: "The play is a scathing condemnation of our Godlessness, blindness, aimlessness, appalling cruelty and, above all, indifference."

The 'trampery' is brilliantly conveyed by Peter O'Toole and Peter Jeffrey. Mr O'Toole, with his concave stomach and stilt-like legs – thin as the gaunt tree he waits beneath – excitingly curls and unleashes his words with the gifts of his native Ireland. It's quite a considerable performance, done to perfection in its superficial clowning and yet with so much more, in the helplessness of his hope and patience.

Peter Jeffrey, though more contrived in manner and accent, nevertheless adds another most notable success to his King Street scoreboard. Here, too, is an actor of considerable versatility and natural talent for characterisation.

Paul Robeson as Othello
Stratford-upon-Avon – Evening World, April 1959

Paul Robeson, back on the English stage after 23 years, astounds us by the way he meets the physical demands of the part. His beautiful voice fills every corner of the theatre with each syllable ... There was inevitably last night much nostalgia in the air. One finds it hard to remember more thunderous first-night applause than that which greeted Robeson at the end. Eventually his solemn face softened and he broke into a wide grin.

He looked down happily on his wife in the front stalls; in his excitement he even got caught up in the curtains. And he deserved the wonderful welcome. Without, perhaps, any great variety in his voice, without looking completely the Shakespeare student's conception of the Moor, he was still splendid. How memorably as the wildly jealous Moor did he lash and rage; all the innate bitterness of his personal life gained expression.

The Hostage by Brendan Behan
Theatre Royal – Evening World, June 1960

This outrageously funny and unwieldy play has all the garrulity of a Dublin public bar – and twice the blasphemy. As a dramatic work it defies any normal description. The chord which holds it together so compellingly is not one of plot; that is non-existent. Rather it is a common streak of humanity, a kindly warmth in the gushing stream of humour.

Here is a play or music-hall revel without a semblance of form. The characters splash their way through the draught Guinness; they abuse each other; they blaspheme; they cock a hearty and irreverent snook at all the conventions. This remarkable theatrical offering of Mr Behan, as bizarre as the Irish themselves, is peopled by tarts and reformers, 'queers' and political fanatics. If we wish we can spot the cynical outlook of the author over the futile political fanaticism which leads to hostages being taken at all.

But he takes precious little seriously. He crumbles the stodgy barriers of convention and hypocrisy in a welter of beer-parlour words and musical profanities. Occasionally one might argue that good taste deserts Mr Behan. But thoughts of this quickly become obscured in the gusto and uproarious tongue-in-cheek tirade on all that's holy.

John Hale's production catches the lusty sing-song mood completely and is his most devastating work since he became director of the company. The cast, too, is excellent. Pat, the lodging-house caretaker, is a made-to-measure part for Leonard Rossiter, and he plays it with tremendous spirit. Margaret Jones is quite brilliant as the earthy Meg, and Annette Crosbie is gloriously effective as the off-beat social worker. Barry Foster, the hostage, gives an outstandingly natural performance as the National Serviceman, and June Watts, in easily her best part with the company, makes a most appealing country girl.

Go and be shocked.

Roots by Arnold Wesker
Theatre Royal – Evening World, February 1961

This is not only the most authentic play about the village working class to emerge in our English theatre since the war; it tackles the problem of groping communication between generations with greater honesty and understanding than we have seen before from one of our native playwrights.

'Roots' is, in part, a political play. Yet Wesker's own passionate Socialism is subsidiary to his concern at the disturbing gulf between a simple but ambitious daughter and her mentally stagnant family. Those moments in the last act when the young woman, idealistically fired by the boy friend who later cruelly ditches her, discovers herself intellectually are thrilling, satisfying theatre.

Mr Wesker has a sharp ear for proletarian dialogue. His lines smell strong of the farmyard. Words which out of context might shock come from these simple farming folk as naturally as the whiff of manure through the kitchen window.

It is because the author has come near the people he is writing about that the very occasional lapses in truth – glimpses of theatrical connivance creep in – stand out so incongruously. One is uneasy, too, in this production about Norfolk accent being widely interpreted. Indeed, there are traces of the Luscombes using the writer's language in a way which is unconventional to the West Country.

This is a play where the humour is broad and lusty. But one looks beyond this and ponders on the trivia, the mental lethargy and the air of futility about this family of farm workers. It might be argued that the comparatively inexperienced Mr Wesker will eventually sting himself by the bees in his bonnet. That is not relevant here. He has written a provocative piece, brimming with humanity, and Duncan Ross directs it with a vital understanding of the problems the author is posing.

Eileen Atkins, as the girl who returns from London, gives a memorably compelling performance, with an 'inner' interpretation allied to an extrovert style. The uncomplicated mother is quite brilliantly observed by June Jago, and there is sympathetic rural playing from Ewan Hooper, Stephanie Cole and Josephine Tewson.

'Roots' is a mile ahead of most similar things of its kind written in this country. The only theatregoers who will not be moved by this production in Bristol are those who don't know about, or don't want to know about, the kind of people in this play.

Variety – on the way out?

Evening World, March 1957

Well, is Variety dead? About half of the variety theatres in this country have or are going to close down. There's another 'obituary notice' in the stage papers nearly every week ...

But despite the obvious danger warnings and trends in entertainment, there are people with faith in variety. They cherish a romantic picture of the days when music hall was booming, when hansom cabs drew up outside the stage doors, when Edwardian fops waited outside in the soft amber hues of the gas light for the exuberant, powdered young ladies of the chorus to step outside.

Perhaps we cannot remember those days. But that's how many of us like to think of the music hall. A world of laughter and robust music, a glimpse of frilly petticoat and a gasp of pleasurable surprise from the stalls. And every seat filled. That's what the optimists believe can happen again, that television will, far from conquering, give the variety theatre a shot in the arm. There are those who feel that our entertainment vogue will do a somersault and that people will once again crave for the live stage.

I, for one, hope so. I love the theatre – and I love variety.

Are the Punch and Judy experts dying out?

Evening World, May 1959

With what may be called Whitsun Week licence, this column switches to a facet of summer entertainment far from the world of stagedoors and greasepaint – the Punch and Judy show. Thousands of children squat on the sand every year to watch the unconventional antics of Mr Punch and his colourful entourage. One might have thought that with its basic child-appeal it could never fail. But I'm beginning to wonder.

I saw a Punch and Judy show on Whit-Monday at a southern resort. It was a bitter disappointment. The dialogue was dull, repetitive, halting. The action was almost non-existent. Indeed, the action had hardly an iota of imagination in it. There was no attempt at even some vague sort of continuity and every character talked in an identical voice.

Now I can remember Punch and Judy shows which had the children so engrossed that they forgot their ice-creams. The diabolical crocodile had us in a frenzy of fear, skilfully relieved by the comical cavorting of the numerous other characters which appeared in an interminable stream from the 'bowels' of the arena.

But it wasn't like that on Monday. The children who were watching seemed only mildly interested. Mr Punch's more aggressive moments brought no shouts of disapproval; the contrived comedy brought few titters.

Maybe the children of today, nurtured by their parents' television sets, are altogether too blasé. Maybe the one-man show on the sands doesn't satisfy them any longer. I don't think so, however. It seems to me that the true artists who for years have made Punch and Judy part of the coastal summer scene are dying out.

AND THAT WOULD BE A GREAT PITY.

Max Miller

Evening World, August 1956

His timing is superb. His unashamed vulgarity somehow never offends. An infinitely less risqué line, delivered by Dad in the drawing-room, might produce embarrassed coughs. But Maxie gets clean away with it. His personality has the irresistibly warm appeal of a brazier fire on the Old Kent Road in the middle of winter ... It's good to have the Bad Boy of Music Hall back in Bristol.

*

What sort of fellow is this Cheeky Chappie himself? Well, he never stops the act. Backstage he talks non-stop. He spontaneously finds a gag – and rocks with laughter. Everyone else laughs too.

He's completely down to earth, friendly and unsophisticated. There's no side with him at all. And he's as casual and unflurried about time as Denis Compton at cricket. How he got on for his second spot only the stage hands will ever know.

Now about those famous innuendos. His face broke into a grin. "Listen, I never say anything wrong. It's what the people think that gets me into trouble."

Backstage – Evening World, August 1957

He adroitly pauses on an innuendo, his eyes do the rest and the audience unleash their laughter. Then, in a flash, he looks pained and asks in all innocence: "What've I said now? You're a nasty lot here at Bristol." As long as there's a Max Miller we can't conceivably imagine the decline of the music hall. And I think that's why I like him so much.

written for the Max Miller Appreciation Society, 2009

What I remember most of all was his wardrobe. He still had his flashy white homburg on. The garish check suit, with plus fours and handkerchief protruding extravagantly out of the great pocket, made him look like a successful bookie (was there ever another kind?). He was strumming his guitar when, a shy young reporter, I made my hesitant entry into his number one dressing room. He put down his guitar – and talked.

And how he talked. It was a good-natured monologue, as ever more cockney than south coast. It struck me – and I recall it even at this distance – that his funny throwaways were observational rather than gags in the conventional sense. I had watched his act and noticed then that he didn't waste time – or material – on set pieces from any well-thumbed joke book. His style was distinctive. Conversational and confident.

George Formby

Evening World, December 1960

A tired-eyed little man in a green silk dressing gown drew hard on his cigarette this afternoon, then painted on a lipstick grin in front of his dressing-room mirror. George Formby was preparing for the hardest stage appearance of his long theatrical career – his first appearance since the death of his devoted wife and business partner, Beryl, this weekend. He had driven through the night to reach the Bristol Hippodrome on time. "Everyone keeps on asking what I am going to do now, I am going to work, that's all. Just work."

It was nearly time. Hastily he touched up his tired eyes with more powder, put a gay pompom hat on his head and slipped on a crazy Chinese costume of blue and red. Then he capered on stage to do his seven comedy scenes, three dialogue spots and two solo acts before a crowded audience who were convinced that he is one of the bravest men in Britain today.

Evening World, December 1960

His music-hall intrusion in the story of 'Aladdin' is hardly relevant. But this unsubtle North Country comic, whose popularity long ago sprang from his endearing moon-face expression and the uncomplicated humour of his ukulele lyrics, is all that the audience asks. As long as he strums away, singing those songs which made him famous before the war, everyone is happy, it seems.

Evening World, March 1961

Jan 14 ... and the curtain came down for the last time on the stage career of George Formby. The packed house at Bristol Hippodrome was still cheering as the moon-faced comic with the broad Lancashire vowels walked wearily up the stone steps to his No. 1 dressing-room.

He tenderly put down his ukulele and started taking off his Oriental make-up. To a stage-hand he said, "I'm not as young as I was." The following day he was in hospital again. And yesterday he died.

Something has gone out of the British music hall. This former racing apprentice – who could then hardly read or write – knew no subtlety as a performer. But he was a skilled professional. He could project the warmth of his personality across the footlights in a way which kept him a top-liner, despite ill-health, infrequent appearances and the Big Beat challenge.

On the first night of 'Aladdin' he grinned and strummed his way to a personal success ... He said he felt fine himself and was making ambitious plans for the future. But this toothy performer was deceiving himself. Bristol was his last booking.

Gracie Fields
Evening World, October 1959

There was just a momentary fear as Our Gracie walked on to the platform last night that she had become sophisticated. She looked astoundingly glamorous – the most glamorous sexagenarian we had ever seen, in fact.

Her dazzlingly opulent dress accentuated a streamlined and youthful waistine, far less matronly than it once was. Her blond hair was beautifully groomed. She made many young girl pop singers look a mess by comparison.

But as soon as she threw her coat aside, whistled characteristically and rubbed a finger inelegantly across her nose we knew that Gracie hadn't really changed. Seemingly tireless she romped through a score of songs, right back to the 'Aspidistra' days and then forward to her latest recording 'Little Donkey'. Those endearing Rochdale vowels were still there. So were the homely asides, the harmlessly earthy innuendos, the dialect jokes.

Her limpid soprano notes are as true as ever. And just occasionally, when she could repress that buoyant sense of fun, she let us appreciate them. She was warm-hearted, sincere and sentimental and she made everyone else sentimental, too. She made two appearances and the tremendous applause proved, if proof were needed, that in these days of slick presentations Gracie leaves most of 'em at the starting-post.

Also on last night's bill were Rawicz and Landauer. In their first spot they gave us music from the ballet – Swan Lake and Nutcracker – and in their second some of the most popular film music.

These two brilliant performers, with their effectively contrasting techniques, helped to make it a memorable evening.

An interview with Noel Coward
Footsteps from East Coker (2010)

But what in honesty has been my theatrical highlight over a lengthy, variegated career? Dodging the understandable taunts of name-dropping, I must nominate my lucky interview with Noel Coward.

He had come to Bristol to supervise the rehearsals for his last musical, 'Sail Away', and I had gone, at my news editor's behest, in search of a word with The Master. One of the Coward aides had seen me lurking. "He's not talking to anyone today. Far too busy. Not a chance. You're wasting your time. Maybe we shall arrange a Press Day just before the opening." There was unbending authority in what he was saying. What he was implying, in less tactful fashion, was: "Clear off. You've got no right to be here in the Hippodrome stalls."

Over the years I had learned how to be resourceful. I hung around in the shadows of the auditorium. And suddenly, after a quarter of an hour, I saw a solitary figure seated in Row K (funny how you remember some things). From the cigarette holder, I knew who it was. But how did one approach him?

"Yes?" He had spoken first.

"I'm from the local evening paper. Will there be any chance of a short chat later on?"

He sized me up as he paused. "Why not now? The rehearsal seems to be going well enough without me. Come and sit down."

I had read of a long history of general rehearsal rows. If such an eminent and revered figure as Coward was specifically involved in any of those excesses of temperamental licence, I was no more than vaguely aware of them. He was full of charm. The consonants were clipped and deliberately fashioned, just as the impressionists of the day copied. It was all straight from one of those patriotic films of his, or the style he preened in front of the French windows in a West End drawing room set.

We chatted for 30 minutes. He put his hand on my knee. "Good to meet you, dear boy." Yes, even 'dear boy' in the style we only pretended he talked. Well, he did. I offered him good luck with the new show and slipped away. My notebook was suitably full as I slipped past his glaring aide who had worked so hard to steer me away.

It was, my friends assured me, an accolade to be treasured for The Master to place and rest a hand on a stranger's knee like that. In fact, Coward was not half as camp as many who come with their mincing walks as part of the oppressive effeminate territory. Frankie Howerd once gave me a similar hand-on-knee treatment after bustling me into a taxi and sitting rather too close to me. I had seen him first in his dressing room to discuss his appearance in 'Hotel Paradiso' and his future plans for Shakespeare's Bottom the Weaver in a season with the London Old Vic. On that brief taxi ride, I had been requested to take him to the pub where a few of the young male actors from the Bristol Old Vic School went, possibly to be picked up. Frankie Howerd, a lonely, talented, promiscuous man, was companionable enough. But I was glad when my mission as cruising advisor was completed and we got to the back-street boozer. I left him, strangely enlightened, in a small group of fawning young men.

9
Peter O'Toole

(top) 'Look Back in Anger': Barry Wilsher (left), Wendy Williams, Peter O'Toole (bottom) 'Waiting for Godot': Peter Jeffrey (left), Peter O'Toole

Six months into David's time as the *Evening World*'s drama critic he submitted a profile of a young actor at the Bristol Old Vic, one who was about to play his first lead role as a professional.

> When 'Look Back in Anger' comes to the Theatre Royal, Bristol, on Monday, Jimmy Porter, the bitter character who really started the 'angry young men' cult, is to be played by 23-year-old Peter O'Toole, Bristol Old Vic's most colourful actor.
>
> Lanky, lean Peter once worked on a newspaper (a copy-boy in Yorkshire). He has thumped a drum in a jazz band. He has sold vacuum cleaners. He has lived in a room with a cistern. He has a rebellious nature. And all these things could be associated with Jimmy Porter.
>
> Peter arrived in Bristol straight from RADA – with less of his native Irish brogue noticeable but with the wild streaks still there. "John Moody has tamed me down. Why, I'm even taking singing lessons from Mrs Moody now" (necessary for his present role, a great comedy success in 'Oh! My Papa').
>
> His first part at the Theatre Royal was in 'The Matchmaker'. He played a fat, drunken cabman and the play gave him seven lines. Since then the parts have got progressively bigger. Recently there was Doolittle in 'Pygmalion' when he made us really sit up. "Now I've got this wonderful part of Jimmy Porter."
>
> This, then, is O'Toole, the young rebel ... He was on a charge the first day in the Navy ... later his ship went and he was left stranded in Sweden (more trouble). And to crown it all – he plays the bagpipes. Of marriage he says: "At the moment I wouldn't want to inflict myself on anyone. But if I did, it would have to be someone from the theatre. Otherwise, it would be bigamy."

How much of this back story is true is debatable. Rather than being born in 1934 in Ireland, as he claimed during his Bristol years, O'Toole was born in 1932 – to an Irish bookmaker father and Scottish mother – in Leeds, spending his childhood in Yorkshire. Yet soon enough he was creating a colourful reputation for himself, a reputation that led David in 1983 – in his review of a biography of O'Toole – to engage in uncharacteristic hyperbole:

> When someone eventually writes the definitive social history of Bristol, interspersing it with such diverse and colourful names as Wesley and Defoe, Chatterton, the boy-poet, and Greenway, the architect convict, there will have to be room left for O'Toole.

He came in 1955, to work at the Bristol Old Vic, and stayed for three years. Later he returned for just three plays. But there are twice as many stories told about him as about WG Grace. And most of them are true.

Soon after he arrived in King Street, a tall, gangling, garrulous young man with an untheatrical voice and an athlete's ability to chase out of the stage door after final curtain in time to catch the last round at the Old Duke or Naval Volunteer, I was told by Nat Brenner: "Here, I promise you, is exceptional material. He's HUGE. He dominates a stage. Just watch him take off."

Brenner, who was number two to John Moody at the Theatre Royal, became O'Toole's counsel and mate. They talked politics, cricket and even theatre together. They drank and philosophised. And I'm sure that wise, old Nat also worried.

From the outset David was an admirer of O'Toole's stage presence. Of his Alfred Doolittle, he wrote: 'He dominates the stage whether he is wearing old clothes or a topper.' Of his Jimmy Porter he observed the brilliance of his 'rasping, colourful turn of phrase', 'contempt for convention' and 'outspoken streak'. Then in the next production, playing Lysander in *A Midsummer Night's Dream*, he was 'happily representing young love ... once or twice speaking poetry with a hint of Jimmy Porter gusto.'

That summer the Old Vic's production of *Oh! My Papa* transferred to the Garrick Theatre in London's West End. A musical comedy in which the characters at a 60th birthday party evolve in a dream sequence into circus performers and animals, it had been a great success in Bristol. David, for one, loved it:

> One can readily understand the fanatical enthusiasm of the cast during rehearsal. Here is a production abounding with simple charm, yet sophisticated; a piece of theatrical craftsmanship which, especially in Act II, breaks into a throbbing, pulsating vitality; an evening we shall not forget for a long time.

He found Peter O'Toole 'riotously funny as the ailing Uncle Gustave' and Rachel Roberts 'splendid, drawing every bit of feeling out of the songs, using that intimate stage manner to advantage and looking always attractive'.

David had already established a friendship with O'Toole:

> We had both been newspaper copy-boys, him in Leeds and me in Yeovil. We shared a similar sense of fun, although I used to tell him he was better company, just the two of us together with

a glass of Guinness, than when he felt he needed to camp things up a bit in a crowd of sycophantic followers from the Bristol Old Vic school.

He came round for supper, at times with pretty girls from the company. With my wife I drove him and Isobel, then a journalist girl friend, to Stratford in the newspaper's ropey Ford Pop, to see one of the tragedies.

Unfortunately David missed the most newsworthy moment of the actor's Bristol years. It occurred when *Oh! My Papa* reached London.

The anticipation in the company was great when the impresario Jack Hylton snapped up *Oh! My Papa* for the West End. David was caught up in the thrill of it, confidently predicting that 'if there's any justice in the theatre, it should run for months.' As he wrote fifty years later: 'In King Street the accountants were totting up the anticipated revenue which should be coming west. The excitement was tangible.'

Alas, it was not to be, the production coming off after only five weeks. The *Daily Express* called it 'a delight', but David's provincial enthusiasm was not shared by the highbrow critics. The *Guardian* condescendingly described the play as 'an achingly homely Swiss musical comedy', calling the popular title tune 'a yowling ballad, one of those tunes which even the tone deaf eventually master'. *The Times* was only a touch more generous:

> Miss Rachel Roberts makes a buoyant character of the circus lady, but otherwise the evening is remarkable only for the varied collection of talents involved in an enterprise so unambitious and so naïve.

David went with a heavily pregnant Anne to the first night, as did several coachloads of loyal Bristolians, and what a first night it turned out to be!

David had heard 'pre-show rumours that an organised clique would be noisily antagonistic to the musical', and so it proved. At the play's close, loud booing and hissing could be heard from the gallery, causing the curtain to be brought down prematurely. David in his report called it 'a deliberate attempt to wreck the first night'. Happily counter-cheers and a seven-minute-long ovation from the body of the audience brought the curtain back up and restored the spirits of the cast.

Peter O'Toole was in no mood to let the matter drop, inviting David to join him in his quest to find the culprits. David, with Anne to consider, declined, only discovering next morning that he had missed out on the night's main news story: the arrest of the 'drunk and disorderly' O'Toole.

Back in Bristol, during that summer of 1957, Peter O'Toole played in the annual cricket match between the Old Vic XI and the Critics. O'Toole's brief cameo role in the contest was a perfect story for David's pen, and he found outlets for it several times over the years.

O'Toole, having grown up in Yorkshire, was passionate about cricket. In the summer of 1974, he turned up during a Somerset/Yorkshire match in Bath, luring David away from the press tent for a drink:

> "I've got a special request," he said over a pint glass. "Can you arrange for me to have a chat with 'Closey' at the close of play?"
> He said it with schoolboy earnestness. Yet here he was, an international film star, asking me to have a word in Brian Close's ear. I introduced them, and it was hard to tell which of them was the more star-struck.

The greatest challenge of O'Toole's career at the Old Vic came in April 1958 when he took on the role of Hamlet. It is said that, filled with anxiety, he lost two stone during rehearsals.

> He seemed to be heading for a nervous breakdown. The company were so concerned about him that they cancelled a crucial late rehearsal. "Go off and forget all about the Prince. See how you feel tomorrow." I was much flattered when he turned up in my office (it was also where Isobel worked) and asked me to go off and have a few pints with him.

Two months later O'Toole, now enough of a friend of David to babysit the young Mark, was gone from Bristol. Soon enough he was in the West End, playing a rebellious soldier in Willis Hall's *The Long and the Short and the Tall*, a performance that won him a Best Actor of the Year award. The following year he was playing major roles at Stratford, with David reviewing his 'outstanding' Shylock. After that came *Lawrence of Arabia*.

David's subsequent encounters with him were few: the day at cricket in Bath, a production of *Uncle Vanya* back in Bristol and, finally, the funeral of Nat Brenner, O'Toole's former 'counsel and mate' at the Old Vic, the man who had recognised from the outset that he was 'HUGE'.

> He saw me, the first time for a number of years, picked his way over the flowers and hugged me as the tears streamed down his face. And one young mourner, in a voice too loud and insensitive for immediate post-funeral sadness, turned to his friend and said: "Who the bloody hell is that? Looks like an out-of-work pro. May have appeared in something with Peter."

"YOU'LL REGRET IT"

After an organised clique boo the first West End performance of 'Oh! My Papa'
Footsteps from East Coker (2010)

The curtain was rapidly brought down and some in the confused audience walked out, mystified by the outrageous behaviour from that vocal faction up in the gallery. Others reacted with a regional fervour that some aged pundits felt was as rare as it was gratifying. They started applauding composer Burkhard, director Warren Jenkins and the cast. It lasted for seven minutes, causing a dramatic rethink backstage. Up went the curtains; Laurie Payne, Rachel Roberts, Sonia Rees and Peter O'Toole among others sang their hit numbers again. The gallery rebels, so well organised, now succumbed.

I realised this was a news story so went in search of the cast. "I so nearly burst into tears, fearing that the show was a flop," Rachel Roberts told me. Then her Celtic fire emerged. "I just wanted to shout back at the demonstrators." O'Toole was typically succinct. "I'll catch up with those bastards."

He proposed that I should trail along with him, presumably for the rest of the night. I explained that I was duty-bound to catch the last train back to Bristol. After all, I had an eight-month pregnant wife with me. We'd already had enough unexpected drama for herself and our new baby for one day.

O'Toole's last words to me were: "You'll regret it." As a one-time aspiring newspaper reporter he possessed a sharp journalistic instinct. And there was Irish fire in his nostrils.

Bleary-eyed, I was in the office by 8 a.m. I'd written on the train my glowing review of the show and my account of the inflamed shenanigans which emanated from the gallery. A colleague greeted me: "Done well to get in so early after all that rumpus."

"How did you know about it?"

"Got it on the PA half an hour ago. Here, have a look at this."

It told me that Peter O'Toole was due in court at Clerkenwell later that morning, charged with being drunk and disorderly in Holborn at 2.10 a.m. He'd been with his sister who with domestic affection had refused to let go of him when he was forcibly put into a police van.

The court case which followed later in the morning claimed he had been shouting in a very loud voice. "Yes I was tight but not disorderly," he argued, adding descriptively that he had gone through several stoneware beakers of home-made mead. He was fined a nominal ten shillings and I was sorry that I had to leave him so that I could catch the last train home. But as he said in those parting words to me: "You'll regret it."

O'TOOLE THE CRICKETER

Western Daily Press, December 1971

Professional actors are apt to be hyper-sensitive souls. But Peter O'Toole was neither especially sensitive to criticism nor revengeful. Not even his one cricketing appearance 14 years ago would persuade me to change my mind.

He had volunteered to play for the Old Vic XI against The Critics. One had known of his affection for soccer – his father had been a professional footballer – but cricket's gentle subtleties and languid charades would, at first sight, have seemed alien to his extrovert nature.

The Critics annually viewed the match as an occasion which carried some prestige; they did not believe in devaluing professional pride with wanton recklessness at the crease against an eleven of indeterminate ability. They arrived early at the ground in freshly laundered flannels and moved with academic intensity into net practice.

The actors arrived 45 minutes late in a crescendo of outrageous sporting bravado, alcoholic belches and attire that would have done credit to the chorus of Pal Joey. Camp followers and young actresses of fragile beauty began to populate the boundary with partisan interest.

O'Toole's contribution deserves contemplation from every student of fate. From the distant position of third man, his fielding appeared to have a singularly negative quality; he preferred his Rabelaisian banter with a taunting stage carpenter. Then, magically, as a certain Bristol critic strode to the wicket, there was a sudden bowling change.

One never discovered whether the change was made in mid-over, but Peter O'Toole, with unpoetic motion and snorting nostrils, started on a 30-yard run of single-minded hostility. The vision will always remain with me. Giant leaps, flailing arms, a face of bearded resolve and moans of muscular agony with every step. The ball flew hard and true and landed, full-toss, on the middle stump. For the bowler, it was a moment of supreme exultation – to match those rare peaks of ecstasy that come to any actor as an audience collectively pays homage to his talents.

He retired almost immediately to third man; his work was done. It was whispered later that he was settling a score for an uncharitable review. But this he vehemently denied. We shall never know.

I prefer to believe his bowling prowess, fleetingly revealed that late-summer afternoon after the pubs had closed, was in many ways just a typical O'Toole performance: grandiose, riveting, amiably cussed, bordering on fantasy and incorrigibly tongue-in-cheek.

PETER TACKLES HAMLET

Evening World, April 1958

O'Toole is the most dynamic thing that has happened to Bristol's Thespian scene for some years. He is a lean, lanky individualist who has been called at various times an intellectual Teddy boy, the untamed lion of King Street and the steadiest drinker of Guinness in Bristol. To that I would add he is, in my opinion, one of the most vital and compelling actors to appear at the Theatre Royal since the war. And one of the most likeable.

To interview Peter O'Toole, you need to sit in the relaxing atmosphere of a bar. Here, he finally 'runs down' after a strenuous rehearsal; here you forget his more ostentatious characteristics and find a genuine warmth of personality.

In many ways he's scared of 'Hamlet'. He has lost weight rehearsing it; he has stayed awake thinking about it. For he knows the famous role is quite the severest test he has faced. In an excited flurry of words he talks about the Old Vic's production: "This is totally away from the Set Piece. We are trying to recapture the Elizabethan spirit."

For half an hour, as he gulped down his Irish brew, he talked about "the complexities of this multi-coloured Hamlet". He has no time for all the technical adornments which go with some Shakespearean productions – elaborate battlement scenes, wind machines, rain effects, fluttering flags, darkness and mist.

"Listen to this ... 'The air bites shrewdly. It is very cold' or, as Horatio says, ''Tis a nipping and an eager air" ... what do you want more than that? Shakespeare paints his own scenery."

Unpredictability is Peter O'Toole's strong point. He suddenly breaks off in the middle of a homily: "Let's have another meat pie. I'll share your sauce." And you both dip into the same plate.

*

Mr O'Toole drained his glass. Costumes' designer Rosemary Vercoe passed him and said: "You're looking more like John the Baptist every day." And everybody laughed.

The relief took his mind from Tuesday – and the most physically, mentally and emotionally gruelling assignment he has been given. He must be one of the youngest professional Hamlets and, in terms of mere months and years, one of the least experienced.

Eagerly await his interpretation. There is one thing you cannot do with Peter O'Toole – ignore him. The West End won't. Just watch!

Hamlet

Bristol Old Vic Company, Theatre Royal
Evening World, April 1958

It's terribly difficult trying to decide how much you like Peter O'Toole's performance as Hamlet. The actor hardly underlines the Prince as a figure of high tragedy; he never quite takes us to the heart of the dilemma in this towering melodrama of vengeance.

Yet it is still an astonishingly fascinating portrayal by a 24-year-old actor of almost the most complex character in Shakespeare. Mr O'Toole's quick imagination flames into life as he flits, often brilliantly, from one emotion to another. In his quiet, contemplative mood, he reveals, with a fair measure of success, the depths of Hamlet's intellect; in the impassioned passages he impresses more.

Peter O'Toole's education does not belong to the speech training academy. But he has the gift of using words – if lacking at times a poetic quality and in danger occasionally of being telescoped together in his enthusiasm – with considerable magic and power. He can lash with an exciting fury few possess.

This is not, perhaps, a great Hamlet. Peter O'Toole is, of necessity, still only a brilliant apprentice at his trade. Maybe his wan, leaping figure does not conform to everyone's physical and romantic conception of the Prince. It is still possibly the best thing he has ever done. And it will grow in stature during the run.

Merchant of Venice

Memorial Theatre, Stratford-upon-Avon
Evening World, April 1960

Peter O'Toole, nurtured eventfully and excitingly in Bristol's King Street and a Hamlet before he was ready at 24, is now a Stratford star on his debut there.

By any standard he is an outstanding Shylock. His powerfully Hebraic performance, with the intriguing accent of a Mile End Road upholsterer and the vast, compelling presence which will never be divorced from him, summits a production which handsomely vindicates the Peter Hall company from the insipid opening of the season.

'The Merchant' troubles one in trying to find the true balance Shakespeare intended between the anti-Semitic and pity for the Jew. Peter O'Toole does not wholly help us. He is a striking and rather noble Jew; we never really despise him. There is only the faintest trace of the malicious and merciless. Even when he sharpens his knife on the steel sole of his shoe and supposedly lusts for blood, we are secretly rooting for human butchery.

Perhaps we are accustomed to seeing a heavier, more ugly and warped Jew. But with the Gentiles such a wretched lot in this delightful, if ludicrous, play, who can blame us offering so much pity to this Shylock?

Uncle Vanya

Theatre Royal, Bristol
The Guardian, October 1973

Peter O'Toole shuffles down the steps into a garden. His mouth sags in geriatric despair: his red-rimmed eyes are filled with Chekhovian pain. It is an entrance worth waiting 15 years for.

In this Bristol Old Vic production of 'Uncle Vanya' at the Theatre Royal, his interpretation is so rich in characterisation that it physically hurts. He meanders in frustration and futility, filling the silence in an unspoken word. He is comic actor enough to dig out, with subtlety, Chekhov's wry humour from the claustrophobic helplessness of the human situation. There's a prelude of Ben Travers when he absurdly chases the Professor, fires and misses. He is sufficiently the crackpot Vanya to get away with this.

Plunder

Ben Travers farce, Theatre Royal, Bristol
The Guardian, October 1974

Forget the physical absurdity of the comparison – and the relationship of Malone the suave crook (Edward Hardwicke) and Darcy Tuck (Peter O'Toole) is not so far removed from Laurel and Hardy. Mr O'Toole is one of our great international comic actors, adept at the subtle touch and scornful of the facile funny face. Every stride is rigidly disciplined and we are never aware of it. The natural inventiveness of the business, with only one over-playing of the hand, is a visual belly-laughing delight. His pairing with Edward Hardwicke's plausibly swaggering rogue is exquisitely played out.

10

Going Freelance

*No regular income and a young family to support
David, Mark, Anne and Julia on a camping holiday in Sussex*

*Getting a foot in the door at TWW, 1963
David with actress Olivia de Haviland*

The closure of the *Evening World* in January 1962 was a body blow to David. On the morning of that ill-fated Saturday, when he boarded the Bristol City coach to Halifax, he had a full-time job and a regular income. By the evening, when he returned home, he had neither. He was 32 years old, with a wife and two children, neither yet at school, and he had no idea where his next payslip would be coming from.

David was not aggressive or thrusting by temperament. His rural upbringing did not give him the easy social confidence of some of his journalistic peers. Yet, beneath his seemingly diffident and gentle manner, he had a burning determination to succeed and he was not averse to taking risks. He wanted to be a writer, and he backed himself to find a way forward as a freelance.

The early years had their share of setbacks, but he worked tirelessly to find outlets for his work. He lived on his wits, cultivating contacts, pitching ideas to editors, finding supplementary sources of income in unlikely activities. At home they took in lodgers and acquired bantam hens to lay eggs. Anne took on part-time market research.

One of David's hopes was that he could become a creative writer as well as – or perhaps even instead of – being a journalist. With this in mind, he signed up for a correspondence course with the TV Scriptwriters' School.

Frederick Oughton, his contact for the course, invited him to submit an outline for a television play, leading David to develop a drama, 'Decision At 5.25', about the friendship between a policeman and a young prostitute whose boyfriend is sent to prison for breaking into a gas meter. The final scene, explaining the title, takes place at a railway station where the girl has to choose between the policeman and the boyfriend returning from jail.

Oughton was worried about David's decision to make the boyfriend – a very small part in the piece – a West Indian, thinking it would lead the play to 'get dismissed as another one on colour'. He suggested that the 'misfit in society' was 'too easy from the dramatic point of view':

> Would it have a contrived look to the television company reader? Mind, I cannot answer the question; I am merely asking it to probe you into a new consciousness, because it is a good idea to try and estimate the reception your work receives when it is read 'cold' by a reader who, in all probability, has a certain quota to get through and report on in a day.

David stood his ground, addressing the issue at the start of his synopsis::

> This is a play about loyalty. It is also a love story. Although one character, seldom seen, is a West Indian, this is in no sense a

play about the colour question. It IS about lonely people trying to connect.

Oughton replied:

> COLOUR QUESTION. Leave it in and risk it after all. If you get people declining, ten to one it will be because of that.

The play was never commissioned, though David was still trying to place it in 1969, now with the title 'When The Train Comes In'. David also submitted the outline of a three-part television series, 'Playing For Kicks', about a professional football side, but nothing came of that, either.

David continued to write short stories, some of which appeared in print. One, 'The Christmas Drink', touched on racial prejudice and homelessness and appeared in a Christian newspaper, *Contact*, for which David also contributed a feature about the religious faith of the Bristol Rovers manager Bert Tann. Among the stories rejected was one about a 61-year-old pianist who had known better days:

> Queenie Roper perspired not with the heat but with a sudden fear. She was gripped with the acrid bitterness of solitude. Tentatively, she surveyed her surroundings. The naked light bulb threw only a cold, amber hue across the denuded room. There was one chair and a tilting, cracked gilt mirror, a symbol of truth unless, like Queenie, you could bravely look without seeing.

It came back from the editor of *Bristol Weekend*: 'I quite enjoyed it, but it's a bit too strong for our more delicate readers (ugh!)'

The correspondence with Oughton lasted two years. A running theme in Oughton's letters was the importance of shaking off the habits of David's trade, what he described as 'the conditioned reflex known as journalism', with its 'facile approach' and its 'sharp and snappy grasp of an idea'. He cited the case of a play returned for revision to another student, also a journalist, who completed the changes within twenty-four hours.

> That is ludicrous and silly. I know that the financial motive is strong, but on the other hand the bullrush does not lead to good work. Journalism is a habit. I know, because I was a journalist myself. It is a very tenacious habit, hard to throw off, but you have to throw it off if you want to get somewhere.

Only Oughton's half of the correspondence survives, but it is clear from the early letters that David was struggling for work and money. 'I do hope that your fortunes pick up,' Oughton writes. 'It takes a long time to make money out of ordinary freelance news reporting.' Then a year later things seem to be looking up for David: 'Perhaps because you are somewhat easier about the job situation, your work shows a great improvement.'

Throughout the exchanges Oughton was forcefully direct in his comments, telling David: 'You can take the truth, I know. And the truth is that you should keep on.'

> Your feeling for people forms the basis of a considerable talent for playwriting. This is not 'flamp'. I am being honest about it. But don't fool yourself that it will be easy. You will require enormous staying power and, when you have completed the Course, a faith in yourself.

He liked David's 'talent for sly humour' and the way in one piece he brought out 'the different faces of man – the public face and the private face. It is always a good theme for a writer who really knows humanity.' In time, that theme would become a hallmark of David's best writing.

Early in 1963, a year after the closure of the *World*, David started to have success in placing feature articles in the local newspapers. In a format he utilised many times in the following years, he created multi-part series on topics. The first two, running weekly in the *Western Daily Press*, were 'The Outsiders', with close-up portraits of ex-prisoners, unmarried mothers and elderly refugees, and 'Eating Out in Bristol', where he stirred controversy by accompanying his profile of the 'boom in eating out' with some damning quotes from diners about the quality of food and service. Then, through the summer of 1964, he was commissioned by the *Bristol Evening Post* to write a Saturday series, 'Cricketers to Remember', in which he penned profiles of former Somerset and Gloucestershire stars, many of them – Charlie Parker, Arthur Wellard, Alf Dipper, Sammy Woods – men about whom he would write in greater depth in later years.

Still yearning to be a cricket writer, especially one who went to the heart of his subjects, David set to work on a biography of WG Grace, aiming to achieve publication in 1965, to coincide with the fiftieth anniversary of Grace's death. 'I do not propose to stack it with statistics and detailed accounts of most of Grace's innings,' he wrote in his submission to publishers. 'The book is far more concerned with Grace as a person.'

With the working title 'Grace – and Favour?', he outlined eight chapters: Gloucestershire (starting the book with WG's acrimonious departure from the county), Cricket, Family, Medicine, Stories, Money, Tours and Judgement. The surviving file contains work on four of these chapters, some 15,000 words, plus a further chapter 'Grace and the Professionals'.

There is a bundle of rejection letters, some quite detailed in their comments. 'It seems that we are just missing by a narrow margin,' his agent reported at one point. 'I would like to go on trying.' Yet the rejections kept coming, leading the agent to ask, 'Do you, by any chance, have a copy of the synopsis as the present one is now looking a little dog-eared?'

Two publishers commented on David being 'an unknown journalist in Bristol', not a well-respected name to sell the work. One felt there was too much emphasis on 'the demolishing of a legend' with 'too little tangible and quotable evidence', written in a tone that was 'a bit too argumentative'. The writing was 'too emphatic', pointing to 'the difference between a book and a newspaper article'. Another publisher recommended a more chronological approach, 'allowing the facts to speak for themselves' and 'ridding the reader of the uncomfortable feeling that the author is breathing down his neck all the time'.

David interviewed some who had known Grace in his later years, and there is material in the surviving work that is fresh and informative. He has researched in detail the circumstances surrounding Grace's falling-out with Gloucestershire, something which had not been much explored at the time, and he has good insights into Grace the doctor. David's approach – non-chronological, reaching always for the inner character of the man, happy to offer his own author's comments – is one for which he came to be admired in his later work. Perhaps the world of cricket books was not ready for such an approach, and perhaps, in fairness, David had not perfected it. There is some truth in the publishers' criticisms. Eventually the project was abandoned, never to be revived.

David was adept at spotting anniversaries with a local angle. December 1965 was the centenary of Rudyard Kipling's birth so, with the writer enduring unhappy schooldays in Devon and, in later life, visiting Bath to treat his wife's rheumatism, David persuaded the *Bristol Evening Post* to give him a full page, in which he tackled head-on the growing discomfort with Kipling's world view:

> He was a slight figure with thick spectacles to offset his short-sightedness and heavy eyebrows to delight a Punch cartoonist. His love of children was reflected in some of his writing. Few could resist the whimsical appeal of his Just So Stories. But it was a deceptive image. For few English Men of Letters have been more bitterly attacked than Kipling.

For David, he was 'a superb story-teller', with 'no equals in evoking the local colour and customs of India', and 'a talented journalist' with 'an uncanny knack of reproducing the speech and thoughts of others'. Yet he was also 'a truculent Imperialist' who 'saw Britain as the Master Race – and everyone else should be taught their place.'

> Maybe it is unfair to allow his outdated Empire-building thoughts to affect his reputation as a writer. Memories die hard but perhaps one day we shall be able to separate the two and prejudices will die. Then it will be possible, belatedly, to measure fully Kipling's literary worth.

The following year was HG Wells' centenary. This time David, picking up on the author's brief spell as an apprentice schoolmaster in the Somerset village of Wookey, secured a feature in the *Bath & Wilts Evening Chronicle*:

> Dreamer Wells, for all his imaginative notions and basic intelligence, was hardly equipped for the part. He swotted up his history dates and learned his weights and measures parrot-fashion. Education in Wookey in those days centred on the three Rs. Young Wells' efforts to instil discipline were none too successful. Once, in desperation, he chased a boy all the way home. The sequel was discouraging for this pupil teacher – the wayward child's mother merely chased Wells all the way back to school.

Right up David's street, as a quirky subject, was AE Housman's brother. Once dubbed England's 'most censored playwright', with 32 of his plays running into trouble with the censor, Laurence Housman was a pacifist, champion of women's rights and one for whom religion and royalty were not off limits as subjects for satire. He had lived in Street, getting his plays performed there and in Glastonbury, allowing David to mark his centenary with a 'Page Five Feature' in the *Bristol Evening Post*:

> He never married. One of his earliest successes was 'An Englishwoman's Love Letters'. Not surprisingly, it was published anonymously. It proved a sell-out. And the publication, which initially received critical acclaim, led to the wildest conjecture about who the author was. Oscar Wilde was mentioned. So was the Queen herself. Housman chuckled to himself. At least the money kept rolling in – and that was something that too rarely happened.

As a spin-off from this article David wrote a 30-minute radio feature on Housman, 'The Last of the Victorians', which was broadcast on the Home Service. With the emphasis on the man, he interviewed people in Street for memories of their unusual fellow resident.

David's persistence and hard work – assisted, of course, by the quality of his output – was starting to pay off. He was taken on by *Melody Maker* to review local jazz and pop concerts; he covered West Country soccer for *Charles Buchan's Football Monthly*, profiled towns for the glossy *Gloucestershire Life* magazine, wrote features for *Radio Times* and had a regular column in the newspaper *TV Weekly*.

For *TV Weekly* he caught up with Bruce Forsyth in a summer show in Torquay, and Morecambe and Wise in pantomime in Bristol. For *Radio Times* he drove to Cheltenham to profile the antiques expert Arthur Negus:

> Arthur Negus gives a wry smile and changes the subject. 'Did I tell you I was the scorer for our 1st XI at school?' And he says it with the kind of genuine pride he shows as he handles a priceless piece of porcelain on 'Going for a Song'.

David also made the first of many forays into ghost-writing, with a three-part series, 'The Tom Jones Story', for *TV Weekly*:

> I like horse-riding. Not a bad rider, either. I served a tough apprenticeship. One of my mates' old man was a dustman with the local council. He had a big cart-horse and we used to take it out to graze. Didn't have any fear of horses in those days. We used to go up into the mountains and get hold of a horse for a ride. They were wild days.
>
> I remember a milkman called Clive, too. He used to get wild horses and break them in. We'd help him. And get plenty of tumbles. It all seems a long way from the bright lights. But even as the frisky ponies kicked out and tossed me up in the Welsh mountains overlooking my home in Pontypridd, my mind was only on one thing ... a singing career.

Through the 1960s, when David was valiantly pressing for work in all directions, he was often on the radio. For a period he was getting up at five o'clock each morning to read the early regional news from the BBC's radio studio in Bristol's Whiteladies Road. Sitting on his own in a room, he had to work a whole set of knobs and other controls, stretching his technological skills. Twice he took the station off air. Then, when *Radio Bristol* was launched, he was in demand as a reporter, mainly for sport.

David also became part of a three-strong, Bristol-based Documentary Research project, undertaking background research for producers of television and radio documentaries. He even picked up work as an extra in the television series 'Softly Softly'.

Another foray away from print journalism arose from David's love of comedy sketches. He had enjoyed making people laugh in the revues he staged as a youngster in East Coker, and he began to send ideas to comedians, among them Dave Allen, Stan Stennett, Charlie Drake and a young Michael Palin, who was particularly encouraging. A few of them were used, and he was even offered a job by Freddie 'Parrotface' Davies. But in the end the fickleness of the work was too great a risk, and he stuck to journalism.

These first years as a freelance were in many respects the making of David as a journalist and writer. Yet, right to the end, he retained a yearning to be a dramatist. In particular, he nursed an unfulfilled ambition to write an anti-war play. It came up in conversation several times when I asked him about future writing. But it was never to be.

By the end of the 1960s he was unable to accept all the work he was being offered. Prioritising his writing, he resigned from Documentary Research. Then he gave up his position as the West Country's concert reviewer for *Melody Maker*, a role for which he had never been an ideal fit. His principal reason, he explained in his letter of resignation, was lack of time:

> My work as a freelance with, of necessity, many markets on many different subjects is reaching the point where I must cut back. I never seem to work less than six and a half days a week and am out, on average, four or five evenings a week. I'm also continually being pulled in as a relief sub-editor and radio reporter for the BBC in the West Region.

As the man from *Melody Maker,* David interviewed and drank whisky with jazz drummer Buddy Rich till three in the morning ('a joyful and thirst-quenching conversation'), admired Otis Redding in his first-ever concert in Britain ('He brought an indifferent show aflame with a wholly exciting 40-minute act') and marvelled at the 'frenzied brilliance' of Jethro Tull's Ian Anderson. But there were many acts, notably The Who at the Yeovil Liberal Club, which left him feeling alienated from the pop scene. He admitted as much in his letter to the editor:

> I have watched in horror – at close quarters – the complete contempt being shown for professional standards. Late arrivals ... no apologies ... in-jokes on stage ... virtually no presentation. And certainly no music! There is a demand for it and it has to be covered. But I don't think I'm the man to do it any longer.

ADVICE TO A SON

In this imaginary advice from a world-weary 'sage' to a son, sent to the Writers' Workshop, David reflects on journalism as a route into creative writing (1963). The conviction for spying of civil servant John Vassall had created a political scandal.

So you want to be a creative writer one day, son, says the sage with an indulgent smile. And you'd like to know whether journalism is the best form of apprenticeship. We're back to that chestnut about the difference between a so-called writer and a journalist. Pull out that fifth-form essay again – the one about the sun setting on the Embankment. Not bad, was it: it fired you with all sorts of starry-eyed aspirations. You decided on the spot what you wanted to do – WRITE. Not ready yet for that first novel, you told yourself. But perhaps a spell on the local weekly paper, and then ...

Not a bad idea really. Certainly better to do that than sell insurance or slide sycophantically onto the conveyor belt of trainee management.

But frankly, son, the local paper won't want any literary nonsense. No place for that lovely flash of imagery. The local paper is in the market for clichés – by the score. After a few weeks, you'll know the drill. You'll be able to churn 'em out ad lib. The rat-a-tat process for all our readers. Nothing creative here, boy.

What about the evening papers or even the nationals? Well, they're a bit better – less stodge, a little more imagination. But you're still restricted by edition deadlines, sadistic subs and unbending style-books.

I don't want necessarily to deter you. Journalism has its merits. It cures wastage and puts you on the way to a zippy, laconic style, if that's what you want. The job is varied, exciting, sometimes stimulating, ego-boosting. You learn to hate cant and Cabinet ministers who hate the Press. In these post-Vassall days, you feel something of a martyr.

But to get back to your original question ... Honestly, son, it'll be a tough transition from journalism to the creative stuff. Newspaper work makes you a superficial, hustling writer. You'll have to unlearn a lot of those neat journalistic tricks; you'll have to think more and probe deeper and not be so reluctant to re-draft. It's no crime to put another sheet in the typewriter – there's no edition to catch this time.

The potential writer, who has listened intently, now looks confused and wary. He thanks the sage and moves off to take another peep at his naïve, pretty little piece about the Embankment. And the sage, once hailed as a young literary wonder, shuffles off contemplatively. He'll push off that application to the 'Surrey Comet' in the morning.

PARADISE IS ALWAYS JUST AROUND THE CORNER

from the series 'The Outsiders', Western Daily Press, January 1963

Our dialogue as we shuffle along the snowy South Glo'shire lane, side by side, is vintage Pinter. Intermittent. Inconsequential. Unreal.

He has a rich Irish brogue, wears two pairs of threadbare gloves, an outsize Army greatcoat and no tie. He never looks at me; his eyes gaze far ahead, unseeing. "Oh yes, it is. Cold, I mean. Real cold tonight. (Long pause). Cold last night, too. Yes, cold in the bus shelter last night. (Pause). Cold for weeks." He punctuates each announcement with expansive mitten-wiping of the nose.

The weather is currently his favourite topic. But he can disconcertingly switch to doss-houses or his lovely Oireland without warning. Once, in the pre-Welfare State days, he would have been called a tramp. He would probably have been dressed more picturesquely – and been stronger on his feet. The modern counterpart, re-styled 'Wayfarer' by some benign civil servant, is less athletic. He isn't averse to hitching a lift and favours a less ambitious itinerary.

My Irish friend nods towards the Winterbourne Reception Centre: "Be warm there tonight. Pipes in the rooms, you know. (Pause). Ah, yes, this snow is real cold." I inquire how long he will be staying. "Must be on tomorrow. Have to keep going. Gloucester tomorrow. It'll be cold there as well."

This is the remarkable thing about the tramp-wayfarer philosophy. An aimless sort of urgency about tomorrow. He has no money, no job – and no destination. And yet all the time he is moving on.

Mr Geoffrey Peck, Warden at the Winterbourne Centre, sums it up: "This is true of all of them. Paradise is always just around the corner."

This sort of Waiting for Godot attitude is beyond the understanding of all but those who have – usually by choice – an unsettled way of life, as the Government handbook has it. A Bristol bus shelter on Monday, Winterbourne on Tuesday, Gloucester Centre on Wednesday, a farm barn burrowing for warmth in the straw on Thursday.

*

I see them again, seated around the trestle tables at Winterbourne, gazing into their china mugs of tea or cocoa with unseeing eyes. And I see again my companion on that snowy Glo'shire lane, murmuring: "Just a night. Must be on my way to Gloucester tomorrow. It'll be cold in Gloucester tomorrow."

Cold, Gloucester, TOMORROW ... what do they mean to this man with a vague past, an aimless present and a strangely abstract future?

CHARLES BUCHAN'S FOOTBALL MONTHLY

The Day Big John Atyeo Cried – *June 1966*

It is the most poignant moment I have ever seen on a football field. The date: April 24, 1965. Bristol City had beaten Oldham Athletic 2-0 in the last match of the season and won promotion to the Second Division.

At the final whistle the 28,000-odd spectators streamed on to the pitch. The City players had to fight their way to the tunnel. But Big John Atyeo was trapped. Everyone wanted to slap his back or shake his hand. Ashton Gate was saluting its hero. It was too much for Atyeo. He broke down and cried!

Finally and reluctantly they made a way for him and, tears streaming down his face, he reached the dressing room where he threw himself onto the bench, physically exhausted. Outside, they were calling for him again.

Atyeo, who had appropriately sealed promotion with a great goal seven minutes from time, pulled himself onto his feet again and went with his team up into the main stand – to acknowledge the cheers and make a short, sincere speech of thanks.

That was his finest hour. More meaningful to him even than his six England appearances. He had taken Bristol City back into the Second Division, the task to which he had dedicated himself.

He has stayed with the club one more season. He has led them again, with all his old enthusiasm – even if the legs were a little less able and the half-chance was not snapped up with quite his former verve.

Now he retires. His 15-year spell at Ashton Gate is over. His future connections with Bristol City will be confined to a seat in the stand. "It has always been my intention to retire while I was still at the top. And now, I have decided after a lot of thought, is the time to step down," he said.

Atyeo, of course, is one of the country's outstanding examples of one-club loyalty. It is possible he would have won more England caps with a more fashionable side. He would almost certainly have earned more money. "Oh, yes, there have been chances to move into the First Division. But I have strong roots in the West Country and have been happy to stay."

After a brief spell as an amateur with Portsmouth, he came to Ashton Gate. And that was where he stayed; slamming in more goals than any player still in the professional game; topping 600 league appearances for the City. His decision to retire means he will not, after all, smash Dixie Dean's record of 349 goals for Everton. But records as such never bothered the big-framed Atyeo.

At his peak he had one of the best body-swerves in the game. His heading is immaculate still and he has a fierce shot in both feet. Above all, he is an intelligent player. Manager Fred Ford sums him up: "He has had so many natural gifts. A great player and a fine team-man. The West Country can be proud of him."

John Atyeo is a friendly, unassuming man. He talks with a quiet, deliberate delivery but it belies a sharp academic brain. He excelled in school exams and later became a quantity surveyor. Now he has started a second career. He is a mathematics teacher at a secondary school in Warminster, Wiltshire, not far from his village home in Dilton Marsh, where he enjoys kicking a ball in the local fields with the schoolboys on Sunday mornings.

Atyeo, married with two young children, was a burly player but he did not run into trouble with referees. His long, prolific-scoring career is an example to any potential Soccer star. He never reaped the benefits of the new players' charter because the maximum wage was lifted too late for him. But basically a quiet village boy, unimpressed by the bright lights, he looked after his money.

As the club he served so well considers plans for a suitable benefit for him, Big John contemplates the future with an open mind: "I'm going to miss it terribly. But I have decided on a complete break with the professional game. I shall try to keep in touch by passing on hints to schoolboys."

Football in the West – *August 1967*

Don't go West, young man! That's the advice probably passed on to more than one professional footballer – and to aspiring managers as well.

Why? What's wrong with Bristol, Plymouth, Exeter and Torquay?

The answer is summed up in one word by a score of people I talked to about this – temperament. It seems that we native West Countrymen are far too easy going. They say we go round with our sunny Somerset smiles, plumping for the leisurely life. Too leisurely. Too relaxed. And this, so we're told, comes out in our soccer.

Cliff Britton, manager of Hull City and himself a native of Bristol, put it this way: "The West is predominantly an agricultural area. And people who live there are more placid and take life at a more leisurely pace than, for instance, in the industrial parts. Footballers from these agricultural areas seem to me to lack the alertness, determination and devil necessary to make the most of their ability. They've been schooled in the easy-going 'life is pleasant' atmosphere which tends to make them less competitive than boys who often have to live by their wits in the hard, industrial areas."

MELODY MAKER

The Who

July 1966

The Who have a kind of bizarre science-fiction appeal – electronically violent, deafeningly strident, all rather removed from reality. There is no other group on the current scene remotely like them.

At the Yeovil Liberal Hall last week, the correct technical balance was never wholly achieved. Words were hardly ever caught, melody was blasted out of existence. True there was a sort of sensual excitement about the performance – this in spite of the group's doleful, deadpan expressions. Occasionally, one detected a pleasant and unexpected sense of vocal harmony.

Keith Moon, t-shirted and intense, bashed his drum skins with unrelenting savagery. Pete Townshend, the most soberly dressed of the four, looked sadly at his audience when not weaving interesting patterns and half-circles with his arms.

Jethro Tull

October 1969

The frenzied brilliance of Jethro Tull underlined the mediocrity and depressing lack of originality among so many of their contemporaries. A packed house at Bristol's Colston Hall on Sunday, never able to remain detached or uninvolved, roared for more.

Jethro Tull offer a tingling repertoire – laced with the outsize eccentricities we have come to expect. If there was ever the faintest hint of boredom – and faint it was – it came with the length of the instrumental solos. The night inevitably belonged to Ian Anderson, whose all-embracing tour de force kept an admiring audience mesmerised. It is not simply his reserve of energy and his limitless extrovert traits. There are his changes of mood: his sensitive flautist movements, his disciplined singing, his confidential jokes and asides.

Every Jethro Tull concert is an event. Here is a group of skilled musicians and originators. There is nothing hackneyed about their performance. They may leave you slightly bemused; you may watch Ian Anderson enact his musical rites with something approaching disbelief. But there still remains a rapport with the audience. And of course the five of them have a driving creative rapport among themselves. Bristol ecstatically welcomed them back, noticed the subtle developments since the last time, and made it clear that they can return as often as they like.

Pop Festival, Bath Football Ground
May 1970

The ten-hour pop and blues festival, staged on Bath City's football ground, ended on a bizarre and eerie note. At midnight on Saturday the floodlights were abruptly turned off – and Fleetwood Mac were left performing in the dark. Bill-toppers Fleetwood should have gone on from 9.30 pm till the scheduled end of the show at 11 pm. But the programme was running late and Fleetwood weren't introduced until 10.45.

When the lights went out drummer Mick Fleetwood provided a lengthy and defiant solo. And a series of small bonfires were lit over the ground.

If the improvised lighting did any damage to the football pitch it was only one of the disappointments for the club who had staged the festival in an effort to raise vital money. But Bath City, the Southern League club who are £50,000 in the red, made a loss on the event. They had hoped for a 15,000 crowd – and less than 5,000 turned up.

Some features of the festival were admirably organised; others flopped. There were embarrassing delays between acts and, even though the organisers allowed the show to overrun by an hour, the build-up to Fleetwood Mac was lost.

Mr Ken Ollis, chairman of the organising committee, claimed that hundreds of people got into the ground without paying and many others were able to watch the show from a nearby hillside. But he also paid tribute to the behaviour of the genuine pop fans: "They were perfect," he said.

As for the performances, a good deal was nondescript and lacking in impact. Quintessence, however, gave the show a teatime boost and there was a nice country rock sound from Matthews Southern Comfort.

Chicken Shack were voted a deservedly big success, not least the animated performance of Stan Webb. They topped the popularity polls, it seemed, with Juicy Lucy, who gave the festival that quality of excitement that had been strangely lacking during a lustre-less afternoon.

And there was still Fleetwood Mac to come. But time was against them and there was inevitably something of an anticlimax about their contribution.

GRACE – AND FAVOUR?

from a part-written and unpublished biography of WG Grace, 1964/5

Sensitivity to criticism

Despite the bluff exterior, WG, like several other members of his family, was hyper-sensitive by nature. It needed only a faint note of antagonism on someone's part for the Doctor to bristle. He saw it as a personal affront – and instinctively sailed into battle.

When fielding in some village matches, he could demonstrate quite extraordinary sense of hearing. Any imprudent spectator – and there were some – who made a jocular remark about the Old Man risked a bitter rejoinder.

As he went into middle-age, he grew extremely sensitive about his waistline and his declining agility. Short singles became a necessary rarity and how he hated the unsympathetic members of the public who urged him, in good humour, to sprint to the other end. Always an active and athletic person, he resented the fact that he was growing old.

It is the spectator's prerogative to barrack a lapsing fielder. As the girth increased, so Grace's fielding declined. I have heard of embarrassing moments, during his last few years with Gloucestershire – and England – when he simply failed to bend sufficiently to make relatively easy stops. Every cry of admonition, although tinged with affection, stabbed straight at his heart.

Once or twice he was known to leave his post at point and walk with slow ponderous steps in the direction of that section of the crowd from where the stinging shouts had come. It was an intimidating sight and no words from the Old Man were needed. There would be no more taunts from that side of the ground.

The doctor

I have been talking to a few of those people still living who know something of his qualities as a family doctor. His manner was gruff and hardly disarming. He was not a sentimentalist. He did not deceive his patients with words of confection intended to postpone the moment of truth. But he was, as his cricket adversaries knew well enough, an innate psychologist. He could talk some patients out of their illness by his apparently perfunctory approach. He had no time for the philanderer and the hypochondriac. Nor did he hold with many of the quack medicines that were coming onto the market; his remedies for the minor ailments were more often based on simple common sense.

Never once – unlike some of the more fashionable doctors of the day – did he turn a patient away. From a purely professional standpoint, he doubtless had deficiencies as a doctor but they were offset by his humanity and conscientious attitude. He did achieve some reputation for his remarkable ability to diagnose smallpox. The disease, which had a high incidence in Bristol at the time, could pose problems for the family doctor because of its similarity in the early stages with chicken pox. WG had this intuitive sense of detecting smallpox. He was rarely proved wrong and he possibly saved more than a few lives this way.

His stamina

WG all through his life practised deep breathing in front of an open window to fortify his lungs; in fact, his stamina was phenomenal. During some of his Herculean innings, with often no boundaries to save his feet, his partner – probably at the crease half as long – invariably flagged before him. His freshness, even in the last few years of active cricket when the girth was spreading, amazed the spectators. His boyish energy was all the more amazing when one realises his night's sleep was often broken. As a doctor, he spent more than one night at the bedside of an ailing patient. Hospital treatment and facilities were far less available then.

The professionals

WG's attitude to the professionals provides one of the most illuminating studies of his character. He was a martinet who castigated in public, a ringmaster who cracked his whip with unrelenting authority. He was a cricketer who demanded reserves of energy to match or surpass his own phenomenal resources.

The pros were his slaves who bowled him into form at the nets, and chased the ball all the way to the boundary when his lobs were clouted to long-leg, and carted the heavy kit from ground to ground.

Yet these same pros, according to Jack Board, Tom Barrow and other spectators of those days I have talked to, had this unwavering respect and affection for him. He for them, too, in his peculiar way.

After he had given up playing, he used to enquire regularly about the health of the pros he had known. One of them, Bill Murch, he took to the Crystal Palace with him to act as head of the groundstaff.

Did Bill discover a less demanding and forbidding WG in those mellowed days? I can only report that the Old Man carried a whistle and blew a long, penetrating blast as he approached the ground each morning.

That was the cue for the former Glo'shire pro to get cracking.

WRITING FOR COMEDY

Footsteps from East Coker (2010)

Away from journalistic aspirations, I wondered at times what other creative scope was open to me. Back in my National Service days, my attention had been aroused when I heard that a group of technicians were planning a variety show for RAF Thorney Island. One of them was Dudley Sutton, later to become a familiar face as a character actor on television. I asked if I could join them and said I would let them see one or two of my sketches. My enthusiasm was for a few days unlimited – I borrowed a typewriter from one of the offices, and to Sutton and his intended concert party I submitted not just one or two sketches but virtually a complete show. I included ideas from my East Coker thespian jaunts and some topical jokes about navigational schools, just like the one where I'd been seeing out my closing months of so-called patriotic enlistment. The variety show concept, alas, died an early death. Several of the entertainers were posted. So were my scripts – I never saw them again.

Alongside my journalism was an unformulated ambition to turn myself into a comedy writer. I landed two pieces on *Braden's Week* and two more, brief and without dialogue, for a late night TV revue show based in Bristol, *Whatever Next*. The going rate seemed to be £46 an item. During a few months at TWW, forerunner of HTV, I was encouraged to do a wedding-day skit for Stan Stennett. Unfortunately the likeable Stan forgot his words and a few decent one-liners were lost.

But I quietly thought there might be a new part-time career for me. Michael Palin, not long out of university and taking his first tentative steps in television, was doing some comedy in a half-hour show for TWW, in the days when regional companies were being invited to originate ideas. The small group, with their virgin Equity cards, used to drink at a decrepit little pub on the Bath Road, between the end of rehearsals and transmission. I went along, too, as a bit of an intruder. I didn't know Palin (still don't) but he struck me as a thoroughly nice bloke. The show didn't last for long and I could see it needed a more expansive budget.

On an impulse several years later, I wrote to Michael Palin, via his agent, and submitted some ideas for no particular slot. His reply came quickly and, with more significance, helpfully. He wrote six pages in his own handwriting. He told me the sketches that he didn't think would work – and why. And he particularly liked one running gag. He suggested how it could be developed. There was no indifference or impatience. He had no show of his imminently on the stocks, of the kind that might be right for my approach, but he hoped it might be possible to explore the idea of mine that he clearly liked.

More or less at the same time, I was hired for a day to assist the playwright Alan Melville, who was acting as the presenter for a bid in Bristol to launch a new commercial radio station, He, too, was marvellously encouraging when I admitted that I was really getting nowhere with my TV sketch-writing aspirations.

He began by telling me who to avoid if I wanted to send sketches and script ideas to performers. The list was a surprisingly long one, suggesting that plagiarising was as rife in light entertainment as in the shadowy corners of publishing. With show business and so many offshoots, I decided it was usually impossible to cite the offender and assemble the evidence. And was it vaguely worth the time and expense?

I made a note of Alan Melville's warning of light-fingered sketch-writers. His most perspicacious advice came when he said: "Latch onto an emerging comic. He's going to be the one looking for new material."

That evening I studied the notice of what was coming soon to the Bristol Hippodrome. Someone called Mike Yarwood was my first candidate. But did impressionists need gags? He apparently didn't; there was no reply to my letter.

An off-beat comedian, Freddie Davies, on his way to the Hippodome the following week, was my next recipient. He had odd-style lips that he puckered incessantly and he wore a bowler. He called himself Mr Parrotface. I'd seen him a few times on television and thought he had an original line in comedy. But the scope he allowed himself was restricted – he would soon need a new direction. A letter from me was waiting for him when he appeared at the Hippodrome on the following Monday. On the Tuesday he phoned me.

Yes, he liked everything I had suggested, especially the new-style children's show. Would I let him have a format straightaway? And – hold on a minute – might I consider packing in my present job, whatever it was, and join him full-time to see how successfully we could work together? That was sweeping stuff, tempting too. But I already knew a little about the pitfalls of show business. My genes, nurtured from generations of canny men on the Somerset-Dorset border, guided me. I thanked Freddie, stalled and, with a few misgivings, put my comedy writing finally to rest.

COMEDY SKETCHES
Michael Palin

COMPERE: Up and down the country, there are all the signs of a boom in ballroom dancing. So we sent one of our tele-reporters to interview a typical ballroom pupil. What, we asked him, in these days of the Big Beat, is the real attraction of the quick-quick-slow variety?

PALIN *(head only as in interview)*: Oh, it's great – it really is, it's great. Look at me, now. I've only been going for three or four months, mate, and it's made a new man of I. Like it's given I poise and self-confidence. Yeah, and glamour. See, it takes you out of yourself, away from the drag of work at the factory – all of us doing the same job there. No individuality. Not like at the dancing, you know. Ballroom dancing, you get all tarted up on a Tuesday and Friday night – and you sail all elegant into the double reverse swivel. You feel you're someone, not just another scruffy berk at the Corn Exchange. I mean, at the factory bench, you're just one of the sheep. But with ballroom dancing, you're a-em ... sophisticated, INDIVIDUAL. Certainly not just a cog in a machine ... CERTAINLY not just a NUMBER.

Camera zooms out to reveal Palin in full 'Come Dancing' drag. Grams come in with Sylvester signature tune. Palin turns and goes into elegant dance with imaginary partner. And on his back ... a large competition <u>number</u>.

Charlie Drake

Charlie seen as school traffic warden. He is carrying his road safety sign flamboyantly as he sees scores of children across the pedestrian crossing. He is then left on one side as a stream of traffic goes by. Charlie obviously perplexed. Finally policeman comes along, moves into the centre of the road ... and beckons Charlie safely across.

Stan Stennett

I expect you've gathered that I'm a home-loving boy at heart. Like it with the wife and kids – or in the garden. I've got a nice garden, you know. Not a bad gardener, either. But when I started out I was so GREEN. D'you know, I thought HYDRANGEAS were a SCOTTISH FOOTBALL CLUB.

I grow marrows – whopping marrows. A pal of mine did the same and he had a nasty end. He had this smashing vegetable marrow. He'd seen it grow day after day, week after week. He tended it like a child. Put straw down to protect it. And when the severe frost came, he was so worried that he stayed out all night, lying close to it to keep it warm. It finished my pal. He was gone in the morning. Frozen to the marrow.

DECISION AT 5.25

PC Bob Ridout befriends the 20-year-old Pat Lawton, a prostitute whose boyfriend has been sent to prison for burgling a gas meter

An unproduced play for television (1965)

Scene 12. Exterior. Cliff top. Day.

Bob gives Pat a hand for the last few yards and they arrive at the seat high above the bay. They are obviously happy though they are not yet completely at ease in each other's presence. They stand behind the seat, looking at the bay.

RIDOUT: Nice view down there. Can see for miles, can't you?

PAT: Yeh. Yeh, lovely.

Wind ruffles her hair and she runs her hand through it.

RIDOUT: Not too windy for you, is it?

PAT: No. I like it to blow and get my hair all over the place, like. Makes me feel all free. *(Laughs self-consciously.)*

RIDOUT: It ... it looks nice. I mean, curly – and pretty.

PAT: You like my hair then.

Ridout nods, shuffles awkwardly, then points hesitatingly to the seat.

RIDOUT: May as well sit down a bit. We're both puffing a bit after that climb.

PAT: *(after a pause)* Any more nice things to say about me? But don't look too hard. They say I've got a hard mouth.

RIDOUT: I – I like it better with less lipstick. I mean, you haven't got on as much today, have you?

PAT: No. *(Grins.)* I didn't think my policeman friend would want me too tarted up. You – ha – you don't like too much paint on, then?

RIDOUT: Well, I don't know much about it really. But I come from the country – and I s'pose we're all a bit old-fashioned. You know.

PAT: This is a different shade from usual. More expensive, too. You could say it was me birthday present to meself. It's .. it's kissproof, you know.

Ridout smiles shyly and fumbles for a cigarette.

RIDOUT: Is it?

PAT: Here, smell behind the ears.

He does so hesitatingly.

PAT: Like it?

RIDOUT: Em – yes, it's all right.

SOFTLY SOFTLY

Western Daily Press, 2006

'Softly Softly' was my favourite cop show on television back in the Sixties and Seventies. It was tightly written, abrasive and character-based, a long way on from dear old PC Dixon who used to patrol the streets of Dock Green with paternal bonhomie. The series was a spin-off of that gritty, ground-breaking 'Z Cars', introduced by the creative Troy Kennedy Martin. With its social realism and Merseyside story-lines, police cars – sirens blazing and occupants arguing – splashed through grimy inner-city byways in search of the villains. Much to the horror of the real police, these cops' private lives could be pretty grimy, too.

'Softly Softly' kept together the two senior officers from 'Z Cars', played by Stratford Johns and Frank Windsor, and it is true to say I was addicted to this new show, which was mostly produced in Bristol and filmed in the West Country. I persuaded myself that there was only one way to see the series at close quarters – and that was by being in it. Astonishingly, I managed to appear in a dozen episodes. In truth, it may have been hard to spot me. I was an extra, paid a not inconsiderable six guineas a day and not allowed – whatever the temptation to offer a pearl of throwaway dialogue – to utter a single word in the presence of the nearest camera or microphone.

That I made any appearance at all is not easy to explain. Professionally I had no obvious thespian aspirations and was not a member of Equity, the actors' trade union and one more militant than most at that time in succeeding to keep non-members at bay. But 'Softly Softly' had logistical problems. It had a pool of extras it could call on, but many lived well away from Bristol. The episodes were filmed on a tight schedule and the need to find someone at the last minute was a constant challenge for the casting people. At the time I was working part-time in the BBC newsroom, so I picked up on the gossip as I eavesdropped on actors in the canteen.

Needing to supplement my meagre freelance wages in those days, I presumptuously applied for an occasional role, however nominal, alongside my heroes – Stratford Johns as Detective Chief Superintendent Charlie Barlow, his quieter, contrasting sidekick Frank Windsor as John Watt, and Norman Bowler, who as Sergeant Harry Hawkins had already acquired a very passable West Country accent.

My cheeky application led to an interview. "But you aren't Equity, are you?" "Erm, well, no." Long pause. "Do you belong to any union?" "The National Union of Journalists."

There was another long delay as the casting woman looked anxiously down her list. "Maybe we can swing it. But don't mention it to anyone else. It's not something Equity approves of. You'd better turn up at eight o'clock in the morning. The coach will be waiting here in Whiteladies Road."

I was there – then and for 11 more episodes. On the first day of filming, the director liked to line up the extras and assess how best they could be used. My craggy, slightly dissipated features apparently lent themselves to sleazy lawlessness. I was a crook four or five times. Shady, salacious … and silent. I also played a gormless copper, a police photographer – with a flash camera I struggled to operate – on hand when a body was pulled out of the Avon in Bristol's Hotwells, and as an observant bystander. There was a commendable versatility about my work. Frank Windsor once complimented me. I stuck to my instructions and didn't reveal my non-luvvie pedigree.

This was not my most embarrassing experience. That happened when we were filming in a field at Dundry, Somerset. I was a young detective and my job was to capture and arrest a villain making good his escape. Ironically, he was being played by a mate of mine in the BBC newsroom, an illustrator for 'Points West' called Peter Andrews, who happened to be an ex-actor and really did have an Equity card.

One of the lessons I learned during my flirtation with BBC Drama was to be wary of young directors on the make. The one orchestrating the fisticuffs in that Dundry field liked rough physical action. "I want this to be a realistic scrap and I'm going to let it run," he said. "Your job is to pitch into Peter. Fists, the lot. But it won't be as hairy as it looks. I'm going to tell him not to resist you, just appear to." He then spoke privately to my workmate-turned-opponent. He told him exactly the same – to give me a thoroughly bad time, but I wouldn't be resisting. It was a crafty and unforgivable move. The fight was for real and lasted for ages. Neither Peter nor I was quite sure what was going on. I suffered a bruised cheek and my raincoat – my own raincoat – was badly torn.

"Great bout," the director said. "I'll feature it." He didn't seem to hear my protests about a coat I wouldn't be able to wear again.

'Softly Softly' was a success – for the quality of its writing, the feuding among the coppers, the breathless tracking of the criminals. South African Stratford Johns was an on-screen bully, admired as an actor and hated by viewers for his aggressive style, but when the cameras weren't running, he seemed to get on well with the more sensitive Frank Windsor.

In fact we all got on well – in my case, because no one ever discovered that I was just a fan living a dream.

11

Local History

Bristol's first horse-drawn tram

The Somerset & Dorset Railway

Local history was a seam David mined as a freelance, regularly coming up with ideas for multi-part series for the *Western Daily Press* and *Bristol Evening Post*: 'Seaport Bristol', 'The Victorians', 'Scandal in the West', 'Murder Most Foul', 'The GWR Story', 'The Somerset and Dorset Railway', 'The Wheel in the West' – as well as the many series he wrote on West Country sport: 'Great Football Matches', 'Like Father Like Son', 'Where Are They Now?' and the life stories of cricketers and footballers.

It was popular journalism, written for a wide audience, nothing over-fancy. Yet there runs through all the articles a vibrant sense of time and place, with the characters brought to life, often in just a few telling sentences. This last skill was exhibited perfectly in David's little book *Famous Bristolians*, in which he penned brief portraits of the city's best-known historical figures. Here is one of his three paragraphs on Isambard Kingdom Brunel:

> He drove himself with the same ruthless single-mindedness that he expected, unreasonably on occasions, from his unskilled workforce. His personal courage, whether below the Thames or in the middle of a railway tunnel threatening to collapse on him, was remarkable. He puffed intermittently on his cigar, never seemed to go to bed and came up with one brilliantly revolutionary scheme after another.

With an intuitive imagination, supported by careful research, David could bring to vivid life moments in the history of Bristol, as in this description of the city's first tram for the series 'The Wheel in the West':

> Bristol came out in the mid-day sun. The church clocks struck 12 – and then the ringers at St Michael's heaved on their ropes to begin a jubilant peal. Perry Road and Park Row were jammed with people. Some of them were waving flags. Then they started to cheer. It could have been a city paying homage to 'W.G.' or a conquering Cup team. But the hero on that warm August morning wasn't a human being at all.
>
> It was the city's first horse-drawn tram. The year was 1875 – and the handsome vehicle with room for 32 passengers was off on its maiden journey. From Perry Road, up through leisured Whiteladies Road, to the fringe of Redland at Blackboy Hill. A good twopennyworth in fact. The occasion could not have been more joyful – or picturesque.

This was local journalism at its best, written for newspapers that boasted circulation figures far in excess of those achieved today.

'THE SLOW AND DIRTY'

The Somerset & Dorset Railway, which closed in 1966
Extracts from a ten-part series, Western Daily Press, February 1974

For 104 years the distinctive locomotives of the Somerset & Dorset Railway puffed, croaked and groaned their way through the rolling hills and buttercup meadows of the West Country. Those who worked for the line swear there was never another one like it. Just over 71 miles of main line from Bath to Bournemouth – and 23 of that single track. It was, in many ways, unbelievably rough-and-ready. But for years, intrepid and skilled footplatemen, their faces caked in sweat and grime, relished the challenge of the appalling operational difficulties.

*

Parts of the S and D were of exquisite beauty. Many railwaymen stopped firing to gaze contemplatively across the verdant fields and restful meadows. Never was it appreciated more than when the train emerged from the Combe Down tunnel. This is North Somerset scenery at its best. The spectacular sweeps of the Mendip countryside captivated thousands of passengers over the years.

And not so far behind – although completely different in character – was the run towards Blandford. Dorset is a lovely county and this stretch of the Somerset & Dorset, threading its way through the undulating county, was another bonus for the passengers.

*

A railway so often reflects an area's economic life. Industrial patterns shift – and bookings drop. One thinks of the former value of the S and D in the context of North Somerset coal-mining. There were the days when the potent, locally-brewed stout from Oakhill was put on the train at Binegar; when the local lime kilns were glad of the railways and when the milk churns were mostly transported by train.

Blandford had an imposing station and was a bustling rail centre, yet still managing to retain the feel of a country town. Every station had its own character. Quaint little halts had too, meticulously maintained. Now most of them have gone. And all the big stations, with their chrome bars and girlie-dominated bookstalls, look the same.

*

Preservationists and other romantics have waxed poetic about the old engines puffing their way round the acute contours of country tracks. But it was hardly a romantic exercise for the fume-smeared men on the footplate.

Imagine an overpoweringly hot summer's day in 1960 as the double-headed Southbound Pines pulls out of Bath station on its way to Evercreech Junction. Almost at once, the crew realise that the brakes are rubbing on the train. That means a stop at Midford for running repairs. But they have to get there first – and there are two single-line tunnels to negotiate on the way. The driver and his fireman look anxiously at each other as they enter the quarter-mile bore of Devonshire Tunnel on a rising grade of 1 in 50.

There are only 12 inches between the chimney top and the roof of the tunnel. The exhaust strikes the roof and rebounds stiflingly around the locomotive. The fireman takes a deep breath and covers his mouth with a damp cloth before squatting on the footboards. For a time the driver sticks to his post and the fumes become so intense that he, too, is forced to sit.

Listen to the fireman as he remembers it: "I sat in the heat-laden atmosphere with my lungs nearly bursting, listening to the Pacific's rasping exhaust as she fought her way up through the Stygian darkness of this hell-hole. Then she slipped. The engine shuddered and vibrated like a trapped lion in a snare. All I could see through the thick, sulphurous atmosphere was a cascade of burning coals, showering all around our cab."

The driver forced himself off the floorboards and tried to slam the regulator shut. But it was stiff because the engine was priming so badly. The fireman staggered to his feet and between them they managed somehow to close the regulator. "Each breath was like swallowing a red hot poker and my chest was tightening up."

It was impossible to tell how fast the train was now going or when they would reach the end of the narrow, claustrophobic tunnel. They made it and continued fighting for breath for some time. The pair were soaked with sweat. They knew it had been a near thing.

*

Sadly few visible signs of the old Somerset & Dorset remain. The famous blue livery went in 1930, and maybe the ominous black that took its place was symbolic of the melancholy future. Scores of famous old signal boxes have now been pulled down for firewood. The romantically curling tracks have become overgrown and unrecognisable.

The tingling sound of the double-headed Pines Express beginning the Mendip climb is now no more than a happy hallucination. The men who worked for the S and D will tell you passionately, there was never another line like it. It was an amalgam of cheery words, financial worries, blind optimism, good-natured chaos (at least in the early days) and a treasured chunk of social history.

SEAPORT BRISTOL

Extracts from a seven-part series, 'One man's view of a city and its history', Western Daily Press, November 1977

This is no history lesson of Bristol. But it is the human, scarred, absorbing story of a great city, once the second in the land. No record of Bristol can be stacked exclusively with affection. It was often weaned on greed, cunning and devious ethics. There were times when it grew pot-bellied on shameless exploitation, sugared by self-righteous words from the pulpit. The city also soared with justifiable civic pride, honest intent, good deeds and an unrivalled spirit of adventure and pioneering zeal.

*

Everywhere we find evocative signs of the maritime past. Cobbled King Street and the wharfside taverns are more eloquent than a score of history books. As are the crescents and terraces of lofty Clifton. Here is the architectural grandeur, less patterned than beautiful Bath, that once made Georgian Bristol 'the most affluent square mile in Europe'.

*

The natural battlements of the Gorge gave Bristolians a haughty independence. Visitors, especially the riders from South Wales in the early days, were offered a hostile reception. The mutual disaffection across the Severn has never wholly disappeared, it seems. But Bristolians aren't by nature belligerent. The rivers around them begat traders. And traders don't like war – it's bad for business. People who were born in Bristol are phlegmatic, mildly suspicious, dry-humoured, canny in a business deal. They are also lacking in ambition and basically good-natured ... once they have accepted you.

*

The snaking Avon served its purpose in making things difficult for the early raiders. But the navigable hazards multiplied as the ships – and maritime intentions – became more grandiose. Just as commuters today curse its tides, so did some of the more enlightened City Fathers in the 18th century. The sad and not uncommon sight of a ship keeling over as the tide went out meant the loss of valuable time and cargo. Overseas traders began to shy away from Bristol. And Liverpool, with more facilities, capitalised.

Bristol remained defiantly, if unrealistically, optimistic. The Great Britain was launched in 1843, five years after the Great Western reached New York from Bristol. Brunel was, by this time, beavering away – telling everyone what was wrong with the docks and usually being right.

And, in the same context of a thriving docks, he knew it was necessary to improve communications with London. The existing Kennet and Avon canal was absurdly slow. A group of Bristol visionaries were thinking the same way. They planned a new railway and wisely chose Brunel as its engineer. The Great Western Railway was on its way.

*

Many rich men generously put their hands into their pockets to make Bristol more beautiful – or better educated. Their benevolence is rightly remembered in quaint annual rituals and speech days. Fresh-cheeked schoolchildren thank God for the goodness of their benefactors. But, frankly, God can't be too happy about some of the methods with which the wealth was accumulated.

Top of the charity league was surely Edward Colston, a somewhat solemn bachelor who stood for Parliament. Maybe he saw it as the waste of valuable time. He preferred devoting all his energies to making money. It was an obsession he justified with the eloquence of his balance sheet. There's nothing wrong in making money, especially if more than £70,000 of it is ultimately given back to the city for schools and almshouses. The unpalatable truth is that a major share of his wealth came from one sordid trade. He dealt in human beings. He made vast sums, in fact, from slaves.

*

John Wesley rode into town, as they say, as a sceptical Anglican parson in 1739. Soon he was breaking away from the established church. He was a dour, often humourless man. He was unwaveringly stubborn and dogmatic. And he was marvellously courageous. The other Church of England clergy were outraged by his methods. Even his own brother was horrified at the way he assumed the power of a bishop to carry out ordination. Wesley, Non-Conformist rebel and individualist, wholly justified the means.

When he arrived in Bristol, his spiritual home, he was a scholarly introvert who carried a book of Shakespeare under his arm as well as the scriptures. But that rhetorical preacher George Whitefield, also shunned by conventional Anglicans, demonstrated the importance of going out into the fields for his services. He didn't bother about Bristol's aristocrats. His congregation comprised slum dwellers and Kingswood's raw, ungodly miners. Wesley watched him at work, pondered for a weekend and then chose the open air, too.

The antipathy towards him mounted. He was abused and stoned; at one Somerset meeting, organised opposition set a bull on him. He was despised for his unorthodox approach. He was feared, by vested interests, for his stand against slavery.

GRAVE RAIDERS

from a five-part series 'Scandal in the West', Western Daily Press, August 1981

Three police constables crept nearer the Bedminster churchyard. They hid behind a tombstone and discovered to their horror that the tip-off had not been a macabre hoax. The moonlight played tricks, as the heavy yew branches swayed in the autumn wind. But the sight before them was unmistakably horrid. They might be on holy ground. Yet their duty was plain. The three policemen looked grimly at each other and then drew their batons.

What followed was a long and vicious battle. At least one pistol was fired. A rapier flashed. And six men caught at their loathsome and lucrative trade fought desperately. They were professional body-snatchers. Their gruesome midnight sorties were well paid, and they worked, without asking questions, for an instant purse and a bellyful of ale.

A young Bedminster woman had been buried earlier that day. "Get her out. We need to cut her up," they were told.

Body-snatching, in the cause of anatomical research, was a black art in the time of George IV. And that midnight free-for-all amid the gravesides in South Bristol happened in 1822.

The consequences were serious if the snatchers were caught. So they fought for self-preservation. The young woman's freshly-interred body was forgotten. Just one escaped. The other five, exhausted and lacerated, were eventually bundled to the police station. They were all charged – and nothing more was heard.

Only a few days earlier there had been an even worse body-snatching scandal. This time a man's coffin had been opened in St Augustine's churchyard in Bristol. Then the body was carried to a room in the precincts of Bristol Cathedral. It had been hired, for a phoney purpose, by several local surgeons. This looked like the classic snatch. No one was alerted. The graveside soil was carefully replaced. And now the surgeons were ready to do their cloak-and-dagger work.

But the recruited labourers had drunk too much. By this time they were belligerent and greedy. They wanted more money for a job that involved so much risk. The quarrel increased and so did the noise. It was unseemly behaviour late at night and next door to a cathedral. Passers-by stopped to listen. Soon there was a crowd. The patrolling constables were told.

The door of that hired room was forced. Inside were no Bibles or ecclesiastical garments. Just one chalk-white man on an improvised slab. There could not have been a more red-handed capture for the police.

For days, College Green buzzed with outraged gossip. Yet, as in the case of the Bedminster snatch, there was no court case. Maybe the surgeons involved were too firmly entrenched in the local establishment.

A few radical voices whimpered in protest. But the missing legal papers remained a nagging mystery.

MERCHANT WHO LOST SIGHT OF AMERICA

extracts from article, Western Daily Press, July 1976

The great American dream faded for one corpulent Bristol merchant in the surprisingly turbulent late-summer waters of the Atlantic in the pre-Columbus days of 1480. John Jay was a winner in nearly everything he touched – as an astute tradesman, a self-confident socialite, a revered elder of the city. But he still goes down in history as one of Bristol's losers. He was the man who didn't discover America ...

John was appointed sheriff in 1472. He relished the civic pomp. He dressed extravagantly and liked to be thought of as one of those merchants with a sense of adventure ...

Sailors who gossiped on the wharfside in the city talked fancifully of 'the isle of Brasille'. Jay liked the sound of that. He estimated that the uncharted land couldn't be so many miles out across the Atlantic ...

The idea of discovering the fabled isle of Brasille obsessed him. There was the status involved – and, of course, the pickings.

He made his plans. He scoured the country and found reputedly the finest pilot, a wizened Welshman called John Lloyd. A Bristol crew was recruited and a modest 80-ton ship, owned by the affluent Jay, sailed down the Bristol Channel on July 15, 1480. It isn't clear whether the sponsor was on board. Several accounts suggest he was.

Everyone seemed optimistic. The crew talked excitedly among themselves of the incentives they had been promised when the new land was discovered.

The ship headed west of Ireland as planned. And it kept going for nine weeks. Without the glimpse of another country. Morale dropped, and the bad weather increased. The 80-ton ship limped back to the nearest Irish port for repairs. There was no thought of renewing the search.

John Jay was baffled. So was Lloyd, 'the finest mariner in the land'. Was it all a fable after all? They returned empty-handed to Bristol and the cynics around the quayside taverns smiled to themselves. Jay, the merchant with the golden touch, had failed at last. He died soon after, still convinced on his death-bed that his ship had got frustratingly near to the Isle of Brasille.

VICTORIAN FARM LABOURERS

from a five-part series 'The Victorians', Western Daily Press, October 1978

Nowhere in Britain was rural poverty more evident than in Somerset and parts of North Devon. The small, isolated farms on Mendip, Exmoor and Dartmoor were run on pitiful slave labour. Up to the 1850s there were many examples of wizened, careworn labourers, still in early middle age, taking home weekly pay packets of seven shillings or less. For that they worked almost round the clock at times of harvest or calving, for instance. There was no mechanisation. And there was little food in their bellies to give them the strength to toss their hay.

Farm workers' conditions became such a scandal that a Royal Commission cited the domestic misery in a stretch of countryside between the Mendips and Weston-super-Mare: 'You can hardly call the dwellings they live in cottages. Some are only lean-to roofs up against the wall.'

In such degrading plight, it wasn't uncommon for a farmworker to live with his wife and up to a dozen children. The wives helped in the fields for a few extra pence. The children got a penny or two for scaring the birds at harvest time.

It was argued by the farmers that the labourers had their accommodation free, that they were allowed potatoes, swedes and milk. And if the worker was a cowman or carter he could earn a bob or two extra anyway. Such blandishments made minimal impact on the downtrodden labourer as he fed his few hens that ran wild at the side of his shack.

The West Country's farmworkers were mostly illiterate. They had no aspirations. They simply existed, hoping that someone more eloquent than they would put their case.

*

When in 1884 farmworkers got the vote it meant precious little. It had come too late. Many by then had been forced to leave the land.

Farmworkers, like coal miners, carry a chip on their shoulders even today. It was made by the yoke. Some, whose families tilled the soil in Somerset, Gloucestershire, Wiltshire and Dorset for many generations, still tell bitterly of the hardship of their ancestors. The stories of struggle in their lean-to hovels have been passed down from father to son.

The one hope for the young lad, if he were bright enough, was to leave home. And the only escape route for the daughter was to go into service.

Yokel jibes were pre-Victorian, of course. But they persisted, and still do today. They are unconsciously cruel and insensitive.

FAMOUS BRISTOLIANS

Two of the 42 vignettes that make up the booklet 'Famous Bristolians' (1979)

Thomas Chatterton

Everyone knows that in 1770 he killed himself by taking arsenic and was buried in a pauper's grave alongside a London workhouse – at the age of seventeen. Who was to blame? Some argued it was Horace Walpole who refused to give this precocious poet the patronage he desperately needed. But philistine Bristol, more obsessed with the wallet than the arts, had been indifferent to his pleas for a hearing.

Academics still can't agree about his literary merit and what he might have achieved. Keats had no doubt at all about this 'martyred genius'. His short, tragic life has since been the subject of theatre and opera; admirers still visit Bristol specifically to see his birthplace, with the schoolroom facade, in Redcliffe Way.

Chatterton, the son of a schoolmaster, had his first poem published in the local paper when he was ten. He went on to invent a 15th century monk Thomas Rowley, and his brilliant literary confidence-trick may never be surpassed for daring or poetic skill. This moody, misunderstood and richly talented youth died suffering from abject frustration, malnutrition and disease.

Ernest Bevin

Once he pushed a mineral-water van around the back streets of Bristol for a few shillings a week. He became a great trade union leader and Foreign Secretary (without losing his West Country vowels or native forthrightness).

Like several of his brothers he left the Exmoor village where he was born in 1881. He took the train to Bristol, lodged in Bishopston and started work in a bakehouse on The Centre. Soon he was a waiter, horse-tram conductor and driver for a lemonade firm in York Street, St Paul's.

His early socialism was touched by Non-Conformist fervour. He was a Sunday School teacher, a Baptist sidesman and even lay preacher. Following in the tradition of Bristol-born Ben Tillett, he became an impassioned champion of the dockers, organising them in fearless, militant style. It was the start of a spectacular climb that carried him to Cabinet status and earned him international respect.

12
Back to the Theatre

Avon Touring Theatre in 'The Football King'
Tim Munro, Tony Robinson, Christine Bradwell, Pauline Kelly

The Crazy Theatre Company in 'Stinkfoot – A Comic Opera in the Grand Tradition' by Vivian Stanshall, staged on The Old Profanity Showboat

For 23 years, from late 1969, David reviewed regional theatre productions for the *Guardian*. There are some 700 in all, pasted carefully into two books, with a few hand-written corrections where sub-editors had mistranscribed him or misattributed his review: to David Frost or, once, to Michael Foot, the leader of the Labour Party. "I've dropped the *Guardian* a line," David told the *Bristol Evening Post*, "telling them I would be happy to get the sort of fee they would pay the other Mr Foot."

In a 1983 article, David set out his approach to reviewing theatre:

> There are no firm rules on how to do the job. I have set only a few for myself: don't walk out before the end, don't discuss the play with anyone in the audience on the first night (however charming or persistent that questioner may be), don't take your seat with a pre-conceived idea.
>
> There is no school of apprenticeship apart from going to – and, less important, reading about – the theatre as often as possible. I made it my business to go to *bad* as well as *good* theatre; I went to tatty music hall and variety as well as Stratford-upon-Avon. It always seemed to me that an accomplished and imaginative comic who could fill an empty stage and hold his audience rapt had much in common with a gifted classical actor delivering a soliloquy.

He expanded these thoughts in an interview the same year:

> I love my reaction to be spontaneous. I frequently go to the theatre without prior knowledge of the play. I like the play to wash over me. I want to see how I respond.

He cited a David Rudkin play portraying a sacrificial beheading in an orchard:

> 'Afore Night Come' left me thrilled and in a state of shock. I hardly remember walking along King Street afterwards, and yet everyone, bar half a dozen or so, hated that play. Now that is the real excitement of the theatre – the way one personally reacts.

The *Guardian* reviews, generally 300 words in length, required in-depth knowledge of theatre, confidence of judgement and an ability to write lively, tightly worded prose. David became a master of the form, finding a delightful way of capturing, in just a few words, fresh perspectives on established playwrights and works.

He was not afraid to identify weaknesses, though almost always he found strengths to balance his review. Only once, reviewing *Dirt*, a university show about pornography, does his generosity of spirit desert him completely. Presumably referring back to *Meet Mr Tombs*, the farce he slated during his

Evening World days, he starts: 'In nearly 30 years' reviewing professional theatre, I can recall only two utterly mis-spent evenings. This was one of them.' Four paragraphs later, he concluded: 'Bizarre theatre is one thing – bad theatre is another.'

The regional edition of the *Guardian* went to press too early for his copy to be wanted on the night so usually he could compose his pieces without hurry the next morning. Yet such was his journalistic schedule, especially during the cricket season, that he did not always have the quiet time he would have liked, as is revealed by a letter from the editor of the Arts Page that David endearingly retained:

> In case I don't have the chance to talk to you on the phone today I thought I ought to tell you that I won't be using your review of the Beggar's Opera, partly because it was fully reviewed when first seen at the Cottesloe Theatre, but partly because it read as if it had been briskly knocked off in a luncheon interval at Taunton.

At the foot of the letter David has written: 'Oh dear – alas, it was!'

He was a regular at the main stages in Bristol, Bath and Cheltenham and, occasionally, further afield at Worcester, Swindon and Salisbury. He also took in a multitude of non-traditional venues. This was in keeping not only with the *Guardian*'s priorities but with his own concern that the theatre should reach beyond its 'predominantly middle-class' audience.

He attended a hall in Thornbury, north of Bristol, where one evening Harold Pinter was among a group of readers of selected prose and poetry:

> Few poets have good actors' voices; Pinter's is rich and resonant, with a tongue that rolls lovingly round the ironies and curiosities of the human condition. The Pinter half of the evening was an opportunity to ponder again the deceptive simplicity of his writing. Short sentences, long pauses; sentiments quarried from the heart and not the more ponderous pages of the dictionary. And that he was there himself added immensely to the enjoyment.

Then there was the Old Profanity Showboat, the former cargo ship Thekla moored in Bristol's Floating Harbour and refitted by Vivian Stanshall, 'erstwhile of the Bonzo Dog Doodah Band', and his wife Ki. There David revelled in Stanshall's eccentric *Stinkfoot*:

> The ideas spill out of him: pastiche, the surreal, visual jokes, and new songs by the conveyor belt. Who are we to complain if the sheer output obscures the narrative and the shape? ... He has

set up the Crackpot Theatre Company and given us an offbeat Christmas show that is funny, bluesy and loony. It isn't always easy to share his wavelength ... but the marvel is that here is an original, unusual musical, smelling of the salt sea: with Coward, Cagney and Mae West around to keep us happily buoyant.

David was also captivated by the spirit of *Yesterday's Island*, a portrait of the St Philip's Marsh area of Bristol, whose inhabitants had been uprooted by the council to create an industrial area:

> 'Yesterday's Island' is community theatre at its best – conceived, written and enacted by Bristolians, some without any previous experience, although you would never know. Professional interpreters would have gone for dramatic effects and inclined to a dreary belly-aching political tract. It would have wholly lacked the heart and tangible integrity of this three-hour 'musical comedy'.

David was drawn to such projects. For the *Evening World* he had called Arnold Wesker's *Roots* 'the most authentic play about the village working class to emerge in our English theatre since the war'. He reiterated that judgement when he saw it again. The lead role in the earlier production had been played by Eileen Atkins; now it was Louise Jameson, 'making a powerful return to the Bristol Old Vic after her loin cloth life alongside Dr Who.' The review gave David the chance to reflect on Wesker's ideals:

> At the time he wrote 'Roots' Wesker was still hopefully extending the hand of culture to the masses. This is no place to argue why, for instance, the theatre is still failing, with much of the fringe providing nothing more than a sop for the visionaries; but the argument and passion of this play, first performed nearly 20 years ago, is almost as valid today. Generation-communication remains so often a faltering and pathetic process. Subservience, allied to indifference, is a negation of knowledge and aspiration.

One group pursuing Wesker's manifesto were the Bristol-based Avon Touring Company, a radical co-operative who, in the spirit of the 1970s, were taking theatre out to the people with lively shows, often with music, on such subjects as industrial picket lines, football and prostitution. Among their early pioneers were David Illingworth, a drama department graduate who died tragically young, Howard Goorney, a veteran of Joan Littlewood's Theatre Workshop, and Tony Robinson, later to achieve fame in 'Blackadder'. David reviewed with sympathy many of their productions; he also previewed Illingworth's play about Nye Bevan which was first performed in Tredegar.

> You don't usually look for theatre premieres in Tredegar. Not in the miners' welfare hall, that flat, functional building of battleship grey where, these days, the colliers' families more often go in search of the flicks than the rhetoric. But this is where Bevan was born, down the road at 32 Charles Street, now boarded up and sadly silent. And it was up on those scarred, protective hillsides, the roads entwining themselves round the clusters of miners' cottages, that he preached his gospels of defiance and hope.

In all of this David was a perfect fit for the *Guardian*. It was less plain sailing for him in matters relating to the new politics of gender and sexuality. A new generation of university-educated radicals was becoming prominent on the paper, in particular women who had no time for the jolly conversations about real ale that David had enjoyed with their predecessors. In one instance, when he put up an idea for a feature, they told him it would be better handled by a feminist writer – or, as David put it in *Footsteps from East Coker*, 'a member of their own uncompromising gender'.

He loved political theatre but only when it worked as theatre. So he may have created editorial unease when he wrote of one play: 'Feminism has often been done a monumental disservice by its surfeit of theatre writers, who have yelled their political case with cliché-ridden, unstructured doggedness.'

He also ran into difficulties on the subject of homosexuality. I was present once when he sympathetically teased out of a mutual friend an admission of long-repressed gayness, and David conveyed no sense of disapproval. But he struggled at times with the new attitudes and the new language. In his scrapbook of theatre reviews he complains of 'censorship by a homosexual cell in the *Guardian* office' when, in a review of a play whose central character is in prison for what we now call 'paedophilia', his word 'pederast' is replaced by 'homosexual'.

David retired as regional drama critic in 1992. He was in his sixties, and he was increasingly feeling the punishing schedule of his work. The task of absorbing a theatre performance, often after a long day, required him to be at his most alert, and this could sometimes be a challenge, as he revealed in his review of Alan Bennett's *Another Country*:

> There is an irritating tendency for Bennett to become almost pretentiously Chekhovian as his disillusioned subjects brood

from the tree-lined verandah. He keeps us guessing about location and motives for most of the first act, and occasionally only just keeps us awake.

His letter of resignation from the *Guardian* referred to only one 'serious' dispute in his 23 years: 'when a pretentious sub (circa 1978) made it clear he was a frustrated reviewer and added opinionated adjectives to my piece. Trouble was I didn't know the meaning of half of them.' His letter went on to make a plea for more coverage of regional drama, which he felt the paper had, in recent years, 'noticeably discouraged'.

As a sports writer he loved the company of players, and so it was with actors and directors. He never recreated the intimacy with theatre people that he enjoyed when he worked for the *Evening World*, but plenty of actors recognised his specialness, as Jane Lapotaire made clear in an 'open letter' to him on the subject of theatre reviews:

> Not all critics are as caring, well informed and sensitive as you, as was evident from our meeting in Bath. Unlike you, David, (your reviews are proof of this), so few of your colleagues really care about or love the theatre. Their columns have become a means of careerism as they develop individualistic literary styles and quirky witticisms at the expense of the health and growth of the profession they can so easily belittle.

David never belittled anybody or anything. That was one of the many endearing features of his personality.

In the interview in 1983 David revealed his own tastes in theatre:

> If I could choose a season of plays, it would be 'Candida' by Shaw, one Arthur Miller – perhaps 'All My Sons', one new play if it's good enough – perhaps a David Hare. Then 'The Recruiting Officer' and finally Brecht's 'Mother Courage'.

There follows a final paragraph from the interviewer, Margaret Ashton of the Bristol Old Vic Theatre Club:

> With this wealth of reporting behind him, David is hopeful that readers appreciate his whims and prejudices and make allowances for them. He prefers to be seen as providing an optional guide. Having said all that, David's shock exit line was, "But then I really prefer the cinema ... and cricket!"

Don't be fooled by David's mischievous sense of humour. He really did love the theatre; the writing tells us that.

EXTRACTS FROM REVIEWS

The Taming of the Shrew

'The Taming of the Shrew' is never more than a sport: a piece of quirky flagellation to titillate the kickster-voyeur rather than anger the sturdy doyennes of the feminist cause. This is tongue-in-cheek Shakespeare. It's a charade with actors relishing the chance to behave like actors.

The Seagull

Chekhov wrote as much for off-stage as on. The scene outside the window is always an integral part of the visual action. The distant sounds – a woodman's axe or the bark of a dog – hold a vital symbolism.

The Cocktail Party

Cerebral drama like 'The Cocktail Party' makes the more fallible among us want for the occasional rush of blood and, metaphorically at least, even a flash of flesh ... Eliot made no noticeable concession to those theatregoers who struggled to grasp his ideas and wanted something more than a brilliant, intense radio play, best suited to a religious slot.

A Streetcar Named Desire

Blanche DuBois's dramatic potency is in her ambivalence. She arrives primly in virgin white and we know that her knickers are really soiled. She affects the haughty aura of a well-bred Southern belle – and we know from the way she immediately stretches for the bottle with that sensual thrust of a generous bust that her mind, quite apart from her hormones, is in utter turmoil.

Abigail's Party

'Abigail's Party' was fine for television: good for a laugh and well worth a retrospective ponder as the coffee cups were being cleared away. On stage the limited dramatic range is exposed. In some ways it is no more than an extended skit on lowering suburban standards where the fitted-carpet existence is stacked with stereos and insensitive jibes rather than brain cells and compatibility.

Entertaining Mr Sloane

Joe Orton wrote without a shred of affection for the human race. His aggressive, anarchic approach came essentially from the Sixties and plays like 'Entertaining Mr Sloane', however riveting, will progressively lose their sting.

A Flea in her Ear

Feydeau is essentially a flawless mathematician. He doodles outrageously with his human figures and teases us with a tangle of sums which defy solution until the last ruffled bedspread has been straightened. Like the most skilful farceurs, he makes nothing too explicit: the best arithmetic is left to the head.

Of Mice and Men

Steinbeck's characters are migrant workers, with nothing to lift their arid hearts but unattainable dreams and an evening in the whorehouse. This is a fine humane play – and a great political one, mostly by what is left unsaid.

Plenty

The play is an essay on the postwar let-down. Most of us would share David Hare's despair at disintegrating idealism and the messy corruption that followed those parachute jumps – and heady day-dreams.

The Master Builder

Ibsen is strong on the male menopause. His Solness, in essence himself, is ever-ready to make a fool of himself over a younger girl or brood erotically over the drawing board. The guilt towers as high as his new house from which he falls at last symbolically to his death.

Mrs Warren's Profession

Only Shaw could have written so absorbingly about prostitution without a whiff of carnal perfume; only Shaw, with that extraordinarily lucid vision of his, could have written in 1894 about woman's need to rise and express herself. He said it definitely with wit and challenging reason.

West Side Story

'West Side Story', based on one of the greatest love stories defiled by bigotry, is ageless in its subject matter – indeed, every time it is seen, it seems to take on, in its uglier aspects, a new modern significance.

Death of a Salesman

'Death of a Salesman' is a considerable work of the theatre, judged by any creative standard and within any era. It ranks, for its agonising and unsparing emotions, not so far short of the mighty Shakespearean tragedies. Miller presents us with a timeless essay on human dignity – and a more specific one on the fearful flaws of the American Dream.

The Football King
Avon Touring Theatre – March 1975

Avon Touring, realistically accepting that professional football is proletarian theatre anyway, come the nearest so far to the realisation of their own concept. 'The Football King' needs neither a glossary nor interpretative aids for those members of an audience unused to or wary of the rituals and intellectual exercises of theatre-going. Here is the language of Eastville and Ashton Gate – and the blokes who stand on the terraces to cheer (and occasionally to ponder the strange political cul-de-sacs of the game).

David Illingworth, the writer who integrated himself with the lingo and the liniment of Bristol Rovers in his sensitive research, has a sharp ear for the clichés of the trade – and the foibles of the manipulative business. Tim Fearon is the King. He is physically right – a surly No. 9 who gets up off his backside to score in injury time. He has, in truth, trained and sweated in his preparation for the part and the result is a portrait, even in the context of satire, which is refreshingly accurate. The manager, loquacious and cynical as Clough in his heyday, is a brilliant comic study from Tony Robinson.

Travesties
Theatre Royal, Bristol – October 1976

From the affectionate way Tom Stoppard discounted the minor traffic offences and chiselled his initials on the Press benches in homely Flax Bourton Court nearly 20 years ago, the rest of us should have sensed that here demonstrably was a Man of Letters. His humour then was surrealist and esoteric – and it hasn't changed. 'Travesties', as seen in this production at Bristol's Theatre Royal, proves the point.

Mr Stoppard is that rare bird of theatre, an original. He is a tongue-in-cheek thinker who invites us to keep our options open about the seriousness of his ideas, political or otherwise. He uses words with loving care and is mischievous enough to play games endlessly with them. The exercise can leave the head spinning, and the jokes – mostly professional giggles – leave me, in this comedy at least, smiling but unsatisfied, way outside the gates of the university.

Robert Knight's direction, although mildly over-ostentatious, is true to the gently eccentric spirit of Stoppard. But I detected a degree of intellectual fawning among the audience in a way that would have embarrassed the vastly talented author. There was more honesty in the reaction of those who hesitated in their response, wishing they could have read the programme notes in advance and deciding that Mr Stoppard should have made things easier for them.

Good Fun
Studio, Theatre Royal, Bristol – April 1982

Victoria Wood invests her work with a fragile, truthful touch. As a musical play to coincide with the Women Live campaign, 'Good Fun' is arguably seen through muted feminist eyes. The eyes seldom blaze: but they are gutsy and vulnerable at the same time. Her men are inclined to be stupid, indolent and unfeeling; yet her girls are also caricatures, whether pink-haired cosmetic vendors or weak-willed idealists.

This production, directed with hilarious ladies' lav bravado by Celia Bannerman, is immensely funny – in support of its title. The gags, falling over each other in gynaecological rotation, have bite, brittleness and Mancunian earthiness. It is a splendid, refreshingly low-brow and yet still sensitive piece of pertinent, lively theatre.

Rowan Atkinson
Bristol Hippodrome – July 1983

It is impossible to categorise him. His brooding blancmange face flits, it appears, from funeral parlour demeanour to that of a gawky adolescent wracked with masturbatory guilt. He has a penchant for mime, embellished with gibberish and surreal moments. The mime is outrageously funny – in the ways of erstwhile continental music hall – rather than technical.

Atkinson is blissfully free from the well trodden paths of satire. Without too much charm or concession to cheap rapport, he is perhaps the most distinctive comic talent in this country since the war. That talent has as yet been only half developed.

Look Back in Anger
Theatre Royal, Bristol – October 1988

This is Jimmy Porter from the Hustings. He harangues and rants – without breath or variation in the decibels. Jonathan Phillips almost certainly qualifies as the noisiest Porter since 'Look Back in Anger' made its mark in theatrical history. He is not necessarily the angriest.

I was an acute observer of anger in the Fifties and it always struck me that, when it came to the Hyde Park soap box, Donald Soper was the most eloquent of the protesters by a mile – he rarely raised his voice. If only Mr Phillips would introduce a few subtle shades to the tirade he delivers.

It is mesmeric and occasionally, alas, reveals how close Osborne was to making his illustrious anti-hero boring.

THE MAKING OF A KING

Early in 1982, for the Bristol Old Vic's production of 'Henry V', David was given privileged access to rehearsals, writing an illustrated booklet 'The Making of the King' and a feature for the Guardian.

They first came together at lunchtime a month ago: excited, subdued, wary, recognising old friends, eyeing strangers with unconcealed curiosity. There are no ostentatious flourishes. They look a good-natured, un-camp lot, encased in woollies. Outside the stage door there are still piles of hard snow.

John David is directing this one himself. He leads them down from the bar to the stage, sits them in a circle and does the introductions. It's a big cast and he hardly hesitates. Morale among some of the supporting actors soars. The director brings out his notes and talks about Henry for quarter of an hour. He sells it to them in his classless, enthusiastic way in two minutes.

David goes on to tell them that Henry was 27 in 1414 when the play began. "And Clive is 27 now." Clive Wood is to play Henry V. He's a gritty, pale-faced young actor with broad shoulders and red hair, and some of the athleticism of a young dancer, which he once briefly was.

"Some say that Henry in this play is less interesting than Hal in 'Henry IV' but I disagree. He's matured. A young and brilliant man is tested like England and emerges victorious," the director goes on. "The play provides a complete anatomy of war – war as a social, historical, moral, physical and emotional occupation. It's all there."

The group of actors, fingering their virgin Penguin copies of the play, look anything but bellicose. There's as yet a light touch to the conversation. David fleetingly confuses his York with his Gloucester and James Cairncross, in rich, sonorous tones of Regent's Park vintage, quips: "Sounds like British Rail's revised timetable."

Cairncross was in the 1953 Bristol Old Vic production of 'Henry V'. "We opened on Coronation Day," he says with reminiscent relish. "The new Queen was making a speech in the evening and it was arranged for this to be relayed to the audience. We changed the interval – and after that the play was killed stone dead!"

*

By the end of the first week the chemistry is working well in the wings. Recurrent concern and mutual advice about digs are exchanged.

There's some levity on stage as Stanley Lebor, a hearty Pistol looking as if he's come straight off the nautical cover of a cigarette packet, works out some vigorous physical business with Nym (Michael Simkins) and Bardolph

(Norman Gregory). June Barrie is pitching Mistress Quickly somewhere between Eastcheap and Mrs Basil Fawlty. She has been everything from Lady Bracknell to Stevie Smith over the last busy decade for her at Bristol.

Over lunch, Clive is aching like hell. He knows he has to be fit for Henry, but he wonders whether he overdid that killing session in a Bristol gym after his usual two-mile morning jog across the Downs in Clifton. The idea of a football match against one of the local radio stations appeals to him. But we're well into the second week and director David is jollying them along. There's less laughter; to his relief, the books have virtually disappeared. "They become psychological props." By now, rich, classical voices are getting dusted off. David Hargreaves's Fluellen is as true as the Arms Park. Graham Sinclair's Macmorris isn't far off Ian Paisley.

Into the third week and the first trace of tension is beginning to show. David is unsettled by some noisy chat in the wings. "If you're not involved, piss off," he says testily. Suddenly there is Clive Wood, spectacled, mug of tea in hand, launching into "Once more into the breach ..." The pulsating set-pieces, whether in tentative rehearsal or not, still pull everyone up with a start. He stumbles on a line and raps out "Shit" in self-rebuke as the poetic momentum is lost.

The run-through of the first half is over and David is not smiling. He strides towards where they are sitting now at the back of the stage. "This is a mammoth play and you are pretty awful." He has more to say and they know that he's right.

*

The scaffolding bridge, which moves backwards and forwards and has many ingenious uses, turns out to be rather higher than expected. Armour-plated soldiers start by swinging like ungainly robots to the distant ground below. Meanwhile, the production manager is rumoured to be checking the insurance cover. But the trainee gymnasts improve immeasurably by dress rehearsal on Tuesday and it's riveting visual stuff – "the best butch show in town".

'Henry V' opens on Wednesday to a full house. In every sense this is a major production and John David, looking tired and quietly triumphant, is glad he did it. The French have been defeated and cobble-stoned King Street is aglow with patriotism. The English soldiers and their victorious king climb out of their armour: talking of Agincourt, imminent pints, sprained ankles and four weeks of creative and remarkably cordial working together in 15th century make-believe amid the cannon fire and the swinging bridges.

13

Outsiders

Victoria Hughes, 'a wholesome, ageing woman', cycles around North Bristol and shares her memories with David over a cup of tea

As a young reporter in Bristol David was quick to see stories beneath the surface of everyday life. One of his first by-lined contributions to the *Bristol Evening World* was a 500-word piece about a tramp he had encountered in the early hours, walking towards Temple Meads railway station.

> Bristol's streets were almost deserted. An occasional taxi went by and solitary policemen tried shop doors. The old man with the luxuriant white beard and the brown paper carrier-bag hobbled on his way at 4 a.m.
>
> He was 80-year-old Tom Walker, former agent and secretary for a Member of Parliament, now surely Britain's most dignified and proud knight of the road. He was returning from Exeter to his 'base' in Rutland – a mere jaunt for this ageless vagabond-philosopher who became a tramp of his own choosing and enjoys every minute of it.

David buys him a cup of tea, which he drinks outside the station.

> It was nearly light when Old Tom set off, with only a little wicker stick to support him along the long road to Rutland, where he will return to an old people's home.

The nether-world of such characters fascinated David. As a freelance writer, he wrote two series of articles on outsiders: for the *Bristol Evening Post* in 1963 and for the *Western Daily Press* in 1970. In them he profiled meths drinkers, drug addicts, homeless wayfarers, single mothers, ex-prisoners in a church hostel. He set each scene with a keen, respectful eye and told the tale with humanity, quick to celebrate those who were trying to help. He outlined his approach at the start of the second series:

> This is a series about unhappy people. Some of them have chosen to opt out of society; others feel that society has rejected them. All of them have lost their way.
>
> There will be no moralising. We can leave that to the self-righteous. Nor will there be any conclusions – or pompous sociological assessments.
>
> I gave myself a simple brief. To listen. Nothing more than that. So in the main this is a simple, objective record of human failure – and the occasional glimmer of hope – in the cosy Seventies.

David wrote often about social issues: the rise of gambling, football hooliganism, the slum conditions of some rented properties, the difficulties encountered by the West Indians who were settling in Bristol. He went in search of ordinary people and listened to their stories.

Always there is humanity in his approach to the subjects of his features, as when he visited a home for refugees:

> Six elderly people, their backgrounds touched by tragedy, are taking part in Bristol's most exciting and least-publicised social experiment at a house in Ashley Down Road. They are refugees – a status conveniently ignored by an affluent society. Their homes and their dreams long ago disintegrated. Now they live with their memories – and a re-discovered peace in their old age. Their refuge is Tudor Lodge, a large house bought by the Bristol and West Council for Aid to Refugees.
>
> They are Latvians and Estonians. Once they were from the equivalent of our middle-class: the senior civil servant, the station-master, the state-registered nurse. War threw them into the gutter. They lost their possessions and most of their pride. They found themselves among the thousands of war's victims, herded without identity or hope into the refugee camps.

His piece ends with words that are, if anything, more chilling to read now than they were in 1963:

> The 70 or so social workers who attended the inaugural meeting in Bristol and those who later arranged for the buying of Tudor Lodge had the necessary vision. But will their work one day become obsolete? History indicates, unfortunately, that it won't.

Not all David's ventures into society's half-hidden corners found their way into print. One, which he sent to the *Evening Post* in 1965, was on the growth of strip clubs in Bristol. David, as well as interviewing a disapproving Methodist minister, visited a club in Clifton:

> On the night I went along, the stripper was a pretty 20-year-old whose real name is Yvonne but is billed as Lizzette. "Perhaps it sounds continental, but the main reason in choosing Lizzette was to hit on something completely different."
>
> Her current dance was a vaguely symbolic one to 'My Boy Lollipop'. She gave away children's lollipops to two or three of the middle-aged males peering up at her on the improvised stage. There was little suggestion of a dance routine. But she had a nice personality, a generous figure and an exquisite sun-tan.

'I am sorry to have to return your article,' the *Post*'s Assistant Editor wrote, 'but frankly I don't think it is our cup of tea. I see no point in the local evening paper drawing particular attention to this subject.'

In the same spirit David sat down with Victoria Hughes who, during the Depression years, had taken a job as a lavatory attendant on the Bristol Downs. There she befriended the women who plied their trade in the evenings, keeping a diary that she shared with David. In its down-to-earth way the resulting book, *Ladies' Mile*, is one of David's greatest achievements, capturing a slice of Bristol life that would otherwise have been lost.

Published as a modest paperback in 1977, it was not well received in official quarters, as David recalled in *Footsteps from East Coker*:

> I don't think it was ever stocked in any of Bristol's many public libraries. One corporation official told me in highly charged, censorious tones: "Not the kind of record we want on display."

Yet it sold out its modest print run, and in time attitudes changed. Visit the Stoke Road toilets today, and you will find a blue plaque: 'Victoria Hughes (1897-1978) who befriended and cared for prostitutes when she worked here from 1929 to 1962.' There is even a campaign to reprint the book, to raise money for the renovation of the toilets.

David's fascination with the darker side of human nature led him to research historic crimes and scandals in the region. In 1973 he secured a three-part series in the *Western Daily Press*, 'Murder Most Foul', to mark the 60th anniversary of the hanging of Bristol chairmaker Ted Palmer. Two years later he contributed a fuller version of the story to a paperback book, *Murder in the Westcountry*, produced by the newly formed Bodmin-based publishers Bossiney Books.

David's great gift in this story-telling, achieved through careful research and intuitive imagination, was to breathe vivid life into his central characters and the seedy world in which they lived. Inevitably there is an element of psychological conjecture, but it has the ring of truth – with compassion for the flawed characters. He achieved the same effect with the story of another murderer, the boxer Del Fontaine, whose tale he told twice: in the *Western Daily Press* in 1982 and the *Bristol Evening Post* in 2007.

Murder in the Westcountry contained a second chapter by David, about the 1876 murder of a policeman in East Coker, a story with which David had grown up. In a second volume from Bossiney Books, *Facets of Crime*, David contributed 'The Scandal of College Green', his account of the 1809 rape of a naïve servant girl by a titled army officer. The fateful pick-up occurred on a Sunday afternoon close to Bristol Cathedral, a setting which allowed David to explore and bring alive the historic underworld of a much-loved city location.

MY NIGHT IN A DOSS HOUSE

from a series, 'The Outsiders', Bristol Evening Post, 1970

Midnight in the dosshouse. I'm in the corner bed, lying in my socks and two sweaters. It's freezing outside. The naked bulbs have been switched off for nearly an hour. I curl in a ball, gaze unseeingly into the darkness … and listen.

There are the snores and the groans, the incessant coughing and the spitting into the chamber-pots. And the snatches of conversation from all corners of the dormitory: "P.J. … Here, P.J. I'm off next week. You can have my bed next week, P.J."

"You've been trying hard, Brummie."

"Yea, got a job at Lichfield. Sounds all right. Kitchen porter and nine quid a week."

And then silence again. You hear a hopeful banging on the door downstairs. But someone is going to be unlucky. All the 53 beds at Rowton House, Cheltenham, are taken. Several late-comers are already kipping on a battered settee. It's a bitter night and the coughing goes on. And the curses. "My bloody chest is done for. It needs the doctor."

Hard to associate this with 1970. Hard to associate it with Regency Cheltenham, where the Young Ladies get the right education and the fashionable Promenade symbolises affluence.

The beds are only a few feet apart. Each with its polythene sheeting as a precaution against bed-wetting; each with its pot underneath. There is no furniture and no lockers. Your trousers are slung under the pillow; you don't take your shirt off.

"Hey, what about Cassius then? He proved to the world, boy, that he's a religious man. It was his religion that done it …"

The voice was unmistakably Irish. Good Catholic sentiments in the doss-house at midnight. There are plenty of Irishmen around me: Noonan and Connolly and Daly and 'Corky' and two P.J.s (Patrick Joseph).

They pay 7s 6d a night (less for the week) for the bed. They cook their food on a gas stove and they crowd avidly round a big wooden table in the evening to watch the telly on a flickering set. It's a luxury that provides the only diversion from lying on the bed or nattering in the communal kitchen.

But they don't talk a lot. When I arrived in early evening, they were watching telly in darkness. Twenty or so of them sitting silently, like indeterminate eerie statues, looking at an old film about cosy family life.

The occasional grunt was the only communication during the film. But they laughed at the commercial about the good strong beer that followed.

Three-quarters of them are regulars at Rowton House. Some have come in from the cold. They shuffle along to the kitchen after the telly and suddenly the little cardboard boxes magically appear, with their irons, their packet of marge and raw onions. It's supper time.

A friendly Scot passes me a mug of strong tea. I finger my week's stubble self-consciously and hope he won't ask me where I'm from. We get on to jobs and I'm assured that Cheltenham is no good – "there's nothing down the Labour."

It's a strangely silent institution. When they talk, the accents are thick and the laughter sparse. But there is a dry humour of a sort in the wash-house where someone has crudely converted a notice into what might be a Limerick racecard.

… It's now the early hours and I stay awake listening to the coughing. And I think of the words of Mary Priday, a warm-hearted woman who with her husband looks after the lodging house: "They're a good lot of lads, really. Perhaps they like a drink at the week-end but there isn't much trouble. If I see them getting a bit naughty down at the pub, I just look at them and say don't let the House down. It usually works." Of the bed-wetting, she says: "What can you expect? Some of them have been sleeping rough. They catch a cold in their kidneys. They can't help themselves."

Christmas at Rowton House will again be a bed for the night. But there will be a special tea laid out on that big bare table. "I've got the lads to pick up blue stamps when they've bought their food at the Co-op. The stamps are worth £5 and this will go towards the tea. It's no point getting anything special for dinner. Some of them will be having a drink and they'll just want to sleep when they get back."

Rowton House is, in the main, a home for the homeless. If there were more beds they could be filled. If there were more money, the basic facilities could be improved. "We're desperately short of cash," says Ald. Charles Irving, chairman of the South West Midlands Housing Society who bought the dilapidated building to make sure the Rowton occupants would still have a roof for the night.

… Long before six in the morning and Brummie is beginning to tell us of his new job again. He's a nice bloke and everyone is glad for him. P.J. will get his bed. No one really knows the time but it's just the start of another day. And every day is roughly about the same as the last there.

But thank goodness, I think to myself, that there is a Rowton House at all.

LADIES' MILE

The story of Victoria Hughes, lavatory attendant on the Bristol Downs
Ghost-written by David and published in 1977

From David's Introduction

This modest book is an extraordinary social document. It is a simple, at times horrifying, record of rough-and-ready prostitution in one corner of Bristol through the grim years of the Depression and afterwards.

During all the years she worked on the Downs, Victoria Hughes recorded her impressions of the people she met and the surreptitious trade they carried on. She made detailed notes in a big, lined notebook. My brief, in editing her notes, has been faithfully to convey how she saw the sordid life about her. Most of the words in the book are her own. I have taken no liberties with the facts. She happened to be a first-class observer with a natural turn of phrase, wry and happily unsophisticated.

Is the book worth publishing? I am convinced that it is. Cities' social histories can be bent and warped to salve civic consciences. Victoria Hughes' unpretentious human document is a facet of Bristol life that needs to be remembered. It may help future generations to understand us that bit better.

First job

I swallowed my pride and became a 'loo lady' on a Thursday afternoon in the summer of 1929. It was the time of the Depression and a net wage of four shillings and sixpence for my two days a week seemed reasonable enough.

My first post was the public lavatories at the Clifton Suspension Bridge. That was reassuring. Good residential area. Nice class of person. No trouble there, I told myself.

Yet it still took quite an effort to go along that opening afternoon at 2.30 p.m. I was worried about people recognising me – and in the days ahead whenever someone I knew came in, I would turn my back or even hide myself away. I could imagine them going home and saying: "I saw Victoria Hughes this afternoon and do you know what she's come down to?"

Gradually I gained confidence. I was kept busy making sure that customers didn't push in without paying their penny. It may have been elegant Clifton but the chance to cheat the Corporation of a humble copper wasn't to be missed, it seemed. Little girls were allowed to use the free cubicle and I was horrified to see women pull them out and take their place.

Moving to the Downs

Eventually my boss asked: "How would you like a change of scenery?"

It was the opportunity I had been waiting for – a full week's wages at last. And that added up to two guineas. It was like gold in those days when thousands were out of work.

My new cloak-rooms were on the Downs. This, surely, was the No. 1 ambition of Bristol's loo ladies in those days. Here it was, surrounded by flowers, gardens and trees, discreetly hidden away behind a fence and bushes – and part of Bristol's lovely, open Downs.

It was to be the start of an astonishing chapter of my life which embarrassed and enriched me at the same time. I found myself an observer and an eavesdropper of a way of life which I hadn't realised existed.

Perhaps I was too naïve for the job. Even at the Suspension Bridge, it took me a surprisingly long time to realise that all the unattached women who wandered in so regularly weren't simply locals on the way to work or the shops. I used to smell the cheap scent and occasionally ponder the apparent lack of personal hygiene. But what were they always comparing notes about? I suppose you could aptly say that the penny eventually dropped for me. They were all on the game.

I couldn't turn a blind eye all the time. There were understandably complaints from the more respectable women who came in to spend a penny. The language from the prostitutes was foul. I got tired of finding contraceptives when I tipped up the hand basins to swill the water away.

There was so much about the girls that I despised. They had a contempt for their own bodies – and the men whose own furtive behaviour was no better than their own. But there was also a cheerfulness and odd kind of warmth about them as they waved me goodbye and moved off to flag down a car in Ladies' Mile or allow a quick, uncomfortable fondle or worse behind one of the stout tree-trunks.

The clients

It was nothing to have as many as twenty tarts, of varying age and appearance, prowling for trade among the tree-trunks of Ladies' Mile. That doesn't take into account those already doing a turn in the back of a car which had driven half a mile into the shadows of the side roads towards Sea Walls. And remember this was simply one concentrated area of twilight Bristol, the one I knew best.

Rivalry among the girls was lively and occasionally heated. Some of the more trusting pros would be unwise enough to tell the others of a planned appointment. If the client was known to be loaded, three or four more tarts would conveniently turn up. The ruse was apt to succeed if the bloke spotted a better-looking girl. This led to some bitter exchanges. "Leave my f—— goods alone," was a rasping order often repeated.

Over the years I was introduced to many of the men. I looked on it as a kind of compliment. It showed the kind of relationship I'd built up with the girls. Coincidentally I knew a few of the men's wives. If they'd only guessed …

One particular man was a director of a very well-known Bristol firm. He was upright and quite distinguished-looking. He had a nice voice. Naturally he was something of a catch. The girls were always ready to jump in the queue when he was about. Sexual intercourse didn't interest him. He was easily gratified. The price for two or three minutes of fumbling masturbation was invariably a five pound note.

His indiscretion astonished me. He must have known people would recognise him. This prominent Bristol businessman was labelled a dirty old man by most of the pros. But without dirty old men, they happily argued, they would be out of business.

Running Mary

Running Mary had sixth sense. At the first hint of a police uniform she was off – at almost sprinting speed. "You can't see her ass for dust when the Law is about," some of the others used to say to me.

*

She was in a mess. Some of the others hinted that she'd caught the disease. A complaint had also attacked both her legs and she needed crutches with which to walk. Crutches for Running Mary? It sounded funny until you thought about it. "You know what's wrong with her legs. 'Tis the pox she's got," one of the tarts confided knowingly. I didn't know whether V.D. could make you lame as well as blind. There were so many theories flying around among the girls all the time.

The next time I saw Mary I couldn't take my eyes off her. The former doll-like face had become a drawn, pasty mask and she snarled at me: "What you staring at me for? Not as bloody odd as all that, is it?"

I lied. "I can't believe it's you again. I haven't seen you for so long. You're looking more yourself again."

She knew well enough that I was lying. Time and again I noticed how people's features changed with the life they led. Mary was now an old hag – and not yet forty. Her cheek bones protruded. Her eyes were slits. Only her vile language was unaltered.

Molly

Romancing. Half of them did it. They lived in a dream world, hoping you would believe them. Molly's line was: "I'm a receptionist in a hotel, you know." The pros used to tease her. "Who you been 'recepting' today, then – anyone one from Ladies' Mile?"

She was tall, very smartly dressed and well spoken. But it struck me that her movements were always nervy and furtive. They gave her away.

Molly was a bit of a snob. She didn't mix much with the other pros. She loved buying new clothes and so needed plenty of money. On the Downs she was good at her job. Gradually she became more communicative with me and she would ramble on, one subject after another in a breathless rush.

One night she came in and announced: "I'm getting married."

She had met a traveller who immediately showed his generosity by giving her six pounds. No doubt it was for a ride in his car across the Downs but she implied it was out of pure love.

Molly introduced me to him. He was about fifty, bald and well-spoken. Just right for a 'hotel receptionist', I should have said! He struck me as very kind and they started living together. That went on for three months and then he dropped her like a red-hot lump of coal. It emerged he was a married man from Bradford with six children.

A piece of the city's history

There's nothing especially sensational about prostitution. Sex has been on sale for thousands of years. As a maritime city, Bristol's whores have usually found it a good market place.

But what went on among the trees on the Downs before, during and after the last war is still, I feel, a little piece of the city's history. I've tried to put it down as straight as I could, direct from my old notebook. It's part of a city's life and only the blinkered would say it didn't happen.

Weeping Mary and Running Mary, Martha and Doris and 'Buggy' ... I knew them all. They were real. Often rotten – but real. I hope I showed some compassion to them. They, in turn, gave me a sort of companionship and warmth. There was goodness, if I looked hard enough, in nearly all of them.

My job was to take the pennies and not to moralise. I never tried to, anyway. I'll leave others to huff and puff about what went on.

I can only say that those thirty-three years among Bristol's shocking and shameless girls enriched my life.

THE MURDER OF ADA JAMES

an extract from 'Bristol boxer' in 'Murder in the Westcountry' (1975)

In the whole trail of contradictions Ada was the biggest paradox of all. She was twenty-one and not pretty. But she possessed an indefinable element of sensuality which apparently attracted men. She regularly attended a mission church whose elders, all brimstone and hell-fire, expounded abstinence and purity for the single girl. Ada was neither temperate in her drinking nor, according to suggestions at the murder trial, in her sex life.

She came from a poor family and probably found an eloquence in her body that she lacked in her tongue. She was born, one of five children, in St Paul's, amid the pubs and the narrow, depressing streets. At thirteen she was ready to leave Wade Street School, St Jude's. Her first job was in an Old Market tobacco store; then she worked for a confectioner in Lewin's Mead. The third and final job for her was at a nail and button factory in St James's Square.

Ada had known Ted Palmer for five years.

He was a bizarre young man. He drank too much and was garrulous company in many of the sawdust pubs in those grimy backstreets. He had a way with words and could summon up an occasional gem of rhetoric to beguile a captive bar-room audience. Occasionally he became belligerent; usually next morning, he was full of contrition.

Ted was a familiar figure in that warren of Bristol streets in the pre-First World War years. He wasn't tall but he had a certain presence with him. The gold-rimmed spectacles he always wore gave him a mildly academic appearance. Yet he had, too, the broad shoulders of an athlete. As a teenager he had been a promising boxer never afraid to enter the Fair booths – for a few shillings and plenty of cheers.

He enjoyed that fleeting experience of adulation. Deteriorating eyesight ended his brief career in the ring. He had to feed the ego elsewhere and he turned to day dreams. 'There's no bloody money in making chairs,' he used to say. 'I'm off around the world.'

In fact, he got as far as Canada. He stayed for nearly a year, wrote a few affectionate letters to Ada and returned to Bristol just before Christmas 1912. His drinking mates thought he was more cocky. And his family at Selworthy Place, Montpelier detected that he was more unbalanced.

He could be arrogant and aggressive. Others remember him when, away from the pubs and people he had to impress, as intelligent, sensitive and tender as a lover.

A SUNDAY AFTERNOON RAPE

an extract from 'The Scandal of College Green' in 'Facets of Crime' (1975)

Bristol's College Green was once more beautiful than it is today – and more wicked, too. Gauche, intrepid girls, inclined towards illicit sex and the avarice that went with it, prowled in pairs after dark. Cynics say that the men strolled there either to see the cathedral in the half-light or catch the clap. This was where Chatterton, the Boy Poet, first foraged in adolescent excitement. This was where the randy and reckless blue-bloods from Clifton and Hotwells came, coins jangling in their pockets, as soon as the port decanter was empty.

In fact, College Green, as it used to be with its leisured, sylvan charm and ecclesiastic respectability, held a paradoxical appeal: somewhere between God and the groin.

It was sordid only in the evening when improvised carnal trades were plied behind the trees. Never brazenly in the full light of day. Never on a restful Sunday afternoon at just the time Bristol's more pious citizens were sauntering across the grass for a final meander before evensong.

But 3rd December 1809 was a Sunday. At 4 o'clock in the afternoon two army officers of the Militia were walking back, briskly in step, towards their lodging-quarters alongside the cathedral. Unlike many of the men who ambled round the streets of Bristol at the weekend, these two were eminently well-heeled and well-fed.

They had been to the post office and were amiably walking off the effects of an excessive lunch in the mess. And as they headed for their lodgings, they heard two girls giggling. They looked at the teenagers who threw back their shoulders and gave them an arrogant grin.

The girls, in their colourful Sunday best, cheap and meretricious, were both passably pretty: good for a furtive fondle outside the servants' quarters maybe on a bad night after the last waltz had been miscalculated at the aristocratic ball. The young officers and the girls carried on a self-conscious conversation in the middle of College Green for a minute or two. The accents were a world apart; their intentions were apparently identical.

'Come on back to the lodgings for a chat,' said the men from the Militia. The girls giggled again – and promptly went.

It was the first act in a full-blooded drama which scandalised Bristol and became the salacious talking-point of every army barracks, not to say Georgian mansion, for miles.

14
The World of Books

David and Bill Andrews

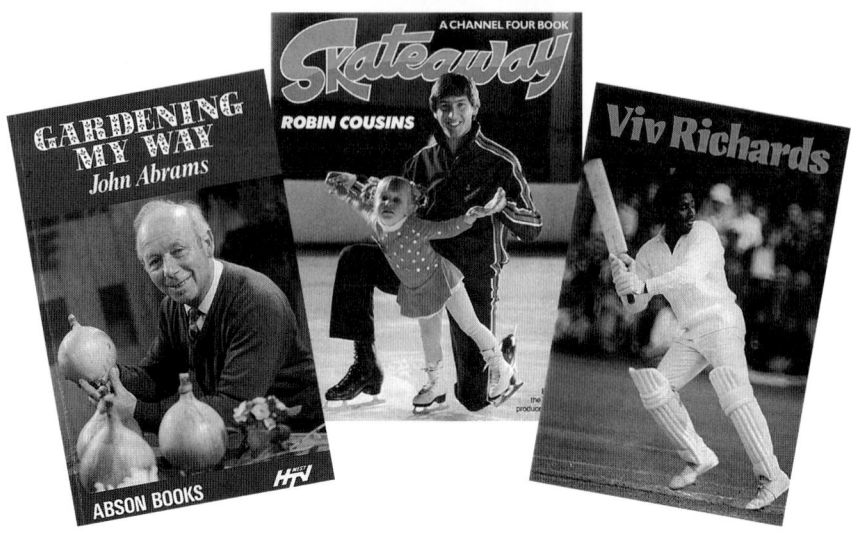

After David's failure to interest a publisher in his biography of WG Grace, he left the world of books till 1973 when the former Somerset cricketer Bill Andrews asked for help with a memoir he was writing in copious longhand. The publishers were complaining that his effort had got out of hand.

"They want me to get it down to 60,000 words."

"How many have you written so far?"

"One hundred and sixty thousand."

And he had. The difficulty was deciding what to leave out, though the libel laws helped.

With his editorial duties completed, David assumed that his involvement was over but, as he related in *Footsteps from East Coker*, the book's highly-strung author was not finished with him.

> On the day Bill's book, 'The Hand That Bowled Bradman', was due to be sent to the printers, I took a phone call at five o'clock in the morning. "Something terrible's happened. Haven't slept all night. I think I got a few facts and tales wrong. I can't let it go – so I've decided to scrap the bloody book altogether. Can I leave it to you, David, to tell the publishers and printers?" He was adamant. I was fully aware of his fragile mental state and feared he might do something drastic. For the life of me I couldn't think of any incident that was libellous enough to pull a book only hours before it went into print.
>
> I needed time to ponder what to do. Bill, in an advanced nervous state, remained completely unyielding. "Stay in bed, Bill. I'll be with you in half an hour." I motored frantically to his home in Weston-super-Mare. And I talked to him in alien marathon style, ignoring his protests. At last I convinced him that no-one had been defamed and there was nothing actionable in his stories. The book came out and, as a simple account of what life was like for a professional cricketer, it was warmly acclaimed. No-one heard of that last-minute scare.

There was a less happy ending to David's next venture into books. Sir George Dowty, aviation engineer and industrialist, had written a memoir which he asked David to turn into a more readable volume. David was flown to the Isle of Man in Dowty's private plane, piloted by Neville Duke, a well-known World War Two flying ace; then he undertook a series of interviews with family, friends and work colleagues. It was a major undertaking, requiring David to absorb information about subjects that were largely unfamiliar to him, but he set to work diligently, sharpening and adding colour to the prose. Among several hundred sheets of paper, preserved in a large folder, is the introduction that David proposed:

> Forty years ago George Dowty took his first tentative step towards business status. He decided to rent a mews loft in Cheltenham for half-a-crown a week. The unpretentious establishment, at 10 Lansdown Terrace Lane, housed a cheap, hand-operated pillar drill, a grimy workbench, a modest set of basic tools ... and a bright-eyed engineering genius.
>
> The description is surely not extravagant. For that cramped loft, forty years and a few sweeping removes later, turned into a commercial giant – the Dowty Group of Companies, stretching out across the world.

After several months, during which David received little in the way of feedback to his chapters, Sir George decided that he did not want to proceed, writing that he was 'unconvinced that it would be of interest to a wider public.' David tried to persuade him otherwise, and Sir George agreed to consider the matter further when his health improved. He died soon afterwards.

David was paid part of the agreed fee, which was more than he received for his next attempt to write a book. The publishers William Heinemann invited him to try his hand at writing a cricket story for '12, 13, 14 year olds who are rather reluctant readers'. David's submission, the 30,000-word 'Spinning Rebel', told the story of a gipsy cricketer, Jack Pucker, whose ability to spin the ball prodigiously led to his playing for Somerset against the touring Australians.

> In the club bar a group of supporters spot Jack and converge. One, who should have known better, says: "Where d'you learn to play like that, Jack – up against the caravans?" He isn't meaning to be offensive. But he is.
>
> Jack feels like saying: "I could empty that jar of beer over your big, fat, ugly head." Instead, he turns away. "Let's get out of this place. Them supporters is gettin' on me wick ... and I don't go much on the beer, either."

Back came a rejection letter. The writing was too detached, and the idea of using the names of current Somerset cricketers – Close, Cartwright, Richards – would date the book too quickly. In fairness, Heinemann are not wrong. The story has potential for young readers, but David never quite discovered a writing style that worked for that readership.

These two books, Sir George Dowty's memoir and 'Spinning Rebel', occupied David during 1975, a year in which he contributed chapters on historic local crimes to two books: *Facets of Crime* and *Murder in the Westcountry*. Busier than ever, he also saw two small publications into print.

First, he edited a booklet, *Ton-Up for Somerset*, celebrating the county cricket club's centenary. In this, unlike in the worlds of aviation and children's writing, he was completely at home:

> An invitation to edit this publication was too good to miss. I didn't want it to be too formal or stuffy. This is a modest record of an extraordinary county whose cricket over the years has been outrageously bad and electrifyingly good. Often, alas, in the same match. At times, the cricket has been touched by genius. Such sublime talent does not apparently bring championship pennants. It does bring the warm glow of affection. I believe the pages of this book reflect that affection. They are full of memories – and humanity.

Then he combined forces with two other West Country sports writers, Alan Gibson and Derek Robinson, to produce *Game for Anything*, a booklet featuring a pot-pourri of sporting articles, accompanied by cheerful cartoons. Selling at 50 pence, with much of the cost offset by advertising, it sadly did not repay the time and initiative that David invested in it.

A light-hearted vein ran through most of the pieces, not least one by David, 'Gamesmanship over Lodway', in which he recalled batting at the village ground when the low sun was shining into his eyes and 'Windy' Thomas – 'who had once played for Somerset at the age of 16 and was now a bank manager' – was 'tossing his dollies into the clouds'.

More intriguing, in light of the pleasure David gained in later years from the company of fellow cricket reporters, is the feature in which he compares cricket's press boxes unfavourably with those in soccer, expressing his dislike of the snobbery and 'inflated literary egos' to be found among the cricket writers of the time.

Following the success of Bill Andrews' book, David attempted to interest publishers in a similar volume of reminiscences by Fred Ford, who had managed both the Bristol soccer clubs, City and Rovers, in the 1960s. Like Andrews, Ford had a fund of good stories, and David set to work on shaping them into a book, to be called 'Laughter In My Boots'. But once more he had no success. 'He does not appear to be one of the major names in football,' wrote one publisher.

Another failure came when, tapping into his own enthusiasm as an occasional conjuror, David pitched to publishers a collaboration with the magician and 'mentalist' David Berglas.

David had long learned to be philosophical about rejection, never letting its prospect discourage him from trying again. In 1977 his book *Ladies' Mile*, based on the memories of Victoria Hughes, was published by a small local firm. The next year the same publishers commissioned him to write *Gardening My Way* for John Abrams, HTV West's expert gardener.

These were local books, but he reached a wider audience with his next venture – with Viv Richards. The young cricketer, at the peak of his powers, was not a conversationalist, nor full of anecdotes like Bill Andrews or Fred Ford, but David worked hard to round out what he was offered. He was given only three weeks to produce the book, and he came close to giving up when the cricketer failed to turn up for a crucial session at his house.

> Against my nature, I went for him. I knew he valued family life so hesitantly I played my sentimental card. "My wife had prepared a special West Indian lunch for you *(true)* and my children, Mark and Julia, have been waiting all day with their autograph books *(equally true)*. And you've let them down."

With Richards suitably contrite, 'The book marginally met its deadline.'

There followed *Zed*, the autobiography of another overseas star who had lit up West Country cricket, Zaheer Abbas of Gloucestershire. In his contribution to Zaheer's benefit brochure, David reflected on such books:

> I must admit I enjoy writing under someone else's name. It's rather challenging and I can relish the anonymity of the strong views I am putting down on paper. In between my journalistic chores I've ghosted for comedians, convicts, one millionaire industrialist (that wasn't, alas, too profitable!), a lavatory attendant, professional footballers and cricketers.
>
> In all cases the work has been carried out with conscientious enthusiasm and a rigid determination not to hoodwink the public. Always the published words have been based on lengthy interviews and an open and friendly liaison with my 'subject'.
>
> I don't like the word 'ghost'. Since last summer I have been co-operating with Zaheer on his book – the result is a collaboration. He has spent hours talking into a cassette microphone. My job has been to listen to the tapes and put Zed's memories into a chronological sequence. To give the story a narrative, if you like.

After *Zed* came *Skateaway*, a book of instruction by the Olympic gold-medal skater Robin Cousins, who had been born in the maternity ward where two days earlier Anne had given birth to Mark.

In these years, when David had not established his reputation as an author, he took the work he was offered, and he continued to do that. Perhaps at times he was too ready to accept projects that took him away from what he enjoyed most, but he was never arrogant. He had known enough rejection not to assume that there would always be work for him.

He wrote a 40th anniversary book for the Lord's Taverners charity, he set down the privately published life story of a local businessman Leslie Gardiner, and, in the aftermath of the extraordinary success of the cricket umpire 'Dickie' Bird's autobiography, he was asked by fellow umpire David Shepherd to collaborate on a similar volume.

Closer to home, when son Mark was compiling *Rough and Smooth*, a history of cider making, David added his distinctive touch to the writing:

> My invitation is to share a sentimental stroll around the hundreds of orchards that have remained a defiant part of our landscape, meeting again some of the timeless characters who have picked the fruit, fermented the juices and quaffed in such joy from their pottery mugs.

Unfortunately David missed out on ghosting one of cinema's greatest stars:

> Roddy Bloomfield, most delightful and gregarious of London's publishers, once phoned and asked me if I was in the mood to travel at short notice to the States.
>
> "Who do you want me to see?"
>
> "Elizabeth Taylor."
>
> No bad way to begin a conversation. I immediately lied and said I was free. One of Richard Burton's brothers was ready to go into print, I was told. But it would need someone to guide his steps. It appeared that Elizabeth Taylor was prepared to offer some thoughts on the Celtic clan. The trouble was that several other publishers were aware of the proposed book. Speed was an essential part of the deal. If we were lucky, how soon might I be available to fly to see Miss Taylor?
>
> "Tomorrow," I said with a flamboyant, unconsciously affected Welsh lilt to my voice.
>
> The book went, I believe, to another publisher. I went to bed only to dream of the violet-eyed Taylor.

TWO SIDES OF THE PRESS BOX

Anything Goes (1975)

Not until I caught Christopher Hollis writing a cricket report for one of the posher Sundays on House of Commons notepaper did I realise the extent of the gulf between the inhabitants of the cricket and soccer press boxes. The two are an era, if not a century, apart. The vowels, the attitudes and the ties are completely different.

The cricket box has none of the human warmth of a Bramall Lane, Gay Meadow or even Sincil Bank. Something forbiddingly Victorian hangs ominously over the typewriters and notebooks. There is even the occasional flourish of a snuff box. A virgin copy of Wisden is handled with ecclesiastical ritual. Last season's averages are contemplated like a chapter from St Luke.

Pipe smoking is favoured; so are formal suits. The *Telegraph* crossword is ostentatiously completed between overs. The occupants tend to fall into social coteries: the pundits for instance who talk pretentiously about the days when there were no off-spinners and the pro's job was to do all the chasing in the outfield. The local scribe's observations are usually received in silence. The Lodge-like clique isn't prepared to encourage such effrontery.

The Saturday-only essayists, a few of them former amateur county cricketers, don't claim to be journalists. Professional newspaper terms are alien to them. They have no wish to know what is meant by Monday morning beats. One sees them cringe at the occasional split infinitive as dictated, usually off the cuff, over one of the press box lines by the evening paper man in his prosaic, unadorned style. They deprecate the chummy pop-paper vogue.

It's journalism's biggest snobbery, worse than that of the denizens of Thomson House who retreat to the lavatories with the *Daily Mirror* for their intellectual elevenses. The hacks and the 'guest' writers are mutually suspicious and disrespectful. The snobbery is indeed two-way and the regulars have their fun at the end of the day when the covers are being placed across the square and the perspiring fielders are downing their first pints. This is when the gentry of the press box are tentatively approaching the phones, armed with a scant knowledge of the internal workings of newspaper offices. Their pedantic deliveries must stimulate a wide range of emotions from the earthy copy-takers on the other end of the line. Tempers are inclined to fray over a nebulous classical quotation that would have been better left at Balliol.

Soccer, although currently acceptable by the intelligentsia, is socially removed from cricket's leisured, contemplative ways. The press box is correspondingly more proletarian, with a homely cuppa at half-time or maybe a hot oxo. We pass our fags round with greater spontaneity and indulge in amicable banter. At Canterbury, Bath or Worcester, with their Godly environs, the cricket writers are inevitably inhibited. Not so Roker Park where we unselfconsciously admire a comely adornment to the stand. This is Association Football, with the players kissing each other like enlightened consenting adults and the reporters swapping Rabelaisian wit in beery bonhomie as they squeeze into their confined seating.

The soccer boxes are busier. Those hungry phones shrill incessantly for sports page fodder. And the arguments continue for 20 minutes, better than an Oxford teach-in and more honest, about whether the final pass really did come from the wing-half. Afterwards there we are again, converging on the manager. We call him by his Christian name and hold on mentally to any dressing-room epigram as he emits his excuses and expletives for another home defeat.

Soccer, comparatively speaking, is a game of short, jerky movements which despite the sophistication of modern tactics has fewer subtleties than cricket. It is swept along by a crowd's passions. The performers resort to histrionics; the referees are subjected to withering insult. In this context, the game's writers are apt to be suitably staccato, brash and pithy in style. Their reports are read in the saloon bar on Saturday night or over a Sunday lunch-time drink.

The nature of cricket is vastly different. The game flows and meanders, full of poetry, lending itself to romanticism and long words. Its atmosphere, in relation to soccer, is sepulchral. And the Saturday essayists, relishing their weekly quota of therapy and this outlet for inflated literary egos, tend to write about everything but the match. They write in meticulous longhand, slipping by the second paragraph – if not before – into self-indulgent autobiography. You need to be a discerning reader to discover any reference to Kitchen's hundred.

If I betray a soccer bias, it is not intentional. I am in love with cricket, too: with its tempo and eccentricities. But I am not wholly in love with its irregular chroniclers. Perhaps one day a cricket essayist with a warm heart will extend a hand and lead me to the bar after the final over. Over our ale, we could trade metaphors for intimate secrets on how to butter up irate newspaper telephonists. The scope is limitless – and we could both benefit. One distant day I might even be lent House of Commons notepaper. Then, seduced by my traditional enemies in the press box, I shall liken the footballers of deposed Barrow and Workington to the gladiators, recapture a Shakespeare sonnet as the pale winter sun brightens a dour defensive battle … and simply throw in the centre-forward's six goals as an afterthought.

GHOST-WRITTEN BOOKS
Viv Richards
The Antiguan cricketer on his early days in England in 'Viv Richards' (1979)

For some weeks after I arrived in Bath I was lost. The weather was cold and uninviting. And not even those lovely terraces in Bath look good when the sun isn't shining. Apart from all that, there was something lacking. Remember I was in my early 20s, a virile black athlete.

Finding girlfriends in a place like Bath, which is dominated by an Abbey and middle-aged, middle-class people understandably set in their ways, wasn't easy. There weren't so many eligible girls of my age group around as far as I could see. Most of those who came to the Lansdown club already had their boy friends or husbands. And I was, after all, a young black man among a lot of white people.

I think there was a touch of desperation in the way I at last found the courage to approach Mr Creed. He'd been taking a fatherly interest in me and seemed the right person to offer me a little guidance on matters personal as well as cricketing. I chose the right moment when we were alone. He knew I wanted to say something to him but couldn't find the right words.

'What is it, Vivian?'

'Well, sir, it's – well – yes, you know, I've been in this country for more than six weeks and …'

'And what, Vivian?'

'I haven't met a lady, you know. Em – can you do anything for me?'

I don't know what the Lansdown chairman thought. He'd already paid for my air fare from Antigua and was trying to turn me into a cricket star. He'd even let me stay in his nice home for a few days.

We have laughed about it many times since. I suppose I thought he had all the right connections. In fact, he didn't let me down.

John Abrams
The television gardener on his philosophy of life in 'Gardening My Way' (1978)

I work in the garden when the mood dictates. And that is the advice I give everyone else. Never let it be a drudgery.

Nature can be a marvellous friend – or a tough adversary. That, to me, is the fun of it. You can never win 'em all. Like life itself, you win some and you lose some. I've no complaints about that. What a dull old place this would be if everything went right.

Fred Ford

The football manager on being Bill Shankly's assistant at Carlisle United in 'Laughter in my Boots', a part-written and unpublished memoir (1975)

Bill's orderliness and tidiness was to the point of fanaticism. In those days the stockings would come back from the laundry shrunk, especially in the feet. He had special templates made out of three-ply wood, the size of a leg and foot. As soon as the stockings came back I would put them on the templates. One could also see if there were any holes. Many a time he would take the stockings home and darn a hole or two himself. He never told anyone. It was just done.

We visited all the lodgings in which the players stayed. One particular house was slightly bigger, a nice one. The woman and her married daughter showed us over. Would we like to see the bedroom? Yes, please. Very good .. twin beds ... nice big room. Then Bill lifted up the couterpane and muttered, "No chamber." The woman said, "Oh no, the bathroom is just down the hall," to which Bill said, "Players cannot walk down the hallway on a Friday night. They might get a draught. Would you put a chamber under the bed, please?" He said to me, "Check on that, Freddy."

The smallest detail was the biggest. He was unbelievable.

David Shepherd

The cricket umpire on the Old Trafford Test in 2000 when, with England batting to save the game on the last day, he failed to spot that three of the deliveries that took wickets were no-balls (2002)

The sun is shining in Devon and I'm up before 6 a.m. to do my paper round for my brother Bill. Then it's a brisk walk with Skip, the dog. I'm quiet and a bit preoccupied as the big match approaches. Yes, I'm a worrier. Nothing changes.

You never quite know what is going to happen with Pakistan, of course. They have so much talent – pace, spin, wristy shots, but they're also the most volatile of cricketing nations. Jabbering away excitedly in a language I can't understand.

As I pack my bag I have absolutely no idea, of course, what a traumatic Test (in the personal sense) is facing me. Especially the last horrendous day. It's going to turn into the lowest point in my cricketing career, leaving me utterly depressed and perilously close to giving up Test and international umpiring on the spot.

15
Harold Gimblett

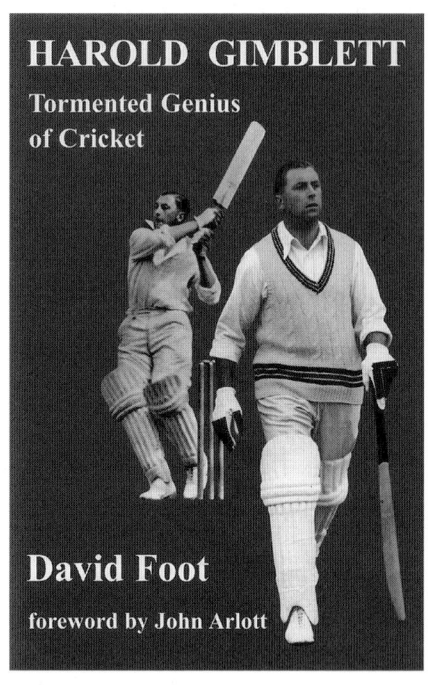

The batsman and the hospital patient

By the mid-1970s David was an experienced ghost-writer. He had also guided the former Somerset cricketer Bill Andrews' autobiography into print. So he was a natural choice when Andrews' old team-mate Harold Gimblett looked for help in writing up his life. Gimblett had been David's first cricketing hero, and he was keen to open up about the mental stresses of cricket – so it was a project that was tailor-made for David.

Gimblett set to work, talking into cassette tapes. His mood, never cheerful for long, grew steadily darker, his speech more rambling and incoherent, till finally he committed suicide. It was months later when David discovered that the tapes had survived and, with the approval of Gimblett's wife Rita, he set to work on the emotionally and professionally challenging task of shaping it all into a book. No longer a ghosted autobiography, it was eventually published in 1982, the first book to bear David's sole name as author.

Heinemann, the publishers, had hesitated before accepting the manuscript. Gimblett was a largely forgotten figure, and David an unknown writer. The book did, however, have a foreword by John Arlott:

> This is the story of a life which, within the small world of cricket, ascended to the heights: but, at the level where life is truly lived, plumbed the ultimate depth. Few would devote so much time and trouble to research as Mr Foot has done – not heavy-handedly, but in making contact with the right witnesses; and in uncovering balancing, and counter-balancing, evidence. Those who knew Harold Gimblett can shed a not unworthy tear into this book; those who did not will find themselves moved by a story the more affecting for being recorded with such dignity.

The book was never a best-seller. Yet, written at a time when mental health was rarely discussed – more rarely still in the world of sport, where such talk was seen as an admission of weakness – the book broke new ground. To this day it features regularly near the top of lists of Greatest Cricket Books. In 2003, after many years out of print, I published a new edition, for which David wrote additional material.

The story of Gimblett's century on debut, in a match in which – rejected by the county – he was playing only because no one else was around, is as close to fairy tale as any in cricket history. Yet it led not to joy but to an inner torment which David captured with humane sensitivity. Both Harold Pinter and John Cleese were keen to create a stage play from the book. But, like Keith Waterhouse's scripts for *Country Reporter* a few years later, nothing ever came of the idea.

THE GENESIS OF THE BOOK

Harold Gimblett – Tormented Genius of Cricket (1982)

Gimblett was my hero; and so he was of every other West Country boy who believed cricket was the best game God ever invented. But schoolboys can be conveniently selective in their idolatry: it does not usually extend beyond the scoreboard. It is based on wondrous innings and tales of outrageous aggression that are exaggerated each time in the telling. We accepted without question that Harold Gimblett ritualistically converted every opening delivery into a half-volley; that he tamed a tiring Larwood, mastered the fiery Nichols and Farnes; that he despatched Miller and Lindwall with disdain; that he was the man to put Ramadhin and Valentine in their place.

Hero worship is healthy; but such doting dreams are fragile. Harold in the flesh, as I discovered some years later, was not always an engaging person. Once during a county match at Street, he stalked to the press tent and rounded on an erstwhile colleague of mine, A.C.H. Smith, the Bristol writer, because he had dared to criticise in print the state of the wicket at Millfield where at that time Gimblett was employed. The reprimand was public and condescending, and it took some years before I privately forgave him.

This book is not a homage. The forthright Gimblett would have deprecated that. I hope it will help to show what a complex person he was and that his troubled mind, which eventually led him to suicide in March 1978, was largely responsible for his vicissitudes of mood, the brusque retorts and the overriding pessimism. There is also much evidence that he could be a man of considerable charm and kindness.

Two years before he died he phoned me one evening from his home, then at Minehead. Would I help him write a book? 'I don't want it to be like any of the other cricket books. I want the public to know what it is really like being a professional sportsman, when you're a worrier. The mental battles for me have been enormous and maybe it would be a good idea to put it on record.' I got the impression that he also saw the exercise as a form of therapy.

We had a long, relaxed conversation and I was concerned about the mounting phone bill. He laughed and said we were on the cheap rate. It was good to hear him laugh, something he had done less and less in recent years. I knew of his increasing anxieties about money matters – unnecessarily so – and I was reassured that he had deliberately chosen when he should ring me.

He told me he had bought a small cassette recorder and I encouraged him to start putting thoughts, as they occurred to him, down on tape. We talked again on the phone from time to time. 'I'm doing it in the middle of the night when I can't sleep … It's going to be very personal.' We agreed that, when he felt he had said all he wanted to, we would have a meeting. He would let me have the various cassettes, and I could use them as the basis for a book.

The meeting never took place. There were intermittent phone calls between us, and he moved to Verwood. I waited for the summons. Then, with a ghastly suddenness, I read of his death.

I assumed that the cassettes, real or mythical, had in effect died with him. But several months later, a relative wrote to me to say they existed. At that point I did not know Mrs Gimblett and, after a decent pause, I approached her rather diffidently. We began to meet; she was helpful and co-operative. With her, I returned to Harold's birthplace at Bicknoller. We walked along the sylvan lanes where they used to do their courting.

At home I listened to the cassettes. They were like very private documents that he wanted now to make public. They were subjective: astute, perceptive, belligerent, unhappy and at times on the point of being irrational. Occasionally I found myself fidgeting in the way of a person caught eavesdropping. The moods were all there, elation and wretchedness. But his cricketing achievements, remembered with consistent modesty, seemed subordinate to other aspects of his life.

The final cassettes, heavy with despair and with Harold's voice trailing away into little pits of agonised reverie, contrasted sharply with his almost chirpy opening words:

> David, this is my attempt at a possible book. The only thing I'm absolutely certain of is the title. At the ripe old age of 62, I feel the title must be 'No More Bouncers' … not that I was ever afraid of 'em.

He took more than his share of bouncers, on and off the field. But this is a slightly different book and the title has been changed. Harold's brutally honest words were the starting point. I have honoured his wish not to make this simply a cricketing record. Rather have I tried to explain why he chose to be dismissive about his own vast talents and the game which gave him a living. He ended up with a contempt for cricket, and I have attempted to untangle some of the complexes that caused this. It was apparently no great thrill for him to play for his country. By the end, as he leaned on his stick and hobbled along the Verwood country roads, he almost appeared to hate the game. He would cut short any conversation about it; sentimental allusions to his maiden century made him both embarrassed and angry. Harold had rejected cricket, the sport he adorned with such dynamic and joyful panache.

FICTION AT FROME

Harold Gimblett – Tormented Genius of Cricket (1982)

West Country schoolboys came to recite the facts and circumstances of Gimblett's magnificent and impudent century of 18th May 1935 with a local vigour never remotely matched in the ritual of the twice-times table. It almost became part of the required curriculum.

The century belonged to fiction. The plot was altogether too thrillingly fashioned: a confectioned scenario that mocked credulity. It came from the genre of sporting stories of excessive heroism on the field, written by Victorian and Edwardian clergy, warmed by their imagination as they sat in draughty rectories. Young readers enjoyed but did not need to believe. It was all part of the romance of cricket.

Yet it did happen, at Frome. A village lad from the Quantocks, turned down by his county, was suddenly asked to play because no one else could be found to make up the eleven. For once, not even an extra from Somerset's intermittent band of strolling players, amateurs who appeared from abroad or the pages of Debrett for a jolly game or two between country house parties, could be spirited up at such short notice. So there was John Daniell saying, without too much conviction: 'Do you know where Frome is, young Gimblett? Can you get there on your own?'

Harold was not too sure that he could. He stammered that perhaps he could catch one very early bus to Bridgwater, and then another to Frome. The secretary pondered the geographical complications. 'You'll never arrive on time that way. Get to Bridgwater by nine o'clock and I'll ask Luckes to pick you up in his car.'

Few centuries have been documented with more detail and loving labour. There have been embellishments at a few thousand cricket dinners since then. The commas and the colour of Harold's pocket handkerchief may have varied slightly, but never the joyful spirit of the day's theatre.

It was a dynamic piece of fledgling cricket by a player so unknown that the scorecard could give no initials for him. Yet his reputation was to be established forever, by what happened on that bitterly cold May afternoon at Frome, where the tents billowed noisily as they do at an early Spring point-to-point. White railings encircled the small playing area, adding to the hint of a rural racing scene.

Frome was proud of its one county match a season. The town had a small population but a lively and loyal support for Somerset cricket. Facilities on the ground were modest, with plenty of functional corrugated iron, and wooden benches transported in for the occasion. There was no room on the scoreboard for individual innings. The voices around the boundary were pure, throaty Somerset: but different from Taunton, Weston or Yeovil. And different from Bicknoller.

On his cassettes, Gimblett talked ramblingly of many things. He chose to give only a brief, factual account of his century at Frome. It occupied just a minute of reminiscence. The dismissive attitude was part of him and we shall return to it. Mrs Gimblett told me: 'I kept the cuttings. Harold would have destroyed them.'

It would be quite wrong for me also to dismiss his maiden innings for Somerset, although in the ways of folklore, everyone will know that he was up well before six a.m. on that Saturday morning and narrowly missed the bus to Bridgwater. The next bus was in two hours' time.

He had a little all-purpose bag within which – you would never have guessed – was his own bruised and discoloured bat and a few sandwiches considerately dropped in by his mother. Maternal kindness had also ensured freshly creased flannels and a clean shirt. He stood, a forlorn figure, on the narrow country road and wondered what he should do now. He started walking, vaguely in the direction of Bridgwater, and then heard a lorry from behind. Harold thumbed it down, something he had never done before. The dialogue that followed had an endearing quality to it.

'Sorry, I've just missed the bus.'
'OK, jump in. Where are you going?'
'To Frome.'
'Why?'
'To play cricket.'
'Who for?'
'Somerset.'
'Oh, ah!'

The lorry driver did not believe Gimblett. How could he have? On his own admission, Harold looked like a wide-eyed innocent, in trouble because he was late for work.

Wally Luckes was waiting for him at Bridgwater, and they reached the ground in good time. Some supporters were already in their places. They recognised the little wicket-keeper and offered a cheery greeting. No one recognised Gimblett.

Then I met the Essex players. Jack O'Connor ... Laurie Eastman ... Morris Nichols ... Ray and Peter Smith ... Tommy Wade ...

Tom Pearce ... I realised I was scared stiff. Wally Luckes gave me the only bit of advice. 'Peter Smith will always bowl you a googly so be ready for it.' I didn't even know what a googly was – I'd never seen one. Wally patiently explained that it looked like a leg-spinner but went the other way.

Reggie Ingle was the Somerset captain and he put Gimblett at number eight. He won the toss and was soon regretting it. Nichols was using all his natural speed, as well as a biting wind that was sweeping across the ground. Jack Lee, Ingle and White were all caught at slip and Somerset were 35 for three. You could hear the groans around the boundary. By lunch, Frank Lee and C.C.C. (Box) Case were also out and the score was 105 for five.

The Bath amateur H.D. Burrough quickly followed. At 2.20pm 20-year-old Harold Gimblett, head down and already pessimistic about what he imagined was a token appearance in county cricket, meandered to the wicket to join Wellard. Someone in the crowd shouted: 'Leave it to Arthur, son.'

During the lunch interval, Wellard had put a friendly hand on Gimblett's shoulder. 'Don't think much of your bat, cock. Why don't you borrow my spare one?' And so he did.

Peter Smith sniffed a novice. His third ball to Gimblett was a googly. The young batsman had not spotted it but he pushed it away to mid-wicket and was off the mark. In his second over from Smith, Gimblett straight-drove to the boundary. That felt good. The Frome supporters rather approved of the way he did that. Who was this lad? Gimb-Gimblett or something? Wasn't he the lad who was always whacking sixes in village matches?

The likeable Peter Smith chuckled silently to himself. He summoned up additional wiles. But so much for cunning. His fourth over after lunch cost 15 runs, all of them to Gimblett. When the leg-break was fractionally over-pitched, the young batsman put his left foot down and heaved the spinning ball over mid-off for six. It landed on the top of the beer tent, a marquee temporarily deserted as the rubicund drinkers moved outside to savour this jaunty newcomer.

Gimblett suddenly realised he was enjoying himself. Nichols was by far the fastest bowler he had ever met, but the young batsman had the clear eyes and nimble feet to keep him out of trouble. In nine overs, Somerset added 69 runs; 48 of them came from Gimblett. He was actually outscoring Wellard, and not many managed that. The ever-bronzed Arthur, jangling the loose change in his flannel trousers, ready for the next poker school, only smiled.

The half-century came with a six. It had taken 28 minutes, and he had received 33 balls. By now the spectators had shed their reserve: they were cheering every shot. The beer was left undrunk.

Wellard miscalculated an off-break from Vic Evans and was stumped. But then came his look-alike and inseparable mate, Andrews. In between, Luckes had been bowled by Nichols, back with the new ball.

New ball? You couldn't afford such niceties around the village greens of West Somerset. Gimblett threshed his way on, swinging and sweeping and driving whenever he could. There was hardly a false shot. Essex fielders rued the short boundary; they were generous enough to applaud some of the sixes.

Nichols dug one in short and the Somerset number eight, with ludicrous time to spare, hooked it for four. Then, oblivious to pace, Gimblett took two more runs through the covers.

He had no idea how many he had scored; the scoreboard gave the minimum of information. But the spectators soon told him. The cover drive had brought him his century. It had been scored out of 130 and had taken 63 minutes. As the fastest hundred of the season it earned him the Lawrence Trophy.

> It was, I suppose, one of those days you dream of. I can't work it out. I took all the praise but Bill Andrews, who got 71, was even faster in his scoring. I savoured the moment – but loathed the publicity that followed.

Gimblett gave a simple return catch when he had scored 123 in 79 minutes.

*

Fleet Street was engaged at that time in a circulation battle of ruthless proportions. Pop journalism carried with it gimmicks and ballyhoo in the bid for new readers. Gimblett's triumph had immense human interest. The photographers and the feature writers turned up at the farm. He posed reluctantly and hated the whole thing.

In a newspaper article, Jack Hobbs congratulated Harold but tempered his compliments by saying it left the young Somerset batsman with a reputation he might have difficulty sustaining. Gimblett knew that only too well.

THE EXPLANATIONS?

Harold Gimblett – Tormented Genius of Cricket (1982)

There is some evidence that he relished controversy, maybe because of his condition, even needed it. He refused to suffer fools and was both impatient and angry with those who, with gossipy mischief, looked for additional flaws in his make-up. When he was living at Barton St David, someone said to a friend of his: 'What a shame Harold drank his way out of first-class cricket.' It was an absurd notion, however much his dreamy demeanour and extremes of manner planted dark hints in the naïve mind of a spectator.

Gimblett's behaviour, with its disconcertingly fluctuating moods, was for more than forty years a source of pain and puzzlement to others. He took many pills, consulted many doctors and maybe confided to too few friends.

Explanation of his mental condition is far from easy. Dr K.C.P. Smith, a consultant psychiatrist in the West Country, has had a great deal of experience in advising on the anxieties of professional sportsmen. In the Fifties and Sixties he was medical adviser for Gloucestershire CCC. Players, not infrequently, came to him to discuss everything from loss of form to insecurity. He found cricketers to be happiest when on the field; there was too much time left for them simply to sit and mope.

Much of Dr Smith's work in recent years has been concerned with the whole spectrum of personality disorders and he has developed the application of a new psychological Reversal Theory, offering fresh explanations for behaviour traits in various walks of life, including sport, the arts and religion. His theory is that the subject has a tendency to treat life as a kind of game, in which he strives to reach feelings of high excitement or arousal. 'Any fall-off is felt as boredom. Some people find themselves constantly bored and frustrated, and they describe this as being depressed. They often think the remedy is tablets.'

A low-key man like Gimblett, he said, needed high excitement. When he failed to reach it, he became phobic: hence talk of too much batting responsibility, ill health, money anxieties. 'He had strong "anti" feelings of aggression. He enjoyed hitting a ball around the ground, having revenge on the world at the same time. He could become enjoyably paranoid – as in the case of the MCC – and play a new type of game against the establishment. But he couldn't keep it up, so became depressed again.'

TWENTY YEARS ON

Harold Gimblett – Tormented Genius of Cricket (revised edition, 2003)

Up to 1982 there had not been so many books which set out to explore the mental anxieties of a first-class cricketer. Runs and wickets have never been a preoccupation of mine. The face of the player, hunched in a corner on the home team's balcony after his latest batting calamity, has been. The true drama of cricket, like no other sport, is played out inside the head. Cricket is intended to be played in the sunshine. It should shimmer with poetry, with relaxed smiles and lyrical images. But at the higher levels there is too much about which to fret and ruminate. It can never quite be called, whatever the romance that affectedly envelops it, a happy sport. The long history of personal animosity, class divisions, insecurity and at times the tragic consequences, bear this out.

*

In the twenty years since the book came out, when driving to or from the county ground in Taunton, I've recurrently pondered still the burdensome bitch that is cricket when the sublime game becomes eroded by money, and physical and psychological demands. Long after Gimblett silently packed his bags and walked out of the county ground for the last time as a player, two capable, intelligent members of the Somerset team, Nigel Popplewell and Nick Folland, decided they had had enough. It was no longer fun to hump a coffin to the other end of the country. In Popplewell's case, he was also probably sick of the incestuous club politics. He got down to a legal career instead, and Folland, having sampled first-class cricket and discovered he could hold his own, returned to teaching. There were aspects of the nominally joyous game from which they temperamentally recoiled.

*

The book brought me an immediate mailbag of emotional reaction. I received nearly 250 letters. A surprising number of readers said the biography made them cry – and these were, I imagine, often unsentimental souls confessing with honesty. One wrote: 'I find it sadder than Hamlet – in fact it has affinities with the Prince.'

The letter I think I valued most came from Harold's brother Dennis, a clergyman who had emigrated with his family to Australia. He had been especially honest in his assessment, doing his best to detach himself from sibling bonds. He wrote of the way I had gone about my biography, in tackling 'the mental and emotional conflicts which he had carried onto the field of battle – not only of cricket but, to a lesser extent, of everyday social intercourse and domestic life.'

His way of seeing, evaluating and talking about people and events used at times to baffle me. As a result of the book, I think I now understand his point of view more clearly. It is a story of a person who strove to release himself from the chains of insecurity and inferiority. What emerges is a picture of Harold, well recognised by the family while revealing much deeper insights into his character than we appreciated before. My wife thought the most valuable part of the book was the way it brought out his caring nature.

Twenty years on, our affection for Gimbo hasn't lessened. He would have blazed away today in one-day cricket and hated it. His contempt for authority and the stiff shirts in the Long Room, as he saw it, would have been as constant as ever. He wouldn't have had much time for the ECB and central contracts. New technology would have driven him to distraction. Politically he would still have been in some confusion – halfway between the minor public school and the 'gentleman farmer' tag on the one hand, and his rebellious Socialist leanings on the other.

Yet what a player (when he chose to be). And what a riddle, endlessly absorbing in his contradictions.

He was once invited to appear as a guest on the popular radio Saturday night *Sports Report*, fronted in those days by Eamonn Andrews.

'If you had your time over again, would you want to be a cricketer?'
Pause ... 'Yes.'
'Anything different from what you've experienced?'
'Yes. I'd make sure I played as an amateur.'
Gasps in the studio.
'Why is that?'
'Because you make more money then.'

A riddle, as ever. Hadn't he told his team-mates enough times that he didn't enjoy being a player? Could the Eamonn Andrews line of questioning have brought out that lurking element of snobbery that his Somerset mates used to detect? Or was he taking the opportunity of a dig at some of those swanky amateurs, who stayed in the best hotels and were supposedly adept at manipulating their expenses?

For Harold Gimblett, a spot of class-conscious rhetoric, tinged with controversy, wasn't to be missed. You seldom got an anodyne statement – or a boring innings – from him. That was part of the genius of the man. Flawed, fragile, bellicose and timelessly brilliant.

NEARLY A STAGE PLAY

Footsteps from East Coker (2010)

Years after my review of his first play, 'The Room', I received a letter from Harold Pinter. He had read a cricket book of mine, based on the gifted and finally tragic life of Somerset's Harold Gimblett. He had, as a cricketing addict, liked the book and saw its potential as a stage play. "What about a one-man character study? The biography, which ends in suicide, has all the strands of a powerful play."

It was marvellously flattering. He said he was too busy at the moment to pursue the idea but, if I shared his enthusiasm, he would come back to me. He never did.

John Cleese was another to see stage possibilities in the sad life and death of Test cricketer Gimblett. He was as eager as Pinter had been. He said he was coming down to Weston-super-Mare for the cricket festival and might it be possible to have a professional chat. By now, my private excitement as a relatively unworldly reporter was understandably growing.

We met at Clarence Park in the tea interval. Autograph seekers had spotted him and were making life intolerable for him. He released choice words and, in a flash of manic temperament not too removed from the *Fawlty Towers* maelstrom, took his famous long, spindly legs off the heightened wooden seat, enough for me hesitantly to introduce myself.

"Ah yes, we've things to discuss. Come to the Grand Atlantic this evening for a drink. Half past eight. We can't talk with all this hubbub."

He had calmed down by then and called in on the way to the hotel to see his mother, who was staying in a local residential home. Clearly sharing my own affection for Somerset cricket and the wondrous batting of Gimblett – at least on one of the ex-cricketer's good days – Cleese pondered the various directions that a stage drama like this one could be explored and written. I got the firm impression that he warmed increasingly to being involved himself in a play about the county's 'tormented genius'. We talked for a long time, or rather John Cleese did most of the talking. He, like Pinter, was too busy at the moment to tackle the project. But he thought he would be back to me. The world of dramatic writing is caught up, alas, in a thousand spurts of transitory effervescence. For so many reasons, good ideas get discarded. The life and death of Harold Gimblett never quite made it beyond the stage of spinning round in the actor's fertile head.

16
Allsorts in a Busy Working Life

An unlikely pairing: Gerry Gow and Lauren Bacall

John Betjeman in old age

Through the 1970s and into the 1980s David was working at full stretch, not only producing books and writing for a range of newspapers and magazines but also working for radio and television. So demanding did his workload become that Anne insisted on continental rather than English camping holidays for the family – to put David out of reach of the telephone. Yet, even when he and Anne made a trip to India in 1982, he made notes with a view to writing an article when he got home.

When *Radio Bristol* was launched in 1970, David was in demand as a reporter, mainly for sport. He also created several half-hour features, including one close to his heart on the years of the *Bristol Evening World*. It begins with David's voice at its most portentous: 'When The Ink Turned Red. The story of one Bristol newspaper – its publicised birth and inevitable death. The beginning and end of the World.' The soundtrack then switches to a street-seller calling out the headlines of the paper's last ever edition: 'Late win by City at Halifax ... Smallpox scare.'

David also undertook broadcasts for Hospital Radio and Caribbean Radio and was a reader for Talking Newspapers for The Blind.

Then local television became a strand of his working life: researching and writing features, also appearing in front of camera as an interviewer. His files bulge with scripts: on subjects ranging from the 1685 Battle of Sedgemoor, the Bristol-born pianist Russ Conway and the music hall entertainer Randolph Sutton to topical issues such as dole queues, gambling and glue-sniffing.

> Trowbridge ... well, we think of the beer, and we think of the bacon. Sausages and dairy products. Bowling clubs – mothers' unions. Good conventional signs of Wiltshire life – a town partly dependent on the rich farmland around it. On the surface a long way from young people with festering anger about having nothing to do ... a long way from glue sniffing.

Glossy local magazines turned to David to profile towns and cities, schools and theatres, and here his eye for the distinctive character of a place would often penetrate deeper than the flannel expected by local dignitaries. Fortunately the editor of *Gloucestershire Life* stood by him when the Tewkesbury Civic Society complained that his feature had misrepresented the town. David, despite his mild manner, knew when to stand his ground, and his letter of reply combined sentences of apparent apology – 'I am sorry you did not like the article ... I am equally sorry that, in your view, I failed to do the subject justice' – with a robust defence of his approach:

> I must dispute your suggestion that I failed to interview key people. Maybe our ideas of interesting people do not coincide. As a trained journalist, I do not consider you have always to go to prominent people in 'key' positions to capture the spirit and essence of a town. I did attempt consciously to take an honest and representative view of Tewkesbury – and the town does not frankly revolve round the Civic Society, eminently worthwhile as this organisation may be.

For a while these profiles provided a strand of regular work, with the *Financial Times* commissioning lengthy features on Bristol and Cardiff.

The request to write the preface to a book of photographs of 'Bristol in the early 1960s' provided an opportunity for David to reflect on the changes he had witnessed in the twenty years since he worked for the *Evening World*:

> There are 272 plates, all taken by the author himself. Many of the scenes are mundane, even unbeautiful; they make up a piece of comparatively recent but too easily forgotten, local history. Here is the Hippodrome when it still had its evocative hat on. Here is Ladies' Mile when it still had its embracing trees (if not its nocturnal ladies). Here are the vegetable crates that we used to have to step over in Baldwin Street. Mr Winstone has the knack of capturing the ordinary – and now fond memories turn it into the extraordinary. So much of what we see in the book has gone for ever.
>
> Nostalgia reaps a dozen different emotions. My own naïve observation: can Bristol really have changed so much so quickly?

This fascination with a lost past is never far away in David's writing, yet he is quick to counterpoint it with some down-to-earth realism.

> A City Council which blindly extols the virtues of a crumbling heritage to the cussed exclusion of the motor car has neither the logic nor the vision to handle my rates. The throbbing vibrations of Bristol's lorries, buses and cars simply could not be ignored.

Almost a lone voice in the 1960s, railing against what David called 'the fashion for demolition', was John Betjeman, whom David arranged to visit shortly before his death in 1984. It was possibly the poet's last interview, recalled poignantly by David in a feature twenty years later.

Then there was his opportunistic meal with the film star Lauren Bacall, which David remembered in one of his last feature articles for the *Guardian*.

From the Battle of Sedgemoor to glue-sniffing in Trowbridge, from John Betjeman to Lauren Bacall, the range of David's writing was wide.

CHELTENHAM

from an article on the town, Gloucestershire Life, June 1970

Cheltenham is elegant and it is gracious. That gets rid, in one initial swoop, of the two adjectives that tumble inevitably into the context. A town has to live with its adjectives. And this lovely Gloucestershire centre basks or squirms, according to the individual point of view, in them.

Those who tend to ridicule the town do so, one suspects, largely out of envy. They mock a leisured haughtiness and a supposed cucumber-sandwich decorum. They imply that the Regency rows are still peopled exclusively by crusty old military men and genteel, if arthritic, old ladies who originally gravitated here to take the medicinal water.

But even those who take pleasure in perpetuating this uncharitable cliché know it to be a gross inaccuracy. The old army officers and Colonial civil servants, if there are still some in the town, can't afford to live on their pensions any longer. The decorum and the gentility may remain but they are hard to discern with the naked eye.

Not really so long ago, it was a village. But suddenly it became fit for a king (every guide-book refers to the status-boosting visit of George III in 1788). It was a village no longer. Instead it presented itself as it spread its superb Regency feathers. The classic frontages remain to be admired; the architectural wizardry of the period, concentrated here in such grandeur, make the town unique.

To the occasional visitor, Cheltenham retains its Regency charm with little visible effort. In fact, it does nothing of the kind. Its buildings all went up together and now they are crumbling together.

CARDIFF

from an article on the city, Financial Times, January 1971

Cardiff, like Wales itself, is big-muscled, warm-hearted, passionate, obstinate and proud. The city is also inclined to be vulnerable. It is soft-centred and wants to be liked, although this would probably never be admitted.

In the context of character, one turns to the dockland community. Many of the homes have physically changed but they still house the acrid memories of flailing fists, off-set by the warm humanity and the unwavering loyalties. Here was racial integration in this country before its time. And the sum total of erstwhile emotions has helped to mould Cardiff's present strong, compassionate features.

LAUREN BACALL IN A TETCHY MOOD

Extracts from a feature, Western Daily Press, February 1979

Lauren Bacall was, they said, in a tetchy mood. Several frustrated photographers put it more strongly. There she was in George's, the Bristol bookshop, signing her new autobiography with nimble fingers and flashing eyes. The eyes were meant for The Media.

Miss Bacall, who has been noted for her strong language, was coldly polite. But in effect she was telling the TV men and the press cameramen that she could do without them. Which is a little odd – not to say ungrateful – from someone whose original screen image was expertly and generously promoted by newspapermen.

*

The book-signing session suddenly ended, and she was out in the street where the engine of her hired limousine was already purring. It was a case for journalistic resourcefulness at least. I jumped in beside the chauffeur.

Miss Bacall knows her Bristol. "Here several years ago, you know, I went to the Bristol Old Vic to see Peter O'Toole in Plunder."

At the Red Herring Bistro in Hotwells, she sipped her gin and tonic and ordered a Dover sole. The tension had gone. And she was prepared to analyse her attitude to the press and television.

The story recalled thirty years on

The Guardian, January 2009

In my more youthful and active journalistic days I worked best with conflicting simultaneous briefs. These involved theatre and sport. The only complication was the logistical one when I had to make the challenging choice between Gielgud declaiming or Charlie George screaming for the ball.

Last week I came across a torn and faded newspaper cutting of an eventful meeting I had in February 1979. It was with Lauren Bacall so, sentimentally at least, it was worth keeping. She was in this country to publicise her autobiography and was in a bad mood. She didn't much like journalists and, no doubt because she had left her make-up case behind in London, she was less than welcoming to half a dozen photographers and TV cameramen who had also turned up at the bookshop in Bristol.

As I arrived, weary from lugging a heavy Uher radio tape-recorder up a long hill, she was leaving. It was an unscheduled early exit. The engine of her swish limo was already purring and her step on to the pavement was as purposeful as that of any Ashton Gate striker. For one impecunious freelance, her face of thunder spelled financial disaster and panic. My presumptuous intentions counted for nothing.

If this sounds like shameless name-dropping, I apologise. But I shall eventually get to the point of this Friday-morning episode involving the style, ageless allure and histrionic range of the actress who once melted Bogart enough to become his wife. It was no time now for rerunning scenes from 'Key Largo' or 'The Big Sleep', which I had studiously researched in preparation. Instead, for one of the few times in a diverse professional life, I let my instincts take over. I jumped in beside the driver and, as if wholly dispassionate about what was happening, I directed him to a small fish restaurant a mile away. My instructions had come out with affected authority. In the back of the limo, La Bacall was spluttering her protests; a young PR woman, equally puzzled, was doing her best to placate her.

There is not a word of exaggeration in this account. The driver clearly thought I was part of the retinue. He pulled up at the restaurant and Bacall, flustered and still confused, followed us in. She rejected and then accepted a double gin, and I ordered a Dover sole for her. Blissfully, her rant at the expense of the Fourth Estate gradually subsided. Perhaps she really was, after all, 'this nice Jewish girl who had been plucked for stardom', as the book blurb told us. I got my lengthy, co-operative radio interview and enough anecdotes for a newspaper piece next morning.

By then we were on more confidential terms. "The trouble is I've got so many things on my mind – like driving back to London and catching my plane at Heathrow," she said. "I know the feeling," I replied with intimate candour. "I have to see Gerry Gow, you know. Yes, another interview." I might as well have said Stanislavsky by the silence my words created.

The revelation made no apparent impact. She must surely have heard of Gerry. Everyone in the West Country had. But I let it pass. He was now top of my agenda, this tousle-haired Glaswegian veteran of 300-plus games for Bristol City who most Saturdays left scarlet stud marks as a ritualistic parting present to his opponents. He didn't believe in fannying about in midfield. He instilled fear: plenty of raw drama there. It is unlikely Gow ever went to a Bristol Old Vic matinée on a free afternoon.

I've no idea whether Gow would be flattered to be bracketed with Bacall. Yet the two of them remain affectionately wedged, at least psychologically, in my memory. From that unconventional audience with Mrs Bogart I kept my appointment with Gerry who went on to oblige me with a goal against Ipswich the following day. I didn't keep a record of my article about him – though I don't fancy 'To Have and Have Not' warranted even a passing mention.

A TRIP TO INDIA

from an article in the Bristol Evening Post, January 1983

How will I forget the hundreds of bundles of rags sleeping in every railway station at night – and on many exposed, uneven pavements? It was the price of timeless poverty. There were the minute hovels from where wizened figures sold nuts or trinkets by day and somehow found room to curl in an unnatural heap at night.

From the comfort of my hotel window, I watched taxi-drivers crawling from their dilapidated cabs at dawn to wash under a street tap – and listless women, holding their frail babies, scavenging with dogs for food in the local dump. I knew it was an indictment of mankind. As were the long lines of money-lenders waiting like vultures to collect their dues outside office and government buildings on payday. You have to be very rich, in fact, to escape the system.

It's hard, back in relatively well-heeled Bristol, to get the sight of those millions of gentle, sunken-cheeked, helpless Indians out of my glazed eyes.

And I leave you with this unpalatable thought for 1983. Despite the increasing unemployment and decreasing compassion of government, there are still too many people in this country eating and earning far too much.

A journey to India should be obligatory for all Britain's selfish graspers – whether from Big Business, the professions or the muscle-bound unions.

LAST INTERVIEW WITH JOHN BETJEMAN

Western Daily Press, October 2004

Almost certainly the last interview given by the late Poet Laureate John Betjeman was to this newspaper. That was 20 years ago, when he was battling Parkinson's disease and trying to recover from a stroke. But the weary, watery eyes twinkled as, between long pauses, he recited snatches of humorous verses about Bristol's Pembroke Road, Bath teashops and the long lost Dilton Marsh Halt.

We were doing a series about famous people, who were encouraged to talk affectionately of West Country towns and villages that had been an influence in their lives. Sir John's undimmed regard for Bristol was well known – but would he be up to 'a gentle chat' about his favourite city, I was asked.

Back in the '60s I had trailed around the antique shops and dusty caverns stacked full of second-hand books with him in Bath, where he was then offering his rambling, eccentric wisdom to the TWW cameras. My job was to write about him. His was to chat about anything, architectural or ecclesiastical, that took his fancy. The problem for the film crew was to keep him in their sights. He'd suddenly wander off to show me a piece of porcelain "in that little shop just round the corner".

The second time around I wasn't sure he would remember me. But his secretary wrote back, inviting me to call on Sir John at his house in Chelsea: "He'd love to talk about Bristol and Bath again – if he's feeling well enough."

There was a folded wheelchair in the hallway. He was slumped in a cushioned chair behind his slightly shambling desk. He spoke slowly and with difficulty, but the mind remained sharp and contentious – and just occasionally that renowned impish or waspish sense of humour or mischief would come through.

The good-natured though rather difficult interview went on for more than an hour. He didn't seem to want me to leave, however, and surprised me when he shouted to his secretary that it was time for elevenses. She appeared not with coffee but champagne. We saw off this early-morning bottle of bubbly as I tried to guide him on a nostalgic trip, waiting at times up to 30 seconds for his considered observations.

Weeks later he was dead and the papers were full of his obituaries. Some hinted that he'd become distant and cantankerous in his final years, that he had lost much of the eccentric charm, natural or partially affected, that had endeared him to so many. I can only say that, whatever his limitations of speech, he was warm and good company.

Before I left, I hesitantly produced three paperbacks of his collected works and asked if there was the remotest chance he would sign them for my children and myself. His right hand wasn't functioning properly, but immediately he stretched for a pen and slowly wrote his name in the three books, with his left hand.

This frail, elderly man, who had once gone on record saying "I'm just an old fraud, you know" and was seen by his detractors as a lightweight poet more amused by the quirks of suburbia than so-called weighty and profound themes, talked with undisguised passion about the West Country towns he knew and loved so much.

On that morning in sunny Chelsea there was none of the teasing, provocative, tongue-in-cheek manner about him. Bristol and Bath were places to be taken very seriously indeed.

That meant he poured scorn on the ugly post-war piecemeal development and architectural vulgarity that he felt had disfigured both cities. He went into one of his numerous reveries and then said: "They are both wonderful places. Bath is conventionally beautiful, and yet it doesn't compare with Bristol. It always seemed to me that Bristol was the livelier city. The people who lived there were also different from Bathonians."

He half-smiled at his memories: "It was Clifton that I found so delightful. I really was in love with it. I used to walk for hours around the Downs and gaze across at Brunel's bridge. Oh gosh, what a marvel that was."

The Downs also reminded him of the zoo. "It was so well integrated into that part of Clifton. And do you know some of the monkeys once escaped? They climbed over a ladder and got over the wall," he chuckled.

Sir John was that rarity: a poet who was also successful. Yet he never seemed to have too much money to spare. His wardrobe, even in his earlier years, was singularly misshapen. There were buttons missing, cigarette ash was everywhere, and an assortment of headgear ranged from Victorian remnants to what appeared to be charity shop giveaways.

His private life was decidedly unconventional. His wife Penelope had her own separate life. His mistress, Lady Elizabeth Cavendish, sister of the Duke of Devonshire, bought him his London home. A recent book confirmed a flirtatious manner he never wholly lost. One or two ex-TWW secretaries would confirm that.

He fell in love with the headmistress of a school in Sherborne where he had gone to give a talk. A bisexual background went back to the day he was seduced by a vicar's son in Malmesbury. At Marlborough School he was bullied and mocked by teachers he refused ever to forgive.

For all that, Betjeman loved the West. He spent days strolling round the pews of local churches or watching in awe the ponderous, romantic Somerset & Dorset steam trains meandering over the Mendips. He could be perverse, juvenile and grumpy when more weighty literary figures patronised him but, against all the trends of poetry, he succeeded in entertaining thousands by his light, evocative touch in verse, and even found times to join campaigns such as the one that saved Clevedon Pier. He always had a passion for seaside Victoriana.

He seems to flit in and out of fashion, but as poet laureates go, he is almost certainly better known than the current one (Andrew Motion), all these years after his death.

But away from the printed page, we should be grateful for the engaging, theatrical way he sparkled in front of the camera. He was the definitive natural performer – and to Bristol and Bath he was a treasured, shambling star.

FARM LABOURER – OR CREATIVE GENIUS?

Westcountry Mysteries (1985)

'Wold Tommy Shayell', as they called him in south Somerset, died more than a hundred and fifty years ago. But a few of the older villagers at Montacute, stirred by the stories about him passed on by succeeding generations of their own families, still pretend that they can remember him.

The tragedy was that Tommy – christened Thomas Shoel – met with none of the deserved recognition during his lifetime, the kind that would have fed and kept alive his careworn, undernourished wife and children.

He was a composer and a poet. And yet he was never taught a note of music and had virtually no schooling.

In Montacute and the neighbouring parishes nestling at the foot of Ham Hill, his contemporaries shook their heads. They watched him composing his verse or his hymn tunes as he sat astride a stile or sprawled contemplatively in the grass. They couldn't understand his poems and had no especial regard for the esoteric mood of church music. But at the same time they marvelled at the pastoral metaphors that he created, the notes that he scored with such melodic ability.

"Where do Tommy get it from? He bain't like the rest of us. He bides for hours up on Ham Hill," they used to say.

The local clergy were rather more forthcoming with their theories. "Thomas is inspired from above," they assured their flocks.

'Wold Tommy' was in many ways an unlikely candidate for divine gifts. He had the voice and the appearance of a simple villager who knew his place in life: and in Montacute that meant unrelenting labours bound by the feudal strictures of the time. No-one could ever remember him going to school. He worked as a farm labourer and a village carter. His health was bad. His face was drawn and his shoulders stooped in the way of most villagers who eked out a living. Yet if he had a sickle in one hand, there was invariably a stub of lead pencil in the other. He was different.

Tom Shoel was born in 1759. His parents died when he was still a small boy. He grew up in acute poverty and was learning to 'hedge and ditch' of necessity almost from the moment he could walk. It was assumed that his life would be as hard, mundane and unfulfilled as other boys of his age in Montacute.

But he grew up 'with music in me head'. He was given a tin whistle and the tunes multiplied. He went to church and learned to read from the Bible. The old vicars to whom he listened entranced were really his only school teachers. Laboriously he taught himself to write. The letters were beautifully formed; the incongruous farm-worker gripped the pencil in his rough-grained fingers and produced copperplate.

He may have been eccentric in some of his behaviour and spent hours on his own wandering the lanes of Stoke-sub-Hamdon, Chiselborough and the Chinnocks. At the same time he longed for the relative convention of a family life. He married a local girl and soon had several children. Their poverty, not unusual in those times among rural communities, was appalling. Child-bearing weakened an already prematurely frail young woman. His wife died; so in the next few years did all the children with the exception of one son.

Tom was distraught. He was left with only his prayers and his 'inner music'. The prayers intensified. The music took on a melancholic element. His emerging poems assumed a surprisingly mature philosophic character.

In his late thirties he married again. There were three more children, all daughters. The collective prayers didn't fill their stomachs. His wife had twins when she was 49. The unequal struggle was eventually too much for her and she killed herself. Her husband was again overcome by grief. "Better fit he do a bit mer work and fergit his writin'," the villagers were apt to say, as if blaming him for the succession of family tragedies.

But Tom couldn't adjust to such harrowing realities. Was he a romantic – or a near genius? Or something of both?

He'd given up all but the token amount of local labouring to buy a loaf or two of bread. His hymn tunes were becoming more prolific. And so were his poems. They were meticulously copied out in his copperplate. A kindly clergyman arranged for three books of his sacred music and several slim volumes of his poems to be published in Bristol. They made him little if any money. He became more unconventional in his habits. He never touched meat, even if he could have afforded it. He talked away to himself, and even those who didn't understand him realised that here was a rare and extraordinary talent.

Tom became 'an instant composer'. When the brass band arrived for a special performance on an annual festival after Trinity Sunday, they discovered that they didn't have their music with them. "Wold Tommy'll do summick for thee," they were told. And so he did. He sat down on a barrel of beer in the yard of the Phelips Arms, according to the late Llewelyn Powys in one of his lovely evocative essays, and composed a new tune for the band. More than that, he scored it for each different instrument. Such a feat of spontaneous creativity was worth sixpence to him. He seldom earned more than half that for one of his hymns.

Thomas Shoel peddled his tunes. He was a hymnsmith who then set off to try to sell his compositions. Occasionally when he headed for Bristol, he would be lucky enough to hitch a lift part of the way on a stage waggon. Often his speculative sorties, with the new hymn in the pocket of his ragged coat, would take him several days. He slept rough on the way, living off turnips and swedes. But there was never a guarantee of a threepenny sale at the end of the journey.

There were many times in earlier years when he penned an anthem or a poem in great haste hopefully to earn a few pence to buy food for one of his sick children. Life never got easier for him.

A few people sensed his rare gifts. He had neither the resources nor the physique to parade his talents before wider audiences. To their everlasting shame, one or two literary figures to whom his work was sent by kindly regional well-wishers hardly bothered to read or assess it.

What could an illiterate farm labourer from a Somerset village know about choral music or literature? If they had only taken the trouble to encourage him, they would have been rewarded. One critic took a look at Tom's poetry and implied that it must have been plagiarised. No 'hedger and ditcher' could have dreamed up those words or had those ethereal thoughts.

Wold Tommy was influenced by no-one save the God he heard about in church. He educated himself – and strolled the country lanes and hillsides to put his thoughts, all spiritually based, onto paper. What did it matter that the spelling was bad, the construction and metre naïve and the occasional word misused?

He died in 1823 and they took his body to a burial place called Five Ashes, on the outskirts of nearby Odcombe and just along the narrow winding lane from his beloved Ham Hill. Five Ashes is an acre of consecrated ground, oddly located in the middle of pasture-land. It is guarded by a high wall, originally built to keep the body-snatchers away. Today the burial place is deserted and overgrown. Here lies Thomas Shoel and some of his family. The names on the leaning tombstones can no longer be read.

He was a remarkable man. He wrote hundreds of poems and hymns. Many of them died with him, unread and unappreciated. We shall never know how near he was to minor genius. A few scholars who came after him studied snatches of his poems and were glowing in their praise. They only regretted that much of his work was lost.

Villagers who grew up with him at Montacute were apt to scoff at his preoccupied demeanour. Others could only wonder at his sheer output – and the depth of thought and sensitivity of a man who never went to school. Till this day, his inspired work remains an absorbing mystery.

Could those erstwhile Montacute churchmen have been right when they pointed to his simple, undeviating faith and said: "He gets it from above."

THE 80s AND I

Bristol Evening Post, December 1989

The drunken yuppie got on the train at Paddington. He had a portable phone sticking out of his pocket and a nasal, cut-glass accent which he was determined everyone should hear before we left London. He was also intent on impressing his Sloane girlfriend, as he preened himself and recounted all his smart-alec remarks of the past day at the expense of lesser and more menial mortals.

When the ticket collector arrived at the yuppie's table, the usual request was cut short. "No, my good man, I haven't a ticket. And neither has my friend. We boarded the train late and no doubt we shall consider paying something or other."

The Sloane giggled. "Oh my God," her companion spluttered. "We've got into a second-class section of the train." He then offered some pretty unoriginal observations on British Rail and its employees.

It happened that the ticket collector was black and diffident. He took the embracing insults in silence. Then he quietly asked the yuppie where he was going and solemnly made out an invoice for the pair. It was handed over – and then scrutinised in exaggerated detail.

"Now look here, my fellow. By an unfortunate mistake, I have climbed into the wrong section of the train. But I am a person of some substance and I think you should know that I travel only first-class. You have made out a second-class ticket."

The little collector paused, eyeing this young whizz-kid phoney who appeared to have a marked social if not drinking problem. Then very deliberately, he said: "A second-class ticket, sir ... for a second-class citizen."

I couldn't help myself. I stood up and applauded. It was a marvellous and dignified put-down. The yuppie and his Sloane got out at Reading.

But, unfortunately, he was one of the ugly metaphors of the 80s: brash, affluent, selfish, insensitive and condescending. He epitomised the ever-grasping tendency, in which materialism is encouraged over good manners, wealth over basic wisdom, high finance over the normal decencies of humanity. Greed above all.

Mrs Thatcher will go into the history books for her positive leadership, her stamina, her unwaveringly dogmatic approach. Yet she is unloved. She lacks humour, the common touch and – surprisingly for a grocer's daughter not always impressed by the surfeit of Etonians around her – a gentle understanding of ordinary people. And never once has she acknowledged a mistake.

The 80s gave us the Falklands, which many still feel could have been avoided. The invasion was patriotically inspiring or economically draining, according to your point of view. Jingoism surfaced to a degree that was both frightening and exciting.

The 80s gave us Doomwatch-style nuclear leaks which, we all fearfully sense, could get worse. They gave us cataclysmic disasters in mid-air and on the ground. Various fundamentalist groups, often in the name of God, were guilty of appalling acts.

Privatisation turned from a long, ugly, rarely-heard word into a rushing reality. Some of us romantically thought that water was almost a God-given freedom. Soon we'll have to say s'il vous plaît to the French every time we want to turn the tap on. What next? Fresh air, maybe.

I hate the way our health care is going. Have you seen some of the cut-price offers? It's getting a bit like a car boot sale. Just how many of our best doctors and surgeons will be creamed off to the private sector? Am I alone in believing that health should never be carved up according to the size of a person's bank balance?

The Greens have vociferously arrived, not before time. They have valuable points to make. One worries about acid rain, insecticides and the number of forests consumed by a few copies of the *Sunday Times*. In the 80s, we seemed to have a new health warning about food every week. Eggs ... fats ... microwaves ... what next?

The 80s? For me, apprehension and pessimism about what I saw happening: too much self-interest and get-rich-quick, and social divisions widening alarmingly.

At least it will be remembered internationally for the stunning shafts of light in Russia and Eastern Europe. But what happens when the dust particles of joy settle, and brave Gorbachev, beset by economic chaos, is brutally pushed aside?

17
Cricket Reporter

*centre: David with Viv Richards, Weston-super-Mare, 1983;
clockwise from top left: fellow reporters David Green,
John Arlott, Vic Marks and John Woodcock*

For more than thirty years, starting in the mid-1970s, David reported on county cricket for the *Guardian* and the *Observer*. At first there were only occasional assignments, then they grew till they became his principal work during the summer months. Mainly he covered the West Country counties – Somerset and Gloucestershire, sometimes venturing into Worcestershire, Hampshire and Glamorgan – but in his last years, when his stamina and mental powers were beginning to fade, the *Guardian* finally realised just how special he was and despatched him all over the country: to Liverpool and Leicester, Headingley and Hove, Scarborough and Southgate.

From 1980 he pasted his reports in a scrapbook, often adding hand-written notes alongside them. These notes died out for a while, but they returned more frequently from 1998 onwards, offering glimpses of the company he kept in the press box and the increasing difficulties he faced as he continued the relentless schedule well into his seventies.

On a Friday night in May 1980 he was in Cardiff to report on a football match that secured the Northern Ireland team their first outright title in the Home International Championships. The next day he was at Taunton to see Ian Botham plunder 228 runs in barely three hours. From Noel Brotherston's 'goal of appropriately jig-like aplomb' to Ian Botham's 'sadism in the sun', he was at the centre of the sporting action, as he drolly observed in a hand-written comment:

> Journalistic grandeur at the age of 51. Ad-libbed two 600-word reports over an appalling line.

There were further heights to scale in 1999 when cricket's World Cup was held in England. David was sent zig-zagging across the country as he reported on eight group-stage matches, then was asked to supply 'colour pieces' for two contests in the later stages of the tournament. He was now a veteran cricket writer, seventy years old, yet his notes recorded:

> Dual peak for me in cricket reporting. Lord's and the Oval. It was the first time I had seen the two grounds in all their glory.

A greater pinnacle was reached three years later when, for the only time in his life, he attended a Test match, reporting on England against India at Trent Bridge for the *Wisden Cricketer* magazine.

Despite what David wrote, perhaps a little tongue-in-cheek, in his 1975 article about the stuffiness of cricket press boxes, he came to love them and to look forward to his days among his fellow scribes on the circuit. When he came home, Anne would ask him not "Was it a good day's cricket?" but "Did you have a good box?"

> The press boxes were where professionally I was happiest. I found myself surrounded by well-fleshed mates who valued fellowship as well as the cricket. Our kinship came naturally. The humour, never far away, could be earthy as well as subtle. There was a bond that allowed us to share jokes, often at each other's expense, and profounder points about the match we'd been sent to watch and comment on. That was in the days, of course, when sports editors believed in decent coverage for championship fixtures, and the writers felt the word allocation justified their presence and judgement. Our faces would light up when, at five to eleven on the first day, we discovered who from other papers would be sharing the box with us.

Despite these warm words in *Footsteps from East Coker*, the notes in David's scrapbook reveal occasional flashes of irritation when a colleague is too full of himself. One, a future BBC sports editor, is described as 'loquacious and journalistically naïve, bubbling away every half-hour for LBC, including nearly every colloquial snippet of press-box gossip'. Another, an old-school regional journalist, gives 'a stunning performance on the phone, complaining about the lunches. His tirade to the Chief Chef went on for 25 minutes.'

David stayed out of, but quietly enjoyed, the class-ridden political clashes when David Green (Manchester Grammar and Labour) locked horns with John Thicknesse and Ivo Tennant (both Harrow and Conservative). David had his own quiet sympathies, but he was fond of all three men. In one note he recorded how, having missed his train home from Truro, he was offered a lift by 'Thickers', who proceeded to drive so fast for 120 miles that David was able to board the same train at Taunton.

Green, the former Lancashire and Gloucestershire batsman, intrigued David greatly: a larger-than-life rebel who held forth volubly in the press box but submitted 'surprisingly straight and dignified' reports to the *Daily Telegraph*. 'They could have come from a country rector,' David wrote in a profile of him in the *Western Daily Press*:

> David Green in full flow is somewhere between Coward and Lenny Bruce. He isn't for those of a nervous disposition or hyper-sensitivity over their favoured use of puritan language. Newcomers to the press box are apt to fall off their chair. Hey, who's this intellectual, they ask, mixing his long words with the salacious asides?
>
> True he was a high flyer at Manchester Grammar School and went on to read history at Oxford. He's brighter than the rest

of us put together. But he never parades that bit of scholarship. In fact, he goes to great lengths to be one of the boys. He takes a dig at the public schools. He prefers a pint of strong lager to a red wine. You suspect he may be a bit of a Leftie.

What is beyond question is his knowledge of cricket. He reads the nuances of the wicket better than half the players. He can spot a phoney a boundary-length away.

In one entry in the scrapbook, next to a 1999 report from Southampton, David has written:

> David Green, the paradox. Between evening pints I guided him onto his beloved modern poetry (Auden, Larkin). Then to Hardy. He memorises long chunks. He suddenly asked for a sheet of paper and jotted down this example of Hardy. No hesitation.

Below, in David Green's neat and gentle hand, are the 14 melancholic lines, word perfect, of a sonnet.

> When you shall see me in the toils of Time,
> My lauded beauties carried off from me
> ...
> Will you not grant to old affection's claim
> The hand of friendship down life's sunless hill?

David's notes record little scenes that do not make it into his reports, such as this of the *Times* editor at Weston-super-Mare: 'Rees-Mogg trying to be informal and persuading Bill Andrews to show his son how to bowl.' Or at Cardiff: 'Wilf Wooller, so unloved by the locals, made his appearance in the press box, to opinionate and talk louder than anyone. Quite benevolent by his standards – but dogmatic.' Wooller would be one of the men whom David would profile in his two books of 'intimate portraits', as would another he encountered that same day at Cardiff:

> Met Carwyn James for the first time. He rolls up his coat sleeves to write. Bit of a mystique about him (Welsh mafia/rugby).

Lengthier is David's account of a visit to the Oval press box from Alec Bedser, a man notorious for his disparaging of the modern game:

> From the inside coat pocket, he took out an action picture of Hoggard. "Just look at that. Everything's wrong. The feet, the body. Just look at the hips." With some passion he pointed out where Hoggard was going wrong. "Now, do you see the difference?" This time he produced a newspaper action shot of

himself, about to deliver the ball. It was not boastful but fairly typical of the reprimands he offers regularly to present coaches.

He had a ready audience and kept talking. Gradually his conversation was extended critically to other aspects of life. He sniffed at the way the country was going. "If I was twenty years younger, I'd emigrate to Australia. No doubt about that." And then back to Hoggard. "No wonder he can't swing it. And look at his head. Everything's wrong. What a bloody action."

In the last years, when David was in his seventies, he was starting to struggle. The long journeys, now often undertaken with Anne sharing the driving, were not without disasters. Trips to Northampton seemed particularly fated. On one occasion a wrong turning on the motorway turned the 120-mile trip into 200 miles; on another he was in Southampton, phoning his copy from a call box at eight o'clock on Friday night when he was told that Vic Marks was at a wedding and he was needed next day for a match between Northamptonshire and the Australians. He drove 100 miles back to Bristol, then in the morning 120 miles to Northampton, only for his car to break down when the fan belt became shredded. With the AA's help, he finally got to the ground.

Five Aussie wickets already gone – and I find from the Observer they want 800 words! Scyld gives me the falls of wickets during the morning. All seats gone in press box. I know I'll have to waffle (even more than usual). I walk round ground and do my piece, leaning on the boot of someone's car. Miss a couple more wickets in the process! On way home car breaks down again (lights go, windscreen won't wipe and it's raining). Eventually towed home from M6 by AA, arriving at 1 a.m.

Needless to say, the report reads beautifully. Here he is on Mark Taylor's innings, little of which he can have witnessed:

The Australian captain is both a popular and a tormented figure these days. There are many cases of Test batsmen, from Bill Edrich to Mike Atherton, driven almost to distraction by miserable sequences. Sporting nations get caught up in the cruel exercise of sadism. But Taylor did himself some good yesterday morning. He was sixth out, leg-before for 76 on the front foot to Kevin Curran. For 158 minutes he played like a sagacious opener, proving things primarily to himself. It was essentially tidy, self-contained and timely batting.

THE DICKENS TOUCH AT TAUNTON

from an article in the Somerset CCC yearbook, 2012

John Arlott used to say that he liked coming to Taunton – because of the press box. In those days he found it irresistibly and uniquely Dickensian. If there was no broadcasting to worry about and no match report for the *Guardian* till late afternoon, he had time to gaze out romantically at the church towers and ponder peacefully over the kind of cricket scene and ambience that he loved. He would have seen off a decent claret at the lunch interval. Now there was a chance to snooze or, with a poet's warm-hearted dreamy eyes, to remember.

Taunton was right for him. It was still a pastoral pleasure, a market town that didn't frantically try to catch up with life's more sophisticated ways. It continued to belong to another era. And the quaintly bijou press box set the mood. The desks were high and, to John Arlott's joy, they had their original inkwells. Bob Cratchit or another member of the Dickens assorted cast list threatened to make an appearance at any time. The prodigious Arlott memory, allied to a naturally companionable nature and that voice of Basingstoke bonhomie, encouraged an enchanting range of conversation. His word imagery would ramble from the turbulent, talented Herbert 'The Colonel' Hewett to the ever convivial Sammy Woods. He had a story about all of them, sounding all the better and more mischievous when given his distinctive, intimate Hampshire vowels.

"What do you want better than this?" he used to say to the assembled audience. We listened and chuckled as the occasional historical indiscretion was slipped in. "I am never happier than when I am sent here. But the steps up to the box make me puff a bit as I get older." He had no real complaints with the ascent, only with the news that the cherished old press box – and the ageless old inkwells – was more than due for an overhaul. Some of us still think of John whenever we recall that dusty beloved room, our spiritual home for years.

It had some distinguished visitors and fellow scribes over the evolving years. Jim Swanton didn't make many professional sorties away from Canterbury or the Test grounds. But John Woodcock came often for *The Times*. He was a popular caller, rich in anecdote and punctual when it came to his ritualistic noontime pint of beer. Brian Close frequently looked in, maybe to persuade a local reporter to put on a bet for him. He, like so many who sat and composed in the Taunton press box, was the most engaging of company.

The first time I saw a county match and peered in awe at the cricket writers, Raymond Robertson-Glasgow, to become my especial literary hero, was on journalistic duty. I hero-worshipped the writers as much as the players. It used to thrill me when the Australians came to the West Country, even more so when Lindsay Hassett or Jack Fingleton would bring some of the famous tourists up to see where we worked.

The Taunton press box wasn't built for comfort. We banged our heads on the low beams. We fought for breath when the tobacco fug obscured us. On cold days we struggled in our great coats as we coped with dear Eric Hill's fetish for fresh air. And we did well to find a chair. When it came to last-minute research, we relied on the generosity of 'Times of London' man Dick Streeton who carried enough reference books to stock a library. How he managed to heave them up the stairs remained a mystery.

But that was now a long time ago. The Taunton box (with more seats) has inevitably lost some of its charm, as well as architectural hazards, in coping with modernity. The lap-tops have taken over and the press boxes have sacrificed much of their social appeal and enduring banter. Arlott, the poet, preferred it as it was.

PRESS BOX CHARACTERS

extracts from an aricle in the magazine Cricket Lore, 2000

In my early self-conscious seasons as a sports reporter the company I was privileged to keep in the press box was of as much significance to me as what was being enacted on the field. At Taunton, where John Arlott was enraptured by the Dickensian inkwells, I took on the role of dormitory monitor as he snoozed through the late afternoon. He woke in a pleasant humour, made a ritual general enquiry about whether he'd missed anything, and always met his *Guardian* deadline. Jack Fingleton liked the ambience created by fellow journalists and amused us with his shafts of acerbity. He wrote well; he talked even better, if we wanted one of his mischievous insights. It wasn't simply Sir Don. He didn't miss a chance to release a sly dig at the expense of fellow broadcaster Alan McGilvray. The diminutive Lindsay Hassett, Irish eyes darting in all directions as if engaged in a Guinness-bar jig, seemed never less than good-humoured. He had given up playing and was back, relaxed and jovial, to write about his successors.

The soccer press boxes could be fun, but they were also frenetic and lacked the warmth and esoteric conversations that cricket offered. In the Doncaster press box I remember sitting next to a Yorkshire lad with a busy pencil. Michael Parkinson. For a game at Brentford, about this same time, a reporter took his seat next to me five minutes into the second half. "London traffic's getting impossible. Been stuck at Hammersmith for an hour, you know. And, by the way, what's the score?" That was Denis Compton, then working for the *Sunday Express*. Tardy or not, he seemed typically unflurried. Hammersmith, one suspects, was regularly defamed.

Compton, too, liked the cordial nature of press box inhabitants. That afternoon at Brentford remains a treasured memory. He was willingly supplied with elusive facts – and he still had time to dispense, at our bidding, snippets of cricket gossip. Only years later did he lose a little of that affability that made him such a favourite. To some of us the occasional intemperate view, often about South Africa, fell uneasily from his lips. Press men are not politicians, at least when sharing a day's sport and banter. Maybe it's unreasonable but we don't want to hear our heroes sounding off with unequivocal disaffection about other segments of the human race.

For more than 45 years I have regularly taken up residence in the press box. To start with, the schoolmasterly presence of Jim Kilburn and a few of the Yorkshire 'heavies' had an inhibiting effect on the rest of us. Jim didn't like too much levity and I was apt to fear that after a gleeful response to a burst of badinage in the front row, he might keep me in for detention. Bill Bowes, despite that owlish face, was much more relaxed. But for the Yorkies, cricket had an ecclesiastical aura, and you didn't laugh too much in church.

Alan Gibson had scant affection for the press box and that disappointed me. He would come and whisper in my ear that he had a double whisky waiting for me in the Stragglers Bar at Taunton. He was inclined to pull us up on our wayward syntax and criticise a Rabelaisian exchange. Alan never quite left academia. John Woodcock had a warmer regard for his fellow scribes. A gentle man of habit – and wise opinions – he liked a pint of beer at mid-day.

Ex-players like Derek Pringle and Vic Marks have integrated easily. Christopher Martin-Jenkins juggles the mike and the lap-top as if he majored in logistics, yet still finds time at Scarborough to chase away for a dip in the sea at the tea interval. Michael Henderson, in his self-confident, engaging way, has an opinion on everything from chamber music to mustard. Some sub-editors and irate *Telegraph* readers say those opinions will be the death of him. He relishes the stir he causes.

What we have in common is an affection for the cricket *per se*: not necessarily the politics and the machinations, but the game. If it hums with the humanity of the press box, so much the better.

CROWD-PULLING CRICKET

England v Rest of the World, Ashton Gate
The Guardian, September 1980

The cheers have been muted at Ashton Gate this season, with Bristol City haplessly exploring the cellars of the Second Division. So there was a cool irony about the way an artificial game, enterprisingly called floodlit cricket and played partly in the daylight, brought back the elusive animation.

They were all there with their mustard pads and sheepish expressions: England and the Rest of the World, playing for £400 plus expenses a man. City, who need the money, had intrepidly staged the match and stood to pick up the profits from the 9,000 crowd.

One trusts that England, put in to bat by Clive Lloyd, did not see it as suitable preamble to the Caribbean tour – at least when the early wickets were tumbling. They lost their first four for 31 runs in no time at all. Then Botham, with sunhat and adventurous intentions, joined Boycott. By the 22nd over the score was up to 135 and they both had half-centuries.

Boycott still looked elegant and was in no mood to devalue his technical skills. Botham was limping from an uncharitable delivery from his Taunton flat-mate Viv Richards, but not before he had evaded the strawberry netting with sixes into the directors' box (what chance has he of a transfer from Scunthorpe to Bristol City?) and other distant parts of the two stands.

The cricket was often bizarre but the entertainment remained engaging in its novelty value and physical power.

It was never too easy fielding in the outfield where Whitehead, Gow and Rodgers are normally hacking away bravely for City. But Gavaskar, perhaps not the liveliest fielder in county cricket this summer, brilliantly held on to a boundary catch to dismiss the ebullient Botham for 84. By now Boycott was entering the spirit of aggressive batsmanship. He unwisely trusted the specially laid wicket, missed the gentle turn of Doshi and was stumped for 68.

Emgland were all out in the 38th over for 214. The batting had been dominated by Boycott and Botham, the bowling by Doshi who teased away accurately to take six for 48 in just seven overs.

The Rest threatened to win by 10 wickets; then Sadiq (64) and Gavaskar (67) were out in the same over to Boycott and the crowd were not after all denied the sight of Richards. He and Zaheer effortlessly moved towards victory in the 36th over. Everything ended with Gooch parodying his colleagues as he bowled from both ends and umpire Bill Alley fielded at short leg. It was that sort of match and the spectators approved.

Double Wicket Competition, Lansdown

The Guardian, August 1982

Len Creed had things on his mind yesterday afternoon – the meetings at Sandown and Chester, and Viv Richards. Creed is a Bath bookmaker and his durable story is that he brought the great batsman to this country from Antigua in 1973. "We'll have you back to Lansdown for your benefit, Vivian, and the whole city will be there," he promised.

Lansdown Cricket Club, where W.G. once played, is one of the oldest in the country. It is hemmed in by the hospital and the bookbinding factory and is a mile from Creed's betting shop. Yesterday he 'hedged' the big ones at Sandown and was still able to chase back to the ground, between the 4.10 and 4.45, to make sure his protegé still knew his way around. King Richards, taking part in an international double-wicket competition, was patently very much at home.

The Lansdown boundary bulged. There were tents retailing strong Somerset ale and good-natured banter. Half Bath's West Indian population, it seemed, was there. They had come mostly to see Viv; but it was a joyful bonus that Ian Botham, Graham Gooch, Kapil Dev and Richard Hadlee were also doing their stuff, of course.

The spectators did not want conventional nonsense like pure international style cricket. They wanted crashing carnival sixes. They were dutifully dispensed in goodly numbers, farther perhaps than ever before. One outrageous blow from Botham cleared the ground, the road, a garden on the other side and smashed straight through an upstairs window. The ball ricocheted across the lounge, spun off a stereo and eventually landed in an armchair. A pretty student nurse, Carmel, arrived home shortly afterwards and, when assured that it was only England's favourite all-rounder, forgot to query the insurance. She even returned the ball.

Parked cars were dented; once the ball was lost in the red roses of the vicar's garden; roofing contractors over the road chose to work from the cover of the chimney pots. This privet-hedged corner of Bath is not used to this and one or two faces glowered from behind the protection of heavy curtains.

The cricket? Oh yes, Botham and Gooch were knocked out, to the dismay of the partisans, by Hadlee and Clive Rice. Botham actually scored a century but who was counting? The England pair lost because they were out more times. Meanwhile Richards and Malcolm Marshall beat Kapil Dev and Peter Willey. The £2,000 competition ended as the crowd hoped when Richards and Marshall beat Hadlee and Rice in the final by 44 runs. The special prize for most sixes was shared by Botham and Gooch.

MATCH REPORTS

Somerset on the verge of a first title, the Sunday League ...

Somerset v Middlesex, Taunton, August 1978

This was a day at Taunton of noisy, good-humoured and arguably premature celebration. But Somerset's rubicund fans, spilling over the boundary of the distinctive market-town ground that has known no title for 103 years, were yesterday scenting success.

... but it is not to be

Somerset v Essex, Taunton, September 1978

Suddenly there was nothing at all. Ten thousand Somerset fans were left crying in their cider at sunny, melancholy Taunton last night. Two titles had slipped cruelly away in two days, and there is still not a trophy to be seen for 103 years of both exasperating and superb cricket in the county.

Somerset lost by two runs to Essex, teasing us to the end. The game finished after 7 o'clock – as television schedules over-ran and Hampshire waited breathlessly. Double defeat, in the Gillette Cup and Sunday League, were accepted with good grace; you could cut the sympathy in the air with a knife.

Six-hitting by Mike Procter

Somerset v Gloucestershire, Taunton, August 1979

Mike Procter yesterday mesmerised a ducking, delirious Taunton Bank Holiday crowd with a display of hitting that surely ranks with some of the tales of great slogging on this intimate ground, passed down from West Country cricketing folklore.

Yet it was too disdainfully scientific to be called slogging. The Gloucestershire captain scored 93 in 46 minutes before playing on to Botham. There were just 23 scoring shots, eight of them sixes and four of them fours.

The hapless Breakwell came on for three overs and then understandably left the Somerset attack, head in hands. All the sixes were off him, half a dozen of them – stretching over two overs – in a ruthless, almost comical row.

The South African survived a leg-side stumping-catch appeal off his opening ball. Then he hunched his broad shoulders and headed hopefully for the record books and the quickest century of the season. In his indecent rush he sent the ball into the car park, the churchyard and the men's lavatories. One six soared through the open window of the players' viewing balcony – and cowed team-mates emerged with the ball, fluttering white flags of surrender.

Joel Garner scores the only century of his career

Gloucestershire v West Indies, Bristol, July 1980

The Big Bird, Joel Garner, no longer kids his West Indian team-mates that he can bat. He demonstrated it with his maiden century against Gloucestershire at Bristol yesterday, often looking more the poet than the predator. More than that, he marvellously saved his side from ignominy.

Garner was out near the end caught at extra cover. He had proudly and attractively occupied the crease for 153 minutes, hitting three sixes and 10 fours in his 104. It was, in any context, an innings of forceful responsibility. He made the ungainly look graceful.

Somerset have always known that he can bat rather than simply slog. He built his innings, overlooking the occasional excusable lapse, as if making out a sturdy case to be viewed as an all-rounder in future. He seemed as tall as the forbidding erstwhile orphanages that surround the ground, he apparently took short singles with a bounding hop skip and jump, and the game belonged to him. The crowd rose to him and he sheepishly came in to a standing ovation and the jocular dressing room backslaps.

Geoffrey Boycott reaches another milestone

Somerset v Yorkshire, Weston-super-Mare, August 1983

Geoffrey Boycott reached 1,000 runs for the season at Weston-super-Mare yesterday. He had done it 20 times before and if the latest statistic passed unnoticed in the Clarence Park heat, the Master Craftsman doubtless knew all about it.

He went on to score 83, with nine well-spaced boundaries over 70 overs before being nimbly stumped by Gard. As ever the technique had been flawless – and still prosaic as the precise small type in a coaching manual. Boycott does not bat; he is in residence, permanent as the pier along the front.

The brutal brilliance of Botham

Somerset v Hampshire, Taunton, May 1985

Taunton marvels at Ian Botham more by the day. His century yesterday, amid the apparent wreckage of a Somerset innings, took him just 76 balls. It equalled the previous fastest of the season, made on this same ground by this same imperious aggressor.

The members rose in doting tribute to his brutal brilliance. It was a glittering, all-embracing collector's item to cherish perhaps almost with the best – certainly the most stunning – in the county's history.

Another West Countryman, Gilbert Jessop, used to describe an extraordinary arc with his bountiful blows without ever looking a slogger. Yesterday, Botham, too, appeared thrillingly in control. Occasionally it seemed that he predetermined his muscular stroke, but that is the nature of the man. His team-mates, who like all county cricketers can be sparing in their praise, say their captain has never played better; he's back to the form of the richest years in that cussed and contradictory career of his.

He's nimbler than he's been for a long time, belying the rural sturdiness of the waist. He has more zest, too, and his England place is what he, as a racing man, might call a cast-iron cert. The blond hair tops a face of buoyant challenge ... The sheer strength of the man is remarkable. Here he was, in the evening, opening the bowling as if he'd been strolling round the Quantock hedgerows with a 12-bore all day. He once hurled at the stumps and Hampshire got four overthrows, but by then he'd have been forgiven anything.

Edmonds ticked off

Somerset v Middlesex, Bath, June 1987

Somerset saved the follow-on. Middlesex, for their part, showed a reluctance to save the blushes of the famous. The mid-afternoon exchange between Mike Gatting and Phil Edmonds, with its marked imbalance in volume, invective and verbiage, offered a theatrical diversion for a festival crowd which had remained rapt and subdued as Somerset painstakingly lessened the formidable deficit.

Edmonds upset his captain with a sluggish piece of fielding on a rough outfield. The spectators, who had not, apparently, taken to Edmonds, cheered. Gatting's reprimand of the fielder was pointed and public. It was hard to get it down verbatim, but the gist was that the Middlesex team did their best to field to the spinner's bowling, and he might return the compliment. Gatting waved in the direction of the pavilion: the implication doesn't bear thinking about.

Vic Marks retires to become The Observer's cricket correspondent

August 1989

Marks epitomises a Somerset cricketer: amiable, gentle-paced, a chuckler-philosopher who stalks the field with hunched shoulders and head down, who scampers singles with the ungainly poise of a startled Rhode Island Red, and who both daydreams and beguiles with his spinners. There is an undeniable literary tradition in Somerset going back to Robertson-Glasgow. But 'Skid' Marks is going to be missed out there on the field.

Umpire Peter Wight at Worcester

Worcestershire v Derbyshire, Worcester, April 1992

Worcester in April: where the tourists used to come, treble-sweatered, to flex their muscles and herald another season. And there was at least still a certain timelessness to the ritual yesterday.

Peter Wight, with phlegmatic face and those surprising, expansive boundary signals, was starting his 25th summer as umpire. He is the longest-serving on the list, appearing unfailingly, unspectacularly like those New Road horse-chestnut buds – and, sadly, with not even a semi-final accolade to show for it. Honours come grudgingly to the journeymen of sport.

No early-morning caution from Mark Lathwell

Somerset v Sussex, Taunton, August 1992

Less than 15 overs of Mark Lathwell at the crease is an event of some significance. Somerset supporters are beginning to take to him in the way they did to another opening batsman with a disregard for early-morning caution, Harold Gimblett.

Lathwell, in his first full season and with the squat, sturdy figure that reminds one more of a North Devon cattle drover than of an occupant of a bank desk – which was once briefly his habitat – was caught at the wicket for 55. In that time he had stroked, punched and glided 11 boundaries.

As usual he did it with a minimum of visible concern. The shots came off the back foot rather more than the front; they were played assuredly late in the style of the exceptional old campaigners.

Lathwell has a temperament sweet as apple dumpling. By the time the St James's clock was striking mid-day he was out, strolling back without self-rebuke or too much analysis – for a shower and probably a game of darts in the recesses of the pavilion.

Play abandoned at Clarence Park

Somerset v Hampshire, Weston-super-Mare, August 1992

There was time for one last sentimental walk round the Clarence Park boundary under the trees for shelter after the mid-afternoon announcement that the match had been abandoned as a draw.

The faithful, some from the Midlands who had for years combined their annual holiday with a visit to the Festival, seemed reluctant to take their leave.

They indicted in all directions like an angry stroke-maker – four-day cricket, the weather, those of the county's ledger-book logicians who believed it was madness to leave Taunton under-used.

No sign yesterday, despite many familiar faces, of that former scorecard seller, the now ennobled Jeffrey Archer, who loves the ground and has been sounded out about the possibility of financial help over recent weeks.

No sign, either, of the local lad John Cleese, who never missed a match here in his school holidays and could be spotted on romantic returns until fairly recent times.

Nearly everyone feels this is the last fixture at Weston. No one is absolutely sure, though.

Whether or not this was going to be the end, David Gower was prepared to do his best to garland the occasion with a memorable innings. Gower hooked Neil Mallender for six deep into the splintery woodwork of the country-style pavilion. He pulled out a quartet of pretty boundaries in no time as he reached 42 not out.

The two sides tried to make a contest of it. There were a few donated runs to start with, then a forfeiture by Somerset. Hampshire were left 324 in 97 overs. It led to some misplaced excitement before lunch, almost as if the elusive tide had been spied.

Tony Middleton, missing some of his intense early-season phlegm, was out leg-before to Andrew Caddick. Kevan James and Gower, one eye on the approaching black clouds, hinted at an eventful afternoon. The languid refinement of Gower could not, one felt, have been bettered as a finale.

But by early teatime the beaches just down the road were deserted and the donkeys were being loaded back into the lorries. At Clarence Park we were left only with the ghosts of cherished locals such as Bill Andrews, Holland Gibbs and Jim Bridges. The tears were in the skies.

Note: County cricket survived at Clarence Park for four more years.

Alleyne saves best till last

Gloucestershire v Essex, Cheltenham, July 1995

The last day of a cricket festival reminds us of faded flowers. By then it has usually lost its colour and new-minted Wisden sparkle. Only the empty seats, discarded beer bottles and romantic regional dreams remain. Yesterday the hoardings had been taken down and most of the tents zipped up, ready to be dismantled and folded in time for the next pony show.

And yet those spectators who bothered to turn up, undeterred by Gloucestershire's seemingly minimal prospects – they needed another 220 with only five wickets left – were wondrously rewarded.

Essex were beaten by three wickets by the 80th over. Thus ended a College Ground festival that had brought two impressive wins for Gloucestershire, as well as record takings of £50,000 net. But the soul of this match had nothing really to do with corporate hospitality or delicately billowing canvas. It belonged quintessentially to a single performance by Mark Alleyne.

He responded to his first championship match as captain with his most consummate innings for the county, taking his overnight 22 to 141. He stayed more than four hours until caught at point.

There were 21 boundaries – rich drives through the covers, perfectly timed strokes off his pads, or deflections. There was nothing flamboyant because that is not the nature of the man. He is almost a reverent figure at the crease, as still as one of those Chapel pews beyond the boundary.

The World Cup brings Scotland to Worcester
Scotland v Australia, Worcester, May 1999

The atmosphere was somewhere between Ibrox and an extended Burns Night. There were more kilts than pyjamas, there were raucous songs and patriot airs and even a quaintly transposed version of 'Away in a Manger', maybe as a concession to the sabbath. It was just an average cricket match in the spirit of the World Cup.

Musical accompaniment to the match was incessant and stridently good-natured. The instruments – trombones, saxophones, trumpets and, briefly, the pipes – varied like the quality and repertoire. Only the mean-spirited would have been affronted by these liberties in Elgar country.

Social evolution at Cheltenham
Gloucestershire v Warwickshire, Cheltenham, July 2000

Nothing reflects our social evolution better than Cheltenham. There stands the Gothic chapel, mellow and constant as ever – just like the towering, protective Cotswolds that frame the College ground.

But the spectators have changed. The clerics and the mustachioed military from the officers' mess who once predominated have virtually gone. Cheltenham has gradually taken on an egalitarian air, with more throaty artisan accents and more relaxed observers who look like out-of-season lock forwards from the Forest of Dean.

The appreciation, however, does not vary. Those who watch here in annual ritual are as knowledgeable as the supporters who worship at Scarborough's festival shrine.

18
Great Innings

Clockwise from top left: Viv Richards, Zaheer Abbas, Brian Lara, Graeme Hick

In the fifty years in which David reported on county cricket, there were perhaps three innings that captured the public imagination more than any other: a blistering 322 scored in only 4¼ hours by Viv Richards at Taunton, an epic 405 by the young Graeme Hick, also at Taunton, and a world-record 501 by Brian Lara at Edgbaston. It was David's happy fate to watch every ball of all three. 'I should like to put it down to journalistic instinct,' he wrote, 'but that would not be strictly true. A cricket writer at my level in a newspaper's structure doesn't choose his matches.'

Having ghost-written Viv Richards' autobiography, David had developed a special bond with the Antiguan. This created one of the truly magical hours of David's journalistic life: the two of them alone in the dressing-room in the aftermath of that magnificent innings.

Hick, if his captain had not declared, would almost certainly have passed the 424 scored by Lancashire's Archie MacLaren at Taunton in 1894, the only other score of 400 made previously in first-class cricket in England. As the chronicler of Somerset's cricket history, David had the opportunity to describe that innings, too, albeit more from the perspective of the wilting and threadbare Somerset eleven.

David also saw a triple-century by Jimmy Cook, the South African who played with stunning success for Somerset for three years. Richards, Hick, Cook, their innings were all played in Somerset matches. But it was much more by chance that David was at Edgbaston in 1994 to see Brian Lara's 501. The runs were scored, with little import, in a match drifting to a draw, but this did not reduce the batsman's greatness for David:

> Genius is not devalued when the pitch is bland and the bowlers are ordinary. He never patronised them; he continued to play his shots on merit. It just happened that the majority of them dripped with attacking grandeur.
>
> Half an hour later, when the TV crews were jostling for vantage points, he was diffident and charming at a press conference. I squeezed in one question and he answered memorably: "One innings like that doesn't make me a great player."

David's timing was also perfect when he found himself on holiday in India in 1982. In mid-holiday he hopped on a plane to Lahore to catch up with the Gloucestershire batsman Zaheer Abbas, for whom he was ghost-writing an autobiography. David arrived in time to see him complete his 100th first-class hundred – in a Test match, a feat only he and Geoffrey Boycott have accomplished.

OH DEAR, ARCHIE'S MATCH!

Archie MacLaren's 424, Lancashire v Somerset, Taunton
Sunshine, Sixes and Cider – A History of Somerset Cricket (1986)

The fixture against Lancashire in July 1895 was Archie's match. It wasn't simply and demoralisingly that Lancashire scored 801. Mr A.C. MacLaren, one of only two amateurs in his side (Somerset had nine) made 424. Such a first-class innings is never likely to be bettered in this country, although Viv Richards appeared to be in hot pursuit of it one sunny day in 1985.

MacLaren won the toss, and Woods scratched his head. Somerset's hapless captain was bereft of support bowlers, not a reassuring prospect on a summer's day when the sun shone and the placid wicket embraced only the batsmen. Sammy turned to the Palairet brothers: 'Well, me dears, I'm going to need both of you – and a few more besides.'

The big Aussie would open the bowling himself with Ted Tyler, fast and slow. He looked with wary pessimism down the team sheet. 'Young Gamlin won't forget this dreadful week in a hurry,' he forecast.

Poor young Herbert Temlett Gamlin, a lad from Wellington, was busily and modestly building a reputation for himself as a rugby full back. He would have been happy to stick to rugby – there was never a more fearless tackler. By 1899 he was making his debut for England, against Wales.

But there he was in 1895, a seventeen-year-old suddenly plucked from village and colts cricket, probably on the impulsive recommendation of Lionel Palairet whom he had dismissed in a Club and Ground trial, coming in to make up the numbers for the games with Essex and Lancashire. Against Essex, he made two ducks and took 0-82. Against Lancashire, he made two more ducks . . . and took the wicket of MacLaren. What matter that the elusive success came off a long hop and that Gerald Fowler, fielding in the outfield, held on to the catch at the second attempt?

Gamlin's career as a professional cricketer was exceedingly brief and no one outside Wellington or a few schoolboy rugby friends had heard of him. But he went into the history books as the nice, naïve young man who got rid of Archie.

My reproduction of the scorecard shows that MacLaren's name was spelt wrongly; it also reveals that Lionel Palairet actually bowled 44 five-ball overs. The supplemented attack included Ezra Bartlett, a Yorkshire-born amateur who fancied himself more as a wicket keeper, Robert Porch, a schoolmaster from Weston-super-Mare who bowled amiable leg-breaks, and Dr John Rask, from Yeovil, who was decidedly better as a middle-order batsman with a penchant for slogging. Not the attack that dreams are made of. Sammy had tried eight of them by lunch. Bowlers, not dreams.

Their virtues had nothing much to do with technical skill, rather more with stamina and sportsmanship. They kept going, while the perspiration dripped, and the scorers frequently scribbled, at the rate of 27 five-ball overs an hour. There was no new ball to await as a psychological gleam of hope, and no tea interval.

Archibald MacLaren was not only a fine captain. He liked to attack from the top of the order in the way, though arguably with more refinements, of Somerset's Hewett. Archie held his bat high as he waited for the ball to be released. His stance brought tut-tuts; none questioned his ability, paraded in turn for Harrow, Lancashire and England.

He found the short Taunton boundary, like the nondescript bowling, very much to his liking. Lancashire were 141 without loss at lunch. Then Arthur Paull took over from Albert Ward and for a long time the cricket turned into, if you were a West Country spectator, an embarrassing exhibition of batsmanship.

Stiff-jointed and unfit fielders exchanged shrugs as they retrieved the battered ball. Archie had passed his 200 in 260 minutes and when those drinks came out in late afternoon the score was 437-1. Palairet had by then gone over from medium pace to lobs, maybe as a realistic piece of energy-conserving. Paull was on 177 when once more he pulled at one of those enticing lobs. Young, confused, wholehearted Gamlin held on to a difficult catch.

Lancashire were 555 for 3 at the close of play; and just before lunch on the second day, MacLaren had cracked W.G.'s record 344. He was then 404 and looked tired. Just 20 more and Fowler juggled with and held the catch, almost apologetically, at long-off. Archie had batted for 470 minutes; the total was then 792-7. There wasn't a large crowd. But those who were at the county ground cheered him all the way back to the pavilion. Sammy led the prolonged applause among the players. 'Thought the old beggar would be out there till Christmas, me dear.'

No innings of that content could be quite flawless. Archie was dropped at mid-on when he had scored 262. Wickham, of all people, put him down early on the second day and no doubt went into clerical retreat on the spot. And after he had reached 400 he offered a venomous return to Palairet. As one of the papers noted quaintly: 'Lionel did not think it advisable to attempt the catch.' It was a magnificent innings. There was one six (remember how difficult they were to score in those days), 64 fours, 10 threes, 26 twos and 80 singles.

OF POWER AND POETRY

Viv Richards' 322, Somerset v Warwickshire, Taunton
The Guardian, 3 June 1985

After the day's play was over and the wedding bells at St James' and Taunton's other boundary churches were at last quiet and the Somerset supporters, palms reddened from applause, had gone reluctantly back to their pint glasses, I went in search of a second assessment of Vivian Richards' historic innings. My own evaluation was too misted by joy and a sense of privilege that sprang from lasting friendship with the West Indian captain.

I sought out the ordinary county cricketers who had earlier marvelled at Richards' wondrous gifts. "It was butchery," they kept repeating, unprompted, uninfluenced by each other. Yet the metaphor was not one of slaughterhouse destruction. Their voices were tinged more with the affection of Christmas shoppers' bonhomie, when surveying the rows of seasonal poultry. Necks had been wrung, but the riches of the feast superseded thoughts of primitive savagery.

This account of an afternoon in the Taunton sun is a personal one, and for this I ask forgiveness. My relationship with Richards has been warm, loyal and not exclusively concerned with cricket. It was getting dark late on Saturday and the Blackdown hills were already a blurred indigo blue when we sat, almost alone, in the dressing room.

It was a gentle, joyful, almost emotional hour. The nephew of CLR. James hovered happily, talking of the film he hoped to make for Channel 4 and regretting that no crew had been present to film his greatest innings.

The other Somerset players had embarrassed – and yet thrilled – Richards as they stood aside in two rows so that he would lead them onto the field for the start of the Warwickshire innings just overs from the close. The Taunton crowd had already embraced him.

Champagne had been passed into the dressing room and now, contemplatively, we shared the still-sparkling dregs in the plastic cups. He was wrapped only in his towel and his solicitous memories: "Oh dear," he said, "we got home from Headingley late. I snatched some sleep and when I woke up I thought I was still in the coach coming home.

"That was probably why I scratched a bit to start with, I was still tired. Then suddenly I knew it was my day. I soared with confidence. I felt great – I can't describe it, and I didn't think I'd ever get out."

It wasn't the voice of a braggard. It was Richards, the best in the world, honestly relaying his feelings. I thought again of what that earthy West

Country philosopher, Bill Andrews, had said to me nearly 10 years ago: "One of these days that lovely bugger Vivian Richards will score 1,000 runs!"

Richards' 322 took him 258 balls. He hit eight sixes and 42 fours. It was his highest score by 31 runs. It also beat Somerset's previous best, 310 by the marvellous Harold Gimblett against Sussex at Eastbourne in 1948. At times we felt it would beat anyone's best but at last, weary rather than careless, he played-on to Anton Ferreira. The driving had been murderous, the ball scorched through mid-wicket like an optical illusion.

ALONE IN THE AFTERMATH

With Viv Richards after close of play
Footsteps from East Coker (2010)

More than an hour after the end of the day's play, by which time most of his team-mates had showered and gone home, I tentatively went in search of him. He took so long over his toiletry and deodorising rituals that he was always the last player to leave the dressing room. There he was, still wrapped in his towel, sitting alone on the bench. No suggestion of celebration or self-acclaim. He had already acknowledged as he came off the field the cheers of the doting supporters, some of whom had come across from the cattle market and stayed to be enraptured, leaving the drovers to load the lorries.

He was tired and reflective. He beckoned me to join him and he found champagne which he poured into plastic mugs. In his own way he was now ready quietly to celebrate. The dressing room was deserted apart from us. And for nearly another hour we talked, our conversation deflecting across unscheduled territory. Viv would never have claimed, I suspect, that he rated notably high in intellectual matters; he was more inclined to leave those more profound affairs to the cerebral Peter Roebuck – in the days, that was, that they were still speaking to each other and in awe of their differing skills. Now, in a smelly dressing room strewn with discarded kit, he unwound. There was no prompting needed from me. I had never seen him so eager to talk and I'm not sure he ever was again in his bountiful life of sport.

A few hours earlier he had scored a triple hundred, so powerful and consummate that one experienced Warwickshire player, in my hearing, said he would give up the game for ever as he realised the enormity of the gulf between them. Now, in the stillness of a cricket ground after almost all the players had gone home, IVA was ready to evaluate what he had achieved. But it had nothing at all to do with cricket.

His innings, indeed, was barely mentioned. Nor was cricket in general. To my surprise he moved onto religion instead. He also talked of his school friends he continued to see whenever he returned to Antigua. He talked lovingly of his family and the influence they had on him. He chuckled as he recalled his days as a waiter, balancing the glasses with a slip fielder's dependable hands. It was a contemplative and spiritual journey that he chose spontaneously to make. It certainly wasn't remotely what I had expected.

THE MOST EPIC OF 20TH CENTURY KNOCKS

Graeme Hick's 405, Worcestershire v Somerset, Taunton
The Guardian, 7 May 1988

First on this same sunny Taunton ground, 93 years ago, came Archie's Match. MacLaren's 424 was one of bludgeoning brilliance and is still talked about graphically by members born a generation or two later.

Then in 1985 came Richards. He scored 322 with mighty and murderous intent against Warwickshire, whose weary bowlers congratulated him with generous spirit and said they were thinking of taking up another sport.

Yesterday it was Graeme Hick's match, as future record books will testify. Worcestershire declared at tea on 682 for seven. The tall 21-year-old Zimbabwean, wondrously talented and still supposedly – and ominously – learning, was 405 not out.

He has scored 815 runs this season and we are still in the first week of May. Records, we suspect, are not of paramount importance to him. "I must admit I didn't even know of the MacLaren achievement," he said, minutes after coming in with a tired step and an exalted face to a members' ovation.

Phil Neale, the Worcestershire captain, also confided that he was unaware how close Hick was to the all-time championship record, set by the irascible Lancashire skipper before the turn of the century. It is hard to guess whether he would have stalled sentimentally for another over or two if he had known. He was not saying but must, in retrospect, agonise over the moment of his declaration.

Worcestershire could not bat too much longer, four-day cricket or not. They still had to bowl out Somerset twice, they argued, and there were optimistic murmurs out of the side of the mouth that the wicket might be eventually turning. For heaven's sake, they might be needing Hick for his bowling. And, as we soon found out in the pale evening sunshine, they did.

He had been at the crease for 9¼ hours. He had given a hard chance or two early on, might have been caught off somewhat tired shots to cover and backward point towards the end, and was perilously near being stumped as he lifted his heel playing and missing at Roebuck.

But it was a magnificent amalgam of timing, discrimination, unflurried temperament and dazzling maturity. "Not as good as my double century at Old Trafford," he said with unassuming candour.

His bolder shots were straight and true. He never resorted to a wanton slog. The emotions were mostly hidden in the nature of this young man, but he wore a third-former's grin and raised his bat high as he reached his 200, 300 and then 400.

Hick faced 469 balls. He hit 35 fours and 11 sixes. He dominated the innings, as lesser mortals stood at the other end to take minor roles and lead the applause. Ian Botham watched with admiration. "It was one of the greatest innings I've seen." The books tell us it was a Worcestershire record and the eighth highest in the first-class game.

There is something quietly engaging about this emerging genius. His style lacks ostentation, just like his persona. He has an old head and relishes the unmitigated strain of concentration that a marathon performance like this demands. As he awaits the bowler's run, he holds the bat horizontally in the way MacLaren favoured.

The Somerset bowlers pounded away with aching limbs, willing hearts and wry looks. The fielding faltered badly as MacLaren did his despotic deeds, but there were only occasional lapses yesterday as the contest veered inexorably towards Worcestershire and the 1,300 spectators – oh, if there had only been more – became obsessed by the sheer statistical grandeur of a feat of historical significance.

COOK'S SPECIAL

Jimmy Cook's 313, Somerset v Glamorgan, Cardiff

The Guardian, 5 May 1990

There was a poetic lilt, full of Golden Age imagery, to the voice of the amiable Glamorgan scorer whose name, after all, is Byron. He garnished a mundane statistic just before tea by telling us that the last wicket had fallen 24 hours earlier. It was that kind of cricket: bountiful for the batsmen, unyielding and even soporific, and yet engrossing in a nostalgic kind of way.

Somerset declared at lunch on 535 for two. Jimmy Cook was then cruising along, in his flawless, one-paced splendour, at 313. He would probably have still been there next week, refusing anything so skittish as a lofted drive, though accumulating attractively because the timing was so exquisite and the sharp eyes ever alert to the fractionally wayward delivery.

Another ten runs for him and the 36-year-old South African, solemn of countenance but warm of nature, would have been Somerset's highest scorer ever. Yet it was time to put Glamorgan in if the match was to take any competitive shape.

Cook batted for nearly 8¾ hours, hitting 43 boundaries. At the other end the county's new skipper, Chris Tavaré, was 120 not out, a particularly poised, correct innings of 255 minutes with 15 fours. Viv Richards, absent because of a stomach upset, lay remedially in the dressing room. He was to learn that his record of 322 for Somerset was safe – for the time being at least.

But records, as the good old Byron reminded us, were broken. Cook's feat had been to score more runs in an innings than anyone in the past against Glamorgan. Wally Hammond had twice got to 302.

FIVE-TON LARA REWRITES EVERY RECORD IN THE BOOK

Brian Lara's 501, Warwickshire v Durham, Edgbaston

The Guardian, 7 June 1994

History was made with surreal splendour in the Birmingham sunshine yesterday. Brian Lara, the West Indies' elfin genius with the Merlin wrists, off-drove the makeshift bowler John Morris at 5.30. The ball skimmed the manicured grass on its way to the fence – and Warwickshire's wondrously gifted overseas player had made the record books redundant.

There were only two balls left, according to the frantic words of his century-making partner Keith Piper, as Lara rocked on his elegant heels for the boundary which gave him a remarkable 501 not out, the highest individual score in the records of first-class cricket.

Gently hit on the helmet the previous delivery, Lara goaded himself into a final flourish of jaunty response as he aimed for the extra-cover area, to beat Hanif Mohammad's total of 499 at Karachi in 1958.

Warwickshire were 810 for four. The records were by then as plentiful as the Midlanders who chased belatedly from work to watch – and journalists, despatched by their offices from Test-match grounds and watering holes.

The biggest irony was that these two counties had failed before the start to reach agreement over a contrived contest. So Warwickshire and Lara simply kept going against Durham's depleted attack.

It seems almost disloyal to the quality of greatness in agreeing with Lara that this was still not, taken all through, one of his better innings. Edgbaston was understandably heady with the reverberations of Brummie-Caribbean cadences, at least in spirit. There has been an aura of worship for him, created in a matter of weeks since he arrived, to compound the most extraordinary frisson since Richards and Botham were savaging in tandem. Bejewelled talent like Lara's must carry any reservations with reluctance.

Yet, by his shimmering standards, he scratched at the start: shivering in Friday's cold, looking weary, as if suddenly confronted by the reality of county cricket's unrelenting pragmatism, after the convivial rum-punch ambience at home.

He should have been caught at the wicket when 18 and was bowled by a no-ball; yesterday, driving a trifle loosely for once through the off-side on 238, he grazed Cummins's fingertips as the ball went on to the boundary. That was a questionable chance; more acceptable was his fallible scoop when on 413, in the direction of square leg. The fielder misjudged badly and did not get under the ball.

There were pained expressions from the tiring, mostly unrewarded Durham players, already regretting that they had not agreed with Warwickshire over artificial forfeitures in pursuit of a result. The fielder, slow off the blocks and – dare one say, confused subconsciously by conflicting allegiances – was the substitute Michael Burns, Warwickshire's reserve wicketkeeper. Lara, assuming he was out, was already racked by self-rebuke. Slowly he glanced towards square leg and the smile of relief that lit up his face was evident, even from under the helmet, at boundary distance.

He is not a batsman of flamboyant persona. There are no fancy tricks to adorn the sublime style of the little man. But the emotion emerged as he got to 400. The bat was raised in boyish joy; he embraced his partner Piper. They are like blood brothers, rooming together, shielding each other on Friday from the cold, when the advertisement hoardings were careering in the wind.

The tentative beginnings, the occasional flaws, had all been superseded by the exquisite grandeur of his attacking strokes, which came with eager and instinctive skill. When he pulled or cross-batted, there was nothing ugly in the execution. The cover drives scorched through, evading fielders with embarrassing ease.

There can surely be few in the present game with better timing, with a greater facility to find the gaps. Durham were mutilated and one could sympathise with them. They were without Graveney (thigh), who could at least have kept going with some attempt at his normal economy, and without Saxelby (back), injured as he practised in the morning in anticipation of a coerced bowling spell.

For Warwickshire, the bit players savoured their own morsel of posterity. Piper finished on 116 himself. Earlier Penney, who for much of the time had stood at the other end rather like a uniformed attendant with innately appreciative eyes at the National Gallery, scored 44 before being taken at extra cover.

But the day belonged imperishably to Lara. "It doesn't make me a great player," he said afterwards with sweet, if unnecessary, diffidence. With 62 fours and 10 sixes – and a timeless exhibition of batsmanship extending over almost eight hours – his place in the game's thoughts and almanacks was assured.

A SPECIAL MOMENT

Zaheer Abbas's 215 (his 100th 100), Pakistan v India, Lahore, December 1982
The Guardian, 15 January 1983

As a batsman inclined to recoil from too much ostentation, he marked the occasion with some style. He reached his hundred with a perfunctory poke for three wide of mid-wicket and held his bat horizontally above his head with both hands – I'd seen Geoff Boycott do that on television when he got his 100th hundred.

Then he went on to score 215 and the Indians, many of them his friends, were glad to see the back of him. Radio commentators shed their accustomed formality as they eulogised the innings. In the lofty open-air press box, where some reporters record their instant thoughts in a Persian-style script that is a thousand times more beautiful than Mr Pitman's, the prose was destined for expansive and affectionate headlines.

Zaheer wiped his spectacles as he walked with a triumphant spring back to the pavilion. His shirt sleeves, surplice-white, were as ever buttoned at the wrist. He smiled like the normally solemn choirboy who knew that he had hit the right note – with purity and grandeur. Imran and the other Pakistan team-mates were there to congratulate him.

*

When he joined Gloucestershire in 1972 he spoke few English words. He is now efficiently bilingual in the way of most of the Pakistan players. "You know how important that innings was to me. Whenever I am scoring runs I am happy. I crack one record and I am already looking for the next."

There is no swagger in the way he says it. His youngest brother keeps the scrapbook and the statistics in Karachi. Home in Bristol, scorer Bert Avery does the same.

Zed invited me into the Pakistan dressing room for the rest of the match. We chatted and then he snoozed in the treatment room – in a pattern which I found endearing. He isn't physically strong and has had problems with his health over the last year or so. You wouldn't think so as he rises on his toes to produce the best square-cut in current cricket. Many would argue that he's the most stylish player in the game. It isn't just romantic nonsense that so many believe he has been inadvertently transposed from the Golden Age of Cricket.

*

Zaheer was born only weeks before the historic and at times acrimonious partition of 1947. His face, studious and preoccupied, carries the complexities of his proud and battle-scarred nation. He has both the gentleness and solemnity of Islam.

A dignified man, with a lofty social standing and a family construction business, to cushion him after he gives up playing, he keeps personal grievances to himself. One, certainly, is the way the Pakistan Cricket Board failed to give him the captaincy ahead of Javed.

But runs for him have always been the wondrous antidote. He overhauled first Fry and Hobbs and then Hammond in Karachi not long ago, by scoring a century in each innings for the eighth time. That was a world record.

"Let's see," he's been apt to ask Bert Avery with that sheepish smile, eyes twinkling behind the spectacles (the same pair as he damaged while fielding several years ago), "how many tons did this Bradman get?" The Gloucestershire statistician responds: "Rather too many even for you, Zed." And they jointly look for a target nearer realism.

Zaheer leaves Richards and Botham to corner the pages of Wisden with the more dynamic flourish. He goes into cricket history almost by stealth. "Where do you bowl to him?" asks his good friend Doshi, to no one in particular. "What are you complaining about – you've just taken five Test wickets," says Zed. Doshi grins and returns to his P.G. Wodehouse.

Far away in Pakistan Zaheer is, at the age of 35, demonstrating once more the receding art of pure batsmanship. "See you back in England," he waves. I edge uneasily past the armed police – one of whom stops me taking some innocuous ciné film as if I were a fugitive from a le Carré novel – and I know instinctively in my heart that the bat is mightier than the gun.

19
Football

The old Eastville ground of Bristol Rovers in 1964

Three West Country football managers: Malcolm Allison (Bristol Rovers), Terry Cooper (Bristol City) and Neil Warnock (Plymouth Argyle)

For almost all of David's working life he reported on football. It provided a steady stream of work, mostly in the local papers but also, when there were high-profile matches, in the national ones. His knowledge of the two Bristol clubs and, to a lesser extent, the other clubs of the south-west, provided him with a rich seam of material, both contemporary and historical.

As a freelance David established a slot for himself, coming up with a string of multi-part series for the *Bristol Evening Post*'s Saturday sports section. Many of these series, often stretching across ten weeks, were ghost-written reminiscences of local sporting heroes. From the world of football there were John Atyeo, Geoff Bradford, Alfie Biggs, Pat Beasley and Fred Ford; from cricket Andy Wilson, Horace Hazell and Reg Sinfield.

In 1971 he developed another series: 'The Great Games', telling the stories of memorable football matches involving the local clubs. Among them were: the FA Cup tie of 1935 when Bristol City, in the lower half of the Third Division South, beat First Division Portsmouth; the quarter-final cup tie in 1951 when Bristol Rovers took the Flying Scotsman train to the north-east and – playing with 'the unbridled zest of a West Country team with a £350 label' – drew with the wealthy Newcastle; and, of course, Yeovil's 1949 victory over Sunderland, 'the most romantic story in the history of West Country soccer'.

Yet David was never one to dwell only on triumphs. With relish he told the story of Rovers' disastrous trip to Luton on Easter Monday 1936 when Joe Payne, a young ex-miner 'pushed reluctantly into the Luton side because three other centre-forwards weren't fit', netted an all-time record ten goals: 'Wags suggested that reporters should be given a cribbage board so that they could keep account of the goals conceded.'

Then there was the cup tie in April 1945, in the last months of the war, when Bristol City travelled to Cardiff's Ninian Park and, long before the introduction of substitutes or penalty shoot-outs, had to keep playing till a winning goal was scored.

> The match started at 3 p.m. and finished, with only fleeting breaks, at 20 minutes to 7! Many were the stories of Welsh supporters who went home for their tea and came back to see what was going on. Players were toppling with cramp and pulled muscles all over the pitch. They were vying for the chance to go out, as injured players, to the wing where they could have a rest. The pace became slower and slower; passes went astray more and more. But it remained an engrossing contest.

David reported regularly on the matches of the two Bristol clubs, where his ability to 'multi-task' was extraordinary. His son Mark recalls a Rovers game at their Eastville ground when David was in charge of the ground's music and announcements, was providing regular updates for *Radio Bristol* and, with the help of Mark and the old Gloucestershire wicket-keeper Andy Wilson, telephoning copy to 13 different newspapers.

The national newspapers – the *Sunday Express*, then for many years the *Observer* and *Guardian* – started to call on him in the 1970s, notably when Bristol City enjoyed four seasons in the top flight of league football. Then in September 1989, when the *Sunday Correspondent* was launched, he was recruited to cover leading matches all over the country. It was an arrangement that broke his long ties with the Bristol clubs, and unfortunately it did not last long, with the paper folding after 14 months.

David's best football reports were for the *Evening World*, which allocated him most of a Monday page to write at leisure about the previous Saturday's game. By contrast, the rush of a deadline after a hectic match rarely left him the time or space to produce the gems that sparkled in his cricket reports.

Football may not have been as close to his heart as cricket, but his feeling for the two Bristol clubs, their history and their heroes, was evident in the many feature articles he wrote – not just for the newspapers but also for such publications as the yearbook of the Bristol Rovers Supporters Club, for whom he submitted an evocative piece when a particular favourite of his, Harold Jarman, 'Best Winger Outside Divsion One', left the club.

> His football has always been a joy because he plays it instinctively. He weaves off down the wing just as he once did for Clifton Villa up on the Downs. He has never bothered his head too much with the theory of the soccer manual ... I'm sorry he's now moving on. I'll miss that glimpse of genius that could lift the dreariest game; I'll miss those nervous mannerisms like the touching of the hair after every duel with a full back; I'll miss the warm and very special relationship he built up with his mates on the North Stand side; I'll miss our bit of banter after the match.

The football article which was closest to David's heart was one he wrote for the *Western Daily Press* on Johnny Hayward, a Yeovil footballer who played on either side of the First World War. A hero of David's father, Hayward was just the sort of sportsman about whom David wrote so well – a man content to play for the enjoyment and to stay true to his roots.

GEOFF BRADFORD

The Bristol Rovers footballer on the club's 1951 FA Cup run, from a ghost-written series in the Bristol Evening Post (1980)

Don Revie was in the Hull side then and Raich Carter was player-manager. We were the underdogs and Raich was so confident he said the game was going to be just a matter of how many goals they scored. But he hadn't seen our great ally – the Eastville mud. The pitch was always heavy in those days, but for this game it was muddier than usual. I remember we were standing in the dressing room tunnel watching the referee go out to inspect the pitch. Someone said: "If he doesn't sink down as far as his knees, the game's on."

We spent some hours on that pitch. Part of our training used to be dragging a sheet of galvanised tin, weighted down by a couple of players standing on it, over the mud to flatten it. It was things like that which helped us to build such a great team spirit.

The mud was so deep by the second half that at one point Ray Warren – what a great skipper he was! – had to give me a push to get me going again. If you stood still a couple of seconds, you'd sink.

They were drawn away to Newcastle United in the quarter-finals

Not thinking we would get so far in the Cup, I had arranged to get married before sixth-round day. Bert Tann gave me permission to go ahead with the wedding. All the lads from the team came and left straightaway afterwards for Southend, where we were to have a week of special training.

I was allowed to stay behind for a one-day honeymoon and joined up with the lads on Tuesday. The next time I saw Betty was after the Cup-tie.

IT'S NO LAUGHING MATTER

Western Daily Press, February 1995

Only twice in my life – when I was still a small boy – did I enter a fancy dress competition. The first time I went as an undertaker, complete with top hat, brass handles and mournful expression, and won first prize.

For my encore, the following year, I decked myself out as a soccer referee. I was unplaced. "You were grinning too much," the judge said. "Referees aren't blessed with a sense of humour."

Maybe that's why they dress in black – just like my undertaker. As a breed they look glum, wary, tetchy and lugubrious. Soccer isn't, I suppose, any laughing matter when you have old pros trying to con you, spectators trying to decapitate you and assessors up in the stand trying to document every flaw.

THE SOCCER STAR WHO SHUNNED THE BIG TIME

Western Daily Press, September 1977

He played his last game of football exactly 50 years ago – and they still talk about him in the Somerset town where he was born and became the idol.

He is extolled in the way that others extol timeless international stars like Puskas and Pele. The First Division clubs held out their tempting inducements. Tottenham, in particular, pleaded with him to join them. They could have turned him into an England player. But he chose to stay with humble Yeovil for 20 years. In that time he scored 548 goals.

His presence on the quaint, sloping Huish ground was guaranteed to excite every soccer fan in South Somerset. He was a gentle, diffident centre forward, uncoached and uncomplicated in his approach to association football. But he had magnetic natural skill and charisma like no Yeovil player before or since. His name: Fred (Johnny) Hayward.

And the question they still ask in the town is why he never left his modest job in the gloving industry to sample First Division football. One of his two sons, Cyril Hayward, too young ever to have seen Johnny play, admits there were private regrets from his father in later life that he did not sample league soccer. "Dad would watch it on television, and I could see what was going through his mind. I think perhaps he felt he didn't make the most of his ability."

There was certainly parental opposition, too. One relative told me: "I don't think Johnny's father ever watched him play. On the one occasion when he walked to the ground, the opposition failed to turn up."

Cyril has a watch given to Johnny by his parents in an attempt to influence his decision to stay at home. And home was important to the quiet-spoken, good-living Johnny. He was happiest of all when surrounded by his family. It was quite a number – seven daughters and two sons.

He was at heart an amateur. There were many county appearances for Somerset. He often recalled with genuine affection his early games for Yeovil Baptists and the Boys' Brigade. Only in the last few years with Yeovil & Petters United, as the club was then called, did he receive any money. He was rather embarrassed about taking it.

A nephew said: "He was never a professional footballer in spirit. It was only that professionalism overtook the club."

Not that the bonuses were likely to make you rich. It was five shillings for a win and half a crown for a draw. The soccer wages went straight into the family budget.

Johnny played in every forward position except outside right. He was born in Wellington Street, just round the corner from the Huish ground, and played his first game for Yeovil in 1907. By 1921, he was knocking in 60 goals a season. Mainly with his left foot. The Hayward left foot was legendary, in fact.

My father watched him in home games and idolised him like every other young lad in his cloth cap on the terraces. He said: "Whenever you saw him brace his left foot, you knew it was a goal. It was lethal."

Arthur Riggs, president of the First Yeovil Company Boys' Brigade, knew Johnny for years. "He was a very nice person in every way, and I never remember him committing a foul."

Yet what was so special about him? Why did First Division scouts from all over the country come to the small market town to see this shy glove-sorter run out in his green and white shirt on a Saturday afternoon? "He had it all – and what a shot," says Percy May, the full back of those days, who still lives in Yeovil.

But, in truth, Johnny was not the all-round footballer. He was not exceptionally fast. Not many of his goals came from headers. Some even called him one-footed. Bill Garrett, of Somerton, watched him "hundreds of times, right back in his Pen Mills days". And he's in no doubt about the one magical skill that made Johnny Hayward a great footballer. "It was his swerve. He left defenders standing. I have never seen a better body-swerve on the field."

For 20 years he enthralled Yeovil crowds and consistently frustrated league managers. He even went out in style. His last game was against Lovells Athletic. And he scored seven goals.

Johnny left others to do the talking and to ponder on why he stayed in Somerset. He died aged 71, but not before he had seen his two sons, Ken and Cyril, briefly play for Yeovil.

Half a century after he kicked his last ball for the local team he chose in preference to Spurs, the Huish supporters – even those who were not born when he played – still talk ecstatically about him.

West Country sport has never had a more unassuming and unlikely hero.

THIS WAS SOMETHING COMPLETELY DIFFERENT
Southampton v Bristol City, 25 December 1941
Bristol Evening Post, January 1973

It reads like a Monty Python sketch. Yet it WAS a great game ... as a story for future generations to cherish and chuckle over. The Bristol City players who took part in it just over 31 years ago will never forget it. Nor will some of those who SHOULD have taken part.

Christmas Day, 1941. City were away to Southampton. Hardly everyone's idea of a Christmas Day. The players were to travel in three cars. First picking-up point: The Hen and Chicken, Bedminster, at 7.30 a.m. Everyone was punctual and the cars set off. There were no sign-posts in those days and it wasn't easy to keep in convoy. Wally Collins, long-standing taxi driver of the City team, took the kit. He also took Clarrie Bourton, Jack Preece and Cliff Morgan.

They arrived in Southampton in good time for the 11 a.m. kick-off. The three changed and waited. And waited. No sign of the other two cars. Southampton manager Tom Parker was pulled in for a hurried conference. Bristol City, he agreed, must rustle up a team somehow or other.

Somehow or other ... they did. Four spare Southampton players of indefinite talent volunteered to turn out. So did three spectators, including a soldier and a schoolteacher. So did the Southampton trainer, Gallagher, who looked as though he hadn't played for years. Cliff Morgan takes up the bizarre story: "When I went to toss up, the referee said that if the rest of the team turned up within 20 minutes, he'd stop this game and start again properly. They actually turned up breathlessly after 23 minutes. There were players like Roy Bentley among them. But the referee had stipulated 20 minutes and he wouldn't change his mind. Well, the rest of our team went up in the stand and started taking the micky out of us. It was a wet, muddy pitch and hard work, I can tell you. Just three City players – and eight others doing their best.

"Lemmo Southway was in charge and he had a brainwave. When I went to take a throw-in, he suggested that I should ask their trainer, who was playing for us, to go down and we'd take him off. 'Then we'll bring Ernie Brinton on in his place,' said Lemmo. Brinton was roughly the same height and build as their trainer. He was sent down to the changing-room to get stripped off. In came their trainer splattered in mud. The mud was scraped off him and smeared onto Ernie."

The daring deception was about to take place. Out ran Brinton, doing his best to adopt the pose of the ageing trainer who had limped off a few minutes earlier. And it worked for a short time. Then the linesman started suspicious glances in the direction of the newcomer who was suddenly playing a little too well. As Cliff puts it, "The game was up."

The referee, who must have been wondering whether he was in charge of a football match or a theatrical farce, ordered the mud-caked Brinton off. Lemmo, with no wish to see his team down to 10 men, rushed back into the changing rooms. But he was too late – the exhausted Southampton trainer was already in the bath. And he wasn't getting out for anyone to play football again. Not on Christmas Day, anyway.

Still the good-natured barracking went on up in the sheltered stand. For the three City players who had imprudently chosen to travel with the kit, the joke was now wearing a little thin. Yet they didn't do so badly. Reports vary as to whether they lost by 5-1 or 5-2. And whether the game Gallagher, exploited trainer that he was, scored an early goal for City by courtesy of the lenient Southampton defenders.

Back in the bath, the weary and mildly irked Ashton Gate trio asked their smirking team-mates: "And what happened to you so-and-sos?" It was discovered that one of the cars broke down and the other pulled up to try to help. That wasn't the end of the day's crises. On the way home one of the cars broke down again. The players got home at 6 p.m.

What a way to spend Christmas Day – and for just 30 shillings a player.

END OF AN ERA AT EASTVILLE

There was talk of Bristol Rovers moving to City's Ashton Gate ground, even of buying it. In the end they stayed at Eastville till 1986 when they moved to Bath.

Western Daily Press, November 1981

There was never another football pitch like Eastville, and not simply because, in such vaudeville fashion, the stand burnt down. For 84 years it has engendered at various times ridicule, mirth, scorn, exasperation, admiration and, above all, warm-hearted affection.

Once upon a time its quagmire surface looked more like a farmyard. Opposing teams joked that they needed wellingtons rather than football boots. Eastville, soon to lose Bristol Rovers to Ashton Gate, was renowned for its mud, its floods and its sprawling referees getting water in their whistles.

It also had its befriending gasometers and unique rose borders that were the envy of the parks department. One First Division star, after failing in a cup match against Rovers, said: "Every time I went to shoot I looked at those lovely red roses and was scared I'd damage them!"

Rovers grew up with adversity at Eastville. The bailiff was never too far away and the thoughts of a £15,000 debt (big in those days) caused the club to sell out to the Greyhound company in 1941 for a give-away £12,000. In fact, after the chairman had done the deal in London, several of the other Rovers directors didn't want to sanction it. But it was too late.

Eastville's approach has always been endearingly down-to-earth and working class. There were never any airs and graces on the terraces. Die-hard supporters were proud of their original Black Arabs nickname – and proud of the long line of great footballers, many of whom the club couldn't afford to keep.

Bristol lad Eddie Hapgood, later to captain England, had to be sold for a few pounds to Kettering. There were also Cliff Britton, Phil Taylor and Ronnie Dix, all great players who made only nominal appearances for Rovers before going on their way in search of fame.

Facilities were never in the five-star category. In the first year after World War One, City turned up at the Rovers ground for a friendly, changed in their charabanc and ran straight onto the pitch. "Your dressing rooms are a blooming disgrace," they said rather superciliously.

In recent years the reputation has apparently persisted. A former chairman called the ground 'a clapped-out builders' yard' and a manager, with a more agricultural turn of phrase, suggested the other day that it was a cowshed. Players in the hungry twenties shrugged off the functional aspects; they were glad to be earning a few pounds.

From 1921 Rovers had had their first manager, Ben Hill from Derby County. They were in business, in the Third Division. Eastville was where the astute Captain Albert Prince-Cox ruled. The club never had a more flamboyant manager. Boxing promotions, music hall, soccer; it was all show business to him. Later came Bert Tann, the dockside philosopher who became the longest serving manager in the game.

Eastville was so many things over the years. It was where Fanny Walden and Jimmy Dimmock came in 1921 as Spurs superstars before their time; where Jesse Whatley kept goal without missing a game in five years; it was the home of Bert Williams and Jackie Pitt, who did everything and are still around. Rovers drew here with Arsenal back in 1903, had a great cup run in 1951 and beat Manchester United in 1955.

Eastville, it will be remembered, was famous for No buy – No sell; a policy born of necessity, that kept rich talents in the Third Division. But controversy was always part of the pattern – and the fun. It will never be quite the same at Ashton Gate, of course. Unless they start growing roses there.

A FANTASY WORLD FULL OF GREAT SPORTSMEN

Western Daily Press, February 2004

Sport is full of fantasists. This week we've had the case of the 76-year-old impostor in Dorset who for years had gone around making presentations and accepting acclaim as the one-time Wolves star Bobby Mason. He has shamefacedly now made his apologies to the local Tories and bowling club – and to the real Wolverhampton player who came down to sort out the man's identity problem.

Five years ago, when Yeovil Town were in the news half-a-century after their historic FA Cup win over Sunderland, I first heard of someone claiming he was Ralph Davis, a member of that famous Somerset side. He lived in Reading but told everyone who would listen that he had been stationed at Houndstone Camp, near Yeovil, at the time of the Cup tie (probably true) and was chosen on merit to play against Sunderland. He then compounded his flight of imagination by saying how upset he was that the present club were refusing to acknowledge his part in the triumph.

After many phone calls I ran Marshall Davies to ground. Even his surname was spelt differently. He steadfastly stuck to his story and said he had written to both the FA and Yeovil chairman John Fry to let them know how pained he was over his lack of official recognition. It was, of course, pure fantasy, though I feel he was by then convinced he had played against Sunderland.

Some of this column's older readers will remember Albert 'Boy' Bessell, standing with his fruit and veg barrow in Old Market and then outside the London Inn, Bedminster. He was a crowd-pleasing fighter of the 1930s who had once walked to London in search of a boxing career, sleeping under the hedge and then staying at the Salvation Army hostel. 'Boy' Bessell, who began in the booths on Horfield Common and St George's Park, went on to fight Eric Boon and appear on the same bill at the Albert Hall as Tommy Farr.

But long after he had given up his colourful career, I discovered someone was impersonating him back in Bristol. I eventually found and confronted him at an old people's home at Westbury Park.

Just like the Davis impostor, this phoney pugilist stuck to his story. What was more, he accurately quoted nearly every one of Bessell's professional fights, the way they ended, the arena and the year. In some freakish way he had taken over the authentic Bristol boxer's personality. He even had a similar name on his pension book. It was pointless to argue or tell him he was a fake.

A QUARTET OF MANAGERS

extracts from four features, The Guardian

Terry Cooper at Bristol City – *August 1983*

By the time I reached his office soon after, Terry Cooper had hoovered the floor, answered a dozen letters in painstaking long-hand, taken a lively training session, picked the team for the following evening's game, conducted a confidential interview with a first-team player and gone on the treatment table himself. It was a pretty normal day.

He played for England 20 times. He was one of the Elland Road elite. Like Big Jack, Norm and Gilesy, he was pampered and rather enjoyed it. Not bad for an introvert lad from the pit at Castleford. Now he was manager of Bristol City who themselves nearly went underground. But how many soccer directors do their own hoovering?

"There isn't any spare cash down in the Fourth Division. I haven't got a secretary so I answer all my own letters. Kids asking for trials. Supporters telling me where I'm going wrong. I never got 'A' for spelling, but I do my best."

Cooper, of the discreetly receding hairline and the creaking joints, is now the oldest player in the Football League. He's apt these days to name himself as substitute. The Ashton Gate crowd cheer him when he ambles on. He then proceeds to take all the corners, never to waste a pass and to bring a whiff of nostalgia to the game. He's usually warming up from about the second minute.

Bobby Gould between jobs – *September 1990*

Gould is back in his Portishead home overlooking the Bristol Channel where the family have lived for nearly 20 years. He is out pounding the lanes of Avon at seven every morning and has lost nearly a stone. He helps Margery with the washing-up, does occasional scouting for Wimbledon if asked, turns up on the local telly and is as restless as ever.

"You know me. I can't sit still. Yesterday is past. It's impossible to say what the future will hold for me. I like challenges, doing new things."

No one would dare doubt his versatility. During his spells out of football he has been an insurance broker and a window-cleaner. He now fancies writing a children's book. When he left Bristol Rovers for Wimbledon three years ago it was, at this reporter's count, his 15th move as player or team boss. It is quite possible one missed half a dozen.

As a nomadic centre-forward of modest skill, he always went in feet first – and with heart not far behind. He hangs his varying emotions out on the line wherever he goes. It is impossible to keep him out of the news for long.

Malcolm Allison at Bristol Rovers – *December 1992*

It was too much to expect to find a well-stocked cocktail cabinet in some corner of this small, sparsely furnished cabin on the edge of a Quaker chocolate factory. But Malcolm Allison was ever a generous host, especially in headier times when he liked to dispense fizzy grapefruit juice along with the pulpy raw material beloved of headline writers.

Here at overcast Keynsham, halfway between Bristol and Bath – the Georgian city where Bristol Rovers play temporarily at Twerton Park – he got up and affected to look beyond the filing cabinets. "There could be a bottle or two left here for me, though I'm not too hopeful. You should have seen the cabinets I had at Maine Road and Palace ..."

Rovers eschew such extravagances at their hired training ground. But you also know that Allison, however much he still savours the reminiscences of his cultivated hedonism, is now at the bus-pass age. There is a bit more flesh around the midriff and, although he retains the sepia handsome-guy appeal of American B pictures, the eyes betray world-weariness, softened by humour.

Neil Warnock at Plymouth Argyle – *January 1997*

Warnock has arrived at his office after a 25-minute drive from his home in Cornwall. The only other occupant is Charlie, the labrador-springer cross who immediately goes to sleep under the table, oblivious to managerial complications and clearly a therapeutic influence.

Home Park has always carried an aura of ambiguity. Its rural past is discernible, not entirely eroded by modern developments. The farm lanes are still there, along with the open spaces and the ground's own evocatively named Barn Park End. Argyle's shirts remain symbolically green. Yet there is also an aggressive resilience about the place. The bomb craters have gone, though the innately gentle, melodic charm of Devonians has often been complemented by a strong temperamental pride which can manifest itself in fiery response. Over the generations Argyle have recruited sailors with heaving hearts like the waves coming in above the Hoe, and swarthy tin-miners from across the Tamar. They did not stand too much nonsense.

"I love the people and this part of the country," says Warnock. "I was actually advised against coming here, you know. Yet I got on so well initially with the chairman. He backed everything I did in the first 12 months as we reached Wembley and won promotion. Now if we pass each other in the car-park we barely speak. It's all done by fax and is sad."

EXTRACTS FROM MATCH REPORTS

Swindon Town 1 Sunderland 1

Second Division – The Guardian, January 1973 (written as 'Matthew Stacey')

There was precious little dignity about this farmyard splash and tumble. The spectators, as if to justify their own dubious good sense in walking to the match in the pouring rain, were prepared to see the funny side. But this was, frankly, no time for comedians. There were puddles everywhere; players gave up measuring their passes after the first few minutes.

A draw was the only result that could carry any justice. The players, their discomfort etched on their faces, were glad when it was all over. Five-yard belly slides are unedifying, and once goalkeeper Allan began wringing out his sodden jersey with all the careworn intent of an old-fashioned laundrywoman.

Derby County 0 Aston Villa 1

First Division – Sunday Correspondent, March 1990

Ian Ormondroyd lunged like a man with his job under threat – which arguably it is. He was named only as substitute, played through the second half (as manager Graham Taylor tried to work out the most profitable way to integrate his vaunted newcomer, Tony Cascarino), and scored the winner after 71 minutes. He threw that beanpole build of his at Daley's centre. His face was that of a Carmarthen farmer who'd found time both to milk the cows and saddle the winner.

Bristol Rovers 2 Bristol City 0

Second Division – The Guardian, April 2000

There has always been something surreal about Bristol Rovers. The intimacy between players and fans is exceptional, and on Saturday one pre-match announcement, amid the birthday greetings, wished a supporter well after his haemorrhoids operation.

The manager Ian Holloway gives long, partial and engaging monologues after games, strong on sentimentality and unusual in imagery. Here he reflected: "The trouble with us is that we've had too many players sitting at the piano, not moving it." Maybe he was simply in an exultant, musical mood. He had just seen his team – only recently "a frightened one" – restate their claim for an automatic promotion place. And the overdue statement was buoyantly made at the expense of tribal rivals.

Exeter City 0 Everton 0

FA Cup 3rd Round – The Guardian, December 1999

It may be difficult to convince those old moneybags of Old Trafford that there is more to the FA Cup than suspect international priorities and the glint of gold. Exeter, where the cupboard is bare and the manager washes the shirts, would point to romance and heroism. The Devon fans would be more specific and translate that as Jason Matthews.

He is a fresh-faced lad from near Bath who gave up a week's wages as an electrician during August to have a trial with Exeter, whom he had impressed in a pre-season friendly. His modest goalkeeping background takes in venues like Mangotsfield, Taunton and Salisbury; this was only his third appearance for Exeter, all as a substitute.

He came on after Stuart Naylor had been told by the doctor not to return because of concussion, suffered as he made one of a number of brave saves.

There was nothing logical about the scoreline. Everton had the polished precision, aesthetic touches and might have had six, though that would have been a cruel reflection on a happy, humble club where girders stand starkly behind one goal as symbols of poverty and unfinished business.

Joyful decibels echoed in compensation from the other corners, so deafening in eternal optimism that the pigeons pointedly sought sanctuary in the crannies of the main stand above the directors' heads.

Many of those cheers were reserved for Matthews. He is on £300 a week, less than he would earn helping his father with the electrics. It is also about 60 times less than one or two of the Everton players. "But to play like this is a dream, the best job I could ever imagine."

He was nominated as man of the match with three minutes to go, not bad for a novice who came on at half-time. "I just heard the Jason from the announcer and assumed it was Jason Rees."

Matthews admitted he calmed down after "a dead nervous" reaction when he was told he would be taking over and made several excellent saves, including an exceptional instinctive one from Kevin Campbell's close-range header. When once fleetingly caught out of position he recovered, scrambled back and turned the ball onto the post.

Exeter had tried in vain to switch this game to Goodison Park. The club's accountants will now get their wish after all.

With Stuart Naylor back in goal, Exeter lost the replay
1-0, conceding a deflected goal in the 85th minute.

20
Boxing and Other Sports

*(top) The jockey Fred Archer (left) and speedway's Billy Hole
(bottom) David with the former boxer Pat Patterson*

David loved boxing. He was drawn to the rawness of it and to its earthy roots. In his teenage diaries it is mentioned more often than any sport except cricket. In his 1948 diary, for instance, he described in detail a heavyweight contest between Joe Louis and Jersey Joe Walcott, he commented on controversial decisions in that summer's Olympic Games, and he wrote a full page on an incident during an MCC tour match in Cape Town when the champion British boxer Freddie Mills, invited into the pavilion by Denis Compton, was denied entry: 'The President said that he took one look at Mills and his party and decided they were not the right types.'

It was an episode that enraged the young David whose diary contains a long diatribe against such 'Victorian era' snobbery. He admits finally that 'it isn't so astonishingly surprising', reflecting that he has noticed 'the same beastly signs of class distinction' when playing for the *Western Gazette* cricket team at Chard and Seaton!

David covered fights for the local papers in Bristol, and in 1988 he compiled a collection of reminiscences of boxing in the city between the wars: *Hungry Fighters of the West*. This was superb social history, where much of David's heart lay, digging deep into the memories of a lost world. He ended the volume with the words of Jack Phelps, a trainer and manager in the Depression years of the 1930s:

> What days! What wonderful scraps! What characters! I feel I've known them all. Coached them as boys, crouched in their corners, cheered at their successes. They weren't all champs by any means. But most of them had something in common. They were HUNGRY FIGHTERS. An empty belly was the greatest motivation of all. It isn't any accident that many of the finest boxers of all time grew up from extreme poverty.

David loved these forays into the past, but he was also ready to report on the sport's changing face. In 1993, for the *Guardian*, he travelled to London to interview the inaugural chair-elect of the British Ladies' Boxing Association, a woman far removed from those 'hungry fighters'.

> There is nothing overtly bellicose about Sue Atkins. She is a landscape gardener who prunes trees and plans rockeries for a living. She used to work at Kensington Gardens and now has her own little business at Mitcham. She is attractive and feminine, with the clear cheeks and fresh complexion of a country girl. But for the past ten years she has been the unofficial British lightweight women's boxing champion.

One of David's great strengths as a writer was his emotional honesty. He was paid to write about boxing but, for all the excitement it stirred in him, he felt it necessary from time to time to express his misgivings about a sport in which, as he put it, 'the primeval intention is to batter an opponent's brain for the entertainment of an insensitive public.'

One can sense some of that ambivalence in David's poignant description of Muhammad Ali at a book signing in a Bristol branch of Waterstones:

> Someone in the crowd with a self-conscious sense of occasion shouted: "Ali!" It wasn't quite the voice of an MC at Madison Square Garden. But everyone turned towards the door and broke into applause.
>
> The winding walk between the countless bookshelves took nearly quarter-of-an-hour. There was not a towel or dressing gown to be seen. Just as much adulation, though, as Muhammad Ali, timeless icon of sporting heroism, walked slowly and at times ponderously. One felt his eyes were occasionally unseeing; he appeared slightly bewildered as he viewed, almost objectively, the recurrent waves of nostalgia and affection all round him.

Between 1978 and 2010 David wrote a regular Friday column for the sports pages of the *Western Daily Press*. Cricket and football featured most frequently, but his brief was to cover all sports. Athletics, wrestling, bowls, lawn tennis, horse racing, snooker, darts – with his gift with words he could bring any of them to vivid life.

For four years, from 1994, he also wrote a weekly feature, 'Where Are They Now?', tracking down local sports stars of the past. Among them were a world table tennis champion, living alone and largely forgotten in retirement, and an England rugby international who had combined his sporting career with duties as an undertaker.

David even accepted a commission from the *Guardian* to write 600 words on a triathlon race in Bath, an event about which he knew nothing. Yet, drawing on his knowledge of the terrain and picking up on the intense rivalry between the two main competitors, he had no difficulty in phoning in an entertaining piece.

If he had a blind spot in sport, it was golf, the often exclusive atmosphere of which never appealed to him. Nevertheless, when a letter from a retired caddie asked David to contact him at his village inn near Tewkesbury, he overcame his prejudice to write a delightful feature.

MIXED FEELINGS ABOUT BOXING

Ambivalence

Western Daily Press, March 1986

Boxing leaves me in an uncomfortable state of ambivalence.

Almost my first job as a news reporter when I came to Bristol in the 1950s was to report on a house fire in the old St Jude's area. The occupant was an ex-professional fighter from Yorkshire. He sat in his charred living room, oblivious to the domestic destruction around him. "I'm the champ," he kept repeating, showing me a succession of ringside photographs which had survived the blaze. I had never met a punchie before and it troubled me for a long time.

He playfully poked me in the ribs and rumbled off a series of names of defeated opponents, real or imagined. As I discovered later, he had always been down the bill and had earned virtually nothing from his fights.

A lifelong bout of guilty pleasure

The Guardian, July 2008

Boxing excites me, let's get that out of the way. I like boxers – their courage, innocent sense of ambition in many cases, vulnerability and the outpouring of sentimentality that causes them to hug their adversary who only minutes before they had tried to knock unconscious. I wrote a book about them, especially those who fought for a pittance in the years between the two world wars. Medical supervision was often negligible. The wan scrappers fought in smoky improvised rings for a fiver a time.

But it seems to me there has always been too much deceit and manipulation in boxing. The crowds were only searching for a semblance of working-class glamour and frisson in that drab aura of national depression.

... As a young wartime schoolboy I went to watch a three-round exhibition given by the middleweight champion Jock McAvoy for the local troops. He belted his opponent without mercy it seemed to me – and then the two, both in the RAF, wandered off together to share a fag. I was left, still wincing, for weeks. But I was also hooked, despite the sheer violence involved and uncertainty about how much the body and head could stand.

It is a rough, gory addiction, not really to be recommended. My reservations continue to lurk. I remember, still too graphically, when as a young reporter I covered a boxing bill and took my place with a hint of self-importance at the ringside. It was only when I got home that I faced justifiable family wrath. My shirt was spattered in blood.

BOXING BETWEEN THE WARS

Hungry Fighters of the West (1988)

Introduction

This is a book about those West Country boxers who fought professionally – usually for a few pounds – between the two great wars. In some cases they fought so that there could be food on the table at home. Apart from being an account of exhilarating bouts in improvised boxing rings and romantically remembered halls, once heavy with Woodbine smoke and throbbing collective excitement, this is a story of marvellous, warm-hearted characters who emerged from the grey working-class ghettos of a city where the dole queues were long and the faces carried the bleak, helpless look of the times.

For scores of wan and wiry boys and young men, boxing provided an elusive whiff of glamour. They crowded into the little gyms dotted around Bedminster and east Bristol. They saved their pennies to go to the regular small-time promotions. They created their heroes, following them week after week from one bout to the next.

Albert 'Boy' Bessell

The South-West featherweight champion who became a popular figure on his fruit-and-veg barrow in Old Market, then in Bedminster

Yes, you're right – I was the bloke who walked to London in search of adventure and a few fights. It's what everyone seems to remember about me! There were four of us ... Gandy Kiswick, Jackie Parker, Sammy Ward and me. It was 1935 and I was 18. All of us out of work and looking for a change of luck. I should say I was the only one who could use his fists. We started out on a Saturday morning. But we soon found that no-one was in a mood to give us a lift. So we split up. I stuck with Gandy. Never seen the other two till years later.

It took Gandy and me three days. Slept one night in a hedgerow and under a haystack. Then in a Salvation Army hostel. I had me boxing kit with me, stuffed in a battered little case. I held on to it like grim death. I made for the Dockland Settlement in London and by then, lost in a strange city, I was wondering what the hell I'd let myself in for. But they gave us a cup of tea, a couple of cakes and a ticket to stay at the Savation Army.

I saw various people including Jack King and Jeff Dixon. They took a look at me and me little bundle of boxing kit and decided to take a chance with me. And soon I was boxing every Sunday.

Tom 'Tosh' Parker

The 'paperweight' boxer who moved to Wales as a boy and worked down the mines, returning to Bristol to box and, later, to become a chargehand at BAC

In the early days I'd work a shift underground from 7 a.m. till 2 p.m., come up and bath, walk across the mountains to Pontypridd and catch the bus to where I was fighting. During the miners' strike in 1926 I had 22 fights over just six months. Three of them on one day. Morning, afternoon and evening. Everyone was unemployed. The doors used to open at 11 o'clock in the morning. The three contests were in different halls – and I stopped all the opponents inside the distance. But Dad told me to slow down. During the strike, the purse went down from 30 bob to a pound.

Medical supervision was a bit slap-happy. If you got a cut on the eye, no-one could care less, it seemed, if the seconds could patch it up between rounds. There were a few dirty fighters. Thumb in the eye. One in the kidneys, you know. And I could tell you of a few boxers who liked the booze too much and went into the ring under the influence. But we all got on well together.

Pat Patterson

The bantamweight, who later in life became a newspaper seller on Union Street ("I got a penny for every three sold")

Not likely to forget me last fight. No bloody fear. I was just back from five and a half years in the Navy. I was a bit short of money and went along to the Colston Hall to see a show. There was always the chance of stepping in for someone at the last minute. 'Seaman' Froggatt from Portsmouth was supposed to be boxing but didn't turn up. George Rose was topping the bill and he said: 'How about you taking on one of these blokes here?' I didn't have much change in me pocket. 'Don't mind, George.'

But when the name of me opponent was announced from the ring, I nearly fell through the canvas. Danahar! Still don't know to this day whether it was the famous Arthur or a brother ... I got beaten in the 4th. Badly cut eye – and the ref stopped the fight. Needed two operations and I've now lost the sight from it.

Prince-Cox, the promoter, slipped 20 quid into me boxing boots afterwards. Then as I was coming out of the Colston Hall, some bloke come up to me: 'While you've been away, Pat, we've kept your licence payments up. You owe us £7.' Just think of that. I'd just bashed away with a feller called Danahar and got me eye permanently damaged. All for 20 quid – and here I was parting bloody company with seven straightaway.

VARIOUS SPORTS

Greyhound Racing

Bristol Weekend, January 1965

Greyhound racing to me is a thousand betting slips, torn in anger or anguish, cascading from avaricious fingers onto the concrete terracing of Eastville.

It's a bookie's banter as, with his contorted features and catarrhal voice, he woos the gullible and chalks up momentary bait to the indecisive; or the tic-tac man with the incongruously ecclesiastical face who semaphores his urgent tidings to a distant colleague.

It's the glint in a trainer's eye as he spots the wet canine nostrils he wants to spot, forging vicariously ahead at the final bend. The tote machine clicking out its message that business is good, the little man emitting his uninhibited oaths as his fancy is baulked in a bad get-away, the hot Oxo to sooth or celebrate …

Greyhound racing is something else to Lady Blanche Douglas, the Glo'shire blue-blood who has her own kennels and track tucked away in the village of Sherston. To her, a greyhound is not a lithe, flashing animal with a number on its back and an obsessive instinct to chase a hare, albeit an electric one. It is an individual: a handsome dog with its own personality, answering to the call of Lady Douglas or her trained kennel staff.

Triathlon

The Guardian, September 1995

Amid the mellow, historic grandeur of Bath, Simon Lessing won the BUPA Triathlon for the third year running, but victory did little to sweeten the sourness of his rivalry with the world champion Spencer Smith.

This is renowned as the friendliest and most informal of events, where thousands come to cheer friends on their exceptional and versatile athleticism and physical courage. But, just as in Georgian times there was liable to be an unseemly exchange or two beneath the veneer of respectability at Beau Nash's gaming tables, the lack of cordiality between the 24-year-old Lessing and his fellow Briton Smith spiced the meeting.

The most gruelling part for everyone yesterday was not the Avon – competitors had the beautiful Pulteney Bridge or Abbey to gaze at therapeutically between strokes – but the 40km cycle challenge, transversing the cruel contours of the old Somerset coalfields and Mendips en route. The seams were notoriously narrow and weary miners often got in each other's way – just like Lessing and Smith yesterday.

Darts

from a series, 'The Boom Sports', Bristol Evening Post, August 1975

Darts was once a slap-happy 301 in a back-street bar – amid jostling pint-swiggers, hearty working-class ribaldry and suspect mathematics. It was where the hops tasted extra sweet when the elusive double-top went triumphantly in. There was only one board and you waited your turn on a Friday night. Today it is played in Britain by nearly three and a half million people.

The top players may not be quite in the league of the pampered First Division soccer stars – but they still travel the world, use their right hand as much to sign autographs as to aim for the double-19, and are feted by their supporters.

Table Tennis

Aubrey Simons – gold medallist in the 1953 World Championships in Bucharest from a series, 'Where Are They Now?', Western Daily Press, December 1994

Aubrey Simons was not the most vaunted member of England's team. Some even said he was a journeyman player, unlikely to win any headlines for himself against the best in the world. How wrong they all were. This studious-looking, bespectacled Bedminster boy, son of a local butcher, was simply indomitable.

Everyone sweltered in the over-heated Iron Curtain hall as the world championships were relentlessly fought out. Simons, a typically phlegmatic figure almost vulnerable in appearance as he kept returning the aggressive shots from the game's most superb players, just kept on winning.

At 3am, weary after the most punishing of schedules, he dared to beat the Czechs' super-star Tereba in the taut deciding match of the semi-finals. He did it with unassuming style: 22-20, 21-18. It was the upset of the competition, leading to an audible buzz of disbelief. England went on to beat Hungary 5-3. In the process Simons out-fought Josef Koczain, who had been in the world singles finals the previous year.

Aubrey kept no scrapbooks and few reminders of his feats in days when table tennis held a genuine glamour. These days Aubrey lives alone in a spacious top-floor flat in Clifton. He modestly keeps his memories to himself. In fact, it's not easy to persuade him to talk about himself. So it was lucky a mutual friend pointed out that Aubrey, as a golfer, holed-in-one twice in a week at Henbury a few weeks ago. "At the same hole."

Aubrey would probably put that down to a fluke, just like that stunning form of his in Bucharest. We all know differently.

Bowls

Radio Times, October 1984

It's bowling's sheer sense of drama that appeals to David Rhys Jones. 'Once you release the wood, there are 12 to 15 seconds before its object is achieved. The suspense is held longer than in most sports.'

That hoary myth about bowls being a game only for older men and women was cracked long ago. He made an eloquent contribution by starting at 11, 'for something to do in the school holidays', back in his native Llanelli. And although his father was a county skip, he didn't wholly approve of young David taking up the game as well. 'Go in for something a little more manly like rugby,' he'd say.

David had a season ticket to watch Llanelli every Saturday. He also played wing forward at grammar school. But there was an absorbing quality, just as exciting in its way, about bowls.

Speedway

Western Daily Press, March 1977

Billy Hole was a West Country speedway legend: a Somerset farmer's son whose nostrils sniffed only the cinders of the racing track. He was idolised by thousands of fans of the speedway team known as the Bristol Bulldogs. His style and ice-cool nerve were as exhilarating a sight as the consummate skills of a soccer super-star. For eight years he was captain, the King of Knowle Stadium.

Distinctively upright on his bike, his ruthlessness, or rather his brilliant judgement after the last bend, helped to make him one of the great names of the early post-war years. His ability to come from behind was the most thrilling spectacle in contemporary speedway. It often looked though as he had left it too late. Miraculously he came from nowhere to win so many races.

The Bulldogs return on Friday with a visit to Wolverhampton. They should roar into action at Eastville, Bristol, on April 29 when the new track will be ready. Not that Billy has shown much interest in the sport since the mid-fifties, when the bulldozers were already rumbling in the distance and the Bulldogs began to disintegrate. The former captain fingered his yellowing scrapbook this week in his Beckington home, near Frome, and said: "It was the collapse of an era, the end of something very special."

He's now a Royal Automobile Club patrolman and he travels in a van. Still, he looks more like a farmer than a man who made his living hurtling almost horizontally round bends. In the golden promotion year of 1949, Billy's face was one of the most photographed in the West Country sports calendar. Is he now forgotten?

"I go out as a service engineer when someone has a breakdown. People are apt to take a long look at me, even after all this time, and say: 'Haven't we seen you before?' And then it clicks. They sit down at the side of the road and just want to reminisce. They're happy to ignore their broken-down car."

Rugby

Austin Sheppard, Bristol & England rugby union prop forward from a series, 'Where Are They Now?', Western Daily Press, November 1995

He's a funeral director, a man of black-suited dignity, compassionate to a degree. "Not that he was quite as considerate to his fellow man in the muscular hurly-burly of a Saturday afternoon at the Memorial Ground," a tongue-in-cheek contemporary was inclined to whisper. Often he had to chase from the graveside to a training session or kick-off. That meant his turning up at times in full mourning dress and topper in the hearse. Once, he told me, he'd had to motor to Harrow to collect a body. Held up in a traffic jam on the way back to Bristol, the team coach passed him in the opposite direction. "I still somehow made the kick-off for the away fixture!"

Golf

Western Daily Press, September 1991

Ernest Hargreaves sat in his village pub near Tewkesbury, a rosebud in his buttonhole and an ageless sparkle in his eyes. He talked about today's obsessively-hyped Ryder Cup on the South Carolina course which has been variously described as a scenic delight and a demanding monster. And he reminisced about the very first Ryder held in this country in 1929 – of which surely he is something of an authority.

Ernest, a 16-year-old Yorkshire lad just out of school, caddied for Walter Hagen. It was the first time he had ever met an American. The way he outwitted a dozen or so rivals for the coveted job also reflected the most resourceful day of his life.

"Those other young caddies were a pretty scruffy lot. And when Mr Hagen drew up at Moortown, Leeds, they converged on him, tapping on his window. I'd dressed for the occasion. In fact, I turned up in my school uniform, neat and tidy. While the others tried in vain to make an impression, I opened the door behind the passenger seat, picked up the golf bag and belongings and boldly marched into the clubhouse with it."

Hagen, extrovert and famous, three times winner of the Open, followed him in, slightly bemused. "What's this young fella like?" he asked the club secretary.

"I'm telling you, Mr Hagen, he's the best little caddie we've got." Ernest, son of an army major killed in the First World War, was engaged on the spot.

He remembers today every detail – Hagen's banter with many in the 5,000 crowd, the sand in the bunkers brought in specially from the beach at Scarborough, the impeccable manners of the spectators.

"From then the relationship was just like that of a father and son. There was the party at the Queen's Hotel where the team were staying. 'Come on down and join us, sonny. I know you won't step out of line.'"

It was unimagined bliss for the young wide-eyed caddie. Soon he was being asked to caddie for Hagen again, at the Muirfield Open. "The average for a caddie was a shilling a round. I was being promised £100 for the Open." He'd have done it for nothing.

Walter won. And so did Henry Cotton when Ernest caddied for him in 1948. "Do you know, I didn't miss an Open from 1929 to 1977," he says.

He's now 79, recently retired after 12 years as official starter at Tewkesbury Hotel Golf and Country Club. It will be hard for him to resist the TV appeal of Kiawah Island today – "although with a few exceptions I don't feel the present-day players compare with the ones I knew so well."

Ernest is a treasury of golfing glory and gossip.

He was asked to attend Henry Cotton's Registry Office wedding in 1938. For some years he was the great golfer's butler, valet and confidant. He never betrayed an indiscretion. For 16 weeks before the war he even toured the music halls, including Bristol Hippodrome, acting as a caddie for Mr Cotton as instruction and a few jokes were nightly dispensed.

"We shared the bills with Ted Ray, Florence Desmond and Nellie Wallace. At Glasgow, we took more money than Harry Lauder!"

Ernest Hargreaves remains blunt and critical of those aspects of golf, like the intrusion of greed and too much money, which tarnishes the game.

"As I remember it, golf was a gentleman's game. It was full of nice people with nice manners. The only snobbery was among the snobs. Today I am appalled by the lack of etiquette and general bad behaviour that I come across. They just don't play in the old-fashioned way."

Horse racing

The Guardian, November 1986

Fred Archer, who rode 2,748 winners including five in the Derby, died 100 years ago this week. He was confined to his bed, depressed and probably delirious. A nurse looked up and saw that he was staggering to his feet, a revolver in his hand. She grappled with him, the gun went off and he collapsed in a heap on the bedroom floor. Archer, a jockey of legendary skill, considerable fame and immense if transitory wealth, had killed himself – at the age of 29.

Officially he'd been suffering from typhoid fever, sent home and put straight to bed after his latest flop on the favourite at Lewes. His friends had for weeks looked at his desperately haggard face and unseeing eyes and feared that he had lost the will to live.

Physically he had been destroyed by years of remorseless wasting. It seemed that almost every minute out of the saddle was spent in a Turkish bath. He pecked only at food, the fragments washed down with self-imposed castor oil. Eventually the sight of meat or bread made him vomit. He was an acute case of what today would be called anorexia nervosa.

Archer looked more like a broken man of 45 or 50 at the end. The facial features, always saturnine, were etched with bleak pessimism. He'd had enough of personal tragedy – the death of his devoted wife from convulsions after child bearing – the malicious innuendoes about his supposedly suspect integrity as a jockey, the incessant demands to pay off his father's debts.

The tragically short life of Fred Archer was full of triumphs and paradoxes. Few denied his vast natural talents as a jockey, though his rival, the hard-drinking George Fordham, was one who did with belligerent frequency. The hate was mutual. They bumped and bored and swore at each other through every race in which they competed. Archer's language, touched by the vowels of his native Cotswolds, was fearsome and crude as his mounts pounded round the bends. It conflicted with the quiet, sensitive side of him off the course.

He was a gentle person – and a cruel one. His need to win was obsessive. In his earlier years, the use of spurs and whip was excessive. He became more considerate to his mounts but the reputation for treating his horses badly would never go away. Apparently it still exists. In a West Country library the other day, as I again read about his colourful and quite romantically chronicled career, I found some impassioned notes in pencil from a reader at the back of the book. "He was a brute and foul-mouthed to everyone in his way ... not the shy, retiring jockey he's made out to be."

That was a sweeping and unfair judgement on him. Archer was a man who, although he could hardly write his name, possessed plenty of basic intelligence and a degree of sensitivity that he acquired from his mother. He was quite good-looking in a dour way. He walked with a slight stoop but had the sort of presence which led to unsubstantiated rumours about his parenthood. Some implied that his mother had produced him from a dalliance with a blue-blood of the time.

He neither looked nor acted like his father, William Archer, a rough-grained, uncouth man, forever quick of temper and short of ready cash. He'd been a tough and successful little jockey himself, with one Grand National win to his credit. Later he took over the King's Arms at Prestbury, near Cheltenham. He knew how to ride a horse but couldn't supervise a till.

The father had little time for formal education. "School bain't no good for you, Fred. Get up on a hoss and make a livin' that way." Archer had his first mount at Newmarket at the age of 12 and his first winner a year later.

Archer was tall for a jockey. He had spindly legs and leaned distinctively forward as he headed for the winning post. He was champion jockey by the age of 17 – and so he stayed from 1874 to 1886. Apart from his Derby wins, he came first in the St Leger half a dozen times, in the Oaks and Two Thousand Guineas four times. His best year was 1885 when he rode an incredible 246 winners out of 667 mounts.

He was sought and competed over to ride the finest horses of the nation's aristocracy. Falmouth, Portland, Rosebery, Beaufort, Westminster ... they all wanted him. The inducements were considerable. The Duchess of Montrose was the most embarrassing of all with her attentions and fulsome compliments. She was well into her sixties and was besotted in the manner of a giggling schoolgirl. Archer rather enjoyed the flattery and accompanying generosity.

He affected a friendship, professional and social, with her but he kept her at a distance. Younger and far more beautiful women nestled in vain for a more permanent place on his arm. He was no womaniser and had no wish after marriage to be unfaithful to Helen Rose. Archer had a special house built (complete, of necessity, with Turkish bath) for the pair of them. But they had less than four years together.

His contemporaries used to say he was a mercenary. You could say the same about many top jockeys. Archer, in fact, needed to keep riding winners. His father sponged on him mercilessly. There were always sycophants hanging around. He was a big gambler himself and not a particularly successful one. He'd put money up against his own mount – and still ride a brilliant race at a demoralising personal cost to himself.

Archer had his critics. They cited his renowned cruelty to a horse. They fanned rumours about his alleged professional misconduct. Certainly he was indiscreet and there was disquiet about his connections with a betting syndicate as consultant. There were bad publicity and headlines – and talk about 'pulling' one of his fancied mounts.

His friends rallied. Lord Falmouth gave him good, legitimate advice on how to invest his money. "We know you're clean, Fred – just keep on riding winners and beat that old drunk Fordham. That's all we ask," his closer intimates used to say.

The mounting criticism added to mental torment and deteriorating health. Happiness became more and more elusive, though he loved to escape back to the West Country in winter, for an occasional ride with the Beaufort Hunt. It also helped him to cast an eye over his father's wayward business affairs – and to pay off the latest debt.

In the end, still not 30, he had had enough. His massive earnings were being spirited away at an alarming rate. His homely, stabilising wife and his older brother William – following a fall in a hurdle race at Cheltenham – had both gone. And now his great gift in life, that of horsemanship, was slipping away. Those years of starvation diet had taken his strength and zest.

He kept his revolver at the side of his bed, ostensibly to frighten off burglars. But Fred Archer privately knew he was finished as a top jockey. His erstwhile analytical skills, as he sized up the rest of the field, had deserted him. The judgement and the nerve had almost gone. The cruel rumours wouldn't go away. He'd first talked of suicide following the death of Helen Rose. The ending, after embarrassing, untypical rides at Brighton and then Lewes, was almost certainly premeditated.

A hundred years on, he still remains one of the great riddles of the English turf.

21

Cricket History

By the mid-1980s, following the critical success of his biography of Harold Gimblett, David was able to spend more of his working year writing books. There were still ghost-written volumes, notably with the cricketer Zaheer Abbas and the skater Robin Cousins, but in successive years he produced *Cricket's Unholy Trinity* and *Sunshine, Sixes and Cider – A History of Somerset Cricket*. Both books gave him the welcome opportunity to research the game's past, an activity from which he drew as much pleasure as writing.

'This isn't quite a cricket book,' he wrote in his introduction to *Cricket's Unholy Trinity*. 'It is a story of three fine cricketers. There is a subtle and important difference.'

The trio were Charlie Parker, Cecil Parkin and Jack MacBryan, men of great talent who in differing ways found themselves at odds with the authorities of their day. All three were at their peak in the 1920s, before David was born, yet by diligent research, a feel for the time and the gift of imagination he was able to bring their stories to life in a way that rose above much of the writing on cricket history in the 1980s.

The following year he was back in print with his history of Somerset cricket in which, with unashamed affection, he revelled in the idiosyncrasies of the county's past. So many cricketers and episodes were brought vividly alive, in a triumph of research, much of it drawn from conversations and interviews across his working life.

The final paragraphs of *Sunshine, Sixes and Cider* were written in the midst of an almighty row following the departure of Viv Richards, Joel Garner and Ian Botham, yet David found a way to end on a cheerfully philosophical note:

> In more than a hundred years of first-class cricket, Somerset have survived such emotional issues as this, floods, flaccid management and an intermittent threat of bankruptcy. All we ask now, in cheerful resilience – and to justify the title of the book – is that the sun continues to shine, the sixes still bounce reverentially off the tombstones in St James's churchyard ... and that the apple juice keeps its especial West Country fizz.

He returned to the players with *Somerset Cricket – A Post-War Who's Who*, in which he penned biographical sketches of all those who had played for the county since the war. With Ivan Ponting providing the underpinning statistics, the book was a modest volume, but it was revamped and much expanded in 2006 as *Sixty Summers*, with David adding to his players' sketches and providing evocative summaries of each post-war season. It won the Cricket Writers' Club's Book of the Year award.

David's most ambitious book was his 1996 biography of Wally Hammond. Arguably the greatest cricketer England has produced since WG Grace, Hammond contracted a debilitating disease during a tour of the Caribbean and underwent a year of treatment before returning to cricket, with many noticing a change in his personality. Over the years David had picked up muttered rumours about the nature of the Gloucestershire cricketer's illness and treatment, and in *Wally Hammond – The Reasons Why* he explored the subject in depth.

For all the evidence he assembled, there was a speculativeness about his conclusions, which was not to the satisfaction of some reviewers, notably Charles Lysaght in the *Irish Independent* who thought the book was 'rather spoiled' by 'slapstick presentation, exaggerated language, unsupported innuendo and outworn clichés', a verdict on his copy of which David wrote: 'That's telling me!'

By contrast, EW Swanton in the *Cricketer* magazine called the book 'a serious sympathetic study of a magnificent cricketer and a difficult, unfulfilled personality'. The book was a great commercial success, aided in no small part by being shortlisted for the high-profile William Hill Sports Book of the Year.

Among the aspects of Hammond's character explored by David was his resentment, almost to the point of paranoia, of the success of the Australian Don Bradman.

> Through the 1930s and again immediately after the war, the Don's massive presence gnawed away at the surprisingly sensitive and fragile persona of Hammond.

It was, therefore, a supreme irony that David's biography hit the bookshops at the same time as a major new biography of Bradman, written by the Labour peer Charles Williams. It, too, was shortlisted for the William Hill prize, with Bradman pipping Hammond to the Cricket Society's annual Literary Award.

David's feeling for, and understanding of, both cricket and society in the inter-war years was exceptional. Even in his eightieth year, when he was conscious of his failing powers, he researched and wrote – at the behest of Scyld Berry, editor of the *Wisden Cricketers' Almanack* – a most intriguing piece about the free-thinking captain of Gloucestershire, Bev Lyon, and his visionary proposal for time-limited cricket.

SOMERSET CRICKET IN THE 1930s

Sunshine, Sixes and Cider (1986)

Making his county debut in 1935 was C.J.P. Barnwell. He was yet another to be surprised by the telegraph boy. 'It was the Bank Holiday game at Bristol and I was petrified. I introduced myself to the team and I don't think they were terribly impressed. The pros were understandably a bit defensive when a new amateur turned up.'

Ingle asked: 'Where do you bat?'

'Where I'm put, sir.'

'Call me Reggie. Now then, where do you bat?'

'Usually at 3.'

'Well, that's where you'll be.'

John Barnwell, who had learned his cricket at Repton, faced up to Charlie Barnett and immediately stroked a four through the covers. Soon he tried to do the same again and played on. 'That was my first lesson.'

The dividing line between amateurs and professionals could on occasion be embarrassing or inhibiting. 'I always found the pros very helpful. One day I confided to Wally Luckes that I was bothered about getting out lbw so often.'

'Glad you asked me that, sir. I didn't like to tell you ...' And Luckes painstakingly showed the amateur where he was going wrong as he played back. 'I hardly ever got out lbw again. The professionals in the thirties really were a grand lot.'

*

Captaincy, in truth, brought nothing but grey hairs. Ingle, who had a gift for what today is rather glibly known as motivation, led the county to nine wins in 1936 and that was the most they had had since 1924. Administrative worries remained on the grand scale, however, and he had to call on – at times in pleading gestures close to prayer – as many as thirty-four players.

After the war, he was closely involved as a solicitor in the defence of Rosina Cornock, the Bristol woman charged with the murder of her husband in the bath. It was a celebrated trial and Reggie Ingle sat through the whole of it as well as visiting Mrs Cornock regularly in Cardiff Prison. 'I always felt that she was innocent and I'm pleased to say she was acquitted. But the case turned my hair white.' And we had always imagined it was due to trying to raise a Somerset side in the late thirties.

WALLY HAMMOND

Reflections on writing a biography of Hammond

Twelfth Man, journal of Wombwell Cricket Lovers Society (1997)

In the six weeks or so that followed the publication of my biography on Wally Hammond, I received more than a hundred letters. This was a far greater instant reaction than I had ever had before. Almost without exception, the writers concentrated on the way I had chosen to deal with a thoroughly difficult subject. And all but two approved.

I needed that kind of reassurance. Anyone who writes for a living works in a vacuum; he is never wholly certain that he has got things right. As journalists, we remain in employment because of the SILENCE of our sports editors. If they don't say anything, it usually means they are satisfied with us. They, like us, know how ephemeral the newspaper industry is. The only time they come on the phone, to mention one of our reports, is when a reader has written in, enraged that we have mis-spelt a name, been careless with a statistic or got a classical allusion wrong.

In my case, the risk is minimised. I try not to litter my reports with too many stats – and I'm not clever enough to quote the classics. But, when it came to a book on Wally, I badly wanted a feedback. This was nothing at all to do with conceit, nothing to do with the quality of my writing. This biography, in my head for 40 years, had caused me to agonise more than ever before.

Research has always appealed to me. It gives me as much pleasure and fulfilment as the process of putting words on paper. As preparation for this book, I talked to dozens of people, most of them cricketers. I went to see a number of his contemporaries – now, alas, dead – and documented their intimate impressions and memories. And before long I found myself confronted with one worrying issue. It was to do with balance.

No-one I spoke to had anything but praise for Hammond's sublime batsmanship. They were altogether more wary when, with honesty, they attempted to assess him as a man. Les Ames was the outstanding exception. He was a wonderfully loyal friend to Hammond and clearly saw him in happier moods. The words of the gentle, kind Ames should in no way be discounted. But the fact that they contrasted so sharply with the judgements of others who played with and against Wally made me increasingly convinced it was time to try to understand the 'Gloucestershire Prince' better.

The two highly critical letters that came my way were angry that I had dared – 'with inconclusive evidence' – to rake up the past and discuss Hammond's illness following his tour to the West Indies in 1925/26.

What they failed to see was that I was attempting, with I like to think sensitivity, to offer some explanations for the irrational mood swings, the remoteness, inaccessibility and the overall complexes that dogged his subsequent cricketing life.

It was surely more than a coincidence that the boyish, carefree 'Tommy' Hammond of his early Gloucestershire CCC days and brief winters with Bristol Rovers was never to be seen again after his return from the Caribbean. I am strongly of the belief that the toxic content of the medication, given him by a caring staff in a Bristol nursing home, was largely to blame for the behavioural contours that followed.

On the very first page I made it clear that this was not a conventional cricket biography. Runs and wickets have never been my abiding interest. But Hammond was a boyhood hero of mine – and it filled me with sadness that he had died far from England, almost forgotten and without any real means of support for his surviving family.

As I wrote the book, so many sub-texts emerged. And I feel the most relevant one of all was the all-pervading presence of the great Don Bradman. "That bloody Bradman – we've got to get him out," Wally would murmur, as if paranoid on the subject. I corresponded with Sir Don. He replied promptly, courteously and, for the most part, monosyllabically to my questions.

They were direct contemporaries, two wondrous batsmen with varying techniques. And two introverts. Most dispassionate judges will put The Don marginally ahead. They did when the two were playing – and that for Wally was yet another complex, another cross to bear in private.

Hammond was a great batsman and could, if he had wished, have been a great all-rounder. He was not a great captain, though his England career in charge was initially encouraging. What more might he – and so many others – have achieved but for the war? His health suffered, and then there was the wretched anti-climax of that ill-conceived post-war tour to Australia. There was much domestic unhappiness and business failure, not all his fault by any means.

One of the saddest stories about him was related to me just after the book came out. A group of England players were on a private tour in South Africa and they went into a bar near Durban. One of our fast bowlers was immediately recognised. Some of the regulars gathered round, asking for autographs. The players looked later across the bar and had a solitary figure pointed out to them. It was Wally Hammond. He was apparently no longer remembered as a Test cricketer and worthy of an autograph. I hope the book goes some way towards redressing with affection that omission.

HAMMOND'S CHANGE IN PERSONALITY

On a tour of the Caribbean in the winter of 1925/26 Hammond became seriously ill. He spent the summer of 1926 in a nursing home, where David thought it likely that he was treated with mercury. He did not return to cricket till the following year.

Wally Hammond – The Reasons Why (1996)

A discernible transformation took hold of him after he made his first faltering steps from the bed in that nursing home of caring staff and perplexed doctors. In a matter of months he had ceased to be a boy. The youthful, impish eyes had suddenly given way to almost world-weary ones, strained, defensive and, for evermore, suspicious. From that ghastly proximity to death and those long hours of silent contemplation, as he lay in the private ward, had come a strange maturity – earlier than nature intended. He was still only 23.

Hammond had never been much of a thinker. At school he had preferred whacking a cricket ball to the prosaic hours in the classroom; he'd enjoyed splashing through the mud of the farmyard with the Neales, during the holidays, rather than any visit to a library or museum, or putting his head in a book.

There had been a carefree indolence about him when he first arrived at the county ground in Bristol. Professional sport wasn't going to demand any particular intellectual effort on his part. That was when he started parting his hair in the middle, in the fashion of famous contemporary sportsmen, especially the glamorous First Division footballers who seemed to have so much spare time once their training was done: golf in plus fours, buckshee seats at the cinema – and, it seemed, not an anxiety in the world.

Wally had found there was plenty of good-natured teasing at both the county headquarters and at Eastville, home of Bristol Rovers. He smiled at the digs about his smart appearance – and what supposedly went on in the back of his spluttering but serviceable old car. He was not adept at dressing room repartee and was hopeless at telling a joke in the style of the lecherous ones that did the rounds amid the pads and shin-guards. But the team-mates all liked him in those early days: he had an appealing presence; he was modest; and everyone sensed that he was capable of becoming a truly exceptional sportsman before too long.

On his return to the pre-season nets in 1927, after the long enforced absence, the change in him was almost tangible. Other players looked at each other in unspoken eloquence. They couldn't quite determine what had happened. Some were effusive in welcoming him back, but Hammond's response was puzzlingly taciturn. Perhaps he was wondering how much they knew.

This transformation would not have been apparent to the general spectator. But I went to see an elderly Gloucestershire supporter in Keynsham. He had watched the county with loyalty and zeal in those very days. He had collected autographs and studied Hammond, idolatrously, at close range. 'I noticed the striking difference in him when he returned to the club after his illness. Not till long afterwards did I personally hear the rumours. What struck me, quite apart from any changes in personality, was the marked manner his complexion had changed.'

As for the players, they remarked among themselves at the abruptness with which his boyish cordiality had at least partially disappeared. He was more withdrawn, less willing to share a harmless confidence. Laymen psychiatrists in the dressing room gave up trying to analyse the reason.

I am convinced that as he lay in his bed and later sat out in the sunshine near the windows of the nursing home, he took stock, for virtually the first time, of his life. The analytical experience left him desperately insecure. That insecurity was never to leave him.

*

In the midsummer months of 1926, Hammond, still badly debilitated by his illness, unable to articulate the metamorphosis taking place, was being gradually gripped by a pervasive inferiority complex. He wished he could string his sentences together more eloquently, like 'Plum' Warner and the well-fleshed, well-educated members of the Gloucestershire County Cricket Club. He wished he was less awkward at the posher gatherings to which the pros were occasionally invited.

He would before long become acknowledged as one of the greatest cricketers in the history of the game. Yet privately he was to become preoccupied by a sense of failure. Indeed, to some extent, his life was later to bear this out – in the wretchedness of his business enterprises, in some of his social aspirations, in his personal relationships. It left him looking over his shoulder, at times needlessly suspicious of colleagues and friends.

... The more we study the outwardly rich and bountiful life of Hammond, the more we find evidence of the insecurity that bedevilled him ... As is so often the case with someone patently unsure of himself, Hammond offset his complexes subconsciously with intermittent shows of arrogance that could make him appear patronising, unfriendly and increasingly remote – especially in the later years of his playing career.

JOHNNY DOUGLAS

The Wisden Cricketer, April 2004

Johnny Douglas was said to be the fittest cricketer of his day. The body was taut and muscular. He would not have been remotely out of place in a 21st-century dressing room where a player's physical condition is too easily a fetish rather than a healthy consideration. Douglas looked more like a boxer than a Test all-rounder. And that was what he was, of course. Those who yawned at his unwaveringly wearisome batting approach argued with some validity that he was worth watching only when he stepped into the ring.

That was a cutting comment on someone who captained his country at cricket and led it to success against the Australians before the First World War. Yet he was never a batsman to ignite a schoolboy's imagination or stir a wing-collared Edwardian scribe to flights of purple prose.

One of the endless fascinations of cricket is the extent of dichotomy among its practitioners. It is the sport in which the brawny blacksmith, romantic icon of rural rampage, does not bowl fast at all but instead pedantically blocks out the last half-hour to earn an honourable draw. It is the bespectacled accountant, pallid of features and delicate of forearm, who crashes four boundaries in an over. In Douglas's case he batted as if losing a competitive stroll with a tortoise – and flung his fists in ferocious combinations of punches to excite black-tied audiences, baying for blood after port, at the National Sporting Club.

He came from a family steeped in the noble art. His father, Johnny H Douglas, was a famous personality in the annals of boxing, a familiar figure at the old Covent Garden Club. Brother 'Pickles' Douglas was a renowned referee, handling title flights. At Felsted School Johnny's own boxing prowess was a matter of approving debate among his fellow fifth-formers. There was never any likelihood of him fighting for money but he boxed proudly for the family name.

In the ringside seats his family shouted encouragement and liked the way, with a pair of boxing gloves, he could look after himself. The dour countenance that he was apt to convey at the crease was a good deal less evident when he was trading blows, usually with some style. He became the best amateur middleweight in England and was crowned Olympic champion in 1908 when he beat Reginald 'Snowy' Baker on points. The fight was so close that a popular myth sprang up (and remains to this day) that the judges could reach no decision and the gold was finally awarded by the referee – Douglas's father. But Douglas was not refereeing at all. He was ringside only so that he could present the medals in his capacity as President of the Amateur Boxing Association.

JWHT Douglas, to allow him his full flourish of initials (the printers gave him the works on the boxing billboards), was also a referee. They used to say he was a martinet as he danced round the two fighters. He was always sparing with his smiles; in the ring, whether boxing or adjudicating, he remained grim-faced, his sleek middle-parting hair unruffled. So he needed to be when handling two adversaries not averse to villainy on the referee's blind side. In 1914 he had whispered a few cautions to George 'Digger' Stanley, once a world bantamweight champion and well known for a range of dark-alley tricks. By the 13th round Douglas had seen enough and disqualified Digger. The defeated boxer's noisy mates, many from the gipsy community from where he came, turned on the referee. But that did not bother Douglas. He played and judged his sport by the letter.

That was why he once rounded on Wally Hammond when captaining an Essex game against Gloucestershire. He and his team-mates were convinced that the 'prince', as Hammond was known in the West Country, was caught in the covers by Laurie Eastman off a ball from the slow left-armer Joe Hipkin. Douglas led the protests when Hammond did not walk. The umpire, caught in a mid-afternoon reverie and uncertain what had happened, spluttered that it had been a bump-ball.

Douglas was seething. At the close of play he went into the Gloucestershire dressing room. He had already offered a few choice words of anger at Wally on the pitch. Now he demanded to know where he was. Reg Sinfield, who was present, recounted with a chuckle that Hammond remained out of sight behind the door. Next morning, when Essex were batting and Douglas was at the crease, Hammond pointedly asked for a bowl. "He went on and hurled them down faster than I'd ever seen from him before," said Sinfield. "He left poor old Johnny black and blue and I felt pretty sorry for him. Yet what courage."

The boxer's pluck was rarely far away. It made up for a somewhat saturnine character and no natural or easy affinity with the players. They still knew that he would battle for them, not wantonly prepared to give his wicket away or be needlessly generous to the other side. The competitive aspect to his play was equally apparent in his not insignificant soccer career, during which he won an amateur international cap.

But his cricket, whatever the groans about his painfully limited batting repertoire, should not be disregarded. He played in 23 Tests and, with

SF Barnes gobbling up the wickets, he led England to an Ashes triumph in 1911/12, having taken over the captaincy when Plum Warner was ill. He played for Essex from 1901 to 1928, scoring 24,531 runs and 26 hundreds. His bowling, with its lateral movement, brought 1,893 wickets. The boxer's sturdy fists held on to 365 catches. The pundits of the day went off his Test captaincy after the 1914-18 war and the records appear to bear that out. But he achieved the season double – 1,000 runs and 100 wickets – five times.

John William Henry Tyler ('Johnny Won't Hit Today' to the Australian public) Douglas may not have been everyone's idea of a shining or inspirational endearment. But his innate courage never deserted him. That was poignantly evident in 1930 when he was drowned at sea trying to save his father's life, after two vessels collided in the fog. The seas were rough and the two did not quite beat the count.

SAMMY WOODS

From Grace to Botham – Profiles of 100 West Country Cricketers (1980)

There is nothing more to write about Sammy Woods. The stories tumble over each other – and most of them are true, or at least in the spirit of this immensely lovable and outsized Australian. Everything about him was bountiful: his shoulders, his smile, the thrust of his bowling arm, the playful swing of his bat, his drinking capacity and the warmth of his heart.

He came over from near Sydney when he was 14 and stayed. So, in time, the West Country vowels took over. No one belonged more loyally to Bridgwater and Taunton, where at some time he lived, and the Quantocks where he hunted and, as everyone seems to know, hid his bottles of ale to refresh many a future ramble. He had no patience with conventional employment and was quickly bored by banking. It is doubtful whether he was able to save much money. But he never turned down a convivial evening, astutely lived for some time at the George Inn and was unfailingly generous with his round of drinks.

Sammy Woods was the most gregarious sportsman of his day. While 'WG' was inclined to drink his whisky amid a coterie of affluent amateurs, Woods was quite indiscriminate in his socialising. If there was something on in Taunton, he was there. When the Fair arrived, he climbed roguishly into the ring. He skittled with rosy-faced zeal and sang, very acceptably in tune, at the village harvest homes. He was extrovert, noisy and offended no one. He came from a big family and always wanted to be surrounded by friends. There was no lack of these. He was not perhaps the most intellectual product of Cambridge but his conversation, which carried a sting and a colourful spectrum of adjectives to complement the natural bonhomie, instantly attracted a captive audience, whether on a beagling sortie, at Taunton cattle market or as he sprawled on the grass between wickets. Before a game he would take a brisk walk around the town. Fellow cricketers, his willing companions, were left incredulous at his knowledge of local industry and custom and a sincere acquaintanceship with nearly everyone he met in Taunton's back streets.

Woods had to be a sportsman. He was beautifully built with shoulder and chest muscles made for physical contact. For a long time, as he put on weight to 15 stone, there was no superfluous flesh. He ran well for a big man. He shoved zestfully as a rugby wing forward and was good enough to play for England. They say he happily chatted away to himself and was fearless in the mauls. He certainly enjoyed the sing-song that followed as much as the match itself.

It is as a cricketer, however, that Somerset remembers him. He was a tall, fast bowler, altogether too fiery for the Oxford batsmen during his Varsity days. The Australians came over in 1888 and reasonably claimed him as one of theirs. He played in three Tests for them. Later he was to play for England. The apparently contrasting loyalties amused him. He was never a great man for boundaries, unless they were those of Somerset.

Woods captained the county for a dozen years, from 1894 to 1906, although he pretended he could not remember how long. During that time he once belted the Sussex attack for 215 at Hove. 'Nice air round here, me old dear. Bracing,' he said as he came off the field.

As a captain he led by example. He bowled his heart out, consistently hostile and mostly accurate. He batted with good-natured aggression and considerable skill. Imprudent hooks and pulls brought banter with a sighing stumper. Imprudent or not, he made 18 centuries for Somerset.

He played 20 years for the county, excelled in some great wins against the almost invincible Yorkshiremen and placed himself alongside the West Country's great all-rounders. Eventually the hips let him down. He continued to play, with a limp and a digger grin, for the local farmers. He still recommended a massage of high-proof spirits for cramp. The arthritis got worse and the style less boisterous. Sammy Woods died aged 62 and there will never be another one.

A CONFRONTATION IN A BRISTOL LIFT

At the end of a dinner at Bristol's Grand Hotel in April 1929, Gloucestershire's Charlie Parker – capped only once by England – made known his feelings about the guest of honour: Pelham 'Plum' Warner, a man at the heart of the game's establishment.

Cricket's Unholy Trinity (1985)

The dinner was officially over. Now was the time for socialising and more drinking. That usually meant the amateurs with the amateurs and, from choice, the pros with the pros. At the top table the Lord Mayor, civic chain sparkling, was preparing to leave. County officials and Corporation aides fussed around him. Wine waiters still glided past with trays of cognac. Parker viewed the scene with visible displeasure and, we can reasonably assume, some political guilt.

He drained his glass with a plebeian flourish. 'It's too stuffy in this bloody place, Reg. Let's go up on the balcony.'

Sinfield opted tactfully for silence. He followed Parker out of the dining room and towards the hotel lift. Parker had discovered on previous visits to the Grand Hotel that it was possible to go out on the balcony on one of the higher floors – to gaze down on Broad Street and take some fresh air.

Hotel guests were milling around in the foyer and the lift was already filling up. Parker and Sinfield squeezed in. Suddenly the lift attendant was creating a stir. 'Make way, mate,' he was saying with fawning effect. 'This is Mr Pelham Warner. We must have room for him in the lift. Make way, please.'

Plum was ready to go to his room and was receiving the VIP treatment, to the apparent detriment of everyone else, of an impressionable lift attendant, especially happy to be subservient when it held promise of a sizeable tip at the end.

Charlie Parker was not going to make way for anyone. His eyes blazed as Pelham Warner gingerly approached the crowded lift cage. It was detonation-point. Reg Sinfield held his breath and even wished he was back playing Minor Counties for Herts. Every person in that lift, men and women in evening dress among them, had the distinct impression that they were about to witness high drama.

The whole incident lasted for no more than thirty seconds. Parker flung his arms out and grasped Warner by the lapels. 'I'll never in my life make way for that bugger. He's never once had a good word to say for me. This so-and-so has blocked my Test match career. I played once in 1921 – and he made sure I'd never play for England again. He even got me up to Leeds in 1926 and then left me out. Make way for him ... ? Mr Bloody Warner will go to bed when I've finished with him.'

The grip on the lapels tightened. There was a nervous hum of agitation from the bystanders. Blows seemed imminent. Warner, always a frail man, said nothing. Here was one of the game's most distinguished figures, a captain of Middlesex and England, a Test selector, founder of *The Cricketer*, cricket correspondent of the *Morning Post*, pillar of the game's establishment, in a highly embarrassing public scuffle.

Sinfield knew that all the compounded rage of Charlie Parker was perilously close to ending in blows. If anything Reg, the former Navy boxer with his broken nose and jutting jaw, looked more the fighting man. In truth he was a gentle soul. There was rather more anxiety than optimism in his voice as he said: 'Come on, Charlie. 'Tisn't worth it.'

Parker held on to Warner's lapels for another ten seconds. His hands trembled. According to Sinfield, Plum was 'as white as a sheet'. Then the grip was released and the county club's former guest scurried away up the stairs this time, to his room. In the lift cage the easing of tension was actually audible.

'The bastard,' Parker repeated. 'He alone ruined my chances.'

By any standards, in any company, it was an extraordinary incident. County officials learned only by second-hand of what had taken place. There were so many conflicting rumours – even though the scuffle took place in such a public place – that Gloucestershire found it hard to substantiate enough to take disciplinary action against their greatest bowler. Only one of Parker's team-mates witnessed it.

I had over the years heard various versions, some more bloodthirsty than others, of what took place on that April night outside the lift of Bristol's Grand Hotel, five days as it happens before I was born. John Arlott, I think it was, over a nocturnal glass of claret, first sharpened my journalistic instincts with a tantalising whiff of that particular scandal.

Reg Sinfield authenticated it for me in detail. I have softened the physical detail and deleted some of the expletives. The rest was as it happened. I imagine Pelham Warner regretted accepting the invitation to the Gloucestershire CCC dinner. As far as I know, he never mentioned the incident to any of his friends.

ARTHUR WELLARD

'My Favourite Cricketer' in The Wisden Cricketer, April 2007

To someone embedded so incorrigibly in the ways, wonders and human oddities of West Country cricket over the decades the choice was one of wavering loyalties. It could have been Harold Gimblett for those instinctive, understated skills, Horace 'Nutty' Hazell for his jovial demeanour and evocative portly waistline, Reg Sinfield for his Tommy Trinder chin and battered boxer's nose or Bill Andrews, so often my confidant, who gave me gossip without a trace of malice. My affection was unbounded. But in the end I went for Arthur Wellard.

The earliest impressions never go away. I still see him strolling off the field at my hometown ground at Yeovil in the late 1930s when Lancashire were the visitors. Winston Place and Eddie Paynter, names vaguely familiar to me, were playing but I did not notice them. It was Wellard I wanted to see up close. I ran across to the modest pavilion at the close of play. He was tall, manly, his dark hair greased back around the central parting, thick, bronzed arms around the neck of a team-mate half his size. What a cricketer, I decided. I already knew he hit sixes and took wickets for a living.

That was my first sight of him. The second, again at a Yeovil ground, was at a Sunday benefit match. In the tea interval I anonymously patrolled the surrounds, in the hope of a fleeting moment of doting proximity. Then suddenly here he was, approaching me. No one else about. If only he would say: "Hello, son, enjoying the cricket?" Anything, in fact. What he did say was: "Hey, son, where's the bogs round hure?"

It was not the most romantic of conversational gambits. I stammered a response and pointed in the right direction. He thanked me and was on his way, no doubt to dispose of a little of the pre-match cheer. The voice, I discovered, carried the suggestion of regional vowels, acquired over the past ten years or so after Kent had been tardy about signing him and Somerset found him digs in Weston-super-Mare.

Wellard was one of Somerset's greatest bowlers and only Farmer White took more wickets for them. He played in two Tests and would have gone to India in 1939 but for the war. My schoolboy contemporaries, like me, loved to ape his leap in the delivery stride. We collected the action pictures and chuckled over the way he seemed occasionally to tuck his left arm behind him at the same time as if scratching his back. In fact the action was orthodox. He consistently swung the ball away from the right-handers; his break-backs were renowned. Many of his wickets came when he clean-bowled startled batsmen – just as well perhaps; too many catches went down ritualistically in the slips from the county's successive clutches of transitory amateurs.

When, after the war, the limbs ached more, he turned to off-spin. There was still native cunning: after he had surreptitiously brought in another slip he would unexpectedly let go an old-style seamer. His fielding, full of sang-froid, was at times as comical as it was intrepid. On hot days he took out his teeth when stationed at silly mid-off. It changed his appearance considerably and, according to several of the pros, his improvised dentistry bordered on gamesmanship.

One of the county scorers worked out that a quarter of Wellard's runs came from sixes. He dispensed entertainment and there were groans when he was quickly out, not just from West Country crowds. His routine was to play back the first half a dozen deliveries with mannered coaching-school correctness. After that, whether the bowling was fast or slow, he aimed for the clouds. A succession of coaches encouraged him to hit straighter. Mostly they let him get on with it.

Arthur, one felt, should have been a jokey extrovert. In fact, he was surprisingly laconic. The voice, when not inclining to Taunton and the Blackdowns, was more cockney than Man of Kent. "Come in a bit at cover, cock," he would say. Everyone was 'cock'. He got animated only when he went racing. That was something he did perhaps a little too often on a Somerset pro's frugal salary.

Andrews idolised him "even though he always bowled with the wind behind him and I suffered at the other end." When the newcomer arrived from Kent, Bill was in awe of his appearance: his gaudy ties, check sports coats and pointed shoes. Not that Wellard was flashy but he carried an aura of self-contained sophistication. Yet he was basically an uncomplicated man. When it rained, he produced a pack of cards. He left the majority of the professionals, fledglings when it came to poker – or, more often, brag – out of pocket. Bill used to say: "He could remember the position of every card in the pack – he was out of our class."

So he was in most cases when it came to cricket. In his first season for the county he took 131 wickets. Three times he did the double. Twice at Wells he belted five sixes in an over, scattering the dreamy young theological students seated at long-on.

Everyone liked Arthur. That included Harold Pinter who wrote affectionately about him and probably considered it a coup when Wellard agreed to play on occasions for the playwright's eleven. Like most of my fellow Somerset friends I was outraged when Somerset chose in 1950 not to re-engage him.

UPSETTING LORD HAWKE

Cecil Parkin, son of a railwayman from County Durham, caused a great stir in 1924 when he put his name to a newspaper column criticising the failure of England's captain Arthur Gilligan to bowl him earlier in a Test. A second article landed him in even hotter water.

Cricket's Unholy Trinity (1985)

Cec Parkin, like many a North Countryman, was blunt and fearless. He hadn't too much time for diplomatic niceties, of the kind you are apt to associate with a pussy-footing southerner. Sports writers in the 1920s quickly detected that he had an undeniable flair for a contentious phrase. He was never unduly reticent when approached for an opinion until his relationship with journalists soured and he had started to walk reluctantly away from a headline.

In the 1920s, the style of the sports pages was changing. Circulation battles were gaining momentum and 'signed' articles by leading sportsmen were proving a notable attraction. The reading public was gullible and had never heard of such an emergent breed as ghost-writers. Parkin was able to supplement his cricket wages with regular postal orders from the papers. His views were avidly read, on a weekly basis, in the old *Empire News*. And those views, at the behest of the wily sports editor, invariably had a sting to them. Poor Lord Hawke was wont to splutter over his Sunday breakfast. For heaven's sake, what right had this nominally educated professional to opinionate on major cricketing issues?

The backlash of anger to his reported attitude to Gilligan as a tactician and especially as a handler of bowlers didn't dissuade him from more published controversy. In one of his articles he was even audacious enough to suggest that England might do worse than appoint a professional captain. Surely Parkin had few equals as a polemicist. He couldn't have said or written anything more likely to arouse the collective wrath of the establishment. He was daring to speak the unspoken. London clubs were suddenly alive with talk of horse-whipping vengeance as heavy-eyed old colonels stumbled from their leather-bound somnolence.

'What's wrong with Herbert Sutcliffe or Jack Hobbs?' he asked with, one suspects, more mischief than naïvety.

This was too much for Lord Hawke. And at the next annual meeting of Yorkshire County Cricket Club he thundered out his protest. It was unfortunate for him that the public remembered only one fervent sentence: 'Pray God no professional will ever captain England.' As a schoolboy nurtured on cricketing rather than historical data, I could quote it more often – and certainly more accurately – than Nelson's valedictory murmur to Hardy.

His Lordship said a good deal more in that impassioned speech. He assured the Yorkshire members, for instance, that he loved professionals 'every one of them'. That must have been an excessive claim and would certainly have been disputed by the two pros he dismissed for good from the Yorkshire dressing room. But there was ample evidence of his affection for the humbler members of the county team. What he wanted to say was that England had always had an amateur captain and it would be a great pity if things changed. In retrospect, we may see him as a blinkered aristocrat but his fashionable defence of the amateur skipper was utterly sincere. His speech won prolonged applause. Cecil Parkin was again cast as the villain.

Parkin, the happy-go-lucky jester, discovered for a second time just how unpopular he had become. At home, he buried his head in his hands and turned to his wife: 'I feel unwanted for no just reason. I think I'll chuck county cricket altogether. There's no joy in being cold-shouldered.'

He was more depressed and miserable than at any other time in his life. When he was told that Hawke had said: 'If he was still a Yorkshire player, I'd make sure he'd never step onto a Yorkshire cricket field again,' Parkin wished with all his heart that he was still back in Norton-on-Tees, working as an apprentice pattern maker.

The gregarious off-spinner sensed that he was being shunned. For several years he had been one of this country's most popular cricketers. His wicket-taking feats for Lancashire were beginning to fill the record books. He was the bowler people came to watch. They were entranced by the sheer variety of his deliveries; they were entertained by the discomfiture of the batsmen who sparred at him and pondered his cheeky spectrum of challenge. And, on top of all that, he was one of nature's jokers. Cricket could always be fun when he was around: palming the ball like the magician he was, under the nose of a gawping umpire, hiding it in his pocket, kicking it up with his right boot in a way all the kids tried to copy. Yet here he was, because of published views that were before their time, being maligned and ostracised.

From this distance none of us would say that Cecil Parkin's bold suggestion was irrational. It was the kind of thing the pros were saying more and more – but mostly from the privacy of their own poky dressing room. The idea that Sutcliffe might eventually lead Yorkshire had even been discreetly ventilated. Parkin's crime was that, for the first time, he had said aloud the things that others had only whispered. He had also said them with a sweeping lack of subtlety, but that was the style of the man.

A LYON-HEARTED EXPERIMENT

Wisden Cricketers' Almanack 2009

Beverley Hamilton Lyon, it was mostly agreed in Bristol, Cheltenham and every sporting corner of the Cotswolds and Severn Vale, was Gloucestershire's finest captain. He was also the county's most imaginative, inspiring and daring leader. Above all, he was one of the great visionaries of our first-class game. In the 1920s and early 1930s he publicly despaired, with a contentious eloquence, at the way county cricket was going. To him it totally lacked a vibrant, competitive structure. He saw it as needlessly somnolent and complacent, as too often it meandered in search of a result. The clock seemed to have a negligible relevance – and that to him was all wrong.

He loved the game and played it well. But despite a cheerful exterior – this model of man-management skills had a natural contempt for cricket's class divisions – he was a restless thinker. To him the current philosophy, however romantic and appealing, was in urgent need of a radical overhaul. By 1930 Bev was saying – and being quoted in the local papers – that it was time to think about playing on Sundays. In Bristol, the city of churches, that was a fearless thing to advocate. Clergy's faces went ashen; the chalices began to rattle in unison.

Yet Lyon foresaw with remarkable clarity how cricket needed to overcome its rigid prejudices, experimenting as it evolved. In the process, he knew how much he would irritate the game's more intractable pontificators, those who resented his facility for creating a headline and his apparent rejection of tradition. Beyond question, however, was the extent of his imagination and his exceptional prophetic skills.

He was appointed Gloucestershire's captain in 1929 and, by the March of 1932, he was the principal speaker at the county club's annual dinner. He spoke for no more than half an hour with a cursory glance at his few notes. In any record of first-class cricket's exercise in vision, it stands as an extraordinary statement of necessary intent. Just a few fidgeted uneasily; the rest, including his team-mates, liked the sound of what he was saying.

Already he was one of the most discussed – and quoted – names in county cricket. The previous summer, when Gloucestershire had gone to Sheffield to play Yorkshire, the first two days were lost to rain. It was a situation made for Lyon. He persuaded the home captain, Frank Greenwood, to adopt a hitherto unheard-of ruse. Both agreed to face one ball in their first innings and let it go for four byes. Then they declared and played in effect for 15 points from a one-innings match. Gloucestershire won and poor Greenwood was reprimanded by his committee. Skipper Lyon led the jollity, never gloating, in the visitors' dressing-room. Cricket's authorities didn't approve, of course. Before long there was a change in the regulations to avoid a repetition.

At that 1932 dinner he mentioned that Gloucestershire had made another loss, as had virtually every other county. Then he went on: "The hard facts are that to run a first-class side costs a good deal of money and 80% has to be taken at the gate. Consequently, something has to go on inside the gate, of enough interest and excitement to attract the crowds. That's the catch. The young man or woman can now spend a shilling watching dirt-track racing, greyhounds tearing round bends, or gangster films by the hundred. That is the type of crowds we have to attract today.

"There are certain respected and very eminent gentlemen who don't understand the changes that have come about in the last 50 years. But then, why should they? Would Bach, Beethoven or Chopin understand Jack Payne? The policy of sitting still and waiting like Mr Micawber for something to turn up seems to me to lack both courage and practicality. The spacious times of the Edwardian era have gone for ever. Lord Hawke can afford to be haughty – cricket cannot. Lord Hawke fiddles while Rome burns.

"I am not prepared to stand by while the game I love dies an unnatural death through lack of support. And I believe there is a great volume of similar opinion throughout the country. There is clearly only one thing to try – the clock must come into the game more. Who can deny that cricket is at its glorious best when time is a factor? Allow a batting side three hours only in which to get their runs. And I challenge anybody to tell me how you have spoilt the first-class game. In that way, you get a decision from 12 hours of cricket. If there has been rain, well then six hours' play will give you a decision.

"Why can't we have a knockout competition on these lines, the final to be played at Lord's or The Oval? Let the profits be divided among competing counties."

Bev's dramatic, unequivocal warnings and advice on what should be done demanded attention. On the drive home from the Grand Hotel, he pondered his next radical step. He had softened up his devotees and doubters; now was the time to put some of his far-seeing ideas into practice. The county's first trial match of the 1932 pre-season seemed the perfect opportunity. It was to be a 12-a-side match at the delightful Stinchcombe ground, high above the Severn. Neither side was to bat for more than two and a half hours. The emphasis was to be on attack and entertainment.

He skippered a full Gloucestershire team. The opposition, Stinchcombe Stragglers, in those days a club of some local status and talent, had Major M.F.S. Jewell, well known as a captain of Worcestershire, leading from the top of the order. His strong side included Bev's brother, Dar Lyon of Somerset, and a pair of Essex professionals, Jack O'Connor and Laurie Eastman. Bev, who never lacked friends in the newspapers, ensured plenty of advance publicity for a match that held so much curiosity value. A crowd of nearly 3,000 turned up at the village ground.

There had been heavy rain and the wicket was 'soft and spongy'. But after a rather slow and self-conscious start, this unconventional county trial match grew in brio and muscular magnetism. Stinchcombe batted first and made 201, best served by the Essex pros, in two and a quarter hours or – such was the over-rate in those days of few fielding changes – 61 overs. Tom Goddard, unaffected by the batsmen's liberties, took five wickets for five runs. There was no limit on the number of overs each bowler could bowl but Lyon sensibly kept his great off-spinner on a leash.

Gloucestershire lost by just five runs and it seemed odd that Lyon juggled the order, partly out of his sense of adventure, partly to share out the pre-season practice. He belted runs himself near the bottom of the order; the rugged New Zealander Charlie Dacre was even lower down, though in compensation he hit five sixes in half a dozen balls. One more would have given Gloucestershire victory by a wicket. Perhaps the experiment might then have been followed up sooner than 30 years later, when Leicestershire's Mike Turner started the Midlands Knockout of 65 overs a side, the forerunner of the Gillette Cup that revived the county game.

West Country accents warmed to the innovations, so different from the po-faced manner in which Championship matches were often played. In the Gloucester evening paper, *The Citizen*, 'S.H.' wrote: 'Time-limit innings can brighten up cricket tremendously ... [it] produced fireworks which sent spectators into the seventh heaven of delight.' The writer quoted Lyon as saying after the match: "It has been proved that under this system players can make runs at a rate which pleases the spectators. Nobody is interested in huge totals being piled up. Three hours' batting is enough for any side."

Arthur Gilligan, the former England captain, wrote in the *News Chronicle*: 'B.H. Lyon's brighter cricket experiment proved a success, and there is no doubt that time-limit matches might be very popular with the public in the near future ...'

One of the players in the Stinchcombe game was less effusive, commenting that "time-limit cricket might be admirable for one-day club matches, but could not be applied to county games." A well-known bowler – was it Goddard? – told Dursley's weekly *The Gazette*: "It would mean that brawn would triumph over brain, and the slow bowler would be eliminated." The editorial in one leading Bristol paper was even more muted: 'B.H. Lyon has proved himself a man of original and revolutionary ideas ... We all want brighter cricket but on this occasion too high a price was paid to secure it.'

Bev must have sensed that Lord's and county committee rooms around the country were becoming weary of what they saw as his gimmicky forays, while he continued to propound the need for a new-look approach. Time-limited innings, knockout competitions, an end to negative batting and bowling: he kept up his attack on cricket's reactionaries. Now it was also time to renew his advocacy for Sunday cricket.

The match on a June Sunday in 1933 was played in aid of hospital charities at Stanway House, near Moreton-in-Marsh, at the invitation of the Earl of Wemyss, president of Cheltenham General Hospital. And it carried the condition that the players would go to church first. Six players who were members of the MCC touring team to Australia the previous winter took part at Stanway. An illustrious opposition line-up included Bob Wyatt, the Nawab of Pataudi, Herbert Sutcliffe, Maurice Leyland and Gubby Allen. Lyon fielded a full county side against the Earl of Wemyss's eleven, who went on to win by 77 runs. Each team had two innings and batted in all for 45 overs. Everything was brisk and entertaining. In all, 763 runs were scored, the sweetest of all by Hammond (127) who hit Leyland for 32 off an over.

Not that there was unanimous approval. Quite apart from ecclesiastical concern, expressed with histrionic fervour from a number of pulpits, Jack Hobbs went on record as saying: "I'm dead against Sunday cricket. The cricketers don't want it. Six days are quite enough." Lord Hawke was more enraged. "It's quite impossible," he spluttered. "Next, you'll be having League football on Sundays. I've never heard of such a thing."

By now Lyon had been dubbed 'The Apostle of Brighter Cricket'. By 1934, after Jardine had gone and Wyatt had a broken thumb, he was an outside bet for the England captaincy. Maybe it was considered he was too unconventional and relied too readily on hunches. Some even whispered that his Jewish blood worked against him. They knew that as a daring tactician, who twice took Gloucestershire to runners-up in the Championship, he sometimes came unstuck. Perhaps there was more than a semblance of panic in the correspondence column of a national newspaper when the writer asked: 'Are Gloucestershire taking brighter cricket to excess? The captain's orders seem to be to hit the cover off the ball in as little time as possible.'

Beverley Lyon was a sophisticated man, a bon viveur, who liked going to the best restaurants, West End first nights, or having a ringside seat for a prize fight. He was gregarious, with a cussed egalitarian streak that endeared him to the county pros when he bundled them into his big Bentley with the instructions to his faithful chauffeur and valet: "We've a win to celebrate – off now to my pub." And it would turn out to be the Dorchester. The amateurs in the game earned no special favours from him. Once, after a snub at Lord's, he deliberately led his players through the professionals' gate onto the field. Hammond was known to idolise and envy him with all that social elan.

Bev died in 1970. As the notice in *The Times* made clear, there was to be no funeral service. He bequeathed his body to the Royal College of Surgeons for medical research. Several obituaries made the same point: 'His bonhomie was thoroughly infectious.' There was appropriate praise for him as a cricketer, one who scored 16 hundreds, two of them in a match against Essex in 1930. He had poor eyesight, so his fielding near to the wicket was all the more commendable. But it was as a thinker and a captain that we remember him best. He had an uncanny sense of the direction cricket needed to go. It could even be argued that he deserves, posthumously, some of the credit for Twenty20.

Stinchcombe, Saturday 30 April 1932
Stinchcombe Stragglers 201 (O'Connor 75, Eastman 62, Goddard 5/5)
Gloucestershire 196 (Lyon 53, Dacre 47*)
Stinchcombe Stragglers won by five runs

BILL ALLEY

Sixty Summers – Somerset Cricket Since The War (2006)

Yes, of course, the craggy old leg-side spellbinder should have played for Australia. He was pencilled in for the 1948 tour of this country and would almost certainly have come, but for a ghastly accident in the nets when his jaw was broken. It coincided, more or less, with domestic bereavements. His Test aspirations were over; he came to Lancashire to play league cricket instead.

And from there, at the age of 38 (as far as one can calculate) this tough, streetwise ex-pug from Sydney surprised everyone by turning to rural Somerset. Very soon he was one of them down there; rolling a lethal ball in the skittle alleys, going out with his 12-bore, following the hounds. He also played his cricket, noisily and never less than entertainingly. He was not once going to be inhibited by convention and accepted style at the crease. He was made for the partisans and not the poets.

Bill had the unfailing eyes of a country fox. He picked up the flight of the ball quickly – and belted, this sturdy left-hander, in the rough direction of mid-wicket. Legside fielders knew it was coming but rarely stood the chance of a catch. He pulled and hooked with immense power and total disregard for the coaching manual. But the repertoire was wider than might have been thought. Many of his runs came from pugnacious chops to third man. He could produce, at times out of sheer mischief, an exquisite cover drive.

This cussed old campaigner took 134 and 95 off the Australians at Taunton. In that extraordinary 1961 summer he scored more than 3,000 runs in all first-class cricket. He never stopped smiting – or talking. Some said he spoke his mind too much, that he belly-ached too much. But he could always be, in that anti-establishment way of his, a most amusing companion. The crowds, not just in the West Country, loved him.

In addition he was the meanest of exponents of medium-paced swing and seam, while no-one remembers him putting down a catch at gully. Later, as a top umpire, his popularity was sustained, even among batsmen who were victims of his propensity for the lbw decision.

Bill became, in spirit, a Somerset man. Yet he resented the fact that the captaincy eluded him, despite promises, and that a small group of pros, upset that he had dropped Brian Langford when standing in as skipper, seemed to have ganged up against him. He was equally resentful over the imposed conditions that led to his departure, and the old welterweight bristled for a long time. Yet what a tonic he had been.

22
Intimate Portraits

Raymond Robertson-Glasgow, Carwyn James, Bill Greswell

'Eleven Intimate Portraits' was the sub-title given by David to his book *Beyond Bat and Ball*. The portraits were all of cricketers, each running to 15 to 20 pages, a length that allowed David to capture the essence of his subjects without any of the suffocating detail that pads out so many biographies of cricketers.

His choice of subjects had no thread to it, other than his personal fascination with each of them, as he explained in his author's note:

> The composition of my team has been a private indulgence. I have wanted to write about most of them for a long time. Almost all were exceptional players in their various ways: by vibrant leadership, warm-heartedness, quirks and fearful insecurities in some cases, and of course often innate brilliance on the field. One, Siegfried Sassoon, may even have been a rotten cricketer by conventional standards; but his enthusiasm could be mesmeric during those matches in a Wiltshire meadow. They offered the sweetest of havens as gnawing thoughts and images of the trenches temporarily receded. The book has been written with much affection as I have searched to explain the whole man, not merely eleven individual cricketers.

Graham Tarrant, who had been responsible for persuading David to write *Country Reporter*, undertook its publication, giving it a 'belles-lettres' look and focusing on specialist cricket outlets. Immediately the book won plaudits. Whereas there are now four Cricket Book of the Year awards, there was only one in 1993 – the Cricket Society Literary Award – and it was won by *Beyond Bat and Ball*. As a result the book was sold on to a mainstream publisher who re-marketed it with a conventional cricket picture on the cover.

EW Swanton called David 'a writer of deep perception and rare sympathy', Stephen Fay said it was 'the best book about cricketers I have ever read', and the veteran journalist Geoffrey Moorhouse, reviewing it in the *Wisden Cricketers' Almanack*, went to the heart of David's special talent:

> The book starts with that mellowing old pug Wilf Wooller and ends with worn-out gypsy Tom Richardson. The team is complemented by Siegfried Sassoon, Jack Fingleton, Bill Andrews, Andy Ducat, Bill Greswell, Big Jim Smith, Bev Lyon, Bertie Poore and Jack Mercer; all but Sassoon fine cricketers, every man rich in his humanity and chosen for that above all. Dennis Silk in a foreword suggests that Foot is as good as Robertson-Glasgow at his best, and I agree. At least as good; not

only because he can describe Ducat handling his bat 'with the respect that a professional violinist shows for his violin' but also for other literary values. This is a sensitive, compassionate writer of originality, of a different order from the tone-deaf hirelings who churn out most of the cricket biographies these days, for quick profit rather than lasting value.

Robertson-Glasgow, whose own portraits of cricketers were of much shorter length, was the first subject in *Fragments of Idolatry*, David's sequel to *Beyond Bat and Ball*. This time there were twelve portraits, of varying lengths, including two writers, Robertson-Glasgow and Alan Gibson, a boxer 'Kid' Berg, a football manager Alec Stock and rugby's Carwyn James. Somerset cricket was represented by Maurice Tremlett, Horace Hazell, Tom Cartwright (partly) and, of course, Robertson-Glasgow; Gloucestershire by Reg Sinfield and Alf Dipper; and there were two forays into Middlesex, to different ends of the social spectrum, with Patsy Hendren and Walter Robins. Again a thread of affection ran through the writing, though it was hard to sense idolatry in the portrait of Walter Robins.

As publisher this time I would have liked to use the word 'essays' about the twelve pieces, but David, as he explained in his introduction, shrank from what he felt to be the grandeur of the word:

> Let no-one flatter me by suggesting that my portraits, character studies if you like, are essays. William Hazlitt, known to veer at times towards the sporting scene, was an essayist. So were Charles Lamb and Robert Lynd, who first ensnared me within the literary pages of the beloved and lamented *News Chronicle*. Some of J.B. Priestley's best phrases and insights are to be found in his essays. Many of Bernard Shaw's wordy, prescient, self-indulgent prefaces to his plays are in their way brilliant essays.
>
> I have never harboured haughty aspirations in my writing, nurtured as I was in the school of journalism and often obsessed with the oddities of human behaviour. When I write about sport – mostly cricket – my reflections emanate usually from somewhere between the dressing room and the psychiatrist's couch. I like to observe how my subject plays; even more how he thinks, what worries him. It is true that I have been inclined to study complex, unfulfilled and, in some cases, sad people.
>
> This is a different collection. Of my twelve 'idols', one did kill himself. Another tried to. One died, a lonely man, in an Amsterdam hotel. But I have chosen them because, in their

varying ways, they have been my heroes. Not all as cricketers, however; not all as practical sportsmen. My group includes a writer and broadcaster, a rugby coach, a football manager and a boxing champion. More than half I came to know well; only one, Alf Dipper, the talented, under-valued Gloucestershire slowcoach, I never met.

My style, I fear, is as discursive as ever. A thread of regard and affection runs through this book – and I hope it shows.

Again the book was met with glowing praise. Ian Wooldridge called it 'sports writing on another plane'; Frank Keating described David as 'our black-belt champ of the unconsidered trifle, the virtuoso of the intricately wrought character cameo'; and Robin Marlar, in the *Cricketer* magazine, went tellingly to the heart of David's talent:

> The real attraction of David Foot's writing is that he is attracted to the loveable without being alarmed by the mysterious. Both he chronicles faithfully as essential features of the whole man.

The two longest portraits in the book feature the two writers, Gibson and Robertson-Glasgow, both men troubled by inner demons but with talents that soared high above most of those who inhabited cricket press boxes. David's comparison of Robertson-Glasgow with Cardus is rich with the insights of a fellow writer.

David's relationship with Alan Gibson was a fraught one, which continued to trouble him long after the *Times* writer's death. Gibson, himself an adopted West Countryman, could be kind and encouraging to the younger David, and David repaid that kindness many times, all too frequently helping his fellow reporter onto a train when the whisky had been too plentifully imbibed during the day. But, as an Oxford scholar, Gibson could also be cruel to David, patronising him for his lack of education and making him feel afresh the inferiority of his roots.

> He claimed he wasn't a journalist, something else that bothered me when newspapers and broadcasting were really his only source of employment.

David, by contrast, was always happy to describe himself as a working journalist. From his humble background he was proud of the profession he served. He had no inclination to assume any trappings of self-importance.

Yet the truth is that, given the right canvas, as he had with these two books, he wrote with rare beauty. In the field of sports writing he was an essayist of the very highest order.

RAYMOND ROBERTSON-GLASGOW ('CRUSOE')

Cricketer and cricket writer in extract from 'Fragments of Idolatry' (2001)

I shamelessly confess that Robertson-Glasgow remains something of an idol. But was he the best? And how do we start to measure, with anything so subjective? It comes back, in my case, to a choice between Sir Neville Cardus and Crusoe – and if we are bandying around high sounding labels like literature, then Cardus must, I say with some reluctance, come first. The brilliance and daring – at times excessive – of his imagery defies challenge. So does the sweep of his imagination and the sheer output that dwarfs Robertson-Glasgow's.

Their styles and backgrounds were of course utterly dissimilar. For Crusoe, the length of a pitch was 22 yards; for Cardus it was all the way from Old Trafford to the opera houses and concert platforms of the world. Cardus could embroider some ornate and beautiful sentences, though I fancy he invariably had half an eye on the effect they would cause in print. There was nothing self-conscious about Robertson-Glasgow. He recoiled from ostentation and his scholarship was obscured. He, too, could write beautifully – but with a brevity that Cardus would never have entertained. His newspaper sub-editors would have liked more words from him. 'Bit short this week, Crusoe. Could you come up with another ... em, hundred words?' For this definitive minimalist, it was not always easy.

One of his envied skills was that he could distil the mood and balance of a match in a few paragraphs. Cardus liked whole columns. The loquacious Mancunian was congenitally discursive, wandering with liberty-taking nostalgia into a dozen by-ways in the course of a match report. Crusoe liked short sentences and was known to drop verbs altogether without any apparent injury to syntax or style. There was no stopping Cardus and his symphonic brasses in full rhythmic flight. A trenchant opinion would then emerge like crashing cymbals. Robertson-Glasgow's word music belonged more to the strings.

No-one back in the *Manchester Guardian* office in Cross Street altered a Cardus comma, or only very occasionally (and discreetly). In truth, not much ever needed to be changed. His lengthy pieces were for the most part exquisitely constructed and his contemporaries knew he was inordinately proud of his reports. He liked to hear the members at Old Trafford discussing them next day. It must be said, too, that after the *Guardian* moved to London, he became increasingly difficult, pernickety and even at times cantankerous; I have that on the word of sub-editors who handled his copy. Where once he'd dutifully dictated his reports over the phone, he now indulged himself by arranging for a chauffeur to take them from Lord's or the Oval to the newspaper offices in Grays Inn Road. At a time when the *Guardian* was anxiously watching its pennies, that was an item of expenditure the paper could have done without.

Crusoe was altogether more self-effacing. It was almost as if he were fearful of boring the reader. For all his classical learning, he could write with a surprisingly light touch, ready to share an esoteric dressing room joke. It might be argued that some of his vignettes – much of his journalism was too short to be gilded with any description as grand as essay – seemed too trivial. Yet he could still illuminate them with wondrous shafts of phraseology and insights that everyone else had missed.

All his life, either as a player or writer, he steadfastly refused to take cricket too seriously. That shouldn't imply for a moment that he tended to patronise those who played for a living. He loved the majority of county professionals, just like he loved mankind; but he edged away from any cerebral interpretations in his reports and minuscule profiles. The unerring perspicacity was there; the judgements, technical and human, were unwaveringly accurate. As someone who taught English and read the classics all his life, he cherished good writing. However seemingly uncomplicated his sentence construction, he would summon up a lovely, original phrase and find apposite, if kindly, adjectives to convey the fruitless endeavours of a sweating, artisan bowler or a sloppy fielder.

He was inclined to write as he talked; and he was a marvellous conversationalist. He used to tell friends of the interminable, meaningless sermons he sat through at matins during his childhood. Heeding the lessons of such clerical insensitivity, he pledged privately to make sure he held his readers' attention. It was significant that some of his finest work was seen in the short *Cricket Prints* and those inconsequential, sparingly written pieces that appeared to have no more than a peripheral association with sport.

Four out of five, asked to weigh the literary merits of one against the other, would plump without hesitation for Cardus. Didn't he revolutionise cricket writing, taking it beyond Victorian and Edwardian cliché and the arid record of a game's chronology? Didn't he give it soul and invest sublime images plucked from some of the great arts of civilisation? Didn't he stand, rightly, as a figure of literature?

I accept all of that without reservation. But for reasons which I can't wholly define I refuse to go with the majority. I simply read Robertson-Glasgow with more enjoyment.

CARWYN JAMES

Welsh rugby player and coach in extract from 'Fragments of Idolatry' (2001)

He died with cruel, mystifying suddenness in a nondescript Amsterdam hotel early in 1983 but that coaxing, mellifluous voice can still be affectionately heard, when we listen hard enough, on a hundred Welsh touchlines. Carwyn, just Carwyn: the name continues to bring a glow of treasured reminiscence, followed by those eloquent, perplexed sighs. There was never a greater influence on the way rugby should be played in Wales. Yet, for complex, contrary, needless, self-induced reasons, he was not appointed the national coach. He was the man everyone knew – and no one knew.

Along every valley, in every pit village, every tucked-away rugby ground of steaming winter breaths amid Saturdays' animated throaty ritual, they doted on his wisdom and the melodic words – about sport or life – which he gave so freely to anyone who asked. They basked in his coaching triumphs for Llanelli and the Lions. They travelled miles, many of them miners' sons like himself, to hear him speak. They revered him as a chapel deacon and a white-robed druid. Many contended he was a rugby guru without equal. They were conscious of the lyrical quality that he insisted on bringing to the game, whether first as an instinctive outside half and then as a gentle, single-minded coach, the mentor to so many. What few of them knew was the measure of the pain he suffered in his privacy.

Perhaps it is the voice that we remember best of all. It was musical and sweetly-tuned, too calm, one would have thought, for the biting winds of an exposed touchline. That voice, fashioned by the hymnal, was rarely raised in rebuke at the expense of a player; it increased fractionally in decibels only when someone, in his cups, took a sly, insensitive dig at Carwyn's undeviating political zeal and 'Welshness'. The voice could be mesmeric, full of crochets and quavers and classical allusions, as his unbridled conversation weaved joyfully in and out of literature, the arts and the brotherhood of man. He loved talking, philosophising, paying homage to genius, whether he saw it at the time as Beethoven or Phil Bennett. He had a reasoned opinion about most things. Backed by scholarship and a sharp brain, softened by the chuckle that was seldom too far away, he was not easily shifted from his stance. There were moods of silence and torment, often obscured from his friends and the general public. To them, the voice of Carwyn James was never idle.

*

My acquaintance with him was relatively brief, though I like to think warm. I had been enjoying his evocative, highly personalised Friday pieces in the *Guardian* and at one of our Christmas lunches – I was a freelance cricket writer on the paper – in the Cheshire Cheese (sawdust and decent beer) off Fleet Street, I found myself sitting next to him. It was a convivial, decidedly liquid occasion, wondrous for me because he didn't stop talking. Yet, I recall, he was not a selfish conversationalist and encouraged me to tell him about my undistinguished schoolboy career as a prop forward who took the kicks in house matches. That amused him.

The lunch went on deep into the afternoon and I worried about whether the paper's sports pages would ever come out that evening. When John Arlott, then our No 1 cricket writer, got up to say the few words that were expected of him, I couldn't decide whether he or Carwyn James looked the more flushed. But they were both in wonderful, anecdotal form and I, a country writer romantically seduced by the Dickensian surrounds, was in awe of both of them.

After that I met Carwyn a number of times, either at St Helen's, Swansea, or Sophia Gardens, Cardiff, where I had gone to cover county cricket and he had wandered into the press boxes to join us. He, too, liked his cricket and had done the occasional match for the *Guardian*. It only occurred to me much later that he might have felt I was perhaps intruding on his new journalistic preserves. But from my experience, he was a man generous in spirit and there wasn't the merest suggestion that he would have liked to be writing about Glamorgan those days instead of me.

On one of my visits to Cardiff, long after the close of play, the two of us were drinking together in the small bar above the dressing rooms. Everyone else had left; the players had sunk their solitary pints and gone. I looked anxiously at my watch and told Carwyn it was time for me to motor back to my home in Bristol. 'Not yet ... not yet. Let's have another drink together. We have much to talk about. Tell me about Bristol Rovers. Or Mike Procter. Or John Blake's Bristol – did he really have that lovely rugby team of his running all the time?'

There was almost a kind of desperation in those cascading questions, as he blurted out the disparate potential starting points of conversation. Before I had offered any kind of reply he was at the bar, buying us another double-gin. I was flattered, of course I was, that he wished to stay chatting with me. At the same time, I came to one irreversible conclusion. He was a painfully lonely man.

Cliff Morgan, Trebanog's mighty icon, was among James' friends. They had similar, decent, God-fearing, unpretentious backgrounds. They traded reminiscences by the dozen; they sang hymns together. On that great New Zealand tour, when Carwyn was the coach and Cliff was heavily involved in broadcasting, there was a knock on Morgan's door at half past eleven one evening. 'And there he was, Carwyn, clutching a bottle of gin with the tonic stuck in his breast pocket. Just to see him there made one feel better. He stayed for hours. We had a Welsh song or two, talked about everything – the scoring of tries, the rights of man.'

*

He died a sick man. He'd put on weight, was still smoking 50 a day and had a consistent thirst, with or without company. Some of the earlier ebullience had disappeared. He now watched matches, as a broadcaster or journalist, and missed the sweat of the dressing room. Always an expert analyst of what was happening on the field, he increasingly pondered – in the privacy of his flat or in the car – what he saw as his lack of fulfilment. Should he have stuck to academia? Why, for a man so friendly by nature, did he lack friends when he needed them most? Worse of all, he used to confess that he was falling out of love with the game that had been the constant factor of joy in his life, his raison d'être.

Carwyn James remains a riddle. There was the personal ecstasy when he was admitted to the Gorsedd of Bards or when, with a rugby ball in his hand, he talked like a vicarious father to a half circle of captive schoolboys. There were times when he wondered whether he talked too seriously about his native beliefs and aspirations, not acknowledging a second point of view. Here was his least engaging (or some would contend his most treasured) quality as a Welshman.

The memorial service at the Tabernacle chapel in his home village was in Welsh. Many of his country's most famous and revered players packed the pews or stood in the chapel grounds as the service was relayed by loudspeakers. In the congregation, too, were the WRU officials with whom he had waged his lengthy, psychological battle. Everyone seemed agreed, amid the sorrow, on one thing. He should have coached Wales. 'The job was his but he wanted too much ...' 'Trouble with Carwyn, he just wouldn't compromise ...' 'A lovely, lonely, cussed, old bugger ...'

That was what they all whispered as they walked away, heavy in heart. And as we began by saying, we still hear his name most Saturdays on every touchline in Wales as the ball goes out of play and there's time for renewed debate. Carwyn ... Carwyn, you wouldn't have allowed that kick for touch. We'd still like you around to show us how.

BILL GRESWELL

Somerset cricketer in extracts from 'Beyond Bat and Ball' (1993)

Bill Greswell was the most brilliantly innovative bowler Somerset ever had. His story is also one of the saddest and least known in the county's variegated history.

There is a case for saying he introduced the technique of in-swing bowling to county cricket, though one or two others arguably preceded him or were contemporaries with those unfamiliar, arcane skills. Bill was perhaps the most adept of all, yet at first it never occurred to him that he was doing anything different with the ball or causing consternation among illustrious batsmen.

He had left Repton in 1908 and in five matches for Somerset in August he took 22 wickets. By the next season, he was earning the grudging admiration of the Australian tourists, finding himself among the most discussed young bowlers in the country. Those who had been inclined to dismiss him as 'just another precocious schoolboy winning premature acclaim' were quickly silenced. The late swerve that he imparted was quite lethal. Wiseacres, sprawled in their canvas chairs in front of the Stragglers Bar at Taunton, stroked leathery faces and said he would walk into the England team.

Greswell in fact played a mere 115 times for his beloved Somerset, never for England. He had a consuming affection for cricket and prodigious, natural gifts as a bowler. He refined those bountiful talents, learning to analyse the curves, diversions and wicked vagaries of his boyishly delivered overs. All he wanted from life was to play cricket. Instead he was sent to Ceylon in work for which he was patently unsuited and he disliked. It must have left him embittered. Yet the public never knew the extent of his anguish.

*

In the year or so he was the county president, I approached him once or twice as a journalist and found him both courteous and taciturn. Members liked his self-effacing manner. Others enjoyed the droll jokes he made to enliven meandering, jejune debates, during his time with Williton Rural District Council. He didn't talk much about his home life. Neighbours occasionally saw him setting off for his long walks up the rust-earthed hillside that dominated, with its distinctive pastoral beauty, that corner of West Somerset. He was a man who needed his privacy. They liked what they saw. They took for granted that his life was contented and balanced.

The reality was so different. If only they had known.

*

He joined the Home Guard with great enthusiasm in the last war. As commander of the local battalion, he welcomed the responsibilities and administrative duties. There were many stories of unorthodox assignments by the motley assortment of Home Guards in the Quantoxhead area – and authentic reports of rifle practice at the expense of the deer population. Major Greswell relayed with wry humour, a quality of his not always evident, some of the escapades. A practice session with live hand grenades, when Bill was in charge, was perilously near to tragedy. He went to infinite pains to explain to a farm worker from Williton how the pin should be removed and the grenade hurled 'just as if it's a cricket ball'. The instructions were not absorbed and the horrified Home Guard commander bellowed for everyone to fall flat on their stomachs. The grenade went off – and the only casualty was an overweight local grocer whose protruding bottom took the major share of the blast.

*

But then the war was over – and once more there was a fearful emptiness in his life. This led to the second of his nervous breakdowns. The first had been in 1931, brought on largely by business failure in the rubber-broking business in London. At Dr Fox's hospital in Brislington, on the outskirts of Bristol, he was one of the guinea pigs for ECT (electro-convulsive therapy). All his life Bill suffered from varying degrees of claustrophobia. This then contentious form of treatment was a thoroughly traumatic experience for him, in the days before the use of anaesthetics in the process. He was strapped down and apprehensive. On one occasion, when he was at the hospital and due for more ECT treatment, he discharged himself.

Much of his life he lacked self-confidence, though significantly this sapping psychological deficiency was never evident when he was playing cricket. A psychiatrist told him more than once: 'You have a dreadful inferiority complex.' Once, visiting the psychiatrist with his second wife, Rachel, the blunt message to the pair of them carried no qualifications. 'You two should never have married – you can't support each other.'

To the public in the West Country he was warmly regarded, a man of gentility. They knew nothing of the blacker side of his nature. His bitterness, which he did his best to hide, manifested itself in oddly teasing actions to domestic pets. His complexes were hard to understand. He was undemonstrative to his children, inclined to greet them with a handshake rather than a kiss. When they were at school, he would write copious letters to them and add illustrations that were well-meaning but had little artistic pretension. He was disappointed that son John was not more of a cricketer. On the morning of the day Gill was due to compete in a gymkhana, Bill took the horse out across the hills and tired it out. That kind of uncharitable action was hard to fathom. At this distance, significantly, the children's affection for him remains strong.

He was, again in sharp contradiction to those who thought they knew him, a person of deep prejudices. His anti-Semitic attitudes were unbending. 'He had only to see an opulent car going by with GB plates and he'd claim it was being driven by a "Jew boy".' He hated all Labour politicians after the war – 'those bleating sheep of the Left' – and Emanuel Shinwell most of all. The dislike of Shinwell could be almost entirely attributed to his Jewish roots. Bill even had suspicions about Jack Meyer, the Somerset cricketing eccentric and Millfield founder, because of the sound of his name. In fact, RJO's father had been an Anglican canon.

The bigotry extended in a number of directions. He didn't like blacks or Yorkshiremen, which must at least show some sort of spectrum of intolerance. When in 1970 Brian Close was invited to come to Somerset as captain, he was appalled.

*

His children's affection for him was considerable. They accepted his whims and the complexes that manifested themselves in oddly cruel, unpredictable actions. They understood his frustrations which at times were almost unbearable for him. He may well have felt he had negligible status in the household. He was lonely and there were certainly occasions when he would have welcomed more visitors to his last two homes – though he had loyal friends with whom he could reminisce.

*

Bill Greswell was something of a tragic figure in the last years of his life. He had always been liked by everyone in sport, and indeed by the local community in the embracing folds of the Quantock Hills. By now Sammy Woods and Farmer White had gone on. His name meant less and less to the successive generations of post-war players at Taunton.

He now spent most of his days in a small, newly built section of the house over the garage at Orchard Combe. He slumped in the armchair, watching television incessantly and often unseeingly. Not too many called to see him. Bill, a religious man, read his Bible, 'Lorna Doone' and his book of devotional thoughts over and over again. Mental decline, at first gradual, became far more marked. Life was not easy for Rachel.

JACK MERCER

Glamorgan cricketer, later Northamptonshire coach and scorer, in extract from 'Beyond Bat and Ball' (1993)

It could be argued that I made a serious error of judgement, in the August of 1981, as the scorers were returning to their improvised conclave after lunch at Clarence Park, Weston-super-Mare, by confessing my childlike love of conjuring to Jack Mercer.

We were walking past a row of parked cars. He put his arm on my shoulder and in almost the same motion spirited a pack of cards from my coat pocket. 'You like a trick, then,' he said in the friendly but embarrassingly amplified tones that suggested his hearing aid wasn't switched on. Before I could reply, he had spread the cards, with a deft little flourish, on the gleaming bonnet of a member's Volvo.

I know of entrepreneurs and professional gamblers who unfailingly take handy calculators everywhere with them; of off-duty barbers who always insist on carrying half a dozen combs, which protrude in neat alignment alongside the biros in the breast pocket. These are symbols of their trade. Between innings, batsmen like to stroll the boundary with a cricket ball deep in their flannels: a sort of stage prop to grip in reassuring familiarity when an insensitive spectator starts to tease.

Jack Mercer's props were his playing cards and a back pocket of loose change that he would pull out, at the merest hint of encouragement, to demonstrate his refined skills of sleight of hand. On that early afternoon, at a match when very few of the illustrious players in the Somerset and Northamptonshire sides could fashion many runs on a disturbingly capricious wicket, scorer Mercer showed me three card tricks and another of mesmeric illusion with half a dozen 10p coins.

He accompanied the impromptu performance with some quite urbane banter and a little wink as he detected my genuine bewilderment. What he didn't appear to notice was my increasing concern that he showed no inclination to forsake his singular, appreciative audience and return to his duties in recording the state of the game. By now Lamb and Yardley were back in the middle, fighting their commendable way to half-centuries. Jack Mercer was still making the aces disappear from the bonnet of a Volvo.

That his audience eventually walked out on him was no reflection of either his dexterity or innate charm. I tactfully shouted, mouth to his ear, that I must get back to the press box; he in turn ambled happily in the direction of his temporarily deserted scorebook, to catch up on three missed overs.

REG SINFIELD

Gloucestershire cricketer in extract from 'Fragments of Idolatry' (2001)

He was not a cricketer fashioned for poets. He even antagonised the supporters of my native county of Somerset. Why then does he remain my favourite?

I suspect I am influenced by the sweetness of his nature. He died in 1988, aged 87, from bowel cancer. Up to a year or so before that he was climbing precariously up ladders to mend a neighbour's roof, mixing cement, tending his and others' gardens, motoring 32 miles a day in a clapped-out Morris 10, still to coach the boys at Colston's School. He doggedly defied his years like no-one else I can recall. His physical strength, contrasting with his innate gentility, was phenomenal.

A few days before he died, at the home of his step-son, I paid one of several visits to his bedside. He was a religious man and he asked me to read some scriptural passages to him. I looked at him as I did so and he seemed restful, his eyes shut as if reflecting on the words. He had been both churchwarden and sidesman at the parish church, attending twice a Sunday and ready to let the vicar know how he disapproved if a sick villager had not been visited. But my call, that last time, was certainly not one of unrelieved piety.

'Come on, Reg, show me that grip again.' A frail hand emerged from under the bedclothes. He grinned and, with an imaginary ball, showed me.

'All a matter of flight. Beat 'em in the air, boy.'

We were back on cricket – and the weary, watery eyes were sparkling again.

'Gloucestershire didn't want to give me my cap, you know, in 1926. They could be mean about that. Colonel Robinson, the captain, said I hadn't done enough to earn it. "Let's see what happens at Trent Bridge then, Colonel," I told him.' Self-justification shouldn't really have been necessary. The single-minded intent was however almost ruined by Harold Larwood. 'He brought one back across my body and caught me in the worst possible place. I went down in a heap and got carted off. But back I came to complete my hundred. And Lol Larwood, bless his heart, later brought me in a double brandy.'

Nothing could have been more eloquent, in Sinfield's murmured argument for a cap. The Colonel handed one over. 'Should damn well think so,' said the team-mates in unison.

On that final visit of mine, he periodically closed his eyes and drifted away. I continued to chat about cricket and he would nod. Once or twice he opened his eyes to put me right on a point. Reg appropriately died in his grey cricket socks.

PATSY HENDREN

Middlesex and England cricketer in extract from 'Fragments of Idolatry' (2001)

Some time after he had given up playing, he'd been appointed Middlesex's scorer. His handwriting was neat, his arithmetic wayward. Fellow scorers used to tell, with benevolent eyes, of instances of faulty mathematics when he did his best to tot up the bowling figures at the close of play. But he liked still being part of the Middlesex entourage, travelling the country just as he used to as a player from 1907 to 1937, and then conveying his limitless enjoyment of the game to successive generations of new players. The pity is that they and many who follow are too absorbed by self-interest, too impatient to pause with their illustrious elders and acquire additional knowledge. Every county has wise old men who were once distinguished cricketers. They stroll the boundaries and receive no more than token acknowledgement from the young pros who are often oblivious to the measure of achievement and experience that would be willingly imparted. All of us make the same mistake: too late we wish we had asked more from our grandfathers.

In Patsy's last season as the scorer for Middlesex, I met him for the only time. It is a presumptuous claim, as I sat some feet away on the other side of a long table. Middlesex were playing Somerset at Glastonbury and it was the custom for the hosts, Morlands, to entertain the two teams to dinner for one night at the George and Pilgrim, in the centre of the town. This was always a convivial evening, with pints of strong ale and a few appropriate, if informal, words from the two captains. I was there as the representative of my evening paper in Bristol and, as far as I can remember, I contrived to sit as close as possible to this distant hero.

His health was not good and it was known he was planning to retire. Yet was I the only one to see him still as a legendary clown? I half wondered, in my naïvety, whether he continued to make jokes about being hit on the head by Larwood, whether he was as funny as everyone said he used to be. The reality was a disappointment. He was a subdued, slightly shrunken man, more like a detached guest at a small town civic luncheon. He seemed quietly to enjoy himself, said little and retired early to his room. I'd wanted someone on the top table to jump to his feet and say in a loud voice: 'That lovely little man just leaving the room is the great Patsy Hendren. Only Jack Hobbs and Frank Woolley scored more runs, gentlemen. Only Jack scored more hundreds. And no-one made us laugh more. Gentlemen, a round of applause ...' Instead, the little man, already a victim of ill health, was on his way to bed. He'd last played for Middlesex 23 years earlier: and now he was almost forgotten.

JACK 'KID' BERG

Jewish boxer in extract from 'Fragments of Idolatry' (2001)

In 1951 I was doing my National Service in the RAF and was stationed for several months at Colindale in London. Most nights I would go down the Northern Line to the West End, to pick up free theatre seats or watch try-out music hall acts at the Nuffield Centre, just off Charing Cross station; or occasionally to prowl, in the wide-eyed ways of country boys, the back alleys of Soho. One evening, I was strolling aimlessly round the corner from Jack Solomons' gym in Great Windmill Street when I saw a man standing in the doorway of his restaurant. He was small, and resplendent in a tuxedo.

I was in uniform, an obligatory form of patriotic identification if I needed seats at the Nuffield Centre. And it was clearly the uniform that attracted his attention. "Where are you stationed, then?"

I was already well-versed in the smarmy invitations from clipjoint operators, pimps and con-men. This was a different kind of conversation. It went on for ten minutes, during which time he told me he'd also been in the RAF. 'Feel like something to eat?'

I gave the sort of helpless shrug that implied a young National Serviceman was really in no position, financially, to go into a Soho restaurant.

'No,' he said, sensing my unease. 'On the house. It isn't very busy tonight.'

In truth it wasn't busy at all. I was the only customer – and I was about to be paid for. He brought me a steak and waved aside my offer to make at least some kind of contribution. While he had been gone – I suspect business may have been so bad that he was the chef as well – I noticed for the first time a number of boxing stills on the walls. I went to examine them: they all featured the same man, the dapper figure who had asked me in for a free meal. Jack 'Kid' Berg.

We talked boxing for a long time after that, or rather he talked. He didn't patronise me in my ignorance. Nor did he boast of his conquests or the acclaim that his flamboyant presence once engendered. At the same time he had a sang-froid about him that I envied. My deferential attitude was probably excessive; village boys aren't very adept at disguising idolatry. When I left, I thanked him profusely and never saw him again. Soon, I was to read he had deserted the restaurant business and was going into films, not for the first time, but now as a stunt man. How he must have hated the sheer inactivity of standing in the doorway of a relatively deserted restaurant. Kid Berg was never a stationary man. He had chased around the East End streets, keeping just out of trouble, as a pallid child. He had been perpetual motion in every ring he entered. On his many voyages to the States he had played games on deck or danced till dawn in the ship's ballroom. When once before the war he was given the lead in a feature film, he'd cockily told the director: 'I hope there's plenty of action.'

I came late to his fighting style: after the rump steak, in fact. I began reading insatiably about him. One can see why the Americans liked him so much. He knew one single, pragmatic way to fight and that was by going forward. He possessed an enormous reservoir of energy. There were times in his early career when he boxed twice a week. He was unfailingly exciting, lifting spectators out of their seats. His methods rarely came from the boxing manual yet the ringcraft could be quite bewildering. His combination of punches staggered opponents steeped in orthodoxy.

Much of his money was made in the States. He became the world junior welterweight champion. Most bouts involving him were memorable. The American promoters struggled to find opponents who had a genuine chance of offsetting his inimitable bravura. Ancient wiseacres out there still talk of his great fights with Kid Chocolate, the talented Cuban Negro, and Tony Canzoneri. In 1930 and '31 he defended his title nine times in America. He was the British lightweight champion at his first attempt in 1934. Such dour historical statistics I can recite – but they tell nothing of his piston fists or gambolling feet snatched straight from an up-tempo Charleston.

His handlers simply glanced at each other and wondered aloud whether he would burn himself out. When he had a bad fight, there was talk of retirement. Those sentiments seldom came from Berg. He enjoyed it too much; he liked making money; he was an easy going extrovert – not so easy going in the ring – who embraced the glamour, the headlines, the publicity and the parties. His first wife Bunty was a dancer in the chorus line with Anna Neagle – and C.B. Cochrane was the best man at the wedding. He used to ride down Rotten Row in Hyde Park on Sunday mornings. His blonde second wife, Moyra, had been a beautician. He always demanded a good-looking young woman on his arm.

The East End threw up some gifted Jewish boxers. Ted 'Kid' Lewis is one cherished name. There was also Harry Mizler, known as Hymie, who surrendered his lightweight title to Berg. The build-up to that fight hadn't been entirely edifying. Here were two Jewish boys of different styles, with their own noisy coteries of East End supporters. There was much talk of grudge and even Jewish monopoly. The ugly aspects of Mosley were starting to emerge too; anti-Semitic emotions were strong in bigoted corners of which there were many.

As the fight approached, Berg was winning the battle of column-inches. He knew how to manipulate the press. He was an altogether more colourful character than Mizler whose family had a fish stall just off the Commercial Road. There was an uneasy tension that preceded the title bout; it never went away and was climaxed when both boxers ended up sharing the same dressing room, neither prepared to concede ground and move out. As controversies were compounded, the wily old Harry Levene was left rubbing his hands.

The Mizler towel was thrown in at the end of the eighth round. There was, I recall, a print of that strange, anti-climactic scrap on the wall of Berg's restaurant. Both boxers had the Star of David emblazoned on their shorts. Berg had badly wanted that fight and asked Levene to obtain it. The Berg-Mizler contest was to me so much more than a boxing match for a title. It was a piece of enthralling social and political history. Judah Bergman's (Kid Berg's) parents were Russian-Jewish. In the early years of the century, the claustrophobic back streets of the East End reverberated with Hebrew cadences. The refugees were starting life afresh. They might have had a sense of relief from racial oppression but they knew there was a minimal guarantee of work. They were defensive and sensitive, quick-tempered and quick-witted. Their business initiative, at even the most humble level, was envied by their Gentile neighbours. They were warm-hearted and sentimental, especially among their own. The ghetto mentality was inevitable but gradually their single minded skills grew – as tailors, stallholders, kosher cooks ... and boxers.

Kid Berg had learned how to defend himself in the mean Whitechapel streets with his restless, flailing arms and fists. He had also learned from his parents how to look after his pennies. It was an ethnic art he never lost, despite the showy lifestyle that he encompassed and the moments of generosity as pretty blondes fluttered their eyelids. He didn't need too many advisors as he kept fighting and the cheques came in. He successfully dabbled in property for a time. When he moved from his first wife to his second, he opportunistically used the same ring.

He was the Whitechapel Whirlwind in a fight game bedecked with melodramatic fancy names. Mostly he was known simply as Yiddle. It carried affection for the man, not a prejudicial sneer for his race. 'Come on, Yiddle,' the crowds bellowed. He responded with a bellicose ferocity that contrasted so sharply with the congenial demeanour of the dandy out of the ring.

Such paradoxes are part of the appeal of boxing that refuses to leave me, despite my nagging misgivings.

HORACE HAZELL

Somerset cricketer in extract from 'Fragments of Idolatry' (2001)

Maybe it's all to do with the name: Horace Hazell. Could there be anything more evocative, rural-sounding, serene? They used to call him simply 'H' or Nutty. His is a name that belongs to Somerset's vibrant hedgerows, fresh, chirpy and wholesome as the morning's dew.

Most of us have a favourite county cricketer, possibly going back to our childhood. He may not be a glamorous sportsman, the archetypal match-winner, fashioned for daily headlines and acclaim. He may even be an ordinary practitioner with bat or ball. We're not always quite sure why we like him best. It's no doubt an amalgam of youthful idolatry on our part, the indefinable appeal of the player's essence and persona, and the subconscious acceptance that he symbolises the spirit of the game we defiantly cherish.

Horace gave up playing for Somerset in 1952 and died in 1990. He remains my favourite, timelessly unrivalled. Yet I never drooled over him or waited in awe for his autograph. There are some aspects of hero worship best left to the second-former; cricket's romantics – an embarrassing breed of which I confess intermittent membership – are, like 'anoraks' and heavy rollers, part of the game's furniture. Sometimes they tend to get a little in the way and obscure the true view.

'H' has always been to me that true view. He has been the metaphor for my appreciation of cricket. Jovial, spiritually uplifting, without malice or artifice. Whenever as a boy I went to Taunton, Horace seemed to be bowling (or Harold Gimblett batting). It was slow left-arm, mostly devoid of tricks. Unlike Jack White, who kept him waiting for a place in the county side, Hazell knew nothing of flight. Nor, come to that, did he spin the ball very much. 'Just look at my fingers,' he used to say. 'They're too small to get any spin.'

So what was there left for him? Accuracy, nagging, unwavering accuracy. Farmer White claimed he could land every ball on a sixpence; with his successor, so different in style and build, every delivery pitched on the eye of a needle. Precision was what he dispensed. It sounds soulless and mechanical. So it probably was for the non-partisan. But the nuances were reserved for his team-mates, as he talked incessantly in a voice nurtured on the pastoral, Somerset side of Bristol and which seemed to become more Quantoxhead or Creech St Michael as the years went on.

*

Somerset cricket was his life: and to me, he was Somerset cricket. He played before and then just after the war when the servicemen had returned, starved of professional sport, to swell the crowds. County cricket still meant something, not yet marginalised by ECB contracts and other pragmatic considerations.

Horace wanted only to play for Gloucestershire or Somerset. He had no other serious ambition. His brother worked on a Bristol newspaper and returned one morning, at 3 a.m., to see the light still on in Horace's bedroom. 'I half-opened the door and found that he'd fallen asleep, with a book of instruction on bowling grips by Fred Root in one hand, a cricket ball in the other. My brother would only have been 13 or 14 at the time.'

Those of us who grew from boys to men, devouring the cricket scores in the daily papers with almost biblical devotion, now glance rather than dally. The game has become more impersonal. There's a transitory aspect to the team sheets. Half the names mean little to us and, in any case, they will be gone by next year. The intimacy and continuity have receded.

I retain images of Horace Hazell, strolling up to the wicket, pretending the ball is turning when it isn't, challenging batsmen to lose their patience and go after him. I see him ambling, tummy bulging and face beaming, from one set of slips to the other. I see him waddling out, the last man and ten to win, with an expression which says, 'Leave it to the Crisis King!' I see him, a trifle sheepishly, driving off in skipper Stuart Rogers' red sports car. ('He took me off to some swanky restaurant and ordered a couple of bottles of wine. D'you know, wine was the only drink I couldn't manage. Made me drunk as a handcart.') I see him, dark hair sleeked back, walking onto the field with Wellard – half as tall and probably half as fit.

His happiness, in the company of his fellow players, was unconfined. He bubbled with cheeky asides while remaining in awe of those who he inherently knew were better cricketers than he would ever be. Away from the ground, among people who spoke with a more refined accent and joked at his 'Bristolese' or gauche expressions, he lacked social confidence. The inferiority complex was never too far away. On the field, there were no airs and graces to trouble him.

'The track's just right for you, Nutty. You'll be on early.'

And he was. As I was saying, he was always on. Wheeling away, looking like a village cricketer. Yet we knew he was much more than that. He was a valued component of a warm-hearted, oddball team. He was a true county cricketer. Patently proud to be an honest pro in the game he loved – a game then which still tingled with humanity.

23
Siegfried Sassoon

Siegfried Sassoon (seated fourth from the right) with the Heytesbury village team, before a match with Netheravon. His wife Hester (far right) has brought the family dog. On Sassoon's right are shepherd Sam Dredge and estate gardeners Bill Gearing and Bert Turner (with pads on).

David was not a literary critic, yet his fascination with human nature could lead him to original insights. Nowhere is this more evident than in his portrait of Siegfried Sassoon, which captured the essence of the poet through the cricket he played in his Wiltshire village of Heytesbury.

Among those who assisted David was Dennis Silk, former Somerset cricketer and Warden of Radley College, whom Sassoon had befriended. On one magical occasion Silk visited the elderly poet, armed with a tape recorder borrowed from Alec Bedser, and enjoyed the rare success of persuading Sassoon to read his poems aloud. 'This is a delightful essay which touches every important spot,' Silk wrote to David. 'I do congratulate you on a superb feat. You wield a most felicitous pen!'

INNER PEACE AT MID-ON

Beyond Bat and Ball (1993)

Siegfried Sassoon's almost comically gawky physique and saturnine features should be discounted. He was perhaps at his happiest of all on the cricket field. The childhood innocence, scarred through as it was by the horrors of the trenches and other private torments, was still discernible as he stationed himself at mid-on to miss his catches and think again of Woolley, his imperishable hero.

Sassoon's cricket, mildly better in his own Kentish days with Bluemantles than when he ambled across the parkland from Heytesbury House, in Wiltshire, to play alongside his estate workers, a few local farmers and boys from the village, was languidly enthusiastic. It was also, whatever he may have believed in his romantic flights, undistinguished.

Tucked discreetly into the late middle-order, he demonstrated an upright stance and an apparent propensity for the off-drive. The stroke carried something of a flourish, lingering on from the stereotyped tuition of his schooldays. His most charitable intimates would not imply it was handsomely executed. There was evidence that he attempted, rather ambitiously, to add the late cut to his quirky and restricted repertoire. It seems to have been no more than a grandiose gesture, alien to the practicalities in hand, to parade suddenly on a sunny day.

His amiable team-mates, not least those who worked for him, did their best to see him into double figures. There was from everyone an obsessive determination not to run him out, though he was known to turn up unexpectedly without invitation at his partner's end. Such aberrations called for a shrug of resignation and saintly self-sacrifice on some bewildered parishioner's part.

Erstwhile partners to whom I spoke described his batting variously as quaint, eccentric, limited and very ordinary. 'Very ordinary' was an evaluation offered without a semblance of malice or even denigration. Dennis Silk, until quite recently the respected and perspicacious Warden at Radley College and a former Somerset cricketer, who knew him well, contemplated Siegfried's aggregate of skills and range of shots, and suggested that he might end up with an average of 17 in a good season. One suspects that friendship lent generosity to the calculation.

Sassoon liked it best of all in the nets. Here he could thrust forward his left foot in the classic tradition and pretend he was a Kent pro, or even one of those ostentatious amateurs from Tunbridge Wells or Canterbury flashing wanton cover boundaries while on leave from the colonial service. He liked the relaxation of the nets. There were no tiresome exertions. Sometimes he'd come out of the Big House at Heytesbury, after a morning in bed reading the papers. He always began with *The Times* – and the cricket scores. They were apt to stir his angular, indolent frame.

'I say, Gearing. Where are young Reynolds and Kitley? I'd like them to bowl at me for half an hour in the nets.'

Bill Gearing was the head gardener. He would stifle an oath, less than pleased at the prospect of losing two able-bodied workers. But at Heytesbury House life was kept in perspective, however confusing that sometimes appeared to the staff. If Henry Reynolds and Jim Kitley were needed to roll up their sleeves and pitch half volleys of obliging pace and direction, rather than hack out the weeds between the onion rows, then so be it. They had no complaints as they pounded up in their hobnails.

When Edmund Blunden, Sassoon's friend for forty years or so, stayed at Heytesbury he was taken to watch him in the nets at Downside. Those were the days when Sassoon also played for the Ravens, a worthy and esoteric team with a formidable membership, emanating from the enthusiasms of the Benedictine community there and especially those of the founder, Dom Aidan Trafford. All the Ravens' home matches were played on the delightful school ground during the holidays.

Sassoon was essentially an introspective man, who saved his talking – whether on theology or the war – for long, nocturnal sessions in the library after dinner. But suddenly, quite out of character, he'd become impish in the nets, and balance a shilling on the stumps in an act of bravado and challenge to the bowlers.

Claims by one or two of his literary friends that he was still turning up in his cream flannels, two or three inches too short for him just like the trousers he wore, when he was into his eighties are a nice but inaccurate notion. One of his last matches for the Ravens was against Ronald Knox's and Christopher Hollis's Mells. Sassoon was about seventy-eight and had announced he was thinking of giving up the great game. The Ravens, in the managerial hands of Father Martin, a housemaster at Downside, were both talented and unconventional in matter of batting order. They still played hard and made great efforts to win in the evening shadows or last over: as a concession perhaps to the local brewery trade. Ideally the opposition batted first; the aim was to leave the Ravens with a total to stretch or inspire them after tea.

The club had a prepossessing skill in stage-management. They would, with an amalgam of cunning and good nature, embrace the confidence of the opposition. The ecclesiastical captain had a persuasive manner. And when it came to the fixture with Mells, there was a corporate ploy of stealth to give Siegfried a valedictory lift towards the elusive double figures. Mells introduced an excessively slow bowler of negligible merit. The ancient batsman played the first four deliveries with wary correctness. He tried to hit the next for six, rather grandly, back over the bowler – and gave mid-on an embarrassingly easy catch.

Sassoon snorted to himself and proclaimed to no one specifically as he came in: 'The bowling was not worthy of me.'

That was his batting. His bowling, essayed in schooldays, wasn't risked at club level. It was his fielding that generated most comment and amusement, mostly out of earshot. Father Martin described it as 'appalling but of immense courage'. He knew only too well Sassoon's lack of mobility and was inclined to act as his runner when batting for Ravens. 'I couldn't trust anyone else – for fear of a mistake.' Could anything be more evocative than this metaphor of Sassoon playing cricket: 'One of those old gramophones with horns, a little cracked … you felt there had been something there at one time.' It was said with much affection.

His absence of coordination in the field, increasingly evident in his last years with Heytesbury and the Ravens, was as engaging as it was hypnotic. Two of his contemporaries recalled his bird-like appearance. Dennis Silk saw him like a wading-bird, picking his legs up high as he walked. Another old friend specified the crane before switching his ornithological preference to the heron. 'I was influenced by that disproportionately large and long head and those angular movements.'

He positioned himself as of right at mid-on, a gaunt, statuesque figure. When the batsman struck the ball firmly in his direction Siegfried remained stiffly to attention, allowing it to crack against his unprotected shins. The rest of the team would wince and do their best to suppress gentle guffaws. He would then, in very much his own time, stoop to pick up the ball and return it underarm to the bowler.

The immobility could be taken to extremes. On his own ground at Heytesbury, he held the unspoken feudal authority without the nominal captaincy. His staff cut the outfield and kept the square manicured, and laden with runs. The club had the facilities for nothing. In return he was allowed to field where he wished – and to go more or less anywhere he chose in the batting order. Sometimes on a whim he went in relatively early to partner Sam Dredge, the Downs shepherd whose pastoral philosophy he shared. Sassoon could perhaps articulate it rather better, but they both had a profound distrust of intellectuals. 'The Captain' was usually put, with some tact, at No. 7, 8 or 9. This met with his tacit approval. No one ever dared to drop the squire to last man.

His Heytesbury team-mates despaired of his catching ability. He would post himself in the dreamy hinterland of the leg side, and on hot Saturday afternoons meander deep into the outfield on occasions. His rambles were accepted. Logic and the state of the game didn't come into it. Roy Newman, later to be the skipper of the village side, played only a few matches alongside him. He was astonished to see him desert the outfield altogether at times, to sit on the iron fence or lean against the gate.

Once when playing for the Ravens on a cold day, he had cussedly kept his hands in his pockets when offered the easiest of catches. In explanation to no one in particular, he said: 'If I'd tried to catch that one, I'm sure I should have strained something.'

This is no more than a warm-hearted vignette of Sassoon as a makeshift club cricketer. But to know him, the most underrated writer of our time in the view of Silk, just a little better, it is valuable to reflect on the game that ran like a stabilising thread through his complex life. He watched country house and village cricket during his privileged upbringing in Kent. In Victorian England he played on the lawn with his less enthusiastic brothers and Mr Moon, his private tutor. He played his first game on Matfield Green when he was still a boy, scoring eight of the team's total of 13. He squeezed into the house team at school and later spent hours at Fenner's, when he found law at Cambridge 'too inhuman and arid'. He bought the evening paper to see the stop press scores.

School life wasn't always agreeable. 'Onion' was hardly the most complimentary of nicknames. He found Marlborough 'moderately pleasant but mentally unprofitable'. His father had left home when Siegfried was seven and that drew him tightly to the bosom of his artistic mother. He was always inclined to be introverted: and cricket was the perfect outlet for the solitary boy and man who still wanted people around him.

It wasn't the same following the hounds in the guise of George Sherston. There was too much noise: their yelps and blood-scented barks, the crescendo of horses' hooves, the incessant bonhomie of the gentry in their hunting livery, flush-faced and stirrup-breathed. Cricket, by contrast, embraced in its quiet all the byways of the imagination. If you were Sassoon, you sat for an hour, pads on and yellowing bat on your lap, waiting your turn and needing to talk. And you could dream when you went out to field – of when the majestic Woolley mended a puncture for you (as he did once for the idolising Siegfried) or played the first of his Tests for England before the First World War.

At cricket you could drift from the game and still be part of it. Surrounded by ten other fielders, Sassoon could look up above Heytesbury House at the dense, timeless woodland that he loved and needed. He knew every ash and beech tree and, if requested, would take his house guests to the trunk of the only oak on the estate. Whenever he walked the woods, he made sure the secateurs were in his jacket pocket. When, twenty years ago, I did the research for a television documentary on the great, often misunderstood poet, his son George told me of the hours Siegfried spent, utterly contented in his chosen solitude, cutting back the bracken.

'Catch it, Captain Sassoon,' would snap him, invariably too late, from his reveries. The 'Oh, bloody hell' from a momentarily exasperated bowler was less audible. His remoteness was accepted. Who was to know whether Mad Jack's darker thoughts of the trench carnage, the loss of dear friends, the wounds and the shell-shocked confusion, and all the self-doubts that clouded his domestic life, remained agonisingly close, ever liable to return and haunt him, whether he was on horseback, in the library or out on the cricket field?

It is quite certain that cricket was a soothing therapy. That serious, still handsome face would break into a look of pure innocent joy when a well-heeled braggart from a neighbouring parish was bowled. He enjoyed the teas at the Angel Inn, this shy man who couldn't talk easily with his workers playing for him but who would sit enthralled, listening to their teatime tales of village life.

When he wrote *The Old Century* in 1936-37, it was above all a simple, domestic chronicle of innocence, 'a happy dream which relieved my troubled mind.' There was a rather beautiful naïvety about 'my simple-minded belief that the world was full of extremely nice people if only one could get to know them properly …'

He liked, almost without exception, the nice people with whom he played cricket. Here, in a way, was his idealism: the kind that caused him to flirt briefly with socialism and to work for the *Daily Herald*. A cricket team was a microcosm of disparate people, blending in peace and good nature amid the tranquility of the countryside. He overlooked the fact that he could relate so much more naturally to other landowners and the schoolmasters at Downside than to the under-gardeners on the estate. One should blame not him but the rigid class structure, and the inhibitions caused by his leisured background, for that.

Sassoon had grown up to believe that the staff should play cricket. Richardson, an early groom, was very good indeed and should, according to the master, have played for Kent. Successive tutors earned his eternal respect if they could pitch on a length on the back garden.

His work force at Heytesbury House was also, one suspects, recruited with an eye to their potential prowess on a Saturday afternoon. The house itself, large rather than attractive, was on the site of a medieval mansion and carried more than a whiff of high drama. Walter, Lord Hungerford, was stopped in his tracks when engaged on enlarging the building. He was arrested, charged with treason and beheaded. Henry VIII seized the whole property. For years it remained semi-derelict. Sassoon was married in 1932; he came to Heytesbury, and stayed till his death in 1967.

When he arrived, Heytesbury was a quiet, isolated village. It was quite an occasion for the parishioners to go the four miles into Warminster. Sassoon loved the sylvan hillsides and decided the new home was conducive to poetry-writing and all those copious entries in his diary. He ensured that the surrounds of the house and the whole grounds were kept immaculate. For that purpose he engaged five men to work in the woods and five more in the gardens. In addition, there were two to look after the stables and the cars – and a staff of eight indoors.

The cricket pitch was tended by his workers. It was much envied 'and everyone wanted to play on it'. The square was almost up to county standard. Captain Sassoon would stroll down to supervise the rolling. 'He was a nice man and it was a treat to work there. The only trouble was that he didn't pay very well.' The Big House never did in those days.

Five of his men played for the team. Old Bill Gearing, the head gardener, was captain. Bert Turner, who as second gardener looked after the greenhouses, was the wicket-keeper. Ernie Stancer, who doubled up as groom and chauffeur, had the build of a jockey which helped when he raced round the boundary. And then 'the young garden boys', Henry Reynolds and Jim Kitley, used to open the bowling. Jim was slightly faster and was allowed to bowl down the hill.

Sassoon liked to involve himself in team selection. It wasn't wholly democratic. But there was always a place for his five strong-muscled workers, who did their best to disguise their eagerness when they learned of a Wednesday fixture. The wages may have been poor but there was time off without question when it came to an important mid-week match.

Sam Dredge, Sam the Shepherd, was a favourite of Siegfried. He was a gentle countryman who opened the innings and had been known to score a hundred with the air of serenity you would expect from a man of the Wiltshire Downs. It seemed equally appropriate that Sam should be the club's spin bowler. As for the Heytesbury farmers who found a place in the village eleven, they were mostly burly of shoulders and thighs, and healthily red of face. One of them, Johnny Perrott, braced himself for massive sixes in a way that caused the poetic chairman of selectors to chuckle and ponder a shaft of romantic imagery.

For away matches and the occasional journey to Warminster, he drove his two-seater Humber. He drove it badly, though no doubt oblivious to the consternation caused to successive passengers and other road users. He wasn't adept at reading the highway signs and assumed a seemingly autocratic, but in truth absent-minded, regard towards right of way. He had the vehicle specially built for his wife in the days when there was still a marital affinity. One companion of his would see the car chugging uneasily into view, and then summon up all the eloquence necessary with a plaintive shake of the head. 'It was too tacky for words. There were yellow joins on the outside to keep the water out.'

Sassoon, after his war poems and the new creative dimension to his work, had become for a time a fashionable figure in literary circles and, certainly by Wiltshire standards, quite a celebrity. Visiting teams would look towards him in awe during the tea intervals at the Angel. Some of them had got hold of the Mad Jack tag and speculated what he might do if a team-mate ran him out.

The villagers didn't see much of him apart from home matches. His lifestyle intrigued them. 'He do stay in bed half the day – and writes them poems all through the night' ... 'He's a bit of a rummun. Leaves the phone ringing, never answers it. His friends get quite annoyed' ... 'He loves playing the piano, you know' ... 'In a dream much of the time, he is. Wanders past you without seeing you at all' ...

But they all knew he was special. They weren't too sure of the details, though they had heard in a vague way of his immense courage as a soldier. Some were convinced he'd won the VC. It was an understandable mistake as he had been recommended for the ultimate award for bravery. 'Captain Sassoon got the MC,' they were told by those with more reliable memories. 'And he chucked it away.'

No one was quite certain why. As this diffident man walked out with his under-gardeners, groom and a few farmers, after losing the toss in mid-July, it was quite impossible to associate him with the valour of a Welch Fusiliers officer who brought back a wounded lance-corporal under heavy fire, and who later captured a German trench single-handed.

He hated the publicity that followed and persisted on and off for the rest of his life. Fleet Street once let him down and he never forgave. When journalists asked if they could call, he said no. If they wanted to talk with him about the war and his poetry, he'd cut them short with a dismissive: 'I'm only prepared to have a word with you about cricket.' That was the last thing they wanted.

The cult of celebrity embarrassed him. Dennis Silk told me: 'It was different if he was in the presence of a great cricketer. There was a boyish excitement about him then – he was totally unaware of his own greatness.'

He loved to be in the company of cricketers. He turned up at Fenner's in 1953 and self-consciously introduced himself to Silk.

'I remember clearly the gaunt, handsome stranger in moth-eaten blue blazer and faded trilby hat, who marched up to the pavilion with a long forked hazel staff in his hand,' Silk was to recall in a Guinness Lecture at the Salisbury Festival of Arts.

Much later he was to tell me: 'Siegfried watched us playing and then took us all to the Garden House Hotel for a slap-up dinner. He entertained us to a virtuoso performance on cricketers' initials. He had a wonderful memory, especially for the initials of Kent players before the First World War.'

In the Cambridge party was the turbaned Sikh, Swaranjit Singh, who was twelfth man in 1954 and won his blue the following summer. A nervous waiter, possibly distracted by the strange drift of Sassoon's unabated monologue, stumbled and deposited a whole bowl of soup on poor Singh.

'Oh, Christ,' someone said.

Siegfried had been in full flow. His mood was jocular. 'Let me see now. Christ J. was it?'

He puffed on his pipe and everyone laughed. A moment of abject embarrassment had passed.

The friendship between Sassoon and Silk grew. It is easy to see why. The Warden of Radley – as he was until his fairly recent retirement and return to the old cricketing pastures of Somerset – is himself a gentle, rounded, civilised man, a scholar without ostentation, literate, a lover of poetry and someone with a similar sense of quiet fun. And in those sunny undergraduate days he was also, to the transparent delight of Sassoon, a cricketer. He got his blue three years running for Cambridge; he went on to play thirty-three times for Somerset. His county team-mates liked him and said he batted with the conscientious efficiency of a pro. At short leg he took all the catches that came his way. He was a big success when he captained the MCC teams in North America and New Zealand. Like Siegfried, he combined the sensitivity of the bookish man with a physical aptitude. When it came to outdoor competitiveness, Silk was rather better, of course. He also played for Cambridge and Sussex at rugby. It was much admired by his mentor.

Dennis Silk was still a student, a learner, a listener in the early days of their friendship. He was invited down to Heytesbury in the August. They talked the night away, or rather Sassoon did. 'My role was to be a listener, he was still haunted by World War One and he called himself the Hermit of Heytesbury.' The ghastly gunfire rumbled on as they sat, the tormented talker and the transfixed listener, until the light of dawn came through the library windows.

> I see them in foul dug-outs, gnawed by rats,
> And in the ruined trenches lashed with rain.
> Dreaming of things they did with balls and bats
> And mocked by hopeless longing to regain
> Bank-holidays, and picture shows, and spats,
> And going to the office in the train …

He needed, even in the mid-Fifties, to go on talking about it as part of the long, painful process of purging the experiences from his system. Occasionally, as in that extract from the poem 'Dreamers', he would interweave cricketing imagery with that of the Somme. Those evenings at Heytesbury were a life's education for Silk. As a historian he chose

Marlborough after leaving Cambridge. The proximity to Heytesbury thrilled Sassoon, who even bought the young schoolmaster an old Austin 10 to make the visits easier.

They played together for the Ravens. This somewhat arcane club, formed in 1921 and relaunched with typical zest by Father Martin, himself a brave sailor turned Benedictine monk, in 1951, had a haphazard but distinguished membership. Ben Barnett, the Australian wicket-keeper, played a game or two. Jack Fingleton, a good friend, only umpired. Tony Pearson, stirringly remembered for the way he took all ten wickets against Leicestershire at Loughborough, when playing for Cambridge, was another Raven, no doubt because of his links with Downside. The Roebuck brothers, Peter and Paul, also played – as did the affable Somerset amateur, Hugh Watts. At the latest count, they could boast over the variegated years one English Test player, eleven county cricketers, a dozen blues and at least four members of Minor Counties status.

It was a club of flawless ecumenical intent, even if the matches were played on the Catholic college ground. Sassoon, who was received into the Roman Catholic faith, there at Downside Abbey in 1957, airily stood his ground at mid-on. Jock Henderson, the Bishop of Bath and Wells, was steadfastly rooted to the lush pastures of mid-off. They exchanged cricketing rather than theological badinage, and left more fleet-footed Ravens to cover for their physical ineptitude. It was a chummy club of sharply varying talents. The chances of selection were helped if you were a friend of the skipper. John Luff, a quarry owner of the Mendips, was one. He never quite got over running out his brother on 99. John made his runs for the Ravens before transporting himself in the spirit of collective immobility to first slip for the rest of the match, either very fine or very wide at the behest of his Benedictine better.

As a club it could be as eccentric as Sassoon himself. There was an element of seriousness about one or two of the members. They were less than enchanted when I once referred to them publicly as oddball. With a misplaced solemnity, they suggested I gave too much of an impression of convivial rural incompetence. I can only report that the Ravens didn't, as far as I could ascertain, have too many rules – if any at all. No one was scolded if a dolly was missed while the fielder was abstractedly admiring the delicate folds of the surrounding countryside.

Cricket is an institution and ritual was important to Sassoon, just as the hunting pink had been. Yet the feudal side of his interest was only nominal, a concession to his background. The war had made him more liberal and he privately wished he could have shown it more as he sat in front of the old pavilion, waiting his turn to bat. He loved the shepherd and the chirpy village boys, especially when they bowled out the opposition by four o'clock. Sadly his classlessness remained theoretical.

Cricket was his game because it gave him space and time. If his eyes misted over as he reflected again on how his best friend died from a rifle bullet, no one knew. Mid-on was as good a cavern as anywhere for introspection: offering as much solitude as he found on his daily stroll through the woodland of his estate. There were times when he needed to unburden himself, to wreak his anger on man's inhumanity: it helped when Edmund Blunden was around to share and do his best to absorb some of the pain, before lightening the gloom with a droll memory of Fenner's.

By the time I went to Heytesbury House, up the long winding gravel drive to research and ponder the life of the late master for that television programme, the flowers, once so profuse, were drooping and less fussed over. The parkland cricket pitch wasn't quite so immaculate. In a few years' time there would be a noisy, intrusive bypass, to cut off the House entirely from the pitch. Whatever would Captain Sassoon have said?

The village team, nowadays without the estate workers, still takes on the neighbouring parishes. The older players still talk affectionately of Siegfried and suspect he'd approve of the consistent artisan skills and playing record. Son George is the president and comes to watch the occasional match. Kindly, apocryphal stories about The Captain, of permanently bruised shins and lamentable fielding, are resurrected every Saturday summer's evening in the two local pubs.

He was 'an English country gentleman to his bones, the echo of a bygone age'. Those who remember him, and the rest of us who pretend we do, still see that mesmeric Edwardian figure: awkward in stature, a decent and good man, a shy, troubled, doubting, complex one.

Sassoon needed his loneliness. The loneliness he cherished most of all was in the crowded, silent company of his timeless trees; in the company of the nuns and monks who could communicate without conversation; and maybe, above all, amid the sublime innocence of a freshly mown outfield.

24
Battling On

At the turn of the century David was working as hard as ever: writing books, supplying regular copy to the *Western Daily Press* and *Wisden Cricket Monthly* and reporting cricket and sometimes football for the *Guardian*, who were now sending him all over the country. In some respects he thrived on the work, but he was in his seventies and he was starting to feel the strain of it all.

Though he had often been to northern football grounds when covering Bristol City for the *Evening World*, he made his first, and only, visit to Headingley in the summer of 2001. For this trip he took the train, laden down with a large bag full of his new book *Fragments of Idolatry*. It seems that I, as the book's publisher, had asked David to offer them to the Yorkshire shop on a sale-or-return basis. This did not go to plan:

> Hotel modest but OK. Less satisfactory was my visit to the club shop with heavy pile of books from Stephen Chalke. Apart from few Wisdens, no space for books. Dreadful shop for Test ground – had to bring books back to Bristol!

In the midst of his own reports David has pasted into his scrapbook one from Michael Henderson in *The Times*. Describing the cricket writers in attendance at Cheltenham, he refers to David as 'looking more than ever like somebody who has just walked out of a Jan Steen tavern scene, a trifle unsteady on his pins, perhaps, and ready for a game of quoits.'

'Surely a case for litigation!' is David's response.

The next year, carrying two cases from the Tunbridge Wells ground to the hotel two miles away ('had been told it was half a mile – no taxis available'), he strains his Achilles tendon and is 'hobbling again'. At Southampton some weeks later he is worse:

> Still walking comically like a lame duck (tendon and sciatic nerve – different legs). Had a few beers with David Green. Twice in the night I had the greatest difficulty getting to the bathroom. Severe cramp added to my physical woes. Took 10 minutes each time. More Chaplin than Cardus!

It had been his life's ambition to be a cricket writer and, despite the aches and pains, he was reluctant to retire on the grounds of physical difficulty. More worrying, however, are the entries in his book of cuttings, from 2000 onwards, when he admits to signs of cognitive degeneration.

> It's going to be a difficult summer. Inner panic and writer's block (which I had always assumed was a phoney term for amateur-writing housewives doing their romantic histories) is

real enough. Can't find apposite words any longer. Wrestle in my head with simple syntax. The memory is by now a bastard and one day I'll drop an appalling clanger.

In September 2001, he tenders his resignation – for the third time, it seems – to the *Guardian* sports editor, Ben Clissitt. This time he is more adamant:

> The time for joking is over. You've indulged me long enough. It is an unforgivably self-important person who doesn't know when it's time to drift away. I can still meet the deadlines and give you the right number of words. But for the first time I'm losing my news instinct, my energies and, whisper it, my accuracy. Memory is letting me down. And I fear that I'm capable of dropping a bloody big clanger. That is unfair to the paper and to me.
>
> I've been churning out my pseudo-lyrical prose for the *Guardian* for probably 30 years. Successive sports editors have been as generous as the subs. It has given me a huge lift and a lot of pleasure: after all the police courts and inquests.
>
> In the past you and Mike Averis both tore up notes of realistic resignation from me. It was good for the ego, but not the logic. A frail self-confidence on my part has been no mannered act, I promise you. I loved being a provincial hack and never really wanted more than that. Please let my resignation just quietly happen.

Back came the reply:

> I am sorry to disappoint you but I am afraid I am going to have to decline your very kind offer. Although it may shatter your illusions about my predecessors, I'm sorry to say it wasn't generosity that led them to reject your previous resignations. Similarly, I would not be able to forgive myself were you to stop writing for us now, just when you are coming into your prime.

Assuring David he made fewer mistakes than most of the others, Clissitt concluded: 'I look forward to reading your first report of the 2002 season.'

And, of course, David is back in place in May 2002, penning a beautifully evocative piece from Southampton, describing the final appearance of the Middlesex bowler Angus Fraser, who is off to share press boxes with David as cricket correspondent of *The Independent*. To the concern of many in the journalistic fraternity, another of cricket's top writing and broadcasting jobs had been entrusted to a former player.

David is still submitting reports seven years on from his letter of resignation. A gentle day at cricket is manageable, but he is tested to the limit in January 2008 when he is asked to cover an evening FA Cup replay between Bristol Rovers and Fulham. Such was his ordeal that, still exhausted, he typed up an account of it the next day.

Difficult football coverage – they don't come worse than Rovers-Fulham Jan 08. Came from Dudley Doust's funeral, driven back by Scyld. Drizzle, thoroughly unpleasant. Went in search of ticket, blissfully waiting for me. First crisis over. Returned to press box, hour before KO to work out my complicated strategy. Talked to *Guardian* – they want 500 words, part at half-time, more at threequarter-time, intro at whistle.

I know from bitter experience that a running story from my normal place is impossible. The tannoy, high decibel, is immediately above our heads. Can't hear a thing on the line. So I go optimistically in search of alternative arrangements. Find a helpful man in charge, at the door, of the President's Club. He agrees to let me use the club's store cupboard/overflow cloakroom at the interval. Works well, though I have teams and formations, too, and the 2nd half has started by the time I go back in the direction of the press box.

No chance of fighting my way back to original seat. Luckily I spot a vacant seat in the crowd near the aisle. Sit there. As before no real elbow room to WRITE a proper report. Miraculously I can hear a faint voice at the other end of the phone, enough to send my next take. Then the worst of all scenarios – extra time and penalty shoot-out.

The office had implied that they could scribble an intro for the first editions. Phone *Guardian* to check on rewrites although it is already late and I hoped they wouldn't need more than a quote or two on Fulham for the London edition. "Afraid we need more than before. It's the best of the replays." How much? 700 words.

Then make the long walk, in drizzle, to the press interview room. Have had no time so far to start on a rewrite. Within a quarter of an hour, Fulham manager Roy Hodgson arrives. London reporters ask a lot of time-wasting questions about foreign players I have never heard of. They also want to know about some potential signings. I want something crisp and relevant to the match I have just seen. After him comes Paul Trollope. Again not particularly strong or useful.

By now it's approaching 11pm. I have not been able to write anything so far, sending my first reports off top of my head, eased by smudgy notes of the game's incidents. Now, with a mixture of shorthand, abbreviations and inconsequential jottings, I knock off an appalling piece.

Ask copy taker how many words so far? 520, he says. A long way short of what is needed. Send a few more pars. How many now? 765, he says. My real fear, though, is that I'm late for the next edition. At midnight, or just before, I check with the office. Was I late? It's all right for the last edition.

At the age of 78, with heart pounding, I could have done without that relentless exercise. Poor report. Impossible working conditions. And a struggle to get my long pieces through on time. Never again, I tell myself. Just what I said once before. It was also a Rovers evening game then.

Because Scyld had brought me to the ground, I had no car. As arranged, I phoned Anne and she came for me. 12.15am.

His last assignment, at the age of 79, is a trip to Cardiff in September 2008, for an uninspiring 40-over cricket match. Glamorgan's rejuvenated Swalec Stadium has won the rights to the first Ashes Test the next summer, yet a washed-out one-day international, followed by the departure of both chief executive and head groundsman, has left the county in turmoil. David, with his rich sense of history, is quick to put it all in perspective:

Glamorgan has seldom been too far away from internal human drama. From the days when Wilf Wooller would raise his voice while practising that distinctive thespian art form at the expense of opposing captains and even rebellious pros in his own dressing room, the county has had this intermittent penchant for surprises and murmurs of confrontation.

Throughout these last years of reporting, David is haunted by his failing memory, his physical struggles and his fear of making mistakes. Early in 2003, volunteering for a first visit to the attractive Horsham ground, he has a wretched day. The game is ruined by drizzle, the promised meal with Anne turns into a fish-and-chip supper and he hits a new low in confidence.

Have increasingly felt I'm a fraud these days, let down by my declining memory. Rushing the intro in my report, I gave victory to the wrong team! Hasn't got that bad before. Told about it on my check call. I was horrified and came home in a state of deep depression. How much longer can they leave me loose on the circuit?

Later in the same summer at Cardiff he has another disturbing experience:

> Memory continues to drift away with a frightening rapidity. Can't remember players' first names (in some cases, their whole name). On the third day I sat in Phil Tottle's BBC box to dictate my early report. And I made FOUR errors. McLeod instead of McLean, Glos instead of Glam. Had great trouble spelling Kasprovitz, tho maybe I can be excused for that! Phil corrected me on the spot so none of the errors reached *Guardian*. But any kind of non-professional conduct like this horrifies me. It is happening increasingly.

The following year his struggle to stay awake at the Cricket Writers' Club dinner leads to an incident that so troubles him that he writes it up not only in his scrapbook of match reports but later in a lengthy typed account entitled 'Unreality'. The story starts on the evening of a match at Northampton, when he was driven down to London by the Birmingham-based journalist Paul Bolton. They were on a tight schedule to arrive at the Inter-Continental Hotel in time and, to David's disappointment, his chauffeur refused to stop for a quick pint. The meal was long, and it was late when the time came for the presentation of the club's two awards: Young Cricketer of the Year ('Ian Bell made a nice and real speech'), followed by the Peter Smith Award in recognition of 'an outstanding contribution to the presentation of cricket to the public'. Previous winners included some of the game's greatest names – David Gower, Brian Lara, Dickie Bird – but only one writer had received this ultimate honour from his peers: John Woodcock of *The Times*, to whom it fell to introduce the 2004 recipient.

> It must be said that John went on a bit. He paused to reminisce about the old players who were present ... "There's dear old Tatters (Roy Tattersall) ... and David Allen, who I remember had a pretty wife ..." Was the award going to one of them? Then John drifted on to West Country writers. Alan Gibson, Robertson-Glasgow and he said, in passing, that neither would have got into a modern press or commentary box because of the number of old players or 'celebrities' who were now employed in that way. Wooders probably spoke for 20 minutes. No doubt most of the gathering had forgotten he was making an award. I was terribly tired and had my eyes closed. Then I heard him say ... "So the award goes to dear old David Foot."

Surreal. Not the remotest idea. And why me? I wasn't as good a player as Lara after all! My first reaction was that it was a practical joke. I looked around the *Guardian* table for a culprit. But everyone was looking at me. "It's YOU. You've got to go up and say a few words." In fact, as I later discovered, everyone on my table knew well in advance. So did Paul Bolton whose role was to make sure I arrived at the dinner – and completely sober. The secret bastards.

It was a crazy recognition for a lad from Bristol who had only covered one Test in his life. But if I'd known, I could at least have thought of some gracious comment and a light-hearted throwaway when I said my obligatory thankyou. As it was, I made a short inadequate speech. Feeling I should lengthen it marginally, I endorsed John's remarks about ex-players.

Oh dear. I returned to my seat to be confronted by Jonathan Agnew who, seemingly enraged, blurted out: "I take great exception to what you've just said about ex-players." I wondered if he was joking but his face told me he wasn't. There followed a mini-monologue, which took the others by surprise. I told him, anxious for no confrontation – I'm too much of a coward anyway – that I didn't have him in mind. "Well then you should have said so." A raw nerve had been touched. He mumbled something about he'd had trouble with John Woodcock on this issue before.

Then he left, with everyone in my surrounds exchanging looks, shrugs and, I really feel, offering me a wave of sympathy for an untimely attack. To my embarrassment/amusement it became the talking point of the post-dinner evening. Journalists can't help themselves; they love anything gossipy.

David was right: he did hate confrontation. When he told me the story the next week, he was still struggling with it emotionally, trying hard to see the funny side of it. He and Jonathan Agnew exchanged warm-hearted letters, putting the spat to bed. But I was left feeling sad that the 'unreal' episode had spoilt the most special of moments in his life as a cricket writer. 'The lad from Bristol who had only covered one Test' had received the ultimate accolade of recognition from his journalistic peers.

As Pat Gibson, chairman of the awards committee, said of David in the press release: 'No-one is held in higher regard in the press boxes of the county circuit. He has his own evocative style that transcends some of the harsher realities of modern sport, and it communicates his affection for the game and his appreciation of its true values.'

CRICKET REPORTS AND FEATURES

Steve Kirby 'more bellicose than balletic'
Yorkshire v Kent, Headingley, June 2001

There could hardly be a more dramatic way to make your championship debut. Steve Kirby, plucked by Yorkshire from the relative obscurity and frustration of second XI cricket at Leicestershire, suddenly found himself as a stand-in for England's last-minute one-day call-up, Matthew Hoggard.

He responded with a variety of emotion and success to fit the occasion. Brought on as second change, he immediately made the ball whistle – to the surprise of Kent batsmen and the murmurs of approval from the Headingley crowd.

Before long, in a second spell of four overs, he was on a hat-trick. He spread his arms extravagantly when in triumph and was smothered by his newly acquired team-mates. Kirby's pace was real enough and ready to take its place, on first impressions, in a side already generously equipped for speed.

The sound of the ball landing in Richard Blakey's gloves made the point. But the accompanying spectrum of ingenuous reaction – and an air of innate belligerence in the best northern traditions – was equally compelling.

Kirby not only beat the batsmen, he glared at them. When an lbw appeal was turned down, he theatrically pirouetted in a way which appeared more bellicose than balletic. His enthusiasm was limitless. When he let go a beamer, amid apologies, he ended on the ground having lost his balance completely.

Angus Fraser's farewell
Hampshire v Middlesex, Southampton, May 2002

Angus Fraser heaved the heavy, long-serving coffin into the boot of his car this week and the handle fell off. "It seemed to be telling me something," he reflected last night, savouring the irony of a faithful bag endorsing his decision to retire.

This was his last appearance for Middlesex, the day after his goodbye ovation at Lord's. Under the leaden skies of Southampton he looked much the same as ever: ungenerous to batsmen though less fiery, lugubrious in expression, lumbering in with optimistic aggression, crossing between overs with that distinctive stride of a village policeman heading for his pension.

It took him five balls for a farewell success. James Hamblin lunged tentatively and second slip took the catch. Fraser allowed himself the semblance of a smile. He came back for a second spell and immediately put an end to Giles White's notable innings.

The crowd clapped, letting imaginations detect more nostalgic venom than the delivery imparted. They applauded again at the end of the innings when he loped in, hunched and happy, his shirt wet and his flannels discoloured by the vigorous rub of the ball and the almost comical dive for a John Crawley shot he was never going to cut off.

Fraser, talented enough to take 177 Test wickets, finished with two for 34, the best for Middlesex. Later he was in pensive mood as he came into the press box, sniffing out the environs of his future career.

"Some days have been harder than others," he said with the hint of a wince. "The hardest thing will be missing the fun of the dressing room." Now 37, he becomes a greenhorn laptop operator. "I'll need a lot of guidance and help," he said, almost in the tones of a promising young cricketer at his first net.

Hampshire, sent in, reached 237, mainly thanks to the composed skills of Crawley, continuing his run of success with his new county. His unbeaten 103 contained nine boundaries and came off 145 balls. White offered excellent support.

It was only just enough. Owais Shah, Edmund Joyce and Simon Cook took the match thrillingly to the last over. In the end Fraser was at the crease, after walking through two lines of clapping Hampshire players. But there was to be no theatrical exit. His side lost by three runs.

David's only Test match

England v India, Trent Bridge, The Wisden Cricketer, August 2002

In many ways this was Vaughan's match. He was mature, orthodox, eminently good-looking, eager for runs. There was no resemblance at all to the once tentative Test greenhorn. Grandiose comparisons were being made as he stroked through the off-side. At times it was coming almost too easily to the artist.

There were, of course, other performances to savour. Virender Sehwag's batting was a revelation in the first innings. One admired the restraint he initially exercised, as if John Wright, India's coach, had had a pleading word in his ear. Then he increased the tempo with much skill. He strikes the ball like Tendulkar; the footwork can be exquisite; and he is happiest when in a hurry. Then came the reliable and resolute trio of the much proven Rahul Dravid, Tendulkar – ominously at his best – and Sourav Ganguly. Only the most inflexibly partial England supporter would have failed to appreciate these three players' virtues, in technique and temperament.

Festival fun at Horsham

Sussex v Nottinghamshire, Horsham, May 2003

It was Chris Cairns, hardly for the first time, who offered most festival fun. He had just flown in from Sri Lanka where New Zealand had been playing and his presence for the match was uncertain until the last moment.

Cairns does not bother too much with the manual's niceties when it comes to Sunday cricket under a cloudy sky. He may have lacked sleep but not muscle. Once he clubbed Billy Taylor over the billowing press tent, a tennis court beyond and into a river. His fifty came off 35 balls, as if he was anxious to get his feet up.

A first view of Twenty20 cricket

Worcestershire v Warwickshire, Worcester, June 2003

It was easy perhaps for some to see this as a joyful evening of self-delusion, altogether too brash and frenetic for Elgar country. But the only valid question is how much this daring, well-intentioned stratagem – to give the moribund aspects of our historic summer game a radical resuscitation – can be sustained. One thing is certain: chief executives are drooling as they count the money.

At the New Road ground last night the anoraks were understandably in some confusion once more, unable to keep abreast of surreal bowling figures and scrambled singles. It is a frighteningly long way from the world of Wisden.

There were nearly 5,000 spectators in a state of constant excitement, good-humoured and, in some cases, new to cricket. Schoolboys had come with satchels still on their shoulders. Choristers arrived straight from choir practice at the cathedral; there were the office workers and whole families, with dads suppressing instinctive qualms.

When Twenty20 was mooted the players saw it as a parody, and recoiled. They had no wish to devalue their professional talents with a frenzy of cross-batted aggression, a negation of everything the successive manuals and coaches had instilled in them.

Then came the gradual rethink. They accepted there would be big crowds and fleeting glamour. In the nets they set out to acquire new techniques to meet the fierce demands of this alien 20-over game. They accepted there was no time here for self-indulgence or purist strokes.

This was in every sense a new concept, equally talked up by the TV teams whose members chased into the rows of supporters to show their versatility in vox-pop roles. This was, in Worcester as everywhere, a jamboree in the sunshine, defying the traditionalists. The music blared, the Jacuzzi bubbled; all around the boundaries electronic speakers were positioned like so many outfielders. The giant screen was not working but no one seemed to mind.

"It's just like when we had Collis King whacking our sixes out of the ground and Ian Botham doing it for Somerset in the same match," said one member nostalgically, as if not everything changed after all.

A supporter in front of the pavilion was unable to hide his protests completely. He knew it was not cricket; it was a high-spirited bastard off-shoot, making it clear to the more perceptive that the game had irretrievably evolved. This was a carnival 'metaphor', indicating that one-day cricket had taken over. It may leave some of us filled with guilt as we watch and do our best to stifle prejudices. Yet how can we discount the initial success of the competition?

There is nothing lyrical nor endearingly anachronistic about Twenty20. It is the beer-match village encounter most of us have enjoyed, here given an added element of skill by paid batsmen who know the value of placement and paid bowlers who do their best to land the ball in the most difficult area. Under the New Road horse chestnuts the fans responded noisily to every muscular blow, every overthrow or flaw. Knowledge may be suspect at times but the spirit is vibrant and ebullient.

As for the detail, Warwickshire won by 20 runs and always seemed to have something in hand. Nick Knight revelled in the evening's levity. The left-hander, demonstrating an array of reverse sweeps and pulls, scored 89 off 58 balls. There were nine fours and three sixes, one of which was adeptly caught by a 17-year-old who was presented with £1,000 for his feat. Warwickshire were all out for 175 after three run-outs and three stumpings by Steve Rhodes.

The South African Neil Carter then took three wickets as Worcestershire did their best to creep near. Kadeer Ali chased to a neat half-century and Ben Smith was 40 not out at the end.

The boys stayed on the field long after the game, many with bats and balls. It was an encouraging sight. Psychologically, at least, cricket did not suffer in any way from New Road's excesses.

Jack Russell retires

Western Daily Press, June 2004

We're all going to miss him – not just for that intuitive brilliance behind the stumps and all the technical skills of his wicket-keeping. For, more than that, Jack Russell is a Stroud boy with all the quaint, defiant independence inherent in those whose homes were bordered by the rolling Cotswolds.

In the Gloucestershire dressing-room he has chivied his team-mates with a challenging conversational style that at times could be almost as military as sporting. He even looks different. For a small man, his big, drooping moustache – one not so far removed from Victorian melodrama – is endearingly disproportionate. He's always been hyperactive, throwing down his bedraggled and faithful gloves to chase a ball almost to the third-man boundary. How he sprinted with such youthful vigour in those outsized pads no-one quite knew.

There was no end to the range of his idiosyncrasies, many of them as comic as they were surreal. His attitude to personal diet and domestic seclusion would put Delia Smith quickly out of business and might prompt the SAS to rewrite its manuals on location subterfuge.

But only now that the throbbing back is making him give up the game, shall we be able to take a fully detached view of his cricketing talents and agree that, at a county singularly rich in the quality of its wicket-keepers, he was the best.

A young Stuart Broad

Gloucestershire v Leicestershire, Cheltenham, August 2006

Everything Stuart Broad does, still as an apprentice fast bowler, adds to the excited speculation about his future. Once he came as a boy to watch Gloucestershire when his father was in his second spell with the county. Now he is briefly in the West Country as a 20-year-old, taking the new balls for Leicestershire and encouraging whispers, however premature, that he could be a legitimate gamble for the Ashes tour this winter.

Here at the College ground, where the Festival had to put on its overcoat as the weather changed, Broad finished the day with four for 47. He was used wisely, not excessively, perplexing several batsmen with his pace and, more so, with his lift.

He is very tall, slim and in a hurry, as is evident in the way he paces back to his mark with those eager schoolboyish strides. Several Gloucestershire batsmen played and missed at some point. He will get faster, if need be, and acquire added skills. But the promise is undeniable.

Marcus Trescothick

The Guardian, November 2006

Loneliness hits hardest of all, even for cricketers, in crowded places. And it was in a sweaty dressing room, wedged in with the coffins and enforced bonhomie of ambitious sportsmen – most of them with their own, varying neuroses just below the surface – that Marcus Trescothick told himself it was time to go.

He has never been gregarious or sharply animated in repartee. He likes a joke but leaves the telling to others. On occasions he has given the impression that he enjoyed the game more with his school chums when playing for Keynsham second XI, with his dad Martyn as the gentle counsellor and his mum suggesting the batsmen get on with it as the tea steamed in the big enamel pot.

Trescothick's seemingly impulsive attitudes over the past year or so have at times been a puzzle to an unknowing public. His previous dramatic Test exit, a matter of unexplained silence, was badly conveyed. The theories inevitably multiplied about why he was coming home. Was his wife, Hayley, suffering from post-natal depression? Was the depression coming from him? How was the marriage going? No one, not even his sporting intimates at Taunton, could initially work it out. The lack of the briefest basic information only fuelled speculation and misplaced rumour.

He is a big man, physically, with a surprisingly fragile mental strength. He is at his best – and then it does show on that normally dour expression of his – when he is standing distinctively upright and challenging at the crease. But more recently that more engaging confidence has been elusive. There is no lustre in the big countryman's eyes.

His England team-mates have noticed it, exchanging glances and sensing the torment which he mostly keeps to himself. Again, on this visit to Australia, he has appeared, at least to the more perceptive, as a painfully lonely figure: missing especially his family, the jokey, uplifting West Country accents, and inwardly recoiling from the rigid disciplines demanded of Test cricketers.

He may not be the most cerebral member of the tour party but, as a light sleeper, he has been pondering for hours the expectations facing a key and most experienced opening batsman pledged to retain the Ashes. He is a worrier. The nerves have been gnawing away at him, however much he has suggested otherwise.

Trescothick badly wanted to take part in this series, perhaps for the last time. Back at Lilleshall and in the Taunton nets he practised unstintingly.

He told himself he could still take on McGrath and that the bat would be broad and fluent once more. At the same time, he was realistic enough to accept that his place was no longer guaranteed; younger players might be ready to open the innings instead of him.

Back in Taunton yesterday supporters were walking aimlessly around the deserted boundary, trying to come up with some kind of explanation for his defection. "Stress-related illness? What does that mean? And he isn't the type anyway. Just remember those days when he used to walk out with Mark Lathwell. Carefree, when the two of them belted all those fours and Somerset's future was wonderfully rosy." Now Somerset are on the bottom of the tables – and Trescothick may be a player without any kind of future.

Another Test opener, the county's director of cricket, Brian Rose, slowly pondered the dramatic events that had Trescothick heading in despair for the airport. "It's a matter of great sadness to me. Marcus has been getting fit here and really looking full of beans. There have been no visible signs of stress. Let's forget the cricket for the moment. His state of health must be the priority and needs to be addressed."

Already there are premature whispers that his England career is over – Duncan Fletcher probably saw him as a risk this time and might not want to take another chance with him – and even that he may be in the mood for walking right away from the game, at least for a therapeutic period. Rose, eager to see and console him as soon as possible, says: "We would love to have him back in our county side and utterly free from stress."

First-class cricketers are a melancholy breed. Whatever their facade they are acutely sensitive, and not just about their form. For the Test players it is worse. Their tour cricket makes deep, disruptive inroads for weeks at a time into their family life. Training is onerous and repetitive. They occasionally get on one another's nerves. Some crack up.

In The Wisden Cricketer two years later, David wrote again about him, ending:

His return to Somerset, its ground timelessly placed between the Tone and its tombstones, is for him the perfect antidote. Trescothick would like, if free of injuries, to play until he is 40.

He is once again a Somerset lad – if still one of the finest batsmen in the country – stroking his runs where he is emotionally and mentally happiest. His fragile temperament needs those gentle roots a lot more than international cricket's oppressive glamour and unforgiving itinerary.

Marcus Trescothick played for Somerset till 2019, retiring at the age of 44.

Graeme Hick retires

The Guardian, September 2008

The lingering image is of Graeme Hick returning to the pavilion at that tea-time declaration. He has just completed his 405 not out, almost prosaically paced over 555 minutes. He should be drained, with traces of elation etching through his weariness. Instead, he walks with a brisk step; the face offers not a flicker of emotion as the smallish crowd, belatedly sensing the proximity of cricket history, converges to applaud. He passes not more than a yard away – and there is not the merest evidence of perspiration on his cheeks and forehead. He could be out for a walk along Worcestershire's Severn.

Hick has never been much for showing his feelings. He is a dutifully courteous and laconic man. You search in vain for a technical insight from his lips or physical nuance. To him the game is not predominantly cerebral or calling for self-analysis. He accepts that nature has blessed him with a wondrous eye-sight, able to pick up the flight, line and pace quicker than most other cricketing mortals. But you fancy that at times such gifts embarrass him.

He has been playing here for a quarter of a century and we suspect that the eyes are starting to let him down; so are the much envied balance and reflexes. It is time for him to choose to go.

Those of us privileged to watch him in his best years have marvelled at the risible ease with which he has played the game. At county level, he has made so many contemporaries look ordinary. His bat was broader than anyone else's. Nothing seemed to get past it. There was always a respect for orthodoxy; with an hypnotic efficiency he took on the bowlers in rotation. The strokes were always clean. For a big man, he was imposing rather than handsome in execution.

We don't truly know why he was a relative failure on the broader international stage. If he ever worked out the temperamental quirks that disrupted his composure and too often undervalued his statistical grandeur and instinctive mastery, he wasn't saying.

One returns to that mighty and, dare one say it, mundane innings at Taunton. It rightly took over the match. Yet it was hard to remember specific strokes or technical peaks. In its special brand of brilliance, it was strangely soulless. He was mocking the game in making it look too easy. Perhaps the West Country spectators, slow to respond as the innings was built, had been spoilt by the ferocity and flamboyance of Viv Richards' bat on this same arena not so long before.

Eventually word got round that Wisden and its records were in business. The crowd became blissfully impartial, unmindful of disintegrating figures among the Somerset bowlers. We shall never know what possessed Phil Neale to declare the Worcestershire innings when Hick was so near to Archie MacLaren's all-time highest individual innings at that point. We can only assume that he was not aware how near Hick himself was or concerned about the accolade of which he had been robbed.

Hick was still only 21, needing to wait another three years before being eligible to play for England. The cricketing politics did not bother him a great deal. Later that evening we asked him about his feat. Politely, quietly, he said he felt a bit tired. And well, that was it. He was not made for profuse prose.

Over the years he has not changed much. He stands tall and erect in the slips, as he does at the crease. He is one of the more introverted occupants of the dressing room. He still makes it all look, if rather less frequently now in his case, absurdly easy. International opponents said they had found him out, capitalising on his frailties at the very top level. He came from a very different Zimbabwe and it is possible his particular background worked against him.

The day after his 405, at the close of play, I saw him lugging with some difficulty his heavy cricket bag down the pavilion steps. He signed an autograph and struggled off to his car, looking endearingly ordinary and unassuming.

Hick has served Worcestershire abundantly. He is one of the great enigmas of modern cricket in this country – and maybe we shall never quite understand why he fell short.

The last paragraphs of David's last match report
Glamorgan v Worcestershire, Cardiff, September 2008

When Worcestershire won the toss and decided to bat on a slow track, at times needing a special vigilance, they moved always with caution to their final total. There was not too much to recall, apart from the half-centuries of Vikram Solanki and Moeen Ali, who posted the only six of the day and looked the more comfortable of the batsmen ... Defensive fields had restricted the scoring, though the approach cried out for a greater sense of adventure.

It was often a dull match, devoid of imagination and finally reflecting too much vulnerable batting. Around the ground, the spectators had other dialogues to discuss – the handsome appearance of their new ground, whatever the short-comings of the recent big match that never was. A Celtic excitement that found some apprehension – about the future Ashes commitments – could be detected.

25
Obituaries

Mike Thresher (left), Peter Roebuck (right), Robert Stephens (below),

As David grew older, he was called upon with increasing frequency to write obituaries. First, there were local people of note for the *Western Daily Press*, then West Country cricketers for various cricket publications, finally a full range of cricketers for the *Guardian*. It was a format that suited him well, though a note written in 2001 revealed his own doubts on that score.

> For the second year running, I was invited to the *Guardian* obit department's Christmas party. This time I turned it down. I'm not sure of the most apposite collective noun for obituarists. In truth, I found them a slightly lugubrious crowd last year. Elderly dons and ageing women with pale faces and too much lipstick.
>
> I suppose obits demand some literary content. I've probably done two dozen or so for the *Guardian* – thespians and, mainly, cricketers. I feel quite unqualified in the case of some of our finest; my technique is to jot down the necessary stats in a column, read a potted biog or two, and then – maybe after a call to a contemporary – weave a few insights and anecdotes around the bare bones. The subs don't seem to have changed much so perhaps I'm doing things right. Doubtless at some point I shall expose myself with a faulty judgement.

David had a great ability to paint distinctive pictures of cricketers in action, with style and personality tellingly knitted together. He loved to celebrate stalwarts of the county game, men such as Dennis Brookes, the stylishly correct Northamptonshire batsman, and Bertie Buse, the Somerset swing bowler with an eccentric run-up. He also loved the outsize characters, such as Glamorgan's Wilf Wooller and Hampshire's Colin Ingleby-Mackenzie, both of whom led their unfancied counties to first championship titles.

Wooller, unusually for a Glamorgan cricketer, came from the north of Wales. A wartime prisoner of the Japanese, he was a man of firmly held and strongly expressed right-wing views. It was ironic, therefore, that when David, feeling ill, was unable to cover a Glamorgan match for the left-leaning *Guardian*, Wooller should agree to stand in for him. "I much enjoyed it," he told David. "They didn't change a word, although I didn't want anyone to see me buying a copy next morning!"

> His influence on Welsh sport has been considerable and a great many, not just on the other side of the Severn Bridge, are going to miss him. Wilf Wooller, whatever the complexes that emanated from those forbidding North Wales mountains, was a man of integrity.

With David there was always a fascination with the wayward characters, such as the highly talented Gloucestershire wicket-keeper Peter Rochford who, with disciplinary issues never far away, left the county 'without explanation' at the end of 1957: 'Alan Gibson used to put him in his all-time Gloucestershire XI; he wasn't alone in that kind of praise.'

> Sometimes outstanding talent in cricket surfaces far too briefly. Personality flaws stifle it – and we are left to wonder what might have been ... Though he didn't realise it at the time, cricket was his life and consuming interest. He missed it immediately he left Gloucestershire. From 1975 to 1977 he was a first-class umpire. After that a void, as he confided in bar-room moments. He never fell out of love with the game, only with fate itself ... He collapsed and died in the arms of a fellow customer in one of the Stroud pubs where he went for company to chat quietly about cricket (never in an egotistical way) and for a drink to help him forget.

The eccentrics were not confined to the field of play. David persuaded the *Guardian* to publish obituaries of two men, both coincidentally Old Harrovians, who added colour to life beyond the boundaries of county cricket: Ed Poore, the hippy friend of rock stars who was often to be seen at Worcester, and Nico Craven, son of a canon at Gloucester Cathedral who each summer for thirty years came down from Cumbria and produced a quirky annual booklet on his days of watching cricket in Gloucestershire.

David was an inveterate attender of funerals, even admitting that he enjoyed them. He loved the opportunity such occasions gave for old sportsmen to renew the lost camaraderie of their younger years. Sometimes, as on the occasion when I gave the address at the Somerset cricketer Ken Biddulph's funeral, he would pen a piece in the *Western Daily Press*:

> In a village church high in the Cotswolds they crowded into the pews, more than 40 years after he'd played his last match for the county ... Ken had dozens of stories about his chums. Now cricket writer and one-time bowling pupil Stephen Chalke told the best of them ... A congregation, all caught up in the mood of nostalgic affection, rocked with hearty, not irreverent laughter. As one, they were dreaming again of past summers and shared friendships.

For the funeral of the Bristol City footballer Mike Thresher, David wrote a full column, using the emotional occasion, 'as much to do with fellowship as sport', to reflect with melancholy on the changed values of the modern game.

A TASTE OF THE 'OLD' TEAM SPIRIT

Western Daily Press, January 2000

In the parish church of Barrington, near Ilminster, at noon yesterday, we were given a cherished view of the Age of Innocence. Mike Thresher's coffin was draped with his No 3 shirt of Ashton Gate. His team-mates from the fifties and sixties crowded the pews to say their warm goodbyes. The full-back, who played 417 times for his beloved Bristol City, had been that enshrined rarity, a £100 footballer. That was what he cost when they found him. Chard and Ilminster couldn't make up their minds who should benefit and they probably still can't. But we know for certain he was a bargain.

'Thresh' was a village boy who played soccer and cricket just like his five brothers and dreamed of a league career. He possessed a big heart and a fearsome tackle, the kind that make timorous wingers quake. What he didn't possess was an agent. No players had their affairs looked after in those ingenuous days, of course. Mike was Chard's first £100 exile, a reluctant celebrity around the pastoral byways of South Somerset.

Yet what was there about professional sport 45 years ago? What caused so many of his Ashton Gate mates, Jantzen and Shadow, Jack and Alec, John, Mike and Alan, to make yesterday's journey with misty eyes and so many fond, if slanderous, memories? This column has too often regretted the fact that team spirit in its truest sense is missing from the modern game. Players are inclined to pick up weighty pay packets and then go their own ways. Rovers in the fifties, for instance, were almost brothers. They went into each other's homes when the day's training was over. Josser played the piano to them. This affected them on Saturday afternoons. And at Ashton Gate the friendship of the players was evident in a way which we no longer see. They shared firesides and domestic confidences. Their wages were low, their laughter voluminous.

'Thresh', John Atyeo and Tommy Burden might occasionally have reminded Peter Doherty of their worth. There were also ructions, it is true, when the Doncaster faction threatened to take over. But for the most part the City Ground was a chummy place and friendships lasted for years.

Mike Thresher's death was a metaphor of what we now so sadly miss. His old team-mates came from all directions to Barrington yesterday, queuing up outside the 13th century church almost as if still waiting for the team coach to arrive for an away match. It was, in its way, blissfully nostalgic and innocent, as much to do with fellowship as sport.

One fears that professional sport has gone irretrievably beyond the point of human contact, stifled by accountants and consumerism instead.

EXTRACTS FROM CRICKET OBITUARIES

Colin Ingleby-Mackenzie (1933-2006)

Hampshire captain

In 2002 Ingleby-Mackenzie became Hampshire's president. Everything he did in cricket, whether on the field or in the committee room, was invested with infinite charm. He was as generous with his racing tips as he was with his declarations, though the latter, however much they looked laden with risk, often seemed to work miraculously in his favour. This was especially true in 1961, when he led Hampshire to the championship title for the first time. Some of the older, rather more cynical pros were inclined to gaze eloquently as one at the ceiling of the claustrophobic dressing room. But his daring – it was instinctive rather than ever calmly analytical – served him surprisingly well.

Eternally cheerful, laughing off the intermittent errors of judgement, he eased the title-seeking tensions. He was a smallish thickset man with thick wavy hair that gave him a rather dashing appearance. He was a better timekeeper than Lord Tennyson, someone known to arrive at the game a trifle unkempt and still in his dinner jacket after a louche night in the West End clubs. For all his eccentric ways, Ingleby-Mackenzie possessed a measure of genuine self-discipline. Northlands Road, the county's former home in Southampton, was perfect for him: chummy and intimate.

Wilf Wooller (1912-1997)

Glamorgan captain

Wilf Wooller was the voice (fearsome and endearing), conscience and embodiment of Welsh sport. He captained his country at rugby and Glamorgan at cricket with an abrasive vigour and competitive zeal, sprinkling his tries and wickets with brave deeds on the field and polemics off it.

In turn Wooller could be intimidating, dogmatic, withering, tetchy and soft-hearted. Like a good Welshman, his emotions were emblazoned for all to see. At centre-threequarter he ran with the ball, 6ft 2in of unquenchable energy, knees pounding up and down almost to his chin in that distinctive battle charge for the line; he had no apparent love for any opponent in his way. At cricket his oaths could be heard on every boundary. He did not go in for the delicacy of language or imitate the outmoded gentlemen of Edwardian demeanour. His spectrum of gamesmanship was legendary and he would justify it with a half smile afterwards.

David Shepherd (1940-2009)
Gloucestershire batsman & international umpire

Rosy-cheeked, distinctively Falstaffian, with the girth of someone who liked food and warm-hearted company, 'Shep' was one of the most familiar white-coated figures on the global cricket circuit.

His duties took him to all the most famous grounds. He found himself staying in exotic hotels and was at times feted by dignitaries of the host nations. Yet he was happiest of all strolling on the sand dunes near his Devon estuary home at Instow with Jenny, his partner, and Skip the dog. He lived only a few boundary lengths away from the lovely North Devon Cricket Club ground where, as a boy, he had first watched games while chasing the rabbits off the outfield, and where he later played in front of the thatched pavilion.

Johnny Lawrence (1911-1988)
Somerset all-rounder

Not too many professional cricketers could cherish the virtues of Johnny Lawrence's best-known hat-trick: he didn't smoke, drink or swear. Another hat-trick of his, carrying lovely irony and the semblance of a cussed streak, was for Somerset against his native county, Yorkshire, in 1948. Both achievements were the subject of endless good humour. It was impossible not to like him.

Johnny was diminutive. He seemed to come only up to the waist of Arthur Wellard and Bill Andrews. His sweaters looked slightly too big for him and the local crowds saw him as an endearing, even comic, figure. He was always tumbling in search of short-leg catches – and encouraging repartee from the batsmen. But his greatest skill was as a leg-break and googly bowler. With Lawrence at one end and rolypoly Horace Hazell at the other, opponents were apt to find batsmanship a bewildering business.

Dennis Brookes (1915-2006)
Northamptonshire batsman

His integrity was as unwaveringly straight as his stance and those unflashy off-drives. He might shake his head at a reckless cut against the spin by a young batsman, but he would answer queries thoughtfully. The voice was quiet, though authoritative, still touched by a Yorkshire vowel or two ... He learned to reject the more fallible shots and decreasingly used the hook. As an opening bat, he was, above all, dependable, a quality acutely needed by his county.

Roy Marshall (1930-1992)
Hampshire & West Indies batsman

Roy Marshall was that rare, marvellous amalgam of gentility and single-minded aggression. It was usually accepted that the reason he went in first for Hampshire was that he simply couldn't bear to hang around for long, pads on and head buzzing over the technical complexities of the pitch and the opposing bowlers. Once he was out there, taking guard and adjusting his spectacles, any mental distractions had been exorcised. He was ready to go. The first ball was at times destined first bounce for the third-man boundary.

For the most part he was a master of style. He square-cut in the grand manner that Greenidge went on to emulate around the same parishes of the Solent. His drives will live timelessly in the minds of Hampshire romantics.

Bertie Buse (1910-1992)
Somerset all-rounder

He was rarely much more than medium-pace. But he was a master of very late in-swing and could often move the ball the other way. Most memorable of all was his approach to the wicket, starting with what seemed like a Sunday-morning stroll along St James Street, followed by the eccentric manifestations of a jig, soft-shoe shuffle and almost belated acceleration. No-one really remembers a wayward delivery; above all, he was reliable.

David 'Butch' White (1935-2008)
Hampshire & England fast bowler

He was, and looked in every sense, a fast bowler – with heart to match his lungs, solid shoulders and a head not too much bothered by the technical subtleties of his trade. He could appear fearsome as he pounded in, leaping with his legs so distinctively stretched in opposite directions that he always threatened to tear his flannels.

Godfrey Evans (1920-1999)
Kent & England wicket-keeper

Many keepers cloak their skills in anonymity, judged by an efficiency that is missed by the naked eye. Not Evans. He possessed an innate theatricality, never too irritating or counter-productive, evident in the marvellous way he hurled himself for those legside catches with those red gloves that seemed slightly too big for him. He was so nimble, so intuitive, that a great many of his legside dismissals were more like optical illusions.

He was the most frighteningly strong cricketer I have ever seen. I remember a slight disagreement at a cocktail party between Godfrey and the giant Hampshire fast bowler Butch White. Godfrey settled the argument by lifting Butch by his shoulders, raising him to the ceiling and hitting his head against it three times.

... and two from beyond the boundary:

Ed Poore (1948-1991)

Worcestershire supporter

No one could miss Ed Poore at a county cricket match. In his Davy Crockett hat and bare feet, with a copy of Wisden and wad of personal records, he was one of the game's few genuine modern eccentrics ... He lived for nearly 30 years at Coddington Court near Malvern. But he increasingly rejected materialism, living frugally and driving a ramshackle car ... He was a collector of mottoes. One was plucked from an Inspector Morse script: "People are dying all over the place. Compared with that, even cricket has to suffer."

He was an idealist whose compassionate nature embraced many causes, including Botham's charity walk. He forgot his cricket to go out to help make known, with his caring and his camera, the plight of the Romanian orphans. His latest crusade was the Gulf Peace Mission. He died in Haifa, a few days after a minor operation.

Nico Craven (1925-2010)

Gloucestershire supporter

Gloucestershire cricket never had a more devoted or sweet-natured fan. He worked until retirement in Cumbria but mocked his declining energies by motoring down to the Cheltenham Festival every summer.

In spirit he belonged to another age and its set of values. His annual returns to Cheltenham were not merely to watch the cricket but to see the same faces in the crowd each year, seated in the same positions on benches and deckchairs, and to swap the same old endearing stories about Tom Goddard and Bomber Wells. It took him three hours to stroll round the boundary, humming snatches of Cole Porter between overs and then returning to shared memories of Mike Procter's wrong-footed pace or Zaheer Abbas's graceful choirboy style.

He hated the uglier aspects of the game and pretended they just did not exist. That kind of felicitous personality, however incorrigibly romantic, gave him a rare and outdated charm.

FRANK KEATING
(1937-2013)

Letter to the Guardian

Frank Keating and I first met on the day in the late 1950s that Frank arrived as a trainee sub-editor at the *Bristol Evening World*. If he was apprehensive about the sweaty demands – up to 13 editions in those days by a team of happily noisy, busy, waspish journos – it didn't show. Our friendship, mine based on a doting affection and regard for this personable newcomer, never wavered.

We enjoyed our rushed, gossipy last-order pints. We played cricket in weekly challenges against local villages, Frank always turned out neatly and occasionally with an improvised cravat.

His iridescent prose, Irish-influenced and often playful, hadn't yet fully surfaced. He could be a lovely, descriptive writer, full of adjectival mischief: over-romantic and eager to take liberties with the language, rather like a slightly self-indulgent jazz pianist at times reluctant to return to the central theme. The subs coped with his excesses. They liked the way, when he felt there was a need, he would reveal a flash of anger at bungling bureaucracy or an official's misplaced self-importance. What we all valued was his humanity.

SEYMOUR CLARK
(1902-1995)

Western Daily Press

Sadly, there has been little mention of the death in a Weston-super-Mare hospital of Seymour Clark at the age of 93. That is no way to remember a former engine driver who might have kept wicket for England, according to former Somerset seam bowler Jim Bridges.

"All you should need to do is take this game seriously, Seymour," Bridges once told him. "And you should accept that contract the county are offering you." Bridges was an intelligent man and he had a very high opinion of the wicketkeeper. Seymour, however, had no intention of tying himself to Somerset. England was in the grip of the Depression and there were thousands out of work. "Thanks very much, but I've got a good job on the railways and I can't risk losing it," he told surprised county officials.

Seymour played five times for Somerset in 1930 and took eight catches, several of them quite brilliant. He had only been rushed into the county side because Wally Luckes was ill and they did not really know where to look for a deputy. "I was just a fish out of water," said Seymour. "My railway pay was stopped when I was playing. It was difficult to get time off, but the station master in Weston helped. He liked his cricket."

Seymour was told to report for four matches on the northern tour. He got on the train at Temple Meads and did not know what he was letting himself in for. "Jack White was the captain and he didn't say a single word to me for the whole of the journey," he said.

"I thought it was up to me. As we were going out to field at Chesterfield I turned to him and said by way of conversation that I would stand up to Arthur Wellard. He gave me a funny look and said he didn't think I'd better."

Those were Seymour's greatest qualities – his reflexes and courage. He did not play in any kind of cricket until he was 25, just three years before his debut for Somerset. In a makeshift railway side, someone suggested he should wear the wicketkeeper's gloves. He did not bother too much about pads in those naïve, early days – nor a box. On green, natural wickets on the local Rec, and village squares which rarely saw a mower, he stood up to everything. Soon he was playing for Weston CC, with proper kit.

Seymour drove a loco on the old GWR. Like all the best men from the nostalgic footplates, he had a sunny disposition. He did not mind jokes about his batting. On his own admission to me, his highest score was three, "helped by a couple of overthrows".

In his nine innings for Somerset he failed to score. That created a priceless cameo for Wisden and all the game's statistical freaks. His minimal ability with the bat got around. Bowlers from the other counties tried hard to get him off the mark – in vain. Peter Smith, of Essex, even dollied down a ball which bounced twice. Seymour swiped ... and was still bowled.

"And do you know," he once confided, "I bought myself a new bat when I played for Somerset. Didn't do me much good, did it!"

So we can forget his batting. Dwell instead on that fearless wicket-keeping, which brought him six catches at Kettering in his third game. If Seymour had signed that contract, the efficient Luckes might have struggled to win his place back.

Seymour had three initials and maybe that was what influenced Somerset to invite him along. But he was very different from some of the old-style amateurs, and more fun. He loved Weston and used to go to Clarence Park, though his eyesight was failing badly at the end. At home in Ewart Road, his garden was as impeccable as his own appearance.

Seymour was Somerset's oldest surviving cricketer – and one with a unique record.

ROBERT STEPHENS
(1931-1995)

Western Daily Press

Robert Stephens broke all the rules of temperate and conventional behaviour. He was married four times and had a dozen lovers. He drank prodigiously, gossiped with indiscreet glee and called for a cigarette hours after a live-saving kidney/liver transplant.

The son of a dockside labourer had gone to Portway Boys' School where he went through the motions of a modest education. He was a shy boy with a Bristol accent – but he revealed an unlikely talent for verse speaking and was sent off to the well-known local drama and voice coach Hedley Goodall for extra tuition.

He was known as Bob to his family and Tubby to his schoolmates. With one chum he gave improvised wartime Punch and Judy shows, doing all the voices himself. They charged a penny admission and gave the money to the Aid for Russia fund. His parents, a big, muscular father and small but authoritarian mother, lived frugally in Priory Road, Shirehampton. They had married in 1930 at St James's parish church. The father, Reuben, had come down to Bristol in search of shipyard work. He ended up a quantity surveyor but the family struggled in the earlier years. Robert wrote: "I had a terrible childhood: no money, no love, no prospects."

It makes his successes and eventual acclaim all the more remarkable. He was knighted for his services to the British stage and was arguably the finest theatre actor ever to come out of Bristol. As late as the 1990s, critics said his Falstaff and King Lear for the Royal Shakespeare Company touched greatness.

Cary Grant was, of course, more famous, but as a film actor. Sir Michael Redgrave, Trevor Howard, Deborah Kerr, Barbara Jefford, Leonard Rossiter, Peter O'Toole, Jeremy Irons, Peter Postlethwaite, Tony Robinson, Daniel Day-Lewis and a score of other big names have strong links with the city. But many of them were only passing through.

Robert Stephens was a genuine Bristolian: a working class boy who lived in a council house and whose mother worked first in Fry's chocolate factory and as a cleaner and help. In the early Seventies I did an interview for 'Woman's Hour' with Robert's mother, Gladys Millicent, who was then living in Coombe Dingle. She said how much he had enjoyed living in Bristol. Home life had been placid, despite brief evacuations to Midsomer Norton and a farm cottage near Bridgwater during the war. Contrast this with his own memories: he claimed that he was excessively walloped by his mother, who had once told him she had never wanted children, anyway.

He left Bristol when he was 17 to train as an actor in the North, and learned his craft in rep. In the wide-ranging career that followed there was a stack of glowing notices for him in his time with the National, the RSC and the Royal Court. At times he was compared with Olivier and Gielgud, but suffered professional setbacks as well as emotional misery.

Much of that came when he was divorced from his third wife Maggie Smith, and strains of self-destruction included a suicide attempt. He spent 10 weeks at a mental hospital.

He died in a year in which things had begun to look up for him, with the public recognition of his knighthood and private happiness of his marriage to his fourth wife, Patricia Quinn. His biographer wrote: "There was no such thing as a wasted moment in his company. He was a one-off, a special case."

ALAN GIBSON
(1923-1997)

from a lengthy obituary in the Guardian

Alan Gibson was a much-admired Test match radio commentator and brilliant broadcaster on a range of subjects, from poetry and the arts to county rugby. He was a Liberal politician and a one-time Baptist lay preacher. He was also an unfulfilled academic and an incorrigible maverick.

A scholarly man, brimming with classical allusions, one felt he might always have been more at home in academia. He was president of the Oxford Union and gained a First in history. The county-cricket circuit never had a more literate occupant of the press box. That, of course, was when he was there for anything more than a nominal appearance; at Taunton, his favourite ground, he preferred the Stragglers' Bar. There, with cherished fountain pen in one hand and treble whisky in the other, he wrote his quaint, distinctive reports that gave him a cult following. Often he had his back to the play; he was as likely to be absorbed in a Hazlitt essay as a *Wisden Almanack*.

He was many things – and many paradoxes. He was the chapel boy who liked to drink, the pacifist with a fiery tongue (usually at the expense of officious cricket-ground stewards), the erudite loner on the boundary seat and the charmer, on a good day, who passed his whisky, in a Johnson's baby bottle, along the press row during the interval at a rugby match. He was an intensely private man, yet was not averse to an audience when he dictated his pieces to London.

PETER ROEBUCK

Somerset cricketer who killed himself in South Africa (1956-2011)

The Cricketer

Peter Roebuck's much-acclaimed diary of the 1983 season, 'It Never Rains', was inspired by reading David's biography of Harold Gimblett. In an early diary entry he quotes from the book: 'Cricket is played very much with the mind. Only the unimaginative player escapes the tension. Many, whatever their seeming unconcern, retreat into caverns of introspection.'

One eerily prophetic, symbolic image remains. The two of us had been standing in the drizzle outside the ground at Lord's. Play had been abandoned for the day and the spectators had gone home. But not Peter Roebuck. Oblivious to the weather, he wanted to talk with some intensity – it was, of course, usually so – about what he saw as my obsession in writing about cricketers' mental miseries and, in too many cases, the taking of their lives.

"Why?" Roebuck asked. "There must be a reason. I'd very much like to talk about it." And we did for half an hour in the rain. He asked most of the questions. What I graphically remember was the way he paused in the middle of one exchange. "It occurs to me that one day you could be writing similarly about me." That to me was a moment of searing self-analysis. I got the impression the grim subject had crossed his mind more than once. We eventually agreed that all the victims died because of their sensitive natures and the game's immense introspection.

Over the seasons we had several more confidential chats. At close of play I would see him walking on his own, not joining his team-mates for their meal. "How about a pizza?" he would say. Conversation surged in all directions. Once he asked me to print his intention to give up cricket so that he could become a Labour politician. He was serious enough but next morning he pleaded with me not to use the story. He acted on impulse and wavered confusingly.

As Somerset's captain he probably suffered from tending to be a cold fish. He recoiled from public speaking and could be prickly with a reply to a persistent member. He was strong on ideas, not prepared to concede ground to an opposing skipper.

His mentor, the legendary Millfield School 'Boss' and Somerset captain RJO Meyer, could see the emerging talent. So could those supporters, who liked the tenacious style with which Roebuck dug in and took on the fast bowlers. With one-paced stubbornness he dusted his spectacles and gave little away. There was a mannered schoolboyish correctness about the way he played his limited repertoire of shots, which he tried determinedly to increase.

Roebuck nearly squeezed into the Test side once or twice, although he acknowledged there were better opening batsmen around. He was even seen by some as the captain of his country, although others may have been overwhelmed by his cerebral line of logic and dry humour. Rather in the manner some of his Somerset colleagues scratched their heads as they worked out one of his stern-faced scholarly jokes.

His parents were teachers at Millfield. They were ambitious for him and for their other children. But Peter's home relationship was apt to be academically claustrophobic. From choice, perhaps, his was a lonely, private life full of self-doubt.

The Shepton Mallet meeting of November 1986, which approved the decision by the Somerset committee to release Viv Richards and Joel Garner (Ian Botham left in protest), was a wretched time for the Roebuck family. Peter remained silent when many members thought he would speak from his position on the top table. Yet there had been a surfeit of words, slander, threats and mutual hate in the weeks leading up to that meeting. It added to the cynicism that was paining and distracting him.

Peter was labelled a Judas. Many Somerset fans forcefully took the side of the deposed trio. Botham and Roebuck never exchanged another word. They contented themselves by trading glowers when they shared media centres around the world. Roebuck had established himself as one of our finest cricket writers, sharp and intrepid in his judgement, perceptive in opinion.

By the age of 35 he had fallen out of love with many aspects of cricket, though not that in Australia. He had already shown skills and moral courage at the wicket and in the committee room. He had chosen to distance himself from England and what he saw as the parochial mentality of Taunton.

It was at Taunton Crown Court where in 2001 he admitted caning three young cricketers he had offered to coach. One can only imagine that as the police questions started once more, he told himself in spontaneous despair: 'Not again. It's more than I can take a second time.'

26

Last Footsteps

*Frank Foot (on the right), East Coker bell ringer for more than sixty years
David outside Verandah Cottage, surrounded by his six grandchildren*

In the early years of the 21st century, despite continuing to write beautiful copy, David was losing confidence, increasingly aware that his memory – so vital to his easy writing style – was no longer reliable. He tried repeatedly to resign from the *Guardian*, but without success. Even when he finally stopped reporting on live matches, he was the paper's first choice for its weekly dose of sporting history when Frank Keating was away. Much of what he offered – Yeovil's Cup triumph, Hammond's ill-fated comeback, his train journey to see the 1948 Australians at Taunton – was in the nature of regurgitation. Yet, served up for a new audience and always with fresh touches, it was still a joy to read.

His wife Anne, through hard work and robust good sense, rose to be Chair of the Magistrates' Bench in Bristol so David was alone at home during his working day. Temperamentally this suited him but, as he grew less assured, it left him too often alone with his inner doubts. Medical problems – his prostate, then his eyes – added to his struggles.

As his publisher I worked with him on a new edition of *Harold Gimblett* in 2003, then *Sixty Summers*, the book about post-war Somerset cricket that he co-authored with Ivan Ponting. What I really wanted him to write was *City Reporter*, a sequel to *Country Reporter*, bringing his alter ego Matthew Fouracre to Bristol for the *Evening World* years. I made several pleas to him but, alas, he did not feel capable of doing it. Nor did he ever write the anti-war play about which he so often talked. All was not lost, however, as somehow, with Scyld Berry and his son Mark also cajoling him, he agreed to write a memoir of his life, taking in those Bristol days.

David, now past his eightieth birthday, needed constant encouragement and reassurance, yet always the chapters, when they arrived, were a delight. He captured the lost pre-war world of rural Somerset so evocatively, he threw a vivid light on his long life in journalism, and his prose was as felicitous as ever. Perhaps, drawing on so much that was personal, it was even better. Years later, when I asked him "Which of your books are you most proud of?", I glowed when he answered "*Footsteps from East Coker.*"

We launched the book in November 2010, with a tea party at his house. His large family all crowded in, together with a few friends, and David made a little speech before retiring to the front room for a session of chiropractice with the Norwegian fiancé of a granddaughter.

He lived for another ten years, still enjoying the love of family and the convivial days with friends. But, with further decline in his memory and his eyesight, he drifted away from the world of words, a world to which, over so many years, he had given so much.

STRAY NOTES
private writing (2001)

For the first time in my life I'm slipping out of the habit of writing. I find an excuse NOT to write. Walking pointlessly into the greenhouse. Vamping my same limited repertoire on the piano and going to infinite trouble to clean the white keys with my pocket handkerchief. I'm not a pedant but I like virginal keys. And what else do I do to put off the one thing I'm supposed to be able to do with some proficiency? I sweep the kitchen floor and wash and wipe individual glasses that could wait till teatime. This domestic role isn't me, yet now I find it therapeutic.

As for the writing, when I fight my way through the chaos of my office to reach the typewriter, the process often frightens me. Simple words become elusive. Apposite adjectives, never a serious problem, just don't come. Now what's that word, beginning with S? Pathetic. At cricket last season, I turned to my dictionary more than ever. When I had the right, evocative word, I couldn't spell it. I've always been a bit dyslexic; it has got progressively worse.

I suppose it could be said that I've become indolent. But that is too easy an explanation. All my working life I've thrived on the hours I put in. This approach, influenced doubtless by the village-boy work ethic, possibly reflects a personality that is not quite as rounded as it should be.

The trouble is – apart from my worrying mental blocks – I have no fluency any longer. I make more notes than ever before (it was hardly a strength of mine) and then I've far too many and can't decide what to use. This is all new to me. I take longer. There's little logical progression in my prose. That is one reason why I'm telling myself I'd like to take a change of direction. If I'm ever going to write this anti-war play of mine, it must be done this winter.

I received a phone call from a relative of Mary Thorne, in a Cruden Bay nursing home. She was acknowledging my card to Mary who will be 97 next summer. Don't think she will make it. Confined to bed, mental faculties impaired. Covered in bed sores. No-one deserves that lack of dignity. Such a sweet-natured person: the office 'mother' at the *Western Gazette*. Imposed on during the war years when, with her impeccable shorthand, she covered the councils and courts and did much of the secretarial work. I once opened the reporters' room door and knocked the heavy typewriter out of her hands. She didn't complain. Back in Aberdeenshire, until her decline, she used to send generous Scottish notes (money) "for the bairns".

The fascinating thing about death is that we never think of it, and its utter finality, when we are young. The subject wanders increasingly into our consciousness – for the most practical of reasons, I suppose – when we get older. I certainly don't fear it. My faith, a marvellous prop for some, has largely deserted me in the conventional sense. I like visiting churches more than I ever did: the fustiness, the faint whiff of incense in those particular parishes where the Pope beckons, the brass plates and undue regard for the local aristos. Just as I did as a boy, I intrepidly step up into the pulpit. The organs are always locked but not the standby piano. To impress my children, I lift the lid and vamp a Jerome Kern refrain; that is if there are no visitors in the building except the family. I like all that and am occasionally moved by the aura of ecclesiastical history. But this is not complemented by faith. We are asked to take too much on trust. Too many wars, too many outrages of bigotry can be directly traced to the pathetic divisions of religion.

So my funeral needn't be solemn, or even especially spiritual. I'd like it to be tuneful, cheerful, warm-hearted, the excuse for non-malicious journalistic gossip and the exchange of stories. Maybe a couple of well-known hymns (a concession to my days in the St Michael's choir) and a bit of jazz and big band on the way out. I may have to leave Mark to find an appropriate bit of Ellington or Basie. I've always liked funerals more than weddings; it isn't an affectation. Subconsciously we are pleasantly selective in our memories. The 'oneness' or unity of regard for the poor old chap in the box is humanity at its best. And why not a timely element of gentle hypocrisy, may I ask?

What is important is that we continue to live in people's minds. I hope my family will remember my nicer qualities and whims. Just as I vividly recall the looks, mannerisms and attitudes of my parents. The faces of my mother and father remain as clear as they have ever been; occasionally I find myself talking to them when I'm in the car on my own. ("Look, Dad, that looks like a decent pub. Free house, too ... Shall we stop?") We've left it too late, of course. Too many things are left too late.

I travelled to London for the *Guardian* Sports Desk lunch. Ben moved in on me to emphasise that he wanted me for another season. And that after three letters of resignation. I shall have to compose yet another, with just a glimpse of compromise, in March. Apart from anything else, I'm sick of telling my cricket colleagues that they won't be seeing me in future. I don't want to be seen as a phoney. My priority is space and time to do a few other things. And I'm just not up to it any longer. I can't find the words, even the simple, commonplace ones, and can't remember players' names. It's time to drift away, Foot.

LAST COLUMN – AFTER 32 YEARS

Western Daily Press, March 2010

Arithmetic is not my strong point but a little research tells me that this is my 1,866th column, some written twice a week, for this paper. That works out at just under a million-and-a-half words. It's a lengthy haul and I feel it is time to put all my favourite adjectives and purple prose finally to bed.

Apart from occasional holidays or illness, I haven't missed a column. And I have agonisingly progressed from cumbersome, portable typewriter to computer keyboard and the highly dubious joys of an email system which has been known to crash in my inexpert hands.

My mostly justifiable range of prejudices, covering the obscenity of high wages, nauseating celebrity status and the sly, cheating inclinations of footballers and cricketers, have defiantly survived.

My first column was in 1978 and the subject was Brian Clough. He was clearly a fine, intrepid manager; yet he irritated some of us as we deferentially queued up for his considered wisdom after the game. He kept us waiting for an hour before a rather mannered appearance, swinging his squash racket like a stage prop. His observations on the football were original and self-consciously clever.

Some of my weekly reflections came easier than others. I liked to sit down on a Thursday afternoon without an idea in my head. Once or twice my sports-loving son came up with imaginative thoughts to get me going. In truth, I have usually been happiest writing about the old days, as when I persuaded my late sports editor, Herbie Gilham, to let me have a month's trial. I'm not sure my slightly offbeat stance on sporting matters really appealed to him. So it surprised me that I managed to sustain it for nearly 33 years.

Styles changed as journalism changed. I enjoyed it most when we had a more relaxed relationship with the players. We hitched a lift back in the team coach after missing the last train home from Middlesbrough. We also had a few rows with the managers and briefly got banned for our pains. That meant we were doing our job.

The postbag was a large one and always warranted a reply. A few readers were inclined to say: "Too much nostalgia. What about City, Rovers, Swindon, Cheltenham and Yeovil now or something about tomorrow's players?" And I tried. One week I attempted to devote my piece to a junior match I dutifully watched. But it couldn't be used. The language from raucous parents was worse than from BBC drama after the watershed.

Journalism can be a pragmatic business as we do our best to meet deadlines or allow officious gate men (not in Bristol) to let us in. Over the years I have used dozens of phone boxes down muddy roads to knock out my columns on a busy week when I was searching for a topic.

I once perched precariously on an uneven lavatory wall when the old Forest Green press box was full. I was there to take a descriptive look at lofty, homely Nailsworth on an FA Cup replay day.

More poignantly, I sat at a hospital bedside to write another column. I read it to my Dad and I think he approved. By the next day, he was dead. While I wrote, he indicated that he wanted a pen and he scribbled what I hoped would be a compliment about my Viv Richards profile. Instead, he penned with his shaky hand: "Try to bring in a drop of whisky next time you come!" Too late, alas.

I had a lovely, if small, core of readers – especially the cricket fans who shared my own steadfast regard for the game and the way it used to be played. But I must have been taking a solemn, downbeat view in successive weeks as I wrote of the Somerset pair, Harold Gimblett and 'Crusoe' Robertson-Glasgow, who committed suicide. The following week, I planned to switch the subject matter and extol the emerging, if introvert, talents of Peter Roebuck. Just right for a column. "Sorry, old chap, but I don't want you killing me off as well."

Every sport got a mention in the column. Golf and tennis are not favourites of mine, though the kindly, tragic Arthur Ashe gave me one of his last interviews, in a Bristol hotel. I went to point-to-points, croquet courts and prize fights. Yet too many things still bothered me. I didn't warm to rugby players who opted for artificial blood or anyone who drove a golf buggy onto the motorway. I also cringed at other sportsmen being banned, or worse, for drugs offences. Petulant footballers who refuse to shake hands don't seem so bad by comparison.

Those 1,866 columns have made up an enthralling, often warm-hearted journey. Thanks for sharing it with me.

FRANK FOOT

Footsteps from East Coker (2010)

My father was inordinately proud of his garden: the size of his onions and parsnips, the way he brought on his Brussel sprouts, the mathematical precision of his rows, those early potatoes planted unfailingly on Good Friday and ready to eat ahead of the neighbours – or so it seemed to me. When relatives came to visit us on the occasional Sunday afternoon, a warm-hearted and yet solemn business, part of the accepted ritual was to go on a tour of the garden. Compliments were rightly paid to Frank. I was usually bringing up the rear of the horticultural procession.

"This young lad of yours. Is he goin' to be a gardener, too?" There'd be a polite little laugh. "Hope so," I'd say, mostly to please my father.

Privately I thought it wasn't at all a bad job. I liked the smell of the soil; liked being entrusted to fork the first new potatoes of the season; liked hand-weeding the rows of burgeoning vegetables so that they suddenly looked neat and attractive. Yes, perhaps I'd be a gardener. The simple operation of planting the seeds and watching them emerge through the freshly raked soil appealed to me.

On weekdays, after school, I would walk along the road past cottages where old men, bent with arthritis, wizened from years of unrewarded labouring, looked into space. They may not have seemed particularly bright and intelligent. In truth, their own education had been grimly superficial. Their conversation was no more than a nod of recognition to the baker as he went past with his horse and two-wheeled bread van. The tin loaves were still warm and they were not long out of the Pulman ovens in Tellis Cross. No-one would ever have dared to call the old, weary men artists as they leaned on their gates. Yet they were. Their flower beds, which they were too modest to display in any ostentatious way, were beautiful, kaleidoscopic, arranged in designs that came, in the manner of a true painter, straight from their heads and imaginations. Nothing in East Coker in those apparently vacuous days was more life-enhancing than the flowers: the gentle manner they were planted, the unself-conscious love bestowed on them by bent, grimy fingers that never needed a brush and easel to portray such a spontaneous achievement of creativity.

The injustice was that they didn't even realise what floral beauty they had created. Their neighbours also trudged past a hundred times a day, offering no more than a token glance. "What's thee tiddies like this year, Bill?" Country dwellers didn't talk about their flowers; that was their secret indulgence.

In the years that followed those back-garden observations, I pondered increasingly the criminal wastage of talent. The old fellers from the village had so much to offer, but there was never really an outlet for their endeavours to be appreciated. It was unthinkable, of course, that there might be. So many, it appeared to me more and more, simply lived, laboured and died. There was no scope to tap their untutored, too often unnoticed talents and embrace their sheepish gifts. Only decades later do we accept the tragedy of such shameful wastage.

I come back to my father again. Almost all of his work was physical. The images I retain of him were of sharpening his scythe at the whet-stone, of proudly surveying his deep trenches as the main-crop potatoes went in, holding his breath as he brought a wheelbarrow load of human excrement from the lavatory to the potential carrot patch. He had a well-muscled body and conversely – endearingly, too – fingers that were, although engrained, pale and delicate. We never discussed music, though I came to realise his frustration that he had no opportunity to learn an instrument. When I was six he went to a music shop in our home town of Yeovil and bought me a piano. It cost £35 and it must have considerably stretched the domestic resources.

I think he had visions of me becoming the church organist in time. "Up to you now, son. Mrs Hackwell has said she'll take you on." She was the organist and choir mistress. In fact, I made reasonable progress and passed the first two exams. Then I confessed to her that I hoped one day to join a dance band. Such a philistine intention took her by surprise. But, with the kindest of responses, she gave me a music book of supposedly tango dancing, for my next birthday. I saw it as a gesture of despair, however, that my involuntary fingers were not cut out one day to succeed Mrs Hackwell at the St Michael's church organ. I just didn't feel I could take syncopated liberties with Purcell – or even with relatively staid Latin-American melodies. The piano wasn't an unnecessary purchase. I painstakingly thumped out my depleted, shallow versions of *I'm forever blowing bubbles* and *Danny Boy* to let my father know I really did have a lingering affection for music, preferably if I could fantasise that I was on the stand with Geraldo or Roy Fox.

My father also possessed a miniature clapped-out accordion which I believe he picked up for sixpence at Sherborne's Pack Monday fair. He would loop a piece of string around his thumb, where once there had been a leather strap, and I would hear him practising, clumsily and inexpertly, Christmas carols and pop songs of his day. I found it very moving and I crept away, not to be seen. I got the impression that he would have loved to be a proper musician. Was that another case of unfulfilled creative desire?

TS ELIOT'S VISIT TO EAST COKER

from one of David's last feature articles for the Guardian (2008)

Eliot was not, as far as I know, a sporting man. His upbringing had been in the United States and one assumes that the wondrous deeds of Hobbs and Hammond made little or no impact on his cerebral imagery. Certainly he did not go around, like AE Housman for instance, in casual wear and a cricket cap. His clothes were more cut for sedentary use than for loping round the boundary.

On that summer's evening he arrived and sat in a pew behind the font. His was an unfamiliar face and my father, who earned £5 a quarter as St Michael's sexton, responsible for cutting the grass between the tombstones, keeping possession of the keys to the tower's spiral staircase and trimming the wicks of the hanging oil lamps, readily engaged the newcomer in amiable conversation.

I have no idea how easy and balanced the exchanges were but am sure that Dad, as usual, wasted no time in offering a comprehensive who's who of local players, cricketers and footballers, and a glossary of their varying skills. There was Tommy Hackwell, who looked like Chaplin, the village undertaker who carved coffins every bit as neatly as he fashioned his punctilious strokes; Roy Haines – "a proper wicketkeeper every bit as good as Ames"; and Cockles Stevens, reserve goalkeeper for Yeovil, who doubled up by reading the lesson at matins.

Cockles, renowned for the depth of his goal-kicks, used to give us the scriptures in a rural voice of sonorous authority, almost as if he was demanding a back-pass from his full-back. My father reasoned that the goalkeeper's familiarity with the Bible was a spiritual titbit worth throwing in.

The parental report, relayed over supper, did not indicate what sort of feedback he got. But he was much impressed with the pious bearing of the man sitting behind the font. "Seemed a nice kind of bloke. Quite religious, you could tell." A few days later the vicar told Dad he knew the visitor had wanted a look at the church. A Mr Elliott or something like that. A bit of a writer.

TS Eliot apparently loved the village but never returned (though his ashes did). As far as we know, the knowledge he gleaned about Cockles' goalkeeping and Roy's stumpings did not find their way into the poet's abstruse wasteland. Dad did not go in for flights of word-music but he always liked the chance of a chat with strangers. He would put down his can of paraffin to volunteer an unsolicited run-down of local sportsmen's achievements. It always seemed to him a perfectly natural form of discussion.

REFLECTIONS

The start and end of the final chapter of 'Footsteps from East Coker' (2010)

Now comes the time for me to reflect – on the village I left in 1955 but never lost.

East Coker did so much to shape me. Its pastoral calm enfolded and nurtured me in those tender years of the 1930s. I still lie awake at night, remembering the timeless cottages and the sight of weary, uneducated, sweet-natured old men, bending their arthritic backs over the garden gate to gossip to a neighbour.

It was my spiritual base. In Verandah Cottage I was born. From here I went to school and later cycled in search of my first proper job. This was my felicitous home, over the little stream bridge and back beyond the laburnum and hollyhocks that framed the front path.

There was the whiff of cider apples and weather-beaten dung in the air. I loved to see the old-style hayricks, the carters on their rounds, still hot bread delivered off the horse-drawn vans. At this distance it may all sound incorrigibly romantic and sentimental, but once it had a wonderful sincerity about it. Village life today may have attracted owners with two or three cars on the gravel drive, lavatories that flush and newcomers who jarringly use non-rural phraseology. But they have disingenuously changed the pattern.

In defiant cussedness, unrealistic as it may be, I don't want too much change. When I return to East Coker now, I want to hear the chimes ringing out their traditional greetings every three hours, just as they did when my father – with some help from me – wound them and the clock for sixty years. I'd like to see the trio of Hughes brothers again, mending their snares and nets and whistling away as they used to, before heading off for a day's rabbiting.

*

I don't think I have ever taken myself too seriously, by trying to set social or intellectual targets that haven't come naturally and would have threatened to lead me off the well-trod rural tracks that enthralled and guided me through my wide-eyed boyhood. My instinct and boyhood have served me well – as have the long lines of oaks that my family first planted generations ago. The trees are as ageless as the parish and Verandah Cottage. My footsteps down the road have been an enthralling adventure.

INDEX *(for reasons of space, close family are omitted)*

Abbott, Stan 59,63
Abrams, John 196,200
Agate, James 42
Agnew, Jonathan 346
Allan, Jimmy 268
Allen, Dave 143
Allen, David 345
Allen, Gubby 305
Allen, Sheila 111
Alley, Bill 236,307
Alleyne, Mark 242-3
Allison, Malcolm 256,267
Amarnath, Lala 29
Ames, Les 288
Anderson, Ian 143,148
Andrews, Bill 29,53,192-3,195-6,203,209, 231,242,249,298-9,309,361
Andrews, Eamonn 212
Andrews, Peter 157
Archer, Fred 270,281-3
Archer, Helen 281-3
Archer, Jeffrey 242
Archer, William 282
Arlott, John 45,53,203,228,233-4,297
Ashe, Arthur 375
Ashton, Margaret 173
Ashton, Marie 89,92
Atherton, Mike 232
Atkins, Eileen 120,172
Atkins, Sue 271
Atkinson, Rowan 177
Atyeo, John 102,146-7,257,359
Auden, WH 231
Averis, Mike 342
Avery, Bert 255
Bacall, Lauren 214,216,218-9
Bach, JS 303
Baker, George 102
Baker, James 36
Baker, Reginald 292
Bannerman, Celia 177
Barnes, Sydney 294
Barnett, Ben 338
Barnett, Charles 99
Barnwell, John 287
Barrie, June 179
Barrow, Tom 151
Bartlett, Ezra 246
Basie, Count 373
Beasley, Pat 257
Beaverbrook, Lord 49-50
Beckett, Samuel 110,118
Bedser, Alec 231-2,329
Beethoven, Ludwig van 303,314

Behan, Brendan 110,119
Bell, Ian 345
Bennett, Alan 172-3
Bennett, John 96
Bennett, Phil 314
Bentley, Roy 262
Berg, Bunty 324
Berg, Jack 310,323-5
Berg, Moyra 324
Berglas, David 196
Berry, Scyld 9,13,232,286,343-4,371
Bessell, Albert 265,274
Betjeman, John 214,216,220-2
Betjeman, Penelope 222
Bevan, Nye 173
Bevin, Ernest 26,167
Biddulph, Ken 358
Biggs, Alfie 257
Bird, Dickie 197,345
Blake, John 315
Blakey, Richard 347
Blizzard, Len 59
Bloomfield, Roddy 197
Blunden, Edmund 330,359
Board, Jack 151
Bogart, Humphrey 219
Bolton, Paul 345-6
Boon, Eric 265
Botham, Ian 229,236-40,251, 253,255,285,350,369
Bourton, Clarrie 262
Bowes, Bill 235
Bowler, Norman 156
Bowles, Stan 63
Boycott, Geoff 236,239,245,254
Bradford, Betty 259
Bradford, Geoff 257,259
Bradman, Donald 42,193,234,255,286,289
Bradwell, Christine 168
Breakwell, Dennis 238
Brecht, Bertolt 110,173
Brenner, Nat 128,130
Bridges, Jim 242,364
Brinton, Ernie 262
Britton, Cliff 147,264
Broad, Stuart 351
Broadis, Ivor 55
Brookes, Dennis 357,361
Brotherston, Noel 229
Browne, Coral 116
Bruce, Lenny 230
Brunel, Isambard 159,162-3,222
Bryant, Eric 55,59-60
Burden, Tommy 359

Burkhard, Willy 131
Burns, Michael 253
Burrough, Dickie 208
Burton, Richard 197
Buse, Bertie 29,357,362
Bushell, Dennis 109
Caddick, Andrew 242
Cagney, James 171
Cairncross, James 178
Cairns, Chris 349
Cameron, John 53
Campbell, Kevin 269
Canzoneri, Tony 324
Cardus, Neville 42,49,311-3,341
Carey, Denis 118
Carmel (nurse) 237
Carter, Neil 350
Carter, Raich 259
Cartwright, Tom 194,310
Cascarino, Tony 268
Case, CCC 208
Casey, Tommy 105
Castle, Fred 29
Cavendish, Elizabeth 222
Chaplin, Charlie 341,378
Charlie (reporter) 107
Charlton, Jack 266
Chatterton, Thomas 127,167,191
Chekhov, Anton 135,172,174
Chopin, Frédéric 303
Clark, Seymour 364-5
Cleese, John 203,213,242
Clissitt, Ben 342
Close, Brian 99,130,194,233,319
Clough, Brian 176,374
Cochrane, CB 324
Cole, Stephanie 120
Collins, Nick 59,63
Collins, Wally 262
Colston, Edward 163
Compton, Denis 122,235,271
Conan Doyle, Arthur 22
Conway, Russ 215
Cook, Jimmy 245,251-2
Cook, Simon 348
Cooper, Jilly 16
Cooper, Terry 256,266
Corbett, Harry H 114
Cornock, Rosie 287
Cotton, Henry 280
Cousins, Robin 197,285
Craven, Nico 358,363
Crawley, John 348
Creed, Len 200,237
Crosbie, Annette 119

380

Coulson, Sylvia	31	
Coulson, William	30-1	
Coward, Noel	124-5,171,230	
Cummins, Anderson	253	
Curran, Kevin	232	
Dacre, Charlie	304,306	
Daley, Tony	268	
Dampier, William	70	
Danahar, Arthur	275	
Daniell, John	206	
David, John	178-9	
Davies, David	117	
Davies, Freddie	145,153	
Davies, Marshall	265	
Davis, Ralph	265	
Day-Lewis, Daniel	366	
Dean, Dixie	146	
Defoe, Daniel	127	
de Haviland, Olivia	136	
Delaney, Shelagh	110-1	
Denning, Byron	251	
Derrick, Jantzen	107,359	
Desmond, Florence	280	
Dicks, HB	69	
Dimmock, Jimmy	264	
Dipper, Alf	139,310-1	
Dix, Ronnie	264	
Dixey, Phyllis	80,87	
Dixon, Jeff	274	
Dodge, Mr	50	
Doherty, Peter	359	
Donat, Robert	75	
Doshi, Dilip	236,255	
Douglas, Blanche	276	
Douglas, Johnny H	292-3	
Douglas, Johnny WHT	292-4	
Douglas, 'Pickles'	292	
Doust, Dudley	343	
Dowty, George	193-5	
Drake, Charlie	143,154	
Dravid, Rahul	348	
Dredge, Sam	328,332,335	
Ducat, Andy	309-10	
Duke, Neville	193	
Dyke, Dickie	57,59,63	
Eason, Reg	96-7,109	
Eastman, Laurie	207,293,304,306	
Edmonds, Phil	240	
Edrich, Bill	232	
Eliot, TS	174,378	
Ellington, Duke	373	
Elliott, Wally	25	
Engel, Susan	117	
Evans, Godfrey	362-3	
Evans, Vic	209	
Falmouth, Lord	283	
Farnes, Ken	204	
Farr, Tommy	265	
Fay, Stephen	309	
Fearon, Tim	176	
Fenner, John	50	
Ferreira, Anton	249	
Feydeau, Georges	175	
Fields, Gracie	114,124	
Fingleton, Jack	234,309,338	
Fleetwood, Mick	149	
Fletcher, Duncan	353	
Folland, Nick	211	
Fontaine, Del	183	
Foot, Michael	169	
Ford, Fred	91,147,195-6,201,257	
Fordham, George	281,283	
Formby, Beryl	123	
Formby, George	113-4,123	
Forsyth, Bruce	142	
Foster, Barry	119	
Fowler, Gerald	246-7	
Fox, Dr	318	
Fox, Roy	377	
Fraser, Angus	342,347-8	
Freeman, EJ	53	
Froggatt, 'Seaman'	275	
Fry, CB	255	
Fry, John	265	
Gallagher, James	262-3	
Gamlin, Herbert	246-7	
Gandhi, Mahatma	42	
Ganguly, Sourav	348	
Gard, Trevor	239	
Gardiner, Leslie	197	
Garner, Joel	239,285,369	
Garrett, Bill	261	
Gatting, Mike	240	
Gavaskar, Sunil	236	
Gearing, Bill	328,330,335	
George, Charlie	218	
George III	217	
Geraldo	377	
Gibbs, Holland	242	
Gibson, Alan	16,195,235,310-1,345,358,367	
Gibson, Pat	346	
Gielgud, John	218	
Giles, Johnny	266	
Gilham, Herbie	374	
Gilligan, Arthur	300,305	
Gimblett, Dennis	211	
Gimblett, Harold	16,25,29,45,49,52,99,202-13,241,249,285,298,326,368,375	
Gimblett, Rita	203,205,207	
Goddard, Tom	304-6,363	
Gomez, Daisy	115	
Gooch, Graham	236-7	
Goodall, Hedley	366	
Goodchild, John	37	
Goorney, Howard	172	
Gorbachev, Mikhail	227	
Gould, Bobby	266	
Gould, Margery	266	
Gow, Gerry	214,219,236	
Gower, David	242,345	
Grace, WG	139-40,150-1,193,237,247,286,294	
Grant, Cary	366	
Graveney, David	253	
Graveney, Tom	100	
Green, David	228,230-1,341	
Greenidge, Gordon	362	
Greenway, Francis	127	
Greenwood, Frank	302-3	
Gregory, Jack	59	
Gregory, Norman	179	
Greswell, Bill	308-9,317-9	
Greswell, Gill	319	
Greswell, John	319	
Greswell, Rachel	318-9	
Griffith, Richard L	111-2	
Gumage (Som. Am. CC)	23	
Hackwell, Mrs	377	
Hackwell, Tommy	378	
Hadlee, Richard	237	
Hafeez, Abdul	29	
Hagen, Walter	279-80	
Haines, Roy	378	
Hale, John	119	
Hall, Brian	59	
Hall, Peter	134	
Hall, Willis	130	
Halliday, Dave	63	
Hamblin, James	347	
Hammond, Wally	36,252,255,286,288-91,293,305,371	
Hanif Mohammad	252	
Hapgood, Eddie	264	
Hardwicke, Edward	135	
Hardy, Thomas	231	
Hare, David	173,175	
Hargreaves, David	179	
Hargreaves, Ernest	272,279-80	
Harold (RAF)	83	
Hassett, Lindsay	234	
Hawke, Lord	300-1,303,305	
Hawkins, Mr	36	
Hayward, Cyril	260-1	
Hayward, Johnny	258,260-1	
Hayward, Ken	261	
Hazare, Vijay	29	
Hazell, Horace	257,298,310,326-7,361	

Hazlitt, William	310,367	James, Kevan	242	le Carré, John	255
Heath, Neville	32	James, MR	27	Lee, Frank	28-9,208
Heathcote, Graham	46-7	Jameson, Louise	172	Lee, Jack	208
Henderson, Jock	338	Jardine, Douglas	305	Lessing, Simon	276
Henderson, Michael	235,341	Jarman, Harold	258	Levene, Harry	325
Hendren, Patsy	310,322	Javed Miandad	255	Lewis, Ted	324
Henry VIII	334	Jay, John	165	Leyland, Maurice	305
Henson, Leslie	24	Jefford, Barbara	366	Liddell, Billy	102-3
Herriot, James	66	Jeffrey, Peter	118,126	Lindwall, Ray	204
Heseltine, Michael	58	Jenkins, Claude	117	Littlewood, Joan	172
Hewett, Herbie	233,247	Jenkins, Warren	131	'Lizzette' (stripper)	182
Hick, Graeme	244-5,250-1,354-5	Jessop, Gilbert	240	Lloyd, Clive	236
Hickman, Arthur	63	Jewell, Maurice	304	Lloyd, John	165
Hill, Ben	264	Johns, Stratford	156-7	Longrigg, Bunty	29
Hill, Eric	53,234	Jones, Margaret	119	Louis, Joe	271
Hindlekar, Dattaram	29	Jones, Tom	142	Lucas, Denzell	38
Hinshelwood, Mrs	104	Joyce, Edmund	348	Luckes, Wally	
Hinshelwood, Paul	104	Kadeer Ali	350		29,206-7,209,287,364-5
Hinshelwood, Wally	104	Kapil Dev	237	Luff, John	338
Hipkin, Joe	293	Kasprowicz, Michael	345	Lynch, Tommy	63
Hobbs, Jack	209,255, 300,322	Keating, Frank	311,364,371	Lynd, Robert	310
Hodges, Commander	53	Keats, John	167	Lyon, Bev	286,302-6,309
Hodgson, Roy	343	Kelly, Katherine	112	Lyon, Dar	304
Hoggard, Matthew	231-2,347	Kelly, Pauline	168	Lysaght, Charles	286
Hole, Billy	270,278-9	Kemble (writer)	51	McAvoy, Jock	273
Hollis, Christopher	198,331	Kern, Jerome	373	MacBryan, Jack	285
Holloway, Ian	268	Kerr, Deborah	366	McCormack (journalist)	39
Hooper, Ewan	120	Kid Chocolate	324	McGilvray, Alan	234
Horne, Lena	86	Kilburn, Jim	235	McGrath, Glenn	353
Hosie, Gordon	49-50	King, Collis	350	MacLaren, Archie	
Housman, AE	141,378	King, Jack	274		245-7,250-1,355
Housman, Laurence	141	Kipling, Rudyard	140-1	Macmillan, Harold	73-5
Howard, Trevor	366	Kirby, Steve	347	Mallender, Neil	242
Howerd, Frankie	125	Kiswick, Gandy	274	Mankad, Vinoo	29
Huddleston, Trevor	98	Kitchen, Mervyn	179	Mann, Bob	104
Hughes (RAF)	83-4	Kitley, Jim	330,335	Mapson, Johnny	59
Hughes brothers	379	Knight, Nick	350	Marks, Vic	228,232,235,240
Hughes, Victoria		Knight, Robert	176	Marlar, Robin	311
	16,180,183,186-9,196	Knowles, David	91	Marsh, Rodney	63
Hungerford, Walter	334	Knox, Ronald	331	Marshall, Fl Lt	84-5
Hunter, Norman	266	Koczain, Josef	277	Marshall, Malcolm	237
Hylton, Jack	129	Lamb, Allan	320	Marshall, Roy	362
Ibsen, Henrik	175	Lamb, Charles	310	Martin, Father	331,338
Illingworth, David	172-3,176	Langford, Brian	53,307	Martin, Troy Kennedy	156
Illingworth, Ray	99	Lanham, 'Cherry'	25,38,67	Martin-Jenkins, Christopher	235
Imran Khan	254	Lapotaire, Jane	173	Mason, Bobby	265
Ingle, Reggie	208,287	Lara, Brian	244-5,252-3,345	Matthews, Jason	269
Ingleby-Mackenzie, Colin	357,360	Larkin, Philip	231	May, Percy	261
Ionesco, Eugène	110	Larwood, Harold	204,321	Melville, Alan	153
Irons, Jeremy	366	Lathwell, Mark	241,353	Mercer, Jack	309,320
Irving, Charles	185	Lauder, Harry	280	Merchant, Vijay	29
Isobel (journalist)	129-30	Laurel & Hardy	135	Meyer, Barry	99
Jago, June	120	Law, Phyllida	117	Meyer, RJO	29,319,368
James, Ada	190	Lawrence, Johnny	29,361	Middleton, Tony	242
James, Carwyn		Leather, Ted	98	Miller, Arthur	173,175
	231,308,310,314-6	Leavis, FR	24	Miller, Keith	204
James, CLR	248	Lebor, Stanley	178	Miller, Max	113-4,122

Mills, Freddie	25,271
Mizler, Hymie	324-5
Moeen Ali	355
Montrose, Duchess of	282
Moody, John	116,127-8
Moody, Mrs	127
Moon, Keith	148
Moon, Mr	332
Moorhouse, Geoffrey	309
Morecambe & Wise	142
Morgan, Cliff (football)	262-3
Morgan, Cliff (rugby)	315-6
Morris, John	252
Mosley, Oswald	324
Motion, Andrew	222
Moyle, Fl Lt	84-5
Muhammad Ali	272
Murch, Bill	151
Murley, Donald	39
Mushtaq Ali	29
Naylor, Stuart	269
Neagle, Anna	324
Neale, Billy	290
Neale, Phil	250,355
Negus, Arthur	142
Newman, Roy	332
Nichols, Morris	52,204,207,209
Nilsson, Gunnar	25
Northover, EH	37
O'Connor, Jack	207,304,306
O'Connor, Joseph	117
Odlum, George	117
Oliver, Vic	93,95-6
Ollis, Ken	149
Ormandroyd, Ian	268
Orton, Joe	174
Osborne, John	110,117,177
O'Toole, Peter	14,114,116-8, 126-35,218,366
Oughton, Frederick	137-9
Palairet, Lionel	49,52,246-7
Palin, Michael	143,152-4
Palmer, Ted	183,190
Parker, Charlie	139,285,296-7
Parker, Jackie	274
Parker, Tom	262
Parker, Tom 'Tosh'	275
Parkin, Cecil	285,300-1
Parkinson, Michael	235
Pataudi, Nawab of	29,305
Patterson, George	59
Patterson, Pat	270,275
Paull, Arthur	247
Payne, Jack	303
Payne, Joe	257
Payne, Laurie	131
Paynter, Eddie	298
Pearce, Tom	208
Pearson, Tony	338
Peck, Geoffrey	145
Peck, Gregory	44
Pele	260
Penney, Trevor	254
Perrott, Johnny	335
Phelps, Jack	271
Phillips, Jonathan	177
Pike, Mr	25
Pinter, Harold	14,110,113,117, 170,203,213,299
Piper, Keith	252-3
Pitman, Isaac	254
Pitt, Jackie	264
Place, Winston	298
Ponting, Ivan	285,371
Poore, Bertie	309
Poore, Ed	358,363
Popplewell, Nigel	211
Porch, Robert	246
Porter, Cole	113,363
Postlethwaite, Peter	366
Pothecary, Sam	53
Powys, Llewelyn	224
Preece, Jack	262
Priday, Mary	185
Priestley, JB	310
Prince-Cox, Bert	264,275
Pringle, Derek	235
Prior, Joe	56
Procter, Mike	238,315,363
Purcell, Henry	3777
Puskás, Ferenc	260
Quinn, Patricia	367
Ramadhin, Sonny	204
Rask, John	246-7
Rawicz & Landauer	124
Ray, Ted	280
Redding, Otis	143
Redgrave, Michael	366
Rees, Jason	269
Rees, Sonia	131
Rees-Mogg, Jacob	231
Rees-Mogg, William	231
Revie, Don	259
Reynolds, Henry	330,335
Rhodes, Steve	350
Rhys Jones, David	278
Rice, Clive	237
Rich, Buddy	143
Richards, Viv	11,16,194,196, 200,228,236-7,244-6,248-50, 252-3,255,285,354,369,375
Richardson (Heytesbury)	334
Richardson, Tom	309
Richardson, Tony	113
Riggs, Arthur	261
Roberts, Cpl	81-2
Roberts, Rachel	128-9,131
Robertson-Glasgow, RC	52,234,240,308-13,345,375
Robeson, Paul	113,118
Robins, Walter	310
Robinson, Colonel	321
Robinson, Derek	195
Robinson, Tony	168,172,176,366
Rochford, Peter	358
Rodgers, David	236
Roebuck, Paul	338
Roebuck, Peter	249,251,338,356,368-9,375
Rogers, Paul	109,116
Rogers, Stuart	327
Root, Fred	327
Rose, Brian	353
Rose, George	275
Ross, Duncan	120
Rossiter, Leonard	114-5,119,366
Rothermere, Lord	89
Rowley, Tony	103
Rowsell, Mr	58,60-1
Rudkin, David	169
Russell, Jack	351
Sadiq Mohammad	236
Sampson, June	93-4
Sanders, JG	37
Sarwate, Chandra	29
Sassoon, George	333,339
Sassoon, Hester	328
Sassoon, Siegfried	7,309,328-9
Saunders, Ron	59
Sawtill (Som. Am. CC)	23
Saxelby, Mark	254
Scriven (Yeovil CC)	53
Sehwag, Virender	348
Seward (Yeovil CC)	53
Shackleton, Len	55,63
Shah, Owais	348
Shakespeare, William	109,116,118,125,133-5, 163,174-5,199,366
Shankly, Bill	201
Shaw, GB	173,175,310
Shearer, Moira	115
Shepherd, Bill	201
Shepherd, David	197,201,361
Shepherd, Jenny	361
Sheppard, Austin	279
Sherston, George	333
Shinwell, Emanuel	319
Shoel, Thomas	223-5
Sibley (writer)	51
Silk, Dennis	309,329-31,336-8

Simkins, Michael	178	Taylor, Elizabeth	197	Webb, Stan	149
Simons, Aubrey	277	Taylor, Graham	268	Wellard, Arthur	53,139,208-9,
Sinclair, Graham	179	Taylor, Mark	232		298-9,327,361,365
Sinclair, Harold	69	Taylor, Mr	43	Wells, Bomber	363
Sinfield, Reg		Taylor, Phil	264	Wells, HG	141
	257,293,296-8,310,321	Tendulkar, Sachin	348	Wemyss, Earl of	305
Singh, Swaranjit	336-7	Tennant, Ivo	230	Wesker, Arnold	110,119-20,172
Smith, ACH	204	Tennyson, Alfred	77	Wesley, Charles	163
Smith, Auriol	117	Tennyson, Lionel	360	Wesley, John	127,163
Smith, Ben	350	Tereba, Václav	277	West, Mae	171
Smith, Bill	50	Tetlow (Yeovil CC)	53	Whatley, Jesse	264
Smith, Delia	351	Tewson, Josephine	120	White (Yeovil CC)	53
Smith, Jim	309	Thatcher, Margaret	226-7	White, 'Butch'	362-3
Smith, KCP	210	Thicknesse, John	230	White, Giles	347
Smith, Maggie	367	Thomas, Windy	195	White, Jack	
Smith, Peter (award)	345	Thompson, Denys	23-4		208,298,319,326,365
Smith, Peter (Essex)	207,365	Thorne, Mary	372	White, Jackie	103
Smith, Ray	207	Thresher, Mike	356,358-9	Whitefield, George	163
Smith, Spencer	276	Tillett, Ben	167	Whitehead, Clive	236
Sohoni, Ranga	29	Tottle, Phil	345	Wickham, Archie	247
Solanki, Vikram	355	Townshend, Pete	148	Wight, Peter	99,241
Solomons, Jack	323	Tracy, Jack	87	Wilde, Oscar	141
Soper, Donald	177	Trafford, Aidan	330	Willey, Peter	237
Southway, Lemmy	262	Travers, Ben	135	Williams, Bert	264
Stainer, N	68	Tremlett, Maurice	37,310	Williams, Charles	286
Stancer, Ernie	3335	Trescothick, Marcus	352-3	Williams, Gerald	68
Stanislavsky, Konstantin	219	Trescothick, Martyn	352	Williams, Harry	68
Stanley, George	293	Trinder, Tommy	298	Williams, Shadow	107,359
Stanshall, Ki	170	Trollope, Paul	343	Williams, Wendy	117,126
Stanshall, Vivian	168,170	Trueman, Fred	99	Wilson, Andy	10,257-8
Steele, Tommy	98	Turner, Bert	328,335	Wilsher, Barry	117,126
Steen, Jan	341	Turner, Mike	304	Wilson, Charles	107
Steinbeck, John	175	Turner, Mr	44	Windsor, Frank	156-7
Stennett, Stan	143,152,154	Tyler, Ted	246	Winstone, Reece	216
Stephens, Gladys	366-7	Vale, Vanda	95-6	Wisdom, Norman	114-5
Stephens, Reuben	366	Valentine, Alf	204	Wodehouse, PG	255
Stephens, Robert	356,366-7	Vaughan, Michael	348	Wolfit, Donald	75
Stephenson, Harold	53	Vercoe, Rosemary	133	Wood, Clive	178-9
Stevens, Cockles	378	Vickery, Tony	53	Wood, Victoria	177
Stevens, W	36	Voyzey (writer)	51	Woodcock, Bruce	26
Stock, Alec	54-7,59-63,105,310	Wade, Tommy	207-8	Woodcock, John	
Stoppard, Tom		Walcott, Jersey Joe	271		228,233,235,345-6
	14,109,112,114,176	Walden, Fanny	264	Wooderson, Sydney	26
Strachey, John	50	Walker, Tom	181	Woods, Sammy	
Streeton, Dick	234	Wallace, Nellie	280		139,233,246-7,294-5,319
Stroud, J	38	Walpole, Horace	167	Wooldridge, Ian	311
Sutcliffe, Herbert	300-1,305	Ward (Yeovil CC)	53	Woolf, Henry	110,117
Sutton, Dudley	152	Ward, Albert	247	Wooller, Wilf	
Sutton, Randolph	215	Ward, Sammy	274		231,309,344,357,360
Swanton, Jim	233,286,309	Wardle, Johnny	99	Woolley, Frank	322,333
Tait, Alex	91	Warner, Pelham	291,294,296-7	Wright, John	348
Tait, Cpl	81	Warnock, Neil	256,267	Wright, Ray	60
Tann, Bert	138,259,264	Warren, Ray	259	Wyatt, Bob	305
Tarrant, Graham	309	Waterhouse, Keith	66,203	Yardley, Jim	320
Tattersall, Roy	345	Watts, Hugh	338	Yarwood, Mike	153
Tavaré, Chris	252	Watts, June	119	Zaheer Abbas	
Taylor, Billy	349	Waugh, Evelyn	112		196,236,244-5,254-5,285